Bolc

Representation and Processing of Natural Language

Natural Communication with Computers

Edited by Leonard Bolc

Carl Hanser Verlag
München Wien

M

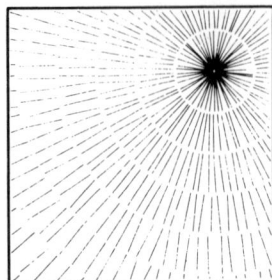

Representation and Processing of Natural Language

Edited by Leonard Bolc

Carl Hanser Verlag
München Wien 1980

M

Editor:
Leonard Bolc, Institute of Informatics, Warsaw University, PKiN, pok. 850,
00-901 Warszawa, Poland

CIP-Kurztitelaufnahme der Deutschen Bibliothek

Representation and processing of natural language
/ ed. by Leonard Bolc. - München, Wien : Hanser;
London, Basingstoke : Macmillan, 1980.
(Natural Communication with computers)
ISBN 3-446-13044-6 (Hanser)
ISBN 0-333-29526-9 (Macmillan)

NE: Bolc, Leonard (Hrsg.)

First published 1980 in Europe
Carl Hanser Verlag München Wien

and

The Macmillan Press Ltd., London and Basingstoke
Associated companies in Delhi Dublin
Hongkong Johannesburg Lagos Melbourne
New York Singapore Tokyo

ISBN 0-333-29526-9 (paper cover - United Kingdom)

ISBN 3-446-13044-6 (German Federal Republic)

Printed in German Federal Republic

TABLE OF CONTENTS

PREFACE

Man/computer communication in natural language requires a thorough knowledge of the natural language. This knowledge can enable nonconformist methods to be used in the examination of natural language.

The book consists of papers by outstanding scientists from the USA, Canada and Europe, who have been engaged in research on natural language problems for man/computer communication.

Richard S.Rosenberg, from the University of British Columbia, Canada gives a general overview of such issues of natural language processing as frames, scripts, etc. His work also describes implementation problems of various systems, such as question answering, speech understanding systems, which have been developed in recent years.

Frank M.Brown, from the University of Texas, USA and Camilla B. Schwind, from the Technical University of Munich, FDR give a detailed examination of a new kind of theory concerning natural language understanding. The basic idea of this new theory is to allow deep interaction between syntactic and semantic concepts and to describe the expressions of meaning representation in the same language, in which the parsing and translation laws are expressed.

Nick Cercone, from Simon Fraser University, Canada surveys the representation for individual items of factual knowledge in the computer. The author also describes the representation in semantic network notation and illustrates his presentation with two mini implementations.

Dietrich Koch and Winfried Heicking, from the Academy of Sciences of the German Democratic Republic, describe in their paper one of the most interesting issues of natural language processing to arise in recent years - ATN (Augmented Transition Network) grammar. This is a special adaptation for the German language. in their contribution, some programs and chosen methods are presented.

Peter Hellwig, from the University of Heidelberg, FDR presents a language processing system PLAIN (Program for Language and Inference). The whole system and the particular components are outlined. The system is appropriate for two types of user: first, linguists for whom this is an examination tool, and second, for users who want to obtain the necessary information from a data base, but only when the PLAIN system becomes part of an information system.

The book therefore describes the most interesting methods of representation and processing of natural language and indicates some important trends for future development.

Warsaw, Spring 1980 Leonard B o l c

APPROACHING DISCOURSE COMPUTATIONALLY: A REVIEW

by

Richard S. Rosenberg
Department of Computer Science
University of British Columbia
Vancouver, B. C., Canada

ABSTRACT

Natural language communication with computers will require a deeper understanding of the nature of human dialogue. Up to very recently, question-answering systems provided the most common framework for the investigation of such communication. Currently a growing interest in the modeling of dialogue and the understanding of discourse has arisen in the Artificial Intelligence (AI) community. It has depended on a variety of contributions from such disciplines as linguistics, the philosophy of language, and cognitive psychology. Our aim, in this essay, is to explore some of these contributions in the light of the unique perspective of AI, the so-called, computational or procedural paradigm. The major part of this presentation will, therefore, deal with such issues as frames and scripts, as proposed by Minsky, Schank, Charniak, and others and their implementation in a variety of systems. The last third will be devoted to such applications as question-answering, in its current forms, speech understanding, expert systems, and computer-aided instruction. The theoretical issues of coherence of text, conversational rules, inference, anaphor reference, and ellipsis represent, in the first instance, the problems faced in the design of conversational systems. It is clear that their solution is an important step on the road to the development of flexible and robust natural language interfaces to large data bases. This is the practical justification of such research; the scientific investigation of the modeling and understanding of discourse requires no such justification.

0. INTRODUCTION

Natural language understanding by computer (NLU) has become a very active field of research over the last few years and indeed is, together with image understanding or scene analysis, probably the dominant area of Artificial Intelligence (AI). Research in NLU has focussed on two main areas as well as a number of supportive ones. These two dominant areas I will refer to as question-answering (QA) systems and discourse, dialogue or text analysis. Although there are a number of topics in common between QA systems and dialogue analysis, their basic aims are quite distinct, a position which will be developed shortly.

Our major purpose is to provide some sense of the range of activity in NLU by attempting to identify the important themes and directions, as well as the less active ones. We will first examine research devoted primarily to natural language understanding itself, that is, to work,the primary aim of which, is the exploration of language phenomena with the ultimate aim being to produce a program which understands* natural language. In this sense, there is (or should be) an obvious commonality of interest among researchers in AI, cognitive psychology, linguistics, the philosophy of language, and sociolinguistics. The issues that must be considered range over syntax, semantics, progmatics, representation of knowledge, the integration of linguistic and extra-linguistic knowledge, the real-time interaction between memory and on-going analysis, conversational strategies, model building, and the overriding question of control.

* There are no quotes on the word "understand" used above but they should always be thought of as present whenever a reference is made to a program or computer understanding. My use is largely operational (with all the attendant pitfalls)in that a computer will be said to understand natural language if it consistently produces appropriate responses where the judgement of appropriateness is by human consensus. Perhaps an alternate word should be used when referring to computers but my hope is that the cautious reader will insert his own quotation marks whenever troubled by some usage.

The second, currently dominant, theme in NLU is research directed towards providing a natural language interface to large data bases for casual or non-sophisticated users. This represents a vigorous revival of one of the earliest research areas in AI. However, whereas the earlier work provided an experimental test bed for ideas in contemporary linguistic theory as well as for ideas and theories developed within AI, the present research has a much more practical motivation. The goal is to build systems that work although, of course, this does not preclude and in some cases even stimulates, interesting theoretical contributions. Nevertheless, the requirements to develop functioning systems largely mitigate against direct scientific exploration in favour of methods with a lingering ad hoc flavour. We will have more to say later.

If we divide NLU into theoretical and applied research, then QA systems are currently the major applied area and the modelling of dialogue or discourse, the major theoretical one. Three or four years ago, however, the title of overall champion would have been awarded to speech understanding mainly because of the size and complexity of systems, as well as the amounts of money, involved. Although support has fallen off dramatically, the legacy of this recent activity is certainly significant enough to require some assessment in this survey.

Two other application areas for NLU which will be discussed are computer assisted instruction (CAI) and advice or diagnosis expert systems. Most of the work in the former area has been developed outside the AI community and its use of natural language is by and large formulaic and of little interest. However, there is some interesting research mainly done at Bolt Beranek and Newman and it is to this work that we will turn.

The development of advice and diagnosis programs has proceeded rapidly in the last few years primarily in the medical sphere. The primary aim is to aid the physician in making accurate evaluations under conditions of incomplete information. As such, problems of decision making with partial knowledge are of major concern and the role of natural language is to facilitate the interaction. It is obviously important that the doctor be able to converse easily with the program; otherwise, its widespread use is likely to be curtailed.

A variety of programs embodying expert knowledge have been developed with differing degrees of sophistication in natural language facilities. As with many other areas, the desire to make a body of knowledge accessible to interested, but casual, users via a computer requires that some form of natural language interaction be made available. Usually, only enough is provided to maintain some reasonable degree of communication. In fact, the very notion of providing just a little natural language reflects the lack of concern for serious issues manifest in many application programs. Nevertheless, many attempts to include a natural language interface to an applications program do make a contribution to the overall goal of NLU, frequently by pointing out the problems faced and the deficiencies unaccounted for.

In the following sections we will discuss theoretical issues in NLU and survey a number of systems to indicate the range and depth of current research. Section I will deal with the theoretical aspects, and Section II with applications, including question-answering, computer-assisted instruction, advice or diagnosis systems as well as a brief look at speech understanding. In Section III, we will briefly discuss a recent critical barrage against the contributions of AI to natural language processing originating with a certain group in the linguistic community.

I DISCOURSE, DIALOGUES, CONVERSATIONS AND TEXTS

I.1 Introduction

During the past two or three years, in parallel to the renewed interest in question-answering systems there has been an effort to develop computer programs which can participate in a dialogue or analyze a coherent piece of text. This effort reflects a consensus among leading researchers in AI that there exist sufficent tools in the AI arsenal to launch a major assault on the problems of language understanding involved in human discourse (Winograd, 1977b). We wish to evaluate this optimism and to describe and discuss these tools.

Another purpose will be to survey briefly contributions from other disciplines relevant to the aforementioned enterprise. Although limitations of space will preclude a detailed discussion, at the very least, an introduction will be given to work in such areas as the philosophy of language, sociolinguistics and ethnomethodology, linguistics, and cognitive psychology. Whether or not research in such diverse areas can be integrated into a coherent approach is one of the questions we shall be exploring. Indeed, a major theme of this section is a critical examination of the computational metaphor as promulgated by, among others Winograd (1976) and Wilks(1976 b).

I.2 A Brief Look at the Past

Almost from the outset, the dominant theme in natural language processing, carried out under the AI banner, has been the question-answering framework. Of two major surveys by Robert Simmons (1965, 1970) of research in this area, the first has "Answering English Questions by Computer" in its title and the second has "Question-Answering Systems". In another important survey by Kuno (1967), titled "Computer Analysis of Natural Languages" the question-answering system is taken as the representative research effect. Figure I, taken from Kuno (1967) can actually serve as the model for the prototype question-answering system and is in effect the linear paradigm, discussed in Rosenberg (1975). It is unnecessary to give a list of systems which fit this paradigm under an appropriate interpretation of PARSER, TRANSLATOR, and RETRIEVER, as this has been done by many people. (See Simmons (1965,1970), Winograd (1972) among others.)

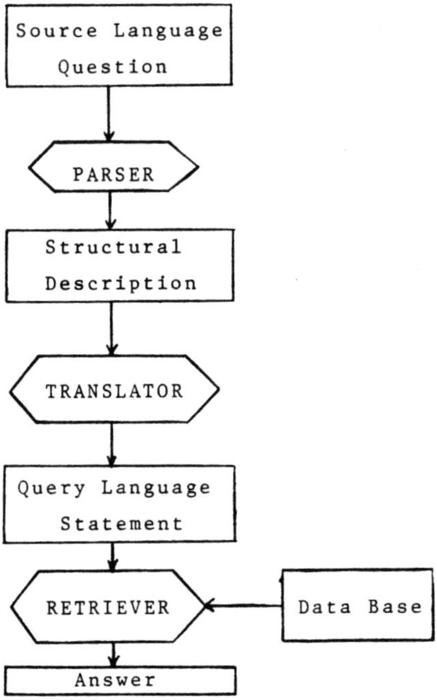

Fig. 1 Question-Answering Systems
(taken from Kuno (1967), Fig. 38, p. 101)

But it is appropriate to consider more carefully the nature of QA systemsand the roots and implications of the associated linear paradigm. One of the major motivations for the development of such systems is the desire to communicate in a more natural way with computers. Given a large data base in some domain, its usefulness is limited to the degree that access to its contents is difficult or forbidding. That is, if special purpose programs or highly restricted and unnatural formats are required in order to retrieve information, the interested but non-sophisticated user is discouraged at the outset. This basic, utilitarian reason for the development of QA systems characterized some of the research supported by the government and various non-profit research agencies but there were other more abstract goals.

Given that the investigation of the nature of intelligent

behaviour is a legitimate intellectual enterprise, certainly a major component of such behaviour is the use of language. Early attempts to investigate natural language processing were largely devoted to machine translation and much of this effort has come to be considered a failure. A more narrowly defined domain was needed and the problem of developing a computer program which could respond to natural language queries with appropriate answers appeared to be more tractable. Considerable impetus was supplied by McCarthy's Advice Taker (1958) which argued extremely well for the QA paradigm. It should be noted, however, that McCarthy was less concerned with natural language than with questions of formal problem solving. His interests were centered in the RETRIEVAL stage of the process wherein, such issues as inference, induction, generalizability, analogy, and learning arise.

But why is the QA framework so attractive for investigating many aspects of natural language? The primary reason seems to be that a "natural" computation model can be associated with the QA approach, as this is depicted in Figure I. This model identified three stages of processing and as a first approximation each can be treated separately. Thus, the first stage, in linguistic terms, is to determine a structural description of the input question. This notion is clearly related to Chomsky's (1965) deep structure concept. Incidentally, Chomsky's work probably provides the underlying principles for most of the QA systems developed up to about 1970. Once having obtained such a representation which is presumably closely connected to the actual meaning of the question, the second stage involves its translation into a form suitable for searching the data base. This final stage can be as straightforward as an indexed search or some kind of pattern matching process, or may require inferencing or problem solving. In some of the more recent systems, this last stage involves the execution of programs which have been constructed in the previous stage (Woods et al 1972).

We should note that QA systems have come to include not only facilities for responding to questions but may also be required to execute commands and to represent new information which has been entered in the form of assertions. Indeed in many cases an assertion is an implicit command to partially restructure the data base. Therefore, QA systems are characterized by their ability to carry out a limited range of actions-questions, commands, assertions - in a fairly limited domain. Let us further note, for future reference, some issues which are not considered. Among these are the intentions of the user, questions of style, of the context of the interaction, setting, etc. But if such issues are raised in the context of criticism of QA systems, they can be dismissed by appealing to the basic ground rules of the QA framework. A user, aware of the nature of the information contained in a data base wishes to determine some fact or sets of facts, to alter the data in some manner, to add new information, or to infer some new fact from what is known. None of these require (or seem to require) any recourse to intentions, beliefs, social context, etc. They seem to epitomize unencumbered communication so that the user, for all intents and purposes, might be another computer making a request.

Certainly the input is framed in a language humans use but the method of treatment makes very few assumptions that humans are actually involved. This is understandable because even within such a restricted framework as the pure QA system, the problems remain extrememly difficult. For most systems the range of acceptable grammatical constructions is quite limited as is the effective range of the semantic representation and the complexity of the necessary inferences. When we come to deal with QA systems, we shall see that one striking feature has been the general abandonment of syntax as a central feature. Probably the major linguistic problem dealt with is ellipsis. In some real sense, basic natural language research has been forsaken. In any case, there is a question whether any serious attack on the processing of natural language can be mounted within the QA framework without the consideration of the matters mentioned previously.

There have been a few systems which have taken into account some wider aspects of human communication. For example,

Weizenbaum's ELIZA (1966) while having very little in the way of facilities for syntax and semantics, did encompass much information about styles of speech. To a surprising degree, Weizenbaum was able to capture a non-trivial fragment of regularity in a particular language context. That he was concerned with the effect of context on understanding is what makes his work interesting. Similar remarks apply to Parkison, Colby, and Faught's(1977) ongoing attempt to model paranoid linguistic behaviour. Here too, the context of a particular situation, in this case a conversant with a psychiatric disorder, provides the major direction for language analysis.

However, most of the earlier research effort had been devoted to systems which excluded all factors save grammar and some limited semantics representation* One of the major claims arising from recent work in linguistics and sociolinguistics is that grammatical analysis cannot be carved out in isolation from such factors as social context, setting, status, and a whole host of other considerations. This runs in direct contradiction to many of the pronouncements of Chomsky (1965), the most important linguist of the past several years and the dominant influence in early computational linguistics.

It is obviously beyond the scope of this section to present a detailed analysis of Chomsky's contributions to linguistics and computational linguistics, but some attention should be paid to the crucial concept of deep structure as discussed in Chomsky (1965). The meaning of a sentence depends on representing its structure at some appropriate level. In conjunction with (or perhaps following) the work of Katz and Postal (1964), and Katz and Fodor (1963), the deep structure is seen as the level of representation at which the meaning can be derived by a semantic interpretation process and from which the surface form of the utterance is produced by a series of transformations**.

*Some important exceptions here are Schank (1972) and Wilks(1975).

**Recent work by Chomsky (1971) and others has argued for a more complex process of semantic interpretation which depends on the surface, phonological form of the sentence. Two contributing factors to this evolution have been the necessity to deal with scope of quantification and focus.

Much subsequent work in linguistics was devoted to the nature and ordering of these transformations as well as the nature of the semantic interpretation rules and lexicon. Such investigations also led to a counter-movement sometimes called generative semantics, which argued that the Chomsky approach which separated syntax and semantics in a fundamental way, was doomed to failure. This controversy is an ongoing one, which at times has become quite strident.

The attractiveness of the Chomsky framework for AI should be quite evident for it sets out a well-defined programme. Because written language is the main object of study, the phonological component can be ignored. This leaves syntactic and semantic components which under the Chomsky framework, operate independently. As such, a linear paradigm, illustrated in Figure I, is quite appropriate. In addition, effort can be devoted to each of these components in a parallel fashion assuming a standard representation for the deep structure.

Because AI researchers have generally been confronted by the exigencies of producing practical systems, compromises have been frequently made. Although a strict separation was maintained between the syntactic and semantic phases in the earlier systems, the nature of these phases was usually very different from the Chomsky conception. For example, the syntactic component has varied from pattern matching rules (Weizenbaum, 1966, Bobrow, 1964), to weak structuralist rules (Green et al, 1961), to context-free grammar (Woods, 1970), to a different grammar altogether (Winograd, 1972). The nature of the semantic component resists classification; in most cases it is so strongly dependent on the particular domain that any attempt at generalization would be hopeless.

Chomsky's emphasis on grammar as the primary object of study in a theory of language seemed quite congenial to the early AI work. It was hoped that a powerful grammar would be the major component of a QA system. Subsequently the necessities of semantics, real world knowledge, inference capabilities, and general probelm solving made the concern with syntax seem to be far too narrow. But still Chomsky's lack of preoccupation with language as only a communication process encouraged the centrality of the linear paradigm and the lack of concern with issues of intention, belief, etc. The waning of his influence in AI corresponds to the growing interest in discourse as an object of study together with a marked awareness of research in cognate areas. Of course, the requirement of producing working QA systems in a variety of domains negates the necessity of following a tradition, the major guiding principle of which, is the primacy of syntax.

I.3. Contributions to Discourse Analysis from Related Disciplines

I.3.1 Introduction

This section will be mainly concerned with contributions from fields other than AI. As such it will range over some of the relevant work in the philosophy of language, sociolinguistics, and linguistics, itself. On the one hand, a cataloguing of purported results from diverse areas may give the impression that a significant confluence is in progress. On the other hand, a common concern may contribute very little to concrete results unless the time is ripe for a serious integration and systhesis. What is the current situation?

First, there are no working systems which incorporate a spectrum of such ideas. A number of systems have been proposed and much of the current excitement and interest derives more from anticipation than accomplishment. And this excitement is not predicated on a powerful emerging theory but rather seems motivated by a confidence in the power of the computational metaphor to implement a number of interesting insights and observations. We will delay our discussion of the computational metaphor and proceed to the purported interesting insights.

It should be noted that for most of the work to be discussed, the term "insight" is quite appropriate. The work we will examine is highly suggestive, highly speculative and largely incomplete. It calls for the incorporation of vast amounts of knowledge and appropriate control processes into any model of conversation or dialogue. The question is how this is to be carried out and the answer is to come from AI.

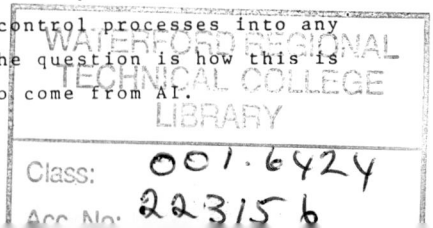

The style of presentation in this section will be meandering and anecdotal. There is no gradual and logical accumulation of evidence leading to the statement of a major discovery. Rather, our purpose is to expose a wide variety of approaches with the aim of sharpening the reader's intuition. It is a difficult task to make discoveries about language and language use appear profound when the subject is one about which everyone by virtue of his skill at execution is indeed an unchallenged expert.

I.3.2 Speech Acts and Conversational Rules

An obvious rich source of ideas for the study of conversation is that stream of philosophy known as the philosophy of language, especially work associated with the names of J.L. Austin (1955), John Searle (1970), and H.P. Grice (1967) among others. In this section we will introduce their ideas, albeit briefly, and comment on their relevance to the task of modelling dialogue from a computational point of view.

Let us begin with John Austin and his very influential book How to do Things with Words. Taking off from the traditional philosophic concerns with the truth value of utterances, Austin outlined a number of communication events which could not be evaluated in terms of truth value but rather required some notion of appropriateness (the so-called felicity conditions). Austin introduced the concept of an illocutionary act, that act which is performed (or may be performed) by a speaker in making an utterance in a more or less conventional manner. For example, if I say that the window is open, I am making a mundane observation with a fairly clear sense but I may also be performing the illocutionary act of stating, or exclaiming or hinting. In fact my desire may be to have someone close the window.

John Searle (1970) catalogued speech acts, the term he used to describe the variety of activities we may actually be performing while making an utterance, in the following manner:

Types of Illocutionary Acts		Possible English Realizates
1. Assertives		assert, state, affirm, deny
2. Directives		order, command, request
3. Commissives		promise, pledge, vow
4. Expressives		apologize, thank, congratulate
5. Declarations	(a)	find, pronounce, appoint
	(b)	declare war
	(c)	fire, resign, excommunicate

Table I Searle's Classification of Illocutionary Acts

Just to indicate the kind of analysis involved in characterizing an illocutionary act, consider Searle's description of a directive. The propositional content of the directive, say a request, involves a future act, A, of the hearer, H. Preparatory conditions are that H is able to do A, and that S, the speaker, believes H is able to do A. Further, it is not obvious to both S and H that H will do A in the normal course of events of his own accord. There is a sincerity condition on S that indeed he or she wants H to do A, and an essential condition as well, that the request certainly counts as an attempt to get H to do A. We might note that if the directive were an order or command, there would be the additional preparatory rule that S must be in a position of authority over H. And in addition the essential condition must be extended to include the fact that the "utterance counts as an attempt to get H to do A in virtue of the authority of S over H". Similar analyses apply to the other illocutionary acts.

This analysis of speech acts certainly has implications for possible computer models of dialogue; to complement this, we might note Searle's belief that linguistic behaviour is rule-governed. Indeed, some attempts have been made to take acccount of these matters; for example see Perrault et al (1978) whose work we will consider in Section I.5. I must apologize for this rather cursory treatment of such important research.

Given that speech acts are the basic conceptual units

involved in communication and are of course realized by the production of sentences, there is a higher level of description which might be related to the organization of the conversation or dialogue itself. Sentences do not appear in isolation and the necessity of deriving rules to govern the coherence of a dialogue is of prime importance. An important contribution in this direction has been made by the philosopher H.P. Grice in the William James Lectures of 1967. What follows is taken directly from this source.

Underlying all conversations (or what should underly all conversations) is the Co-operative Principle.

> Make your conversational contribution such as is required at the stage at which it occurs, by the accepted purpose or direction of the talk exchange in which you are engaged.

As a means of explicating this principle, Grice proposes four Conversational Maxims which are given as follows:

1. Quantity (of Information)
   (1) Make your contribution as informative as is required (for the current purposes of the exchange).
   (2) Do not make your contribution more informative than is required.

2. Quality
   Try to make your contribution one that is true.
   (1) Do not say what you believe to be false.
   (2) Do not say that for which you lack adequate evidence.

3. Relation
   Be relevant.

4. Manner
   Be perspicuous.
   (1) Avoid obscurity of expression.
   (2) Avoid ambiguity.
   (3) Be brief (avoid unnecessary prolixity)
   (4) Be orderly.

These maxims seem to be more prescriptive than descriptive, in that their violation in ordinary conversation is probably the usual state of affairs. However, such maxims must at least be given lip service by people at large; otherwise, conversation would be impossible if, for example, everyone lied. In any case, the assumption that the maxims are observed, provides a superstructure for conversations. Unfortunately, the maxims, as formulated, are so far removed from preciseness and rigour as to be almost useless for purposes of computer modelling. The task of formalizing the third maxim, "Be relevant", is itself probably equal in difficulty to the entire task of developing a computer program to participate in a conversation. Nevertheless, Grice's work is an important contribution to a problem of extra-ordinary difficulty.

In a somewhat similar vein, Robin Lakoff (1973) has introduced "Rules of Politeness", namely, the following:

1. Don't impose
2. Give options
3. Make addressee feel good - be friendly

Clark and Lucy (1975), cognitive psychologists, have performed experiments in order to determine how a listener comes to understand a sentence such as "Must you open the door?". They claim that the listener first constructs the literal meaning, checks its plausibility, and if there is a difficulty applies a rule of conversation to determine the conveyed meaning. Their experimental findings show some evidence that a literal meaning is constructed first. This might suggest that a computer program should follow this strategy; indeed, it is not easy to see how an appropriate interpretation would be possible from the outset. Other important work in this area, sometimes called indirect speech acts includes Gordon and Lakoff (1971), Larkin and O'Malley (1973), and Searle (1975).

Within the domain of text analysis, there have been parallel attempts to extend grammatical analysis beyond sentence boundaries through the development of text grammars (van Dijk, 1972). With respect to stories, David Rumelhart (1975) of the LNR Research Group has proposed a story grammar with the following rules:

Rule 1: Story→Setting + Episode
Rule 2: Setting→(State)*
Rule 3: Episode→Event + Reaction
Rule 4: Event→{Episode|Change-of-state|Action|Event + Event}
Rule 5: Reaction→Internal Response + Overt Response
Rule 6: Internal Response→{Emotion|Desire}
Rule 7: Overt Response→{Action|(Attempt)*}
Rule 8: Attempt→Plan + Application
Rule 9: Application→(Preaction)* + (Action + Consequence)
Rule 10: Preaction→Subgoal + (Attempt)*

Rule 11: Consequence→{Reaction|Event}

where Setting is a statement of time and place as well as an introduction to the main characters and is a series of stative propositions, and

Episodes are special kinds of events which involve the reactions of animate (or anthropomorphic) objects to the world.

Associated with each syntactic rule is a semantic rule so that corresponding to the syntactic structure of a story will be a semantic one which will be used to draw inferences and make approprite connections. Rumelhart comments that his approach to stories is an attempt to systematize Propp's (1968) analysis of Russian folk tales.

In conclusion, we might note that the ongoing work of Roger Schank, his colleagues, and students, although relevant to questions of story analysis, will be discussed in Section I.4.3.

I.3.3 Linguistic, Sociolinguistic, and Psychological Contributions

A number of linguists including Fillmore (1976), G. Lakoff (1974) have recognized the necessity of going beyond syntax in order to deal with the 'real' problem of linguistics which is how people understand language. The centrality-of-syntax advocates have certainly slighted the role of semantics, and ignored the problem of pragmatics. Such a position is not possible for AI researchers interested in modelling natural language understanding which goes beyond the boundaries of single sentences. And it is linguists such as Fillmore and G. Lakoff who have supported the AI endeavour by pointing out the degree to which a wide variety of knowledge sources are necessary even to determine the appropriate structural description of individual sentences to say nothing of coherently connected sequences. In this regard, it is worth sampling the viewpoints and suggestions of these researchers who share a common interest with natural language researchers in AI.

Although it is not necessary for those of us in NLU to be reassured that the transformationalist or standard program in linguistics has limited applicability, it is, at the very least, interesting to find leading linguists opposing it as well.

Consider these remarks made by Charles Fillmore (1976) to an audience of computational linguists:

> ... I am convinced that an enormously large amount of natural language is formulaic, automatic and rehearsed, rather than propositional, creative or freely generated, (p9)
>
> ...a grossly underestimated portion of speech behavior consists of the performance of rehearsed speech routines. Many of these formulas or routines or cliches are learnt in connection with particular topics, particular social roles, and particular social occasions; the interpretation of texts containing them requires the interpreter to draw on sometimes highly specific kinds of knowledge. (p 23)

Fillmore's proposals for the kind of knowledge necessary to understand text echoed ongoing work in AI especially Minsky (1975), Schank and Abelson (1977), and Charniak (1975) among others. Speaking in a language that sounded very much like that of an AI researcher, Fillmore outlined the requirements for a text understander.

> The interpreter needs to be able to construct a scene or sequence of scenes that matches the text he is processing. He does this by having access to an enormous number of <u>cognitive schemata</u> and by knowing which words and morphemes (if any) are associated with each of these schemata. Again borrowing from others, I will say that the words and morphemes "activate" the associated schemata in the interpreter's mind. I refer to this associated linguistic knowledge and its organization as a <u>linguistic frame</u>, a collection of linguistic forms or processes related in precise ways to specific <u>cognitive schemata</u> and which might impose certain perspectives on these. (p 13, my underlining)

In section I.5, we will discuss attempted AI implementations of these ideas but now we turn to important and related work in sociolinguistics (or ethnomethodology).

Again, we should note that the reason for introducing sociolinguistics to this discussion is not to name-drop, but to support the argument that there is a convergence of ideas from a number of diverse fields and it may be that the time is ripe to test the usefulness of these ideas by writing computer programs. In any case, it is somewhat remarkable that the views expressed by Erving Goffman (1974) should be so similar to those of Marvin Minsky (1975), as we shall see.

We wish to consider Goffman's definition of what he calls primary frameworks:

> Primary frameworks vary in degree of organization. Some are neatly presentable as a system of entities, postulates, and rules; others - indeed, most others - appear to have no apparent articulated shape, providing only a lore of understanding, an approach, a perspective. Whatever the degree of organization, however, each primary framework allows its user to locate, perceive, identify, and label a seemingly infinite number of concrete occurrences defined in its terms. (p 21)

Comparing Goffman's notions with those of Fillmore's, we see that there is an attempt to characterize, in a similar way, the structure and use of the built-in-knowledge necessary to understand the variety of situations, both linguistic and other which are encountered in everyday life. Granted that these ideas are imprecise (although both Fillmore, and especially Goffman present a wealth of supporting evidence), nevertheless, they are highly suggestive and have stimulated particular computer models for knowledge organization.

Psychologists have long been concerned with the nature of cognitive structures involved in such ordinary activities as perceiving and remembering. As a final contribution to this section's theme, two quotations from Barlett's (1967) classic Remembering, first published in 1932, seem appropriate. Again the similarity to previous quoted remarks should be obvious. In some concluding remarks to a chapter containing experimental evidence on perceiving and imaging Bartlett notes:

> As we have seen, in certain cases of great structural simplicity, or of structural regularity, or of extreme familiarity, the immediate data are at once fitted to, or matched with, a perceptual pattern which appears to be pre-existent so far as the perceptual act is concerned. This pre-formed setting, scheme, or pattern is utilized in a completely unreflecting, unanalytical and unwitting manner. (p.45)

Later in the book, when developing a theory of remembering, Bartlett proposes the following definition:

> 'Schema' refers to an active organization of past reactions, or of past experiences, which must always be supposed to be operating in any well-adapted organic response. (p.201)

Although Bartlett's schema were not directly motivated by linguistic phenomena, their action certainly parallel's Fillmore's cognitive schemata, Goffman's primary frameworks, and (as we shall see) Minsky's frames (primarily motivated by visual phenomena).

We now turn to the treatment of concrete problems in the representation of knowledge.

I.4 Problems of Representation

I.4.1 Introduction

It is difficult to separate a discussion of general problems in the representation of knowledge from the employment of these representatives in specific NLU systems. Nevertheless, it does seem worthwhile to identify the attempts to implement knowledge representations that correspond in some degree to those structures discussed in the previous section. Specific proposals originating with a variety of researchers, with differing goals, will be outlined and in a subsequent section working systems employing these representations will be analysed.

If the impression is being created that the major concern is with the problem of representing knowledge, let me dispel it immediately. One need not be an expert in AI to realize that there are of course two issues at hand and furthermover that they are intimately related. These issues are representation and control. A motto for researchers in AI might be: "No representation without control". That is, whereas other related disciplines can afford the luxury of emphasizing the nature of required knowledge structures to the almost complete exclusion of how they are used, AI has not and cannot follow suit. By its very definition, AI requires that its ideas be tested by the development and eventual execution of programs. Thus the organization of knowledge is in and of itself insufficient to account for a working program.

In fact, it seems strange even to talk about first deciding on a means of representing the necessary knowledge and then worrying about how to use (or control) it. At the very least, the design of data structures, whether declarative or procedural, is conditioned from the outset by a fundamental concern with issues of control. In the discussion to follow, the emphasis will be on knowledge structures for the simple reason that it is easier to describe how things are represented than how they are used. However, wherever possible the relevant issues with respect to control will be pointed out and evaluated.

I. 4.2 Minsky's Frames

About five years ago, Marvin Minsky (1975), one of the most influential thinkers in the AI community, proposed a framework for representing knowledge, commonly called a frame theory. Although the primary motivation is towards the problem of recognizing and understanding visual scenes, he does attempt to show its application in the area of discourse analysis. Minsky's proposal stimulated a flury of research aimed at more clearly specifying the nature and control of frames. But first we turn to a brief examination of Minsky's theory.

We will let Minsky himself set the stage for a discussion of his theory.

> When one encounters a new situation (or makes a substantial change in one's view of the present problem) one selects from memory a substantial structure called a frame... A frame is a data-structure for representing a stereo-typed situation like being in a certain kind of living room, or going to a child's birthday party. (p. 212)

So far this description is not unlike those of Bartlett and Fillmore. But it is Minsky's task to specify a computational theory with the necessary detail that it requires.

A frame must contain a variety of information related to its use, to what one can expect next and what steps should be taken if these expectations are not confirmed. One can view a frame as a network of nodes and relations organized in terms of levels of detail. The top levels represent the most static or stable information in the frame, in some sense, the central concept being represented whereas the lower levels contain terminals or slots which must be instantiated by the specific details of the phenomenon being confronted. Since these terminals themselves can specify a variety of conditions for their satisfaction, they can be viewed in some cases as being sub-frames. In the opposite direction, groups of frames dealing with a related area can be grouped together into frame systems.

If the initially hypothesized frame fails because its terminals cannot be satisfied, the problem is which frame to try next. Associated with the frame is an information retrieval network which taking into account the nature of the failure of the initially chosen frame to succeed, selects a possible replacement and uses the information previously computed in the process of evaluating the newly chosen frame. Note that the choice of an alternate frame will use information derived from the failure of previous frames to apply.

An initial, useful way of thinking about frame networks (and this is really Minsky's main thrust) is in the domain of image understanding for scene analysis. For a particular scene, say a living room, a frame might be a view of the room. The network represents a collection of views of the room organized in a systematic way to reflect regular transitions of viewpoint around the room. But given that NLU is our main interest, we must turn to Minsky's discussion of the applicability of frames to language understanding, especially discourse analysis.

As a working hypothesis, Minsky suggests that frequently visual images are evoked in the understanding of sentences and associated with these will be purposes, attitudes, functions and other non-visual aspects. Furthermore such aspects can be represented by terminals and their default assignments. So the basic argument is that there is a strong similarity between image understanding and language understanding with respect to the organization and use of knowledge. There is an additional assumption, not unique to Minsky, that for purposes of understanding, the distinction between syntax and semantics must be blurred.

Consider Minsky's summary of his view of NLU:

> The key words and ideas of a discourse evoke substantial thematic or scenario structures, drawn from memory with rich default assumptions The individual statements of a discourse lead to

> temporary representations which seem to correspond to what contemporary linguists call "deep structures" - which are then quickly rearranged or consumed in elaborating the growing scenario representation. (p. 245)

In somewhat more detail but quite insufficient to be implemented directly, Minsky suggests that the language processing system can be organized into a hierarchy of frameworks which deal with various levels of the understanding process. Minsky suggests that the following levels, among others, are necessary:

Surface syntactic frames:	Mainly verb cases. Prepositional and word order indicator conventions.
Surface semantic frames:	Deep syntactic frames. Action-centered meanings of words, etc.
Thematic frames:	Topics, activities, portraits, setting.
Narrative frames:	Stories, explanations, and arguments. Conventions about foci, protogonists, plots, developments, etc. (p. 245)

At the outset of his presentation, Minsky apologizes for the vagueness of some of the proposals. However, his purpose was to stimulate both discussion and research for it is obvious that definitive answers are still in the future. And indeed within the spirit of frame theory a number of extended proposals and implementations have emerged both in vision and natural language research. We will turn to some of these systems later but next we will consider the world of concepts, scripts, and plans.

I. 4.3 Scripts

I. 4.3.0 Introduction

A frame by some other name may be a script. Indeed as Schank and Abelson (1975) note

> The ideas presented here can be viewed as a specialization of the frame idea. We shall refer to our central constructs as "scripts". (p. 15)

Before we are able to adequately discuss scripts we must step back and briefly consider the work (mainly by Schank and his students) which led to their development. Because Schank (1972,

1973,1975b,Schank et al 1975), has written extensively on this earlier work, it does not seem necessary to say very much about it, perhaps just enough to make the subsequent efforts understandable. The earlier system is called MARGIE.

After having laid the groundwork, we will examine the concepts of episodes, scripts, and plans as developed by Schank and Abelson. To provide a comparison and a contrast with this version of scripts, we will consider the work of Charniak (1975) which is also presented as an elaboration of Minsky's frame theory. There are other versions of the frame concept of course, but only a few of these will be mentioned (but not used) here.

I 4.3.1 Conceptual Dependency

From the outset Schank has not been modest about either his ambitions or his accomplishments,

> The goal of the research described here is to create a theory of human natural language understanding... The task as I see it is primarily to understand human understanding and secondarily to create computer programs to actually understand. (Schank, 1972, p. 552, 553)

If that is the goal, the basic premise of Conceptual Dependency theory is that there exists a level of meaning underlying natural language, that in some sense is language independent, into which linguistic structures map during understanding. To derive an appropriate meaning representation, Schank argued for the existence of primitive concepts and underlying canonical forms. That is, independent of surface form, two sentences which have the same meaning must have the same representation in terms of the primitive concepts. This representation is called a conceptualization.

Basically a conceptualization represents an actor (ACTOR) performing an action(ACT) under a variety of constraints and elaborations. In one sense, although the comparison is minimized by Schank, conceptual dependency bears a resemblance to Fillmore's (1968,1971a) case theory. As such it is largely verb (or action) driven and the most important primitives are the ACTs. Although the actual number of primitive ACTs has varied over the years, there appear to be about eleven or twelve divided into four groups:

Physical ACTS

PROPEL:	apply a force to (e.g. push, throw)
MOVE:	move a body part (e.g. scratch, kiss)
INGEST:	take something inside you (e.g. eat, drink)
EXPEL:	take something from inside you and force it out (e.g. sweat, cry)
GRASP:	grasp (e.g. hold, grab)

Global ACTS
PTRANS: expresses a change in the physical location
of an object (e.g. go, put)
ATRANS: operates on abstract relationships
(e.g. ownership and possession, give, buy, take)

Instrumental ACTS
ATTEND: takes sense organs(eyes, ears) as objects (see,
listen)
SPEAK: produces sounds; its objects are sound (e.g.
say)

Mental ACTS
MTRANS: to handle the flow of information to and from
the conscious mind (underlies verbs like recall
memorize, perceive)
MBUILD: accounts for thought combination
(e.g. conclude, resolve, solve)

The complete language of conceptual dependency includes conceptual
cases (objective, recipient, directive, and instrumental), ACT categories
(physical, emotional, communication, state, etc.), conceptual relations (causality, time, location), conceptual tenses (past, future, conditional, continuing,
etc.), a whole host of conceptual rules, and two different kinds of dictionaries.
Before concluding this section, we will give examples of conceptualizations:

(1) John moved the table to the wall.

$$John \Longleftrightarrow^P PTRANS \xleftarrow{0} table \xleftarrow{D} wall$$
$$table \Longleftrightarrow^R LOC \text{ (wall)}$$
$$\overset{\wedge}{near}$$

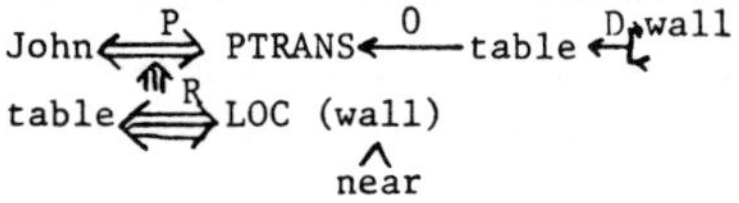

Gloss: John physically moved the table from
somewhere to the wall and the reason for
this action was to cause the table to
be near the wall.

(2) Mary sold her car to Beth.

$$Mary \overset{P}{\Longleftrightarrow} ATRANS \xleftarrow{0} OWNERSHIP:car \xleftarrow{R} \begin{matrix} Beth \\ Mary \end{matrix}$$
$$Beth \overset{}{\Longleftrightarrow} ATRANS \xleftarrow{0} OWNERSHIP:money \xleftarrow{R} \begin{matrix} Mary \\ Beth \end{matrix}$$

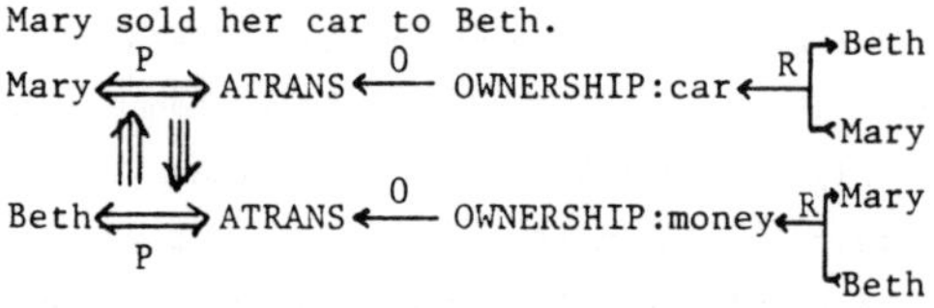

Gloss: Mary transferred ownership of the car from
herself to Beth which caused Beth to transfer
her money from herself to Mary (or the transfership of money from Beth to Mary caused
Mary to transfer her car to Beth)

(3) I walked to the cafeteria.

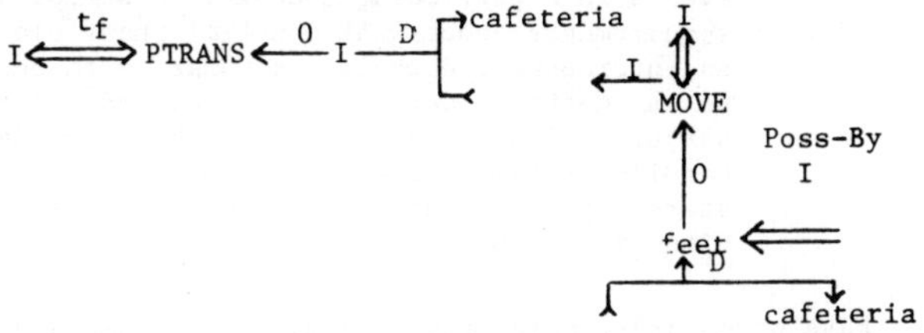

Gloss: I physically moved myself to the cafeteria (from somewhere) and I performed that action by moving my feet in the direction of the cafeteria.

The main reason for the use of primitives in a representation scheme is that it allows for a reasonably small set of processes to operate on structures built from these primitives in order to determine reasonable inferences to be drawn. For example in its inference mode, MARGIE makes the following inferences from the input sentence: "John gave Mary an aspirin":

1. John believes that Mary wants an aspirin.
2. Mary is sick.
3. Mary wants to feel better.
4. Mary will ingest the aspirin.

These inferences are only a few of the number which can be drawn from the input sentence by the inferencing mechanism developed by Rieger (1975). Furthermore, he believes that all such inferences should be made everytime a sentence is encountered. The potential explosion of inferences does not appear to be of major concern to him.

So far all the effort has been devoted to the processing and representation of single sentences. Obviously, all this apparatus has not been developed for the analysis of isolated sentences, the understanding of which will hardly consititute a theory of human understanding. The extension of this work to the domain of texts follows fairly naturally but requires the explication of causal and temporal relations in order to deal with the coherence implicit in connected discourse. To deal with the overall structure of texts, Schank and Abelson developed their version of frames, namely, scripts.

I. 4.3.2 Scripts and Plans

We will begin this section with a quotation from Schank and Abelson (1977), which clearly describes what they mean by a script.

> A script is a structure that describes appropriate sequences of events in a particular context. A script is made up of slots and requirements about what can fill those slots. The structure is an interconnected whole, and what is in one slot affects what can be in another. Scripts handle everyday situations. They are not subject to much change, nor do they provide the apparatus for handling totally novel situations. Thus, a script is predetermined, stereotyped sequence of actions that defines a well-known situtation. (p. 41)

As we have noted previously, there seems to have emerged a general consensus on the form of knowledge representations required to understand natural language. Large, coherent, active data structures seem to be necessary and their elaboration represents a major, current research task.

In section I.5.4 we will go into more detail about scripts but for the present purposes a sketch of a script for a restaurant, from the point of view of a customer, will suffice. (Schank 1975b)

script: restaurant
roles: customer; waitress; chef; cashier
reason: to get food so as to go down in hunger and up in pleasure.

scene I: entering

PTRANS - self into restaurant
ATTEND - eyes to where empty tables are
MBUILD - where to sit
PTRANS - self to table
MOVE - sit down

scene 2: ordering

ATRANS - receive menu
ATTEND - look at it
MBUILD - decide what self wants
MTRANS - tell order to waitress

scene 3: - eating

ATRANS - receive food
INGEST - eat food

Scene 4: exiting

MTRANS - ask for check
ATRANS - receive check
ATRANS - give tip to waitress
PTRANS - go to cashier
ATRANS - give money to cashier
PTRANS - go out of restaurant

Each primitive ACT stands for the main action in a standard set of actions. It should be clear that the above sketch is probably a caricature rather than a characterization of activities associated with dining in a restaurant. This also raises the fundamental question associated with scripts (or frames) which is how to account for the potentially infinite variations of a simple activity. Recall that if a script is meant to represent the central or stereotyped event but to deal adequately with real world phenomena, it will be necessary to go beyond such simple characterizations. Additional necessary pieces of the system are goals and plans.

To achieve a desired goal under unusual circumstances an appropriate script may be invoked and the sequence of steps followed. But suppose there does not exist a script for the particular situation encountered. The system must construct a plan to achieve the desired goal. Available resources are called PLANS, and may be viewed as sequences of actions, similar to mini-scripts, which can be used to achieve the given goal (or GOAL). We will return shortly to the Schank and Abelson system of scripts, plans, and goals but first we turn to another proposal for representing knowledge in the frame "formalism".

I 4.3.3 Charniak's Frames

Over the past three years Charniak (1975, 1977a, b, c, 1978a, b) has written several papers on an approach to representing knowledge for language understanding with an emphasis on common sense inference. He freely acknowledges the inspiration of Minsky (Charniak, 1975) and in fact calls his structures, frames. There is also a strong similarity to the independently developed "scripts" of Schank and Abelson. First, to set the stage, a brief quotation by Charniak (1975) follows:

> I take a frame to be a static data structure about one stereotyped topic, such as shopping at the supermarket, taking a bath, a piggy bank. Each frame is primarily made up of many statements about the frame topic, called "frame statements" (F.S.)... <u>The primary mechanism of understanding a line of a story is to see it as instantiating one or more F.S.'s</u>. (p. 42)

Here is a simple outline consisting of some frame statements about shopping in a supermarket.

```
Goal(SHOPPER own ITEMS)
SHOPPER be at SUPERMARKET
SHOPPER have use of BASKET
do for all ITEM ITEMS
      SHOPPER at ITEM
      BASKET at ITEM
      ITEM in BASKET
end
SHOPPER at CHECKOUT COUNTER
BASKET at CHECKOUT COUNTER
SHOPPER pay  for ITEMS
SHOPPER leave SUPERMARKET
```

Note the implicit assumption that shopping is only done with a cart (a BASKET). This is not necessary of course and a simple modification of the frame allows for a generalization. One can view that part of the supermarket frame devoted to the use of shopping carts as a sub-frame.

Instead of actually instantiating FS's in the process of story understanding a separate data structure called a "frame image" (FI) is created. This means that different shoppers, each using the supermarket frame will develop separate FI's. Since one of Charniak's major goals is dealing with problems of inference, we should consider, however briefly, his method for using frames for this purpose. Charniak (1972) has long claimed that some inferencing must be done as the story is being processed but obviously the question is how to limit the potentially infinite number of inferences which could be made to those which should be made. Charniak proposes something he calls the "Dual Usage Rule" to deal with part of this question; that is, when should an FS be instantiated and put into the data base? An answer proposed is that typically an FS is instantiated in the data base if it is in an active frame and appears in the semantic representation of the text.

More recently Charniak (1978b) has discussed a computer program called Ms. Malaprop, which is based on "framed" knowledge. Without attempting to describe this system, we might list some of its major points as follows:

1. Frame comprehension hypothesis - a major part of understanding is the matching of incoming story information against the framed knowledge of what normally occurs.

2. Matching - The purpose of matching is to identify the prototypical event eluded (sic) to by an occurrence in the story.

3. Read time inference - Many inferences are made while reading. There are three kinds of deductive inferences: (a) when a contradiction is noticed, (b) when a frame expectation is confounded, and (c) when the input implies a state or event which is important for the activities discussed in the story.

4. Undoing wrong conclusions - A system which makes inferences while reading will invariably make some false ones. Should Ms. Malaprop later discover that a particular conclusion is wrong she will correct it, as well as anything which might have been derived from it.

--taken from pages 225-226 (Charniak 1978b)

We will now turn to one final form of representation usually referred to as semantic nets.

I. 4.4 Semantic Networks

I. 4.4.1 Introduction

Given the wealth of information on semantic networks, viz. Woods (1975), Simmons (1973), Schubert (1976), and Brachman (1977) among others, it hardly seems necessary to provide yet another survey. But our purpose is to introduce just enough detail in order to show how this structure can be used to represent knowledge for discourse processing.

The first use of semantic networks in AI is generally credited to Ross Quillian (1968) in his attempt to encode the meanings of individual words. Since that time the variety of applications has been enormous and the variations in notation almost as large. The simplest characterization might be that a semantic network is a labelled directed graph for which the nodes represent concepts and the arcs, relations among the concepts. For example, the sentence "John gave Mary a book in the park yesterday", might be represented by the following structure:

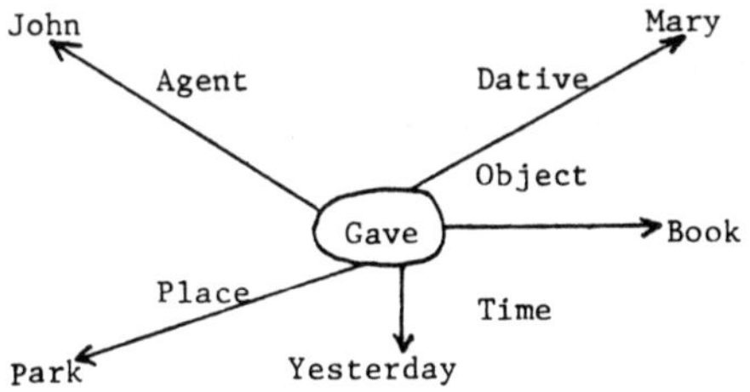

This semantic network might represent the structure generated by one version of a case grammar.

There have been a variety of arguments expressed about the supposed virtues and defects of semantic networks. One of the earliest and still perhaps a major claim in their favour is their supposed "perspicuity". Supposedly knowledge represented in terms of lists of predicates in some formal language or attribute-value pairs does not carry the same visual impact for the system designer. It should be clear that the arguments for perspicuity really have to do with paper representations or discussions rather than with a particular use of data structures in a programming language. Given the large amounts of knowledge which must be represented in current systems, it is not clear that the visual aids provided by a semantic net are at all helpful. For example, see

Fig. 13.10 in Scragg (1975).

A more important argument, and a basic question for any representation scheme is the ease of access of relevant data. Semantic nets are supposed to shine with respect to this issue. Once having entered the net at some node, it is to be expected that additional associated information is easily accessible along neighbouring arcs. That is, there is some notion of "semantic distance" (implicitly) defined over the network. In comparison, list-based representation schemes are thought to be neutral with respect to the relationship between successive or neighbouring data items. But this difference may also be illusory, for one can associate with any storage scheme a retrieval network organized along any desired lines.

There have also been complaints raised that the "semantics" of semantic nets are usually ill-defined (Woods, 1975), that there is difficulty in representing logical constructs (Schubert, 1976), and that there is a confusion over what nodes and properties are (Brachman, 1977). We will examine next the use of semantic networks in their guise as scenes, episodes, and scenarios, as used by Norman and Rumelhart (1975) and their associates.

I. 4.4.2 An Application from Cognitive Psychology

We are concerned here with the work of Norman and Rumelhart (1975) and the LNR Research Group at the University of California, San Diego. And they are concerned, from a psychological perspective, with such issues as language comprehension, memory structures, both long term and episodic, perception and problem solving, reasoning, and question answering. At the risk of being superficial, we can only mention a few of the aspects of this large project, but perhaps enough to indicate the aims and accomplishments of the group.

While it is impossible to provide a detailed description of the system, let us consider some of the following features:

1. There are obvious similarities, acknowledged by Rumelhart, Lindsay, and Norman (1972) to work by Schank (1972), Fillmore (1968), Quillian (1966, 1969), and Anderson and Bower (1973). Familiar notions such as case, nodes as concepts, arcs as relations are common to all these systems.
2. Here is a network representation from Rumelhart, Lindsay, Norman (1972) of the short story:

Yesterday at school, the boy hit the window with a stone. The man scolded him.

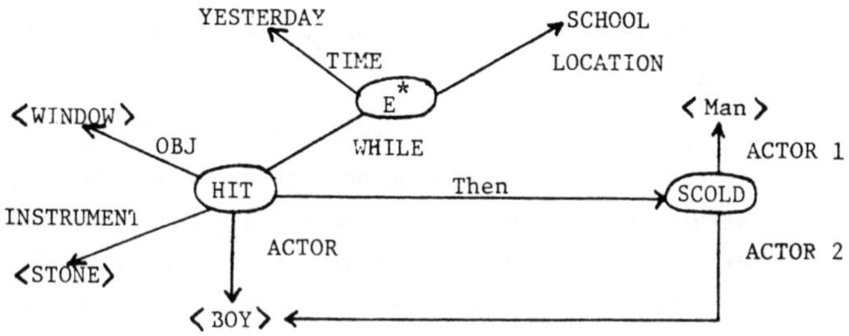

There are two types of nodes in the system, primary nodes and secondary nodes. A primary node refers directly to the natural language word and may contain a definition of the word in a relational format. A secondary node can be thought of as a token of a primary type node. The printed words in the circles and in the angular brackets denote secondary events and concept nodes which are connected to their primary nodes by the act and isa arrows respectively (but not shown here).

3. The representation distinguishes among three classes or levels of information, namely, concepts, events, and episodes, Concepts, which refer to particular ideas, are constructed using such relations as isa (for set membership) and has (to define properties). An event would represent a simple sentence consisting of actors, actions, and objects. For example that part of the network representing the boy hitting the window with a stone is an event. An episode is a cluster of events with such interrelations as then and while, examples of which are shown in the given network.

4. The LNR group argues for a single system approach to the study of cognitive processes:

> One system has to be capable of handling the representation and processing issues in syntactic and semantic analysis of language, in memory, perception, problem solving, reasoning, question-answering, and in the acquisition of knowledge (Norman and Rumelhart 1975, p 160).

Their computer implementation, called MEMOD (memory model) consists of a knowledge representation, a semantic network of the type discussed previously, a parser which using an augmented transition network (ATN, Woods, 1970) transforms input sentences into active network structures within the semantic net, and an interpreter which performs a variety of operations on the semantic network itself which correspond to updating and learning.

5. The parser is based on ideas derived from Fillmore's (1968) work on case grammars. This means that verbs are the main syntactic structures and are represented by case frames which are used to drive the parser to seek satisfactory arguments. See Taylor and Rosenberg (1975) for another version of a case-driven parser for natural language.

6. MEMOD has been used in a variety of applications to buttress claims for its universality. Among these are the following:
   (i) in a system that understands and can answer questions.
   (ii) in modelling the human problem-solving processes involved in the playing of board games such as GO with an emphasis on the perceptual and cognitive aspects.
   (iii) in self-examination of the operation of its own processes.

I.4.5 Comments and Criticisms

Frames, scripts, and schemata have not been greeted with universal acclaim as the answer. The proponents were among the first to recognize some of the problems which faced the designers of frame-based systems. Here are some of Minsky's (1975) concerns taken from his original paper:

Expectation:	How to select an initial frame to meet some given conditions?
Elaboration:	How to select and assign subframes to represent additional details?
Alteration:	How to find a frame to replace one that does not fit well enough?
Novelty:	What to do if no acceptable frame can be found? Can we modify an old frame or must we build a new one?
Learning:	What frames should be stored, or modified, as a result of the experience?

(pp. 247-248)

It is the first of these issues that has received the most attention. In the area of computer vision, Mackworth (1977) has referred to the chicken-and-egg problem. In the same domain, Palmer (1975) has described the parsing problem as one of deciding between a bottom-up or a top-down approach, or in other terms, is it the whole that interprets the parts or do the parts lead to the recognition of the whole? More concretely, he phrases the dilemna or paradox as:

> How can someone recognize a face until he has first recognized the eyes, nose , mouth, and ears? Then again, how can someone recognize the eyes, nose, mouth and ears until he knows that they are part of a face? (p. 295)

Schank and Abelson (1977), of necessity, address themselves to this problem as well. In their formalism, the script header is crucial in determining which script to apply to the current situation. What is important is that, for example, the use of the word 'restaurant' out of context should not lead to the invocation of the restaurant script. Now if we can determine what 'out of context' means, we are done. Most likely the sentence, 'The man fell near the restaurant', has very little to do with restaurants. They also raise the notion of 'fleeting scripts' to refer to scripts which are mentioned and presumedly proceed normally; that is, default paths are assumed and not developed or instantiated so that a pointer to the appropriate script suffices.

To instantiate a script, it is required that not only the header occur but one other line as well. Schank and Abelson (1977) propose a variety of headers which differ in the strength of the prediction that their associated contexts will in fact be instantiated. The first type which makes a weak prediction is called a Precondition Header (PH). Its use is illustrated by the occurrence of a sentence such as 'Mary was very hungry'. This sentence serves as a PH for the restaurant script because it is the goal condition for one of the main activities of this script, namely, the ingestion of food (INGEST food). A reasonable prediction is that the restaurant script may be appropriate because it is a common way of acquiring food. The other types of headers depend on activities in which at least one acts as an instrument for the others, the explicit mention of a time or place, and most strongly predictive, the occurrence of a conceptualization which matches a conceptualization internal to the script.

So far we have been concerned with technical problems related to the use of frames in story understanding. But Wilks (1976a) raises a more general question which challenges the fundamental assumption underlying the packaging of knowledge in frames. Simply put, the claim is that to a large measure, language understanding requires linguistic knowledge (syntax and semantics), general world knowledge and inferencing ability. The reliance on relatively large coherent chunks of knowledge may be relatively infrequent. This is obviously in direct contrast to the position of Schank and Abelson, Charniak, and others.

Wilks, in a rather amusing example dealing with a puberty rite, attempts to minimize the necessity of frames in story understanding. He outlines a male puberty rite script in a notation similar to Charniak's (1975) supermarket frame and then presents the following very short story:

> Little Kimathi's mother accidentally
> { touched his arm / dropped her shoga / looked away } during the puberty rite
> The crowd drew back in horror.

The claim is that any speaker of English is able to understand this story and it is highly unlikely that he or she uses anything like a puberty rite script. How then is it understood? In ordinary terms, we might say that given the behaviour of the crowd we infer that the mother touching Kimathi accidentally during the puberty rite is a bad thing. Wilks expands upon this argument but for our purposes the main point has been made.

Other criticisms have to do with the claim that frames are too static a form of knowledge representation to deal adequately with a rapidly changing and dynamic world (Feldman, 1975). Further along this line they seem to be a retrogressive step, a retreat from powerful procedural methods to older declarative representations such as thesauri which had earlier been found severely wanting (Wilks, 1976a). With these and other criticisms in mind we turn to a survey of some current systems.

I. 5 Some Current Systems

I. 5.1 Introduction

It should be stated from the outset that none of the systems described here (or for that matter any other) is complete in any real sense. The major limitation is the domain of discourse which is chosen for its narrowness to permit the construction of an entire understanding system. This is especially the case for frame-based systems which require the detailed representation of large chunks of knowledge. Given a restricted enough subject it is possible to construct a few comprehensive frames or scripts and then explore problems associated with their application to simple stories.

But again the simplification implies that such serious issues as frame selection and/or replacement do not really arise. Although the designers suggest a variety of methods for selecting initial frames (see Section I.4.5), in reality their systems only contain a few frames and do not provide a real test for their control strategies. Basically what is explored in most of these systems is the internal structure of frames, their interaction under limited numbers, and their ability to deal with a few linguistic and inference problems.

There is no suggestion in any of the systems of how frames are learned, acquired, or modified except for some casual suggestions by Schank and Abelson (1977). This observation is not meant to be a criticism, given that learning is not a major research area elsewhere in AI. We will first examine two rather old systems, Weizenbaum's ELIZA (1966), and Colby's PARRY (Parkinson, Colby, Faught, 1977) because although they are designed to carry on conversations, they do opperate on quite different principles than the other systems discussed. The other systems described are GUS (Bobrow, et al, 1977), the proposed conversational system of McCalla (1977, 1978), and SAM (Schank and Abelson, 1977). A number of additional projects will be mentioned briefly including the work of Grosz (1977 a,b; 1978 a,b), Sidner (1978 a,b), and Cohen (1978).

I. 5.2 Two Early Systems

The purpose of including Weizenbaum's (1966) classic paper in this discussion of contemporary NLU systems, is certainly not to describe the structure of the ELIZA program; rather, in the light of recent theoretical developments, it may be possible to view it in a new light. If one assumes that a basic purpose of recent systems is to participate in conversations then ELIZA satisfies this requirement. Moreover, although its performance is not very sophisticated, it is reasonably robust and the domain of discourse is quite unrestricted. However, it has one major drawback; in human terms, it doesn't know what it is talking about.

In computer terms, it has almost no semantics, limited syntax, and it does not represent in any real way anything that it discovers about the human participant. How then is ELIZA able to be an active, almost believable conversant? One answer is that it depends very heavily on its conversational partner to be forgiving and to want the conversation to continue even when anomalous responses are encountered. Another answer is that Weizenbaum has indeed captured, in a simple and perhaps even trivial way, something interesting about the nature of conversations. It may be the case that, except for goal-directed interchanges, many conversations proceed from sentence to sentence with only an occasional reference to previous discourse.

We do not wish to read more into ELIZA than actually exists but it is, at the very least curious, that such a simple program can exhibit a range of behaviours that eludes the most sophisticated current systems. Most of its behaviour is illusory, however, since its gross inadequacies are immediately apparent when questioned about its responses. Of course, ELIZA cannot respond to questions other than to treat them in a uniform manner; that is, pattern matching is performed and a canned response is produced.* ELIZA has no memory, no inferencing power, no linguistic knowledge, hardly any world knowledge, but is nevertheless, interesting.

Turning to Colby's PARRY (Parkison, Colby, Faught, 1977), we encounter a recent exposition of a long ongoing project, directed by Colby, for purposes quite different from those of Weizenbaum. Colby, a psychiatrist, has been developing a computer program which incorporates a theory of paranoid behaviour. To test this theory the program must be able to communicate in natural language with an interviewer such that the transcripts of these interactions are indistinguishable from those produced by a paranoid human. As such, the program must be equipped with sufficient linguistic ability to engage in a conversation which is an exercise in paranoid delusions.

PARRY's language understanding component is driven by a few thousand general patterns and probably represents the most extensive use of patterns in a NLU system. By patterns we mean a rule with a left and right hand side such that if the left hand side matches the input, then the right hand side becomes active and produces a response. Once the input has been appropriately matched, its relevance to the program's sphere of interest must be determined, the information adequately represented, and a response made. The program's interests are the source of its paranoid behaviour and in many of its responses, this feature appears quite prominently.

In some sense, the thousands of patterns underlying PARRY's linguistic abilities, comprise a very large frame or script appropriate to its paranoid bent. From our point of view, however, PARRY is somewhat deficient in its linguistic versatility and certainly lacking in broadly based world knowledge. The ability of pattern-directed matching to deal with syntactically ill-formed

*One might view ELIZA's Script as a collection of mini-frames but this does not really explain very much.

structures is exploited but a coherent and principled approach to natural language understanding is sacrificed. Nevertheless Colby's system does carry out quite convincing conversations and is, therefore, a contribution to this area.

I. 5.3 GUS(Genial Understander System)

GUS, developed by Bobrow et al (1977), represents the initial experimental NLU system in a promised series of such systems, from a most distinguished group of researchers in AI and cognitive psychology.. GUS has quite limited abilities and knowledge as befits an introductory system. It is supposed to schedule roundtrip airline journeys originating in San Jose and remaining within California. As such, it has attributes of a CAI (computer-aided instruction) system in that it attempts to extract sufficient information from the user, via a dialog, in order to plan the limited trip.

The CAI component is a mixture of menu-driven and mixed-initiative strategies. On the one hand a fixed number of pieces of information must be acquired (menu-driven) but the order of acquisition can vary (mixed-initiative). GUS is advertised as a 'Frame-Driven Dialog System' with the mandatory reference to Minsky (1975). Sufficient knowledge must be embedded in the frames in order to direct the conversation, determine the required information whenever it appears by syntactic and semantic processes, and produce appropriate responses which either confirm or solicit new information. Perhaps an appropriate starting point for our analysis is to annotate a transcript of a dialog with GUS.

GUS: Hello. My name is GUS. I can help you plan a simple trip by air. Where do you want to go?
(1) Client: I want to go to San Diego on May 28.
GUS: What time do you want to leave?
(2) Client: I must be in San Diego before 10 am.
GUS: Would you like P.S.A. flight 102 that arrives at 9:15 am?
(3) Client: What is the next flight?
GUS: Air California flight 310 that leaves at 8:30 am and arrives at 10 am.
(4) Client: I'll take the first one.
GUS: In what name do I make the reservation, please?
(5) Client: Dan Bobrow
GUS: I have confirmed the following flight: P.S.A. flight 102 on Wednesday May 28 from San Jose to San Diego that leaves 7:30 am and arrives at 9:15 am.
What date do you want to return on?
(6) Client: On Friday in the evening.
GUS: Would you like the flight that leaves at 7:45 pm?
(7) Client: That's fine.
GUS: I have confirmed the following flight: P.S.A. flight 307 on Friday May 30 from San Diego to San Jose that leaves at 7:45 pm and arrives at 9:30 pm. Thank you for calling. Goodbye.

(p 157, Bobrow et al, 1977)

GUS opens with a standard introduction and a question concerning the client's destination. The client responds but provides not only the destination but a date as well. Although in GUS's 'script' the departure date is next on the agenda, it recognized that this has been supplied already and so it jumps to the next item it requires, namely, the departure time. The client's response (2) is somewhat oblique and requires GUS to infer and suggest a possible departure time which suits the client's preferred arrival time. This demonstrates GUS's ability to accommodate indirect answers.

The client (3) is not satisfied and inquires about the 'next flight'. GUS interprets this to mean the next departing flight as listed in a standard airline schedule and gives its times of departure and arrival. The client's response (4) contains an anaphoric reference, 'the first one', and this is correctly interpreted by GUS to mean the first of the two flights mentioned so far. The ability to deal with anaphora is one of the major problems facing any NLU system; we will consider some of these issues later. After having obtained the client's name, GUS confirms the depart-information and begins the process of obtaining the return data by asking for the return date. This time the client responds with 'Friday' which is certainly not a date and it is up to GUS to determine which date Friday refers to.

Given that the departure takes place on Wednesday, May 28, the program infers that the probable return date is Friday, May 30. This requires GUS to have knowledge about the way people make such time references as 'next Thursday', 'this Monday', or 'the coming Wednesday' and how the interpretation of these is dependent on the context in which they were uttered (see Fillmore on Deixis, 1971). As soon as the program acquires a return time, it has complete information and summarizes it for the client.

It should be apparent that GUS's terms of reference are quite narrow but that even so some interesting problems must be solved. To begin with, we will first examine the structure of frames and then some of the control issues involved in their use. Consider the following two key frames, <Dialog> and <Trip Specification>:

Slots	Fillers	Servants	Demons
<Dialog>			
CLIENT	<Person>	Create	Link to TRAVELLER
NOW	<Date>	Get date	
TOPIC	<Trip Specification>	Create	
<Trip Specification>			
HOMEPORT	<City>	Default: Palo Alto	
FOREIGNPORT	<City>		Link to OUTWARDLEG, AWAYSTAY, INWARD-LEG

Slots	Fillers	Servants	Demons
OUTWARDLEG	<TripLeg>	Create	
AWAYSTAY	<PlaceStay>		
INWARDLEG	<TripLeg>	Create	

(taken from Bobrow et al, 1977)

Names in angle brackets (e.g. <Date>) are frame names, representing pointers to other frames, not shown here. A dialogue commences as the system attempts to instantiate an instance of the dialog frame. It must fill the slots of the frame and does this in a depth-first, recursive manner using the associated fillers. As we have seen, slots may be filled out of sequence. It is the responsibility, usually, of the associated servants to fill the slots either by calculating a value from known data, by creating a new frame, or by asking the client. The notion of demons, originated with Charniak (1972); they can be thought of as programs-in-waiting. As soon as conditions (read specific data values) are appropriate the demons execute. For example, as soon as a departure is specified, a demon calls a program which determines a proposed flight to be presented to the client. The embedding of procedures in the frame data structure, is called (by Winograd) procedural attachment.

The entire process is initiated with the attempted instantiation of the <Dialogue> frame. This requires the filling in of the slots of this frame, initially in sequence. Thus a <Person> frame is created by the appropriate servant and a demon is actuated which puts the same instance of person in the TRAVELLER slot. Next the NOW slot is filled by a servant which constructs a <DATE> frame for the current date. Finally, a <Trip Specification> frame is created to fill the TOPIC slot, which completes the <Dialog> frame; the process continues with the filling of the slots in the <Trip Specification> frame.

As mentioned previously the control process is basically depth-first, recursive. Thus attempts to fill the slots of a frame can cause another frame to be created and its slots to be filled first. It does not seem likely that such a simple regimen will be adequate for systems with large data bases expecially in circumstances of non-directed interaction. Given the domain in which GUS operates, the control process used is appropriate, because a rather small set of data items is required and there really is not much deviation allowed (or expected) from the standard sequence of request-response pairs. However, as a first step, GUS performs quite well and the structure of its frames is particularly interesting.

It should be pointed out that an important goal in the GUS project was the testing of the KRL language (Bobrow and Winograd, 1977). KRL (Knowledge Representation Language) is an ambitious attempt to provide a universal language for a wide variety of applications in AI. Its major aim is descriptive adequacy and this explains, perhaps, why questions of control are not given first priority.

As a final comment about GUS, we might note that in experiments with it, people frequently exceeded the capabilities of the system in ways not expected by the designers. Many people tend to be a somewhat verbose and provide information which the program not only does not expect but cannot accommodate. This is a problem for all conversational systems. What can be done when the program encounters a response beyond the range of its competence? How does it even recognize that such an event has occurred? GUS, which represents an initial step, should not be expected to deal with such problems but they cannot be ignored for very long.

I.5.3 Modelling Conversation

McCalla's (1977, 1978) concern, as it is many others as well, is to investigate the organization of knowledge necessary for a system to participate in a dialogue or conversation with a person. The term 'organization' is taken to include both the structure of the knowledge and the control processes which manipulate it. This required the development of yet another language called |LISP), embedded in LISP, to provide the necessary control structures. At the time of this writing, the language was not completely debugged; hence, the system was not implemented. However, most of the system was represented in |LISP even though it has never been run.

Some of the issues which McCalla wished to deal with in his research are as follows:

(1) Whether world and linguistic knowledge can be effectively combined?

(2) How the goals of a conversant affect what he/she says and understands.

(3) How the knowledge of a conversant about him/herself and other conversants affect what he/she says and understands.

(4) How the conversant is able to use context to enable him/herself to focus on the relevant and ignore the irrelevant.

Related to these are some issues more specifically associated with AI concerns, namely:

(i) the integration of procedural and declarative knowledge.

(ii) the ability to access this knowledge (problems of when and how to search)

(iii) the necessity of a context mechanism (see (4) above)
(iv) the need to maintain a record of processing decisions (see (2) above)
(v) the building in of robustness
(vi) the spectre of complexity and combinatorial explosion.

McCalla organizes his analysis of conversation in terms of the following four levels:

1. Non-linguistic Goals

   Any conversation is usually driven by non-linguistic goals. Clearly, planning is important as well as the need for extra-linguistic information.

2. Scripts (cf. Schank and Abelson, 1977)
   These represent the highest level of linguistic goals and are usually invoked as subgoal of 1. Their primary task is to keep track of utterances on both sides of a conversation.

3. Speech acts
   Scripts, in turn, can call in subgoals that involve interpreting or generating the speech of a single speaker. Such single verbal subgoals are called speech acts (after Searle, 1970). Examples of these are inquire, respond, agree, etc.

4. Language Level
   This level deals directly with the surface utterance. Basically, it involves syntactic analysis but in the context of differing subgoals generated at the other levels.

As a real-world context for exploring his ideas, McCalla chose the conversations to be expected when purchasing, at a box-office, a ticket for a concert, the ordering of a drink at intermission, and the commenting on the first half performance. There is a strong similarity between the first two situations which are goal-directed and involve the buying of something. The third is undirected and as might be expected is treated in considerably less detail than the first two. Consider Fig. 2. which gives the dynamic linkages of some concert scenario, |PEXPR's. The latter are the equivalent of frames in McCalla's system. A typical ticket-buying conversation which would invoke this structure is given below:

Ticket-Seller (TS): "Yes?"
Model (M): "I'd like a ticket to the concert."
TS: "How about K-5? It is right centre about 10 rows back"
M: "Fine. How much is that?"
TS: "10 dollars."
M: "O.K." (hands over the money)
TS: (hands over the ticket)
M: "Thanks"
TS: "Thank-you sir."

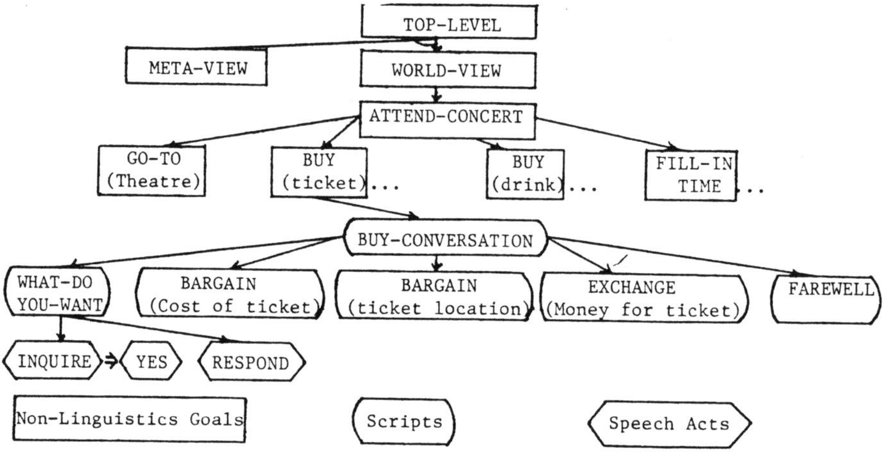

Fig. 2 Dynamic Linkages of Some Concert Scenario |PEXRS (taken from McCalla, 1977, p. 89)

We might try to briefly characterize the representation of knowledge in McCalla's system. The basic data structures are called <u>objects</u> which can communicate to one another by passing messages. The most interesting of these are the |PEXPR's, referred to previously. These contain both static information, in the form of patterns, which can be matched in the PLANNER/CONNIVER manner, as well as active or procedural information which can be actuated during message passing. Failure of a message pattern to match can cause a variety of activities including the inheritance of certain properties along implicit links of other |PEXPR"s. That is, there is an underlying semantic network in which the |PEXPR's are embedded.

Successful message passing activates the associated |PEXPR and creates an activation network (or an instantiated network) which corresponds to an execution environment. This serves as a very powerful kind of context mechanism important in accessing current goals. Once activated, execution instances remain, usually in chains, and provide something like episodic memory.

There are serious questions to be asked about this work in terms of the combinatorial explosion issue referred to earlier. I discuss this problem now, not because McCalla's system is more prone to it than others, but just because it is representative of the approach we have been concentrating on. There is no question that a large, comprehensive system with thousands of objects (frames, or scripts) will most likely grind to a halt if sophisticated control methods are not used. The initial frame selection problem, and the shifting to new frames place a great burden on the processing resources of a NLU system. Various mechanisms have been proposed, including parallel processing in which by an associative activation scheme all possible relevant objects are interrogated. However, there have not been any serious (i.e. very large) systems which are actually running except perhaps for some speech understanding ones.

I.5.4 SAM, FRUMP, and PAM

We introduced the notion of scripts as defined by Schank and Abelson (1977) in section I.4.3.2. Except for a brief discussion of problems of script selection, very little was said about how the scripts were used and which domains were chosen. In this section, we wish to examine a number of applications of the script framework, as developed by Schank and his students, including Lehnert (1976, 1977a,b), Cullingford (1976), and Willensky (1978).

The first program to be discussed is SAM (Script Applier Mechanism), a story understander, followed by FRUMP (Fast Reading Understanding and Memory Program, and finally PAM (Plan Applier Mechanism) a story understander that uses plans, goals, and themes. Of all the work on NLU systems in progress, that of Schank, his students, both current and past, represents the most coherent and single-minded. Under the prevasive influence of Schank's vision and determination, this major and comprehensive research programme looms large in AI.

I. 5.4.1 SAM

SAM is a program which takes a story as input and produces a large conceptual dependency network as an internal representation from which paraphrases and summaries can be generated. Also a question-answering program developed by Lehnert (1977a) can access this representation to answer questions about the story. As might be expected, the stories used are well-characterized by the available scripts such as the restaurant one described previously. SAM operates in four stages, the first three of which interact as co-routines. One way to gain some sense of the operation of this program is to follow its operation in processing the first two sentences of a simple story. This trace is taken from Schank and Abelson (1977). The entire text is as follows:

> John went to a restaurant. He ordered a hamburger.
> The waiter said they didn't have any. John asked
> for a hot dog. When the hot dog came, it was burnt.
> He left the restaurant.
>
> (p. 190, Schank & Abelson, 1977)

We will be making reference to the following three modules:

(a) PARSER - the analyser, an extension of Riesbeck's (1975) parser developed for the MARGIE system (Schank, 1975a) which translates sentences into a conceptual dependency representation.

(b) MEMTOK - a memory module which contains information about objects or actors which may appear in stories.

(c) APPLY - the script applier, which attempts to select an appropriate script to be used in processing the text.

After the story text has been put in a file, PARSER is called and parses the first sentence into the conceptual dependency structure,

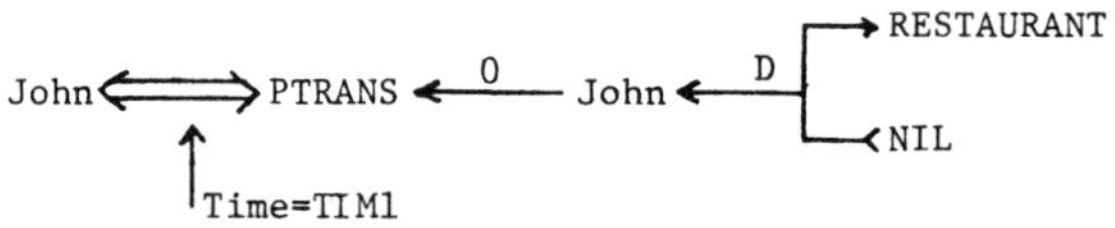

Now MEMTOK is called with this structure as input and attempts to identify 'John' and 'restaurant'. Given that this is the first sentence of the story it knows nothing about the human, 'John', and the location, 'restaurant', and so calls APPLY, with the above structure and a suggestion that the restaurant script may be appropriate because of the word 'restaurant' in the input.

APPLY, in this case, finds the suggestion well-made, invokes the restaurant script, checks to see if any preconditions have been violated (which is not the case here), instantiates the default conditions, 'has money' and 'is hungry' binds 'John', 'restaurant', and 'money' in this script, informs MEMTOK, and finally calls PARSER on the next sentence.

In this sentence, 'He ordered a Hamburger', PARSER uses the sense of order corresponding to 'order a meal (in a restaurant)', a result of the previous invocation of the restaurant script. At this point the PARSER does not know the referent of 'he'; it calls MEMTOK to 'internalize' the present parse but cannot deal with 'hamburger'. It is now the turn of APPLY, to use the restaurant script, to interpret the input sentence. The result of APPLY's analysis is to identify 'he' as 'John', to tentatively link 'order' to order a meal, not a check or a menu, and to tentatively bind order to 'hamburger'. In addition, instantiating further items in the restaurant script, it gets tokens for 'table', 'chair', and 'waiter' from MEMTOK.

The remainder of the analysis is similar but as more of the story is processed the accumulated constraints limit the range of possible interpretations. The given text was quite simple in that the correct script was chosen initially and was the only one necessary. However, the system has the ability to bring scripts in and out as needed. Once the processing is complete, the control program, CP, produces a paraphrase of it which is output in English using a generator module. Now, the system is ready for questions.

Consider the question, 'Did John eat a hot dog?', which cannot be answered directly from the story text. The question is parsed, and MEMTOK is called. It identifies 'John' as having been created earlier but it is unable to identify 'hot dog'. The question is recognized as of type yes/no. Having been unable to locate the phrase 'eating a hot-dog' in the top-level story representation, the question-anwsering program, QA, hypothesizes that 'eating' may have been prevented for some reason. It eventually goes on to discover that the fact the hot dog was burnt is a good reason for its not having been eaten and produces an appropriate answer.

I.5.4.2 FRUMP (Fast Reading Understanding and Memory Program)

FRUMP can be thought of as a program which just skims stories in contrast to SAM which really understands them. It does this by using what might be called sketchy scripts, which are sparse both with respect to the number of conceptualizations contained and the relations among them, compared to the corresponding script SAM would use. FRUMP operates by skimming the newspaper story until it obtains sufficient information to select an appropriate script. The script is in effect composed of a list of facts, called requests, which it expects to find in the story. It demonstrates its competency by producing a simple summary for each story.

I.5.4.3 PAM (Plan Applier Mechanism)

This program was designed to understand stories which involve goals, plans, and identifiable themes. In interpreting such stories, PAM will treat each character's behaviour as an attempt to achieve specific goals. Schank and Abelson (1977) present the following story as an example of PAM's operation.

> John loved Mary but she didn't want to marry him. One day, a dragon stole Mary from the castle. John got on top of his horse and killed the dragon. Mary agreed to marry him. They lived happily ever after. (p. 217)

PAM is able to answer the following questions:

> Why did John get on his horse?
> BECAUSE HE WANTED TO BE NEAR MARY.

Why did Mary agree to marry John?
BECAUSE SHE WAS INDEBTED TO HIM.

Why did John kill the dragon?
BECAUSE HE WANTED MARY NOT TO DIE.

In order to answer such questions, PAM must make a number of inferences of which the following are a few:

John wanted to marry Mary.
Mary was endangered by the dragon
John wanted to save Mary from the dragon.
Mary became grateful to John for rescuing her.

To make these inferences, PAM must have knowledge about how plans, associated with specific goals, can be achieved. There is also knowledge about themes which generate goals such as the love theme which generates, perhaps, a marriage goal. We will not pursue the details here, the reader can refer to Schank and Abelson (1977) for a brief review, or to Wilensky (1978) for much more detail.

I.5.5 More Systems

To accommodate the conflicting aims of completeness and space limitations, we will mention and briefly describe a few examples of other systems or approaches to modelling dialogue. These vary from Grosz's (1977a,b,1978a,b) study of task-oriented dialogues, developed as part of SRI International's speech understanding project (see Walker, 1978) to the work at the University of Toronto directed at incorportating speech act theory into a computational framework. (Allen and Perrault, 1978; Perrault, Allen, Cohen, 1978; Cohen, 1978). Other work includes the design of a frame representation language (FRL, Roberts and Goldstein, 1977) and two NLU systems, built on this language, by Sidner[Bullwinkle] (Bullwinkle 1977; Sidner 1978a,b) and Rosenberg (1977).

I.5.5.1 Task-oriented Dialogues

Barbara Grosz's (1977a, 1977b, 1978a, 1978b) contributions are to the dialog component of SRI International's speech understanding project. However her work can be evaluated independent of its original context. As such her major concern was with the structure of dialogues and in particular a subclass called, task-oriented dialogues. These are characterized by the fact that there is a major well-defined task underlying the goal of the dialogue and furthermore, the dialogue usually follows, not necessarily in a predetermined order, the sub-goal structure of the original goal. In such situations, this sub-goal hierarchy provides an important tool in language processing. There does seem to be some relation between task-oriented situations and scripts or frames in that some notion of stereotypic behaviour is important.

Locating the current state of the dialogue within a subtree corresponding to a particular subgoal of the dialogue provides an important clue to the focus of the conversation. If the focus, roughly the global theme, is determined accurately, it will provide an important handle on resolving a variety of reference problems. Indeed, the problem of anaphora (abbreviated reference) is one of the most difficult problems facing any NLU system. If the system can keep track of the shifting focus of the dialogue, it will have considerable constraints available for understanding the discourse. In particular, knowledge of focus is a crucial element in determining referents of pronouns occurring in the discourse. For a comprehensive survey of anaphora problems see Hirst (1979).

Grosz's focus representation uses Hendrix's (1975) partitioned semantic nets. She has extended this notion of partitioning to allow a network to be partitioned in more than one way. Grosz argues that a focus representation must satisfy a number of criteria including the identification of that part of the representation relevant to the current discourse, the reflection of the dynamic nature of discourse by a corresponding shift in focus, the focussing on implicitly mentioned items, and the recovery of previous foci. Her major contribution, is the development of a system which allows for the representation and monitoring of the focus of the discourse.

I.5.5.2 Planning and Speech Acts

A group at the University of Toronto including Perrault, Allen, and Cohen have been exploring the interrelations among the choice of a particular speech act in a conversation, the speaker's model of the hearer, and the planning process necessary to achieve certain goals. Cohen (1978) has developed a program called OSCAR which can, when it wants the user to perform some action, plan the appropriate request speech act, plan inform speech acts in order to get the user to believe some fact, and also plan multiple acts, and questions. This work represents one of the first attempts to incorporate speech act theory into a computational framework and also to link this approach to a planning mechanism.

I.5.5.3 Frame-based Systems at MIT

As a direct outgrowth of Minsky's (1975) speculations, Roberts and Goldstein (1977) (Goldstein and Roberts, 1977) designed a language called

FRL (Frame Representation Language) for building frame-based systems. Rosenberg (1977) developed a frame-based system for processing text and Sidner (also known as Bullwinkle) worked on the PAL personal assistant program; more specifically she was concerned with discourse pragmatics and reference.

Basically, as Roberts and Goldstein (1977) state,

> FRL extends the traditional Property List representation scheme by allowing properties to have comments, defaults and constraints, to inherit information from abstract forms of the same type, and to have attached procedures triggered by adding or deleting values.

Rosenberg (1977) uses FRL as a representation language for his text-processing system. His basic concern is to link the new knowledge, derived from parsing successive sentences of a text, into the growing representation. First, the appropriate context must be found and second the new information must be mapped into that context. He presents some examples of frames and shows how slots are filled and linkages created. However, his program takes as input, what he calls deep case frames. He assumes another program which maps from the surface case structure into these deep frames.

Sidner (1978a,b; Bullwinkle 1977) while primarily interested in problems of reference, arising in discourse, has been involved in the design of a computer assistant, called PAL, which is supposed to be able to plan meetings among a number of people at specific times, dates, and places, (c.f. GUS discussed previously). PAL operates by interpreting each input sentence via a parser, a case frame interpreter and representation mapping program, into a set of FRL frames. For a careful discussion of the reference aspects of Sidner's work see Hirst (1979) Another major concern of this system is the determination of the focus of the discourse in order to determine the purposes of the discourse

I.5.5.4 Other Systems and Approaches

We wish to include these references in order to bring to the reader's attention as many different strands of research, on discourse analysis, as possible.

At the Information Sciences Institute at the University of Southern California a group including Mann, Moore, and Levin (Levin, Moore, 1977; Mann, Moore, Levin, 1977; Moore, Levin, Mann, 1977) has been developing a model of human communication sufficiently well-specified to be used in man-machine communication.

Reichman's (1978) research effort is to determine how participants in a conversation maintain coherency. She introduces the, not unfamiliar, notion of a context space which represents a group of utterances related to a single issue. The development of a discourse model including the context space structure, the discourse topic, and the items in focus serves as a basis for determining whether or not coherency is being maintained.

At MIT, a group under the direction of William Martin (Hawkinson, 1975) has been developing a representation system for natural language, called OWL. Using this representation, Brown (1977) has designed an expert NLU system in the domain of programming. She has used structures called methods to model both linguistic and non-linguistic activities.

Although this reference might better be included in the subsequent discussion of question-answering systems, we mention it here because it is based on the script concept of Schank and Abelson (1977). This is the work of Hemphill and Rhyne (1978) at IBM, San Jose. They believe that a script-based representation scheme can deal adequately with such pervasive problems as ambiguity, multi-sentence queries, goal-directed behaviour, and presuppositions in the queries.

Jerry Hobbs (1976,1977) currently at SRI International has been working on discourse analysis for several years. He has also done extensive work on anaphor resolutions.

An important source of information on discourse analysis is the Proceedings of the 13th Annual Meeting of the Association for Computational Linguistics held in 1975 (Diller, 1975). Particularly important papers were given by Philips (1975) on coherency and Bruce (1975) on discourse models.

I.6 Comments and Conclusions

To help place the work just discussed into perspective, we might pose a number of questions. What characterizes the AI point of view towards natural language understanding? Is there some reason to believe it will be more successful than other approaches? With respect to the previous question, when will the systems developed move beyond the toy stage, to actually confront the problems of dealing with large amounts of knowledge? One answer to this last question is that researchers developing natural language interfaces to large data bases are dealing, to a certain extent, with this issue. (We will continue our analysis of QA systems, shortly).

Wilks (1976b)refers to an 'AI paradigm' and, Winograd (1976) and

Johnson-Laird (1977) talk about 'a procedural understanding of semantics' and 'procedural semantics', respectively. The important points of the 'AI paradigm' as Wilks sees them are testability via programming, the recognition of the primacy of viewing language in a communicative context, and the importance of the organization of knowledge. In terms of a distinction made famous by Chomsky (1965), that of competence-performance, AI comes down heavily on the performance side.

To emphasize this point of view, Winograd (1976) notes that the procedural paradigm is "based on the belief that there is a level of explanation at which there are significant similarities between the pyschological processes of human language use and the computational processes in computer programs we can construct and study" [my underlining]. Winograd (1976) echoes Wilks' remarks when he presents a basis for a procedural theory. For AI a theory of language should be focussed on cognitive processes rather than linguistic objects. Given that context is important, it should be formulated in terms of cognitive structures not linguistic texts. Finally it is possible to study the processes involved in cognition and language use, scientifically.

This position as articulated by Wilks, Winograd, Schank, and others has aroused considerable opposition in the linguistic community, especially among the transformationalists and their supporters. In the final section of this chapter we will examine some of these arguments. For now, we turn briefly to our question about the limited systems so far developed. The simple answer is that the study of discourse in AI is quite new and obviously much needs to be done before large systems can be developed. It is also the case that the detailed structure of all the knowledge must not only be determined by the researchers but must be hand coded by them as well. Moreover this will probably remain the case for the near future.

The real test for the AI approach is yet to come. But for now, we can say that the discipline imposed on theory construction by the writing of programs may turn out to be one of the most important contributions of AI. Furthermore, the necessity of integrating linguistic and non-linguistic knowledge, the fundamental problems of directing processing, of efficiently accessing vast amounts of knowledge, of making appropriate inferences are all part of the daily concerns of researchers working within the AI paradigm.

II APPLICATIONS OF NATURAL LANGUAGE PROCESSING

The major emphasis of this chapter is the contribution of AI to the study of human discourse through the development of NLU systems. In section I we attempted to present a comprehensive survey of work in this area. However, there are other areas of research (and development) from which contributions to discourse will emerge. These are being grouped under the general title of applications, and, while the treatment will be somewhat cursory, we hope to identify some specific contributions. As mentioned in the introduction, the purpose of such systems is to carry out specific and limited tasks. It is in this context that one encounters linguistic problems although very frequently their solution applies only to very narrowly-defined situations.

We will consider, first, the design of natural language interfaces for large data bases. This has become a very active area and has attracted the interests of a number of research groups in industry and the universities. One interesting aspect of this increased activity in QA systems is that a significant amount of research funding originates with the Defense Department in the United States. Thus typical data bases include repair and flight records of airplanes, and type and location of naval vessels.

This will be followed by a brief review of the recent major research effort in speech understanding and an equally brief examination of the natural language components of expert systems and computer-aided instruction (CAI) systems. In these last two areas the ability to interact with the user in natural language is an important ingredient in their potential usefulness. For expert systems, say medical diagnosis ones, it is necessary to provide a natural form of communication to attract experts to use them. It is especially the case for CAI that unless natural language communication is possible, the form of interaction is likely to be menu-driven, with very little initiative allowed to the user.

II.1 Question-Answering Systems

As mentioned previously, QA systems represented one of the earliest attempts to process natural language by computer and with the achievements of Winograd (1972) and Woods et al (1972) seemed to reach a reasonably high level of performance. As speech understanding moved to the forefront to be followed by a concern with discourse, it seemed that the stage was set for a serious, concerted attack on the problem of providing a useful natural language interface for potentially unsophisticated users of large data bases. Such data bases had emerged in a wide variety of areas - military, industrial, medical, educational, government, judicial, community, etc.

A possible research programme which might have been pursued was to conceive of a domain independent natural language front-end. If we believe that there is some core of language competency independent of specialized knowledge, it is not hard, at least, to conceive of a language module which can be applied to a given data base in a coherent, principled manner. That is, if the semantics of the data base are sufficiently well-defined, it should be possible to specify a collection of 'hooks' for the front-end which the data base specialist can use to interface his data base.

If such a front-end were possible it would represent a significant demonstration that the state of the art of NLU had reached a high level. Even if not possible at the present time, the attempt would reveal some of the inadequacies of the current approaches. Among the systems to be discussed, only Harris's ROBOT (1977a,b, 1978) is presented as a partial realization of this programme. And interestingly enough only ROBOT is a commercially available product, the proprietary software of Artificial Intelligence Corporation, and Software AG of North America. Perhaps the pressures of the marketplace are a greater spur to a coherent approach than the current sponsored research environment.

As we shall see, although a number of important and interesting discoveries and observations have emerged in the course of developing a variety of natural language interfaces, many aspects of these systems can only be characterized as ad hoc. Taking advantage of as many features of the data base as possible, the designers have carefully tailored the syntax and semantics of the individual systems. Thus their portability is limited and new applications require considerable rewriting. But what has emerged is a number of design principles which surely are a step in the right direction.

For the purposes of this section we will examine four representative systems. Our main concern is to identify their contributions to natural language understanding and as such we will have little to say about data base organization, retrieval strategies, or other programming issues.

II. 1.1 RENDEZVOUS

Codd (1974), important for his development of relational data bases

(Codd, 1970), saw the importance of natural language communication with such data bases. In an influential paper, Codd (1974), he proposed the necessary steps in order to make this communication possible. Two of these argue for the virtues of the relational structure but the following five serve as important goals for any QA system*:

1. Introduce clarification dialog of bounded scope:
   Given that one cannot expect the system to know very much except its own data base, any attempt to clarify the user's request by means of a dialogue must stay very close to what the system knows.

2. Introduce restatement of user's query:
   After the process of clarification dialog is complete, the system should restate the query in its own terms and determine if it matches the user's intended meaning.

3. Separate query formulation from data base search:
   The process of clarification dialog and query restatement should not require access to the data base. The search is only initiated when the extracted query is correct. This aspect should contribute to the domain independent front-end.

4. Employ multiple choice interrogation as fall-back:
   If analysis of the user's query fails because of his use of idioms or other unknown words, the system should have a menu of choices to present in order to extract the users intentions.

5. Provide a definition capability:
   If the system can detect that the user is employing a term it does not understand, it should have some facility to allow the user to define the term. It is obvious that for most situations, the system will only have limited capacity.

These goals suggest a considerable expansion of power over the earlier QA systems. The attempt here is to provide facilities to enable the system to engage the user in a goal-directed dialogue, the purpose of which is to interpret the question to the user's satisfaction. Thus, the analysis of discourse, discussed previously, which appeared somewhat abstract, certainly has ready application for QA systems incorporating a dialogue facility. The initial task for the RENDEZVOUS system is to process the user's question and this it does by employing a partitioned collection of phrase tranformation rules.

Before these are used, a morphological routine reduces each word, independently, to its root form. Then lexical classes are assigned to each

* The goals themselves are taken from Codd (1974) but the comments are the author's.

word which reflects its semantic function, such as attribute, relation name, comparator, rather than its syntactic category. There is also a considerable effort to reduce all words to a normal form (e.g. SAN JOSE is reduced to the single word SAN-JOSE), to correct simple spelling errors, and to issue warnings about words not recognized by the system.

In the phrase transformation rules, the left hand side specifies a pattern which if matched in the input string, invokes the right hand side which specifies one or more replacement patterns and may also cause functions to be called which extract information from the user or the knowledge base. The end result of this process is a formal query which can return an answer when evaluated on the data base. Given that the data base is relational, one can imagine the structure of this query. But before the data base is searched the formal query must be passed to a generator whose goal is to produce an English language version for the user's approval.

If at any point in the interaction, the user changes his mind or runs into a problem he can call on a menu driven editor which allows him to modify his question, by replacing a word or phrase. If any other kind of difficulty arises there is a 'help' facility available to the user by pressing the HELP key. Given that the major aim of the designers of RENDEZVOUS is to help the user to precisely formulate a question which expresses his intention, they are willing to depend heavily upon menus to achieve this. It appears, from the examples presented that the natural language processing serves mainly to determine which pre-formulated menus of choices are to be presented to the user in order to refine his question. Much of the previous description is taken from Codd et al (1978).

II. 1.2 ROBOT

As mentioned in the introduction to this section, Harris's ROBOT (1977a, b, 1978) comes closest to the notion of a domain-independent, natural language interface. We will be concerned here with Harris's arguments for using the data base as an adjunct of the natural language lexicon and, of course, with the specific linguistic phenomena dealt with in ROBOT. With respect to the former point Harris (1977a) notes:

> Specifically the goals of the project are to refine the natural language processing capability to the point where only dictionary changes would be necessary to move from one area of discourse to another.

Because users cannot be expected to be aware of the structure of the data base, the burden must be borne by the query translator which transforms the natural language query into appropriate data base management system commands. The basic structure of the ROBOT system is shown below:

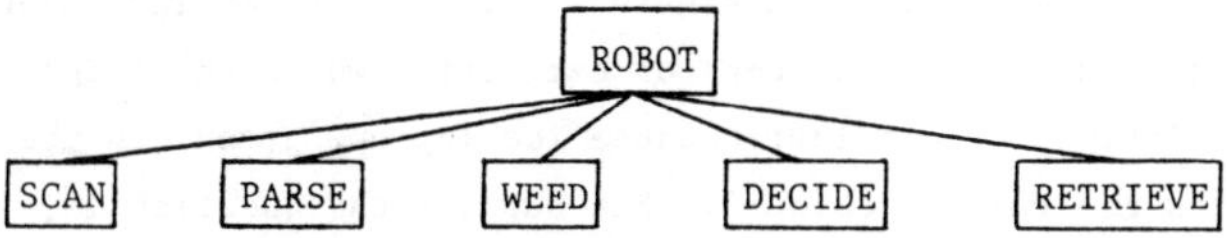

We will briefly describe the role of each of these modules.

SCAN - changes the input string into a list of words, treats groups of words as a single word where appropriate (e.g. NEW YORK is treated as a single word). It may need information from the data base.

PARSE - An augmented transition network (ATN) grammar (Woods, 1970) is used exhaustively to produce every possible parse.

WEED - By interacting with the data base discards those parses with semantic discrepencies.

DECIDE - By consulting data base chooses most likely interpretation. If there is no clear winner, the user is asked to resolve the ambiguities.

RETRIEVE - Intended interpretation used to find final answers.

The dictionary contains mostly linguistic terms and, this is quite important, entries in the data base act like extended dictionary entries. Given that large data bases contain thousands and even millions of words, it is infeasible to try to include them in the dictionary especially when the data base, because of changes, may require frequent updating. This suggests that if the natural language interface is not to be domain dependent, there should be some way of using the data base itself as part of the dictionary. The immediate problem is that a word in the data base does not contain typical dictionary information such as syntactic category, morphological information, or composite word information.

The ATN parser can be modified so that it only builds the syntactic structure of what it recognizes. Subsequently when semantic analysis begins, sufficient semantic knowledge may be available to allow the necessary structure to be built. It is at this point that the data base serves its second function, in the language processing phase, as a repository of world knowledge. Under the usual organization of a data base into fields and values, a word appearing as a value of a given field has that field as its 'meaning'. For example, the question, 'What cars are green?', would cause the colour field of the entries for cars to be searched for the value green.

Finally, how does the system know that 'green' is in the colour field? Harris claims that as obvious and simple a structure as an inversion index for the data base can serve as a means of extracting world knowledge. So the system knows that 'green' is a colour because looking up 'green' in the inversion index returns the result 'colour'. But suppose the question is, 'How many mauve cars are there?", and 'mauve' does not appear in the inversion index. Of course, mauve is a colour, but the fact that it is not in the data base means the system will return the answer, none. Thus the user will not know whether there are mauve coloured cars in existence but none currently listed in the data base or whether the entire concept is impossible.

It remains only to consider some of the linguistic features of ROBOT. Since users may interact with the system using fragments of complete sentences in order to lessen the typing burden, ROBOT has two ATN's (which are run in sequence), one for full sentences and one for fragments. A sentence fragment will cause the first ATN to fail quickly with very little overhead resulting in a call to the second. Sentence fragments are sometimes used elliptically to further restrict a previous query or to retrieve similar information for another category of objects. For example, for a data base of employees, and for each the address, marital status, sex, city, salary, and telephone, consider some sample questions: (Harris, 1977a)

SINGLE IN CHICAGO
  This yields the names of all single employees in Chicago [Sentence fragment]
THEIR SALARIES
  For all the previous persons, print their salaries. [Sentence fragment, pronoun reference]
WHO ARE THE SECRETARIES?
  Print names of all employees who are secretaries.
WHICH OF THEM LIVE IN CHICAGO?
  Of the above secretaries, which live in Chicago [anaphor reference]
WHICH OF THEM LIVE IN DETROIT?
  In this case, the pronoun must refer to the original secretaries, not the ones living in Chicago. [anaphor reference]

The use of the data base itself as a source of knowledge is believed by Harris to be an important idea. He notes that we may have to wait too long for such knowledge representation languages as KRL (Bobrow and Winograd 1977) to solve our problems. Unfortunately, his solution does not offer much promise for serious linguistic and inference issues. For the sample data base, the semantic representation is quite trivial; in fact, it is similar to that of an early QA system, BASEBALL (Green et al 1961), a list of attribute value pairs. If such a representation is appropriate then methods such as Harris's will work. However, the limitations are obvious and cannot be finessed. For simply constructed data bases and for questions which can be answered by more or less simple test and generate methods, ROBOT works.

II 1.3 PLANES

The PLANES system, a QA system for a large relational data base, is under development at the University of Illinois, by a group directed by David Waltz (Waltz et al 1976, Waltz and Goodman 1977, Waltz 1978). The data base is a subset of the U.S. Navy 3-M (Maintenance and Material Management) data base of aircraft maintenance and flight data. First we present some examples of the program's linguistic abilities.

Ellipsis:

How many flights did plane 003 make in Feb. 73?
During April?
March?
All of 1973?

Anaphor reference

How many flights did plane 48 make during Dec. 1969?
How many flight hours did it log?

Non-grammatical input

January 1973 plane 3 damages.

It should be noted that PLANES takes advantage of some particularly helpful features of its world; namely, there is very little lexical ambiguity, the vocabulary is quite small (about 900 words), there are very few modes of interaction, people generally use simple sentences, and the designers have a reasonably good idea what users want. This last point is quite important because, in essence, PLANES operates by using a set of patterns to match question types and an ATN to parse the subpatterns. If the number and variety of question types can be identified then the first stage in answering a question is to perform pattern matching of a rather mundane kind.

There are some features of this system worth mentioning especially from a linguistic point of view. The lexicon has two parts, a standard dictionary, with words and features, and a dictionary manager which accesses, maintains, and updates the dictionary. Some of its functions, when given a word for which no entry exists in the dictionary, are to do morphological analysis and if this fails to follow it with a punctuation checker, a spelling corrector, a composite word recognizer, and a word substituter.

When a subnetwork ATN matches a phrase, an associated context register is set. For example, when a date is parsed, the structure (date(month +)(day +)(year +)) is set. Context registers are used to keep track of past history, to paraphrase a request, and to deal with anaphor reference and ellipsis. Associated with the question patterns are concept case frames, similar to those specified by Fillmore (1968). Each case frame consists of the act, related to the verb, and a list of associated noun phrases. This system of case frames and subnetwork ATN's forms a semantic grammar in the sense of Burton (1976).

A final comment on pronoun reference will reveal some of the limitations of this system. First, only references to the previous request are permitted. The results of this request are saved in a temporary file, so that when a pronoun is recognized in a subsequent sentence, it is this file which will be searched using the newly formulated query. There are two limitations to this process:

1. Pronouns can only reference noun groups.
2. If the pronoun references information in the previous request, not available in the temporary file, the request fails.

Remedies are proposed but as might be expected they are somewhat ad hoc.

The justification for much of this approach is that a practical, working system must be built. The designers admit that the linguistic component does not capture much of the regularity of natural language because it is highly domain dependent. In addition it may be quite difficult to extend the system when syntactic and semantic knowledge are so tightly linked.

II 1.4 LADDER

LADDER (language access to distributed data with error recovery) is a system developed at SRI International. It is described in Hendrix (1977), Sacerdoti (1977), and, in most detail, in Hendrix et al (1978). LADDER represents a large research effort to make communication with very large distributed data bases possible in natural language. Emerging from this research is an engineering strategy for the design of natural language interfaces. The data base for which this system was designed involved data from the U.S. Navy and indeed its purpose was to aid Navy decision makers. LADDER is a very large system and it will only be possible to sketch its organization and performance.

The natural language interface has been constructed, using a language processing package, called LIFER (Hendrix 1977). It is designed to apply state of the art techniques in computationallinguistics to practical data base applications. LIFER has two parts: a language specification facility and a parser. The grammar rules are context free, augmented by an arbitrarily complex output expression, which gives the grammar Turing machine power. The parser is non-deterministic,top-down, left-to-right, similar to the ATN's of Woods (1970).

The grammar is characteristic of that class of linguistic systems called semantic grammars (a term guaranteed to outrage transformationalists). For example, lexical items are classified by semantic categories rather than syntactic ones. This allows the designer to take advantage of whatever structure he can in the domain of interest. In its treatment of ellipsis, LIFER depends on the apparent semantic similarity of similar syntactic structures. For example the substring'OF SANTA INEZ' in the sentence 'WHAT IS THE LENGTH OF SANTA INEZ?', is abstracted, from the parse of this sentence as 'OF <SHIP>' and can be used to match a subsequent elliptical expression such as 'OF THE KENNEDY' or 'OF THE FASTEST NUCLEAR CARRIER'. (See Hendrix et al 1978, p.125).

As is to be expected, the set of productions defines a class of input questions and commands which may not be suitable for every user. The LIFER system permits new productions to be defined and the applicability of the system, extended. We have said nothing about the retrieval or data base aspects of this system because it is beyond the scope of this treatment but important issues are involved which will have a major impact on any program which purports to deal with natural language communication.

II. 1.5 Conclusions

Current QA systems are being designed to incorporate sufficient linguistic ability in order to accommodate a variety of situations such as discovering the user's intention by engaging in a clarification dialogue, recognizing anaphoric references, and allowing elliptical expressions. Clearly, all of these are also relevant to the modeling or analysis of dialogue. Before concluding this discussion we wish to acknowledge the important, ongoing research on REL (Rapidly Extensible Language) by Thompson and Thompson (1975, 1978). In a sense REL is similar to LIFER in that it provides the necessary tools to build a natural language system tailored to the user's needs.

An important consideration in natural language understanding is for the system to recognize possible misconceptions or presumptions that the user may hold. Kaplan (1978) (and Kaplan and Joshi, 1978) has been concerned with this problem and has developed methods to identify such situations. So that if a question is asked which makes an incorrect assumption, the system will note this and so inform the user, rather than return the default negative answer. As noted previously, Harris's ROBOT (Harris 1977 a, b) makes the default response.

Finally, we recommend a good collection of brief descriptions of natural language interfaces which appeared in the February 1977 issue of the SIGART newsletter (Waltz 1977). Also recommended is a discussion of natural language interfaces by Petrick (1976), in which he cautions against facile optimism with respect to the early appearance of useful, working systems.

II. 2 Speech Understanding

Speech understanding represents one of the most concerted (and well-funded) research efforts in AI. The design goals were specified by a study group lead by Alan Newell (Newell et al 1973). The project was to understand speech, albeit constrained to a restricted vocabulary (1000 words), a quiet room, a highly artificial syntax, in a few times real time, with less than 10% semantic error. There were three sites at which major systems were developed:

1. Bolt Beranek and Newman - SPEECHLIS
   - Woods and Makhoul 1974
   - Woods et al 1974
   - Nash-Webber 1975
2. Carnegie-Mellon University - HEARSAY, HARPY
   - Erman and Lesser 1975
   - Reddy et al 1976
   - Erman et al 1976
   - Lowerre 1976
   - Lesser and Erman 1977
3. SRI International and Systems Development Corporation
   - Walker 1976
   - Walker 1978

It is obviously impossible to say very much about any of these systems in this limited space. In addition, the major difficulties faced by these systems were related to the processing of an acoustic signal and the associated phonetic, phonological, and prosodic problems. The reason for including this reference is twofold, to say something about the role of discourse analysis and to comment on the methods of control which have been developed for extremely large systems. With respect to the former, only the SRI system was concerned in any systematic way with the use of discourse analysis to resolve anaphora and to handle ellipses. We have already referred to the work of Barbara Grosz (1978b) on the use of focus in anaphor resolution.

It is in the area of devising strategies for dealing with large amounts of knowledge and controlling many and diverse processes that developments in speech understanding may make important contributions to future research in discourse modeling. The HEARSAY-II model (Lesser and Erman 1977) confronts this problem by isolating knowledge in large, distinct modules and providing a global working memory, the blackboard, which acts as a structure on which competing hypotheses (and their confirming evidence) can be stored. Changes in the blackboard initiate responses in the knowledge sources which may offer new hypotheses or criticisms, resulting in a new blackboard configuration. Consider this description of the control process as described in Reddy (1976), an important survey:

> What we have here is an activity equivalent to a set of cooperating asynchronous parallel processors even when it runs on a uniprocessor. Generating and verifying hypotheses using several KS's [Knowledge Sources] is analogous to several persons attempting to solve a jigsaw puzzle with each person working on a different part of the puzzle but with each modifying his strategies based on the progress being made by others (p. 513)

When systems for modelling discourse achieve the size and complexity of such speech understanding systems, they will certainly require similar control strategies. Of course higher level knowledge sources concerned with progmatics, conversational strategies, and discourse structures will play a more important role.

For a brief but useful survey of speech understanding from both a pattern recognition and AI point of view, see Robinson (1979 a,b).

II.3 Expert Systems

These represent an increasingly important research area in AI. Perhaps, one of the earliest and most important was DENDRAL (Buchanan, Sutherland, and Feigenbaum 1969), a program which generated possible molecular structures for organic compounds, given mass spectra as input. There was no natural language component to this system. However MYCIN (Shortliffe 1976), a medical consultation system, does depend on natural language communication for a variety of reasons. The system accepts questions from the user for the following purposes:

1. Informational questions with respect to the status of current knowledge about the patient.
2. Questions about the deductions MYCIN has made on the current consultation.
3. General questions about MYCIN's judgemental rules.
4. Explanatory questions about MYCIN's previous output.

5. Confirmatory questions about the user's own decision rules.

The representation of knowledge in MYCIN is in the form of rules embedded in a production system, a highly modular structure. MYCIN's control strategy is essentially backward chaining so that the solution tree to a given problem provides a context for answering questions about the deductions made. Questions about rules used will elict the rules in an English language version although they are stored internally in LISP form. The expert user can even add new rules to the system in English for translation into LISP. It is interesting, therefore, that MYCIN has no sense of discourse, anaphora, or complex syntax. It depends on rather simple pattern matching using keywords and for this reason is not really a contribution to advanced language processing. However, expert programs provide a rich environment for discourse modeling if sufficiently efficient systems can be designed.

II.4 Computer-Aided Instruction

This section will be devoted to a single system, probably one of the most successful and useful programs ever created within the AI community. SOPHIE (A SOPHisticated Instructional Environment) was developed at Bolt Beranek and Newman under the direction of John Seely Brown (Brown, Burton and Bell 1974,1975; Brown and Burton 1975). The innovative aspects of this system are best described in the words of the designers (Brown and Burton 1975).

> Unlike previous AI-CAI systems which attempt to mimic the roles of a human teacher, SOPHIE tries to create a "reactive" environment in which the student learns by trying out his ideas rather than by instruction. To this end, SOPHIE incorporates a "strong" model of its knowledge domain along with numerous heuristic strategies for answering a student's questions, providing him with critiques of his current solution paths and generating alternative theories to his current hypotheses.
>
> pp. 311-312

We wish, of course, to consider the natural language understanding aspects of SOPHIE. It is clear that in the context of dealing with a supposedly intelligent system, a student will expect a high level of linguistic competence. Therefore SOPHIE will have to deal with such familiar problems as ellipses, anaphora, and sentence fragments. Instead of depending heavily on a complex syntactic component, the designers of SOPHIE chose to rely on a semantic grammar (Burton 1976). In such a grammar, the usual syntactic categories such as noun, verb phrase, etc. are replaced by categories which are semantically meaningful with respect to the concepts of the domain. The resulting grammar expresses constraints among these concepts. There is also informationabout which constituent concepts can be pronominalized or deleted.

The result of parsing using a semantic grammar is a semantic representation since the semantics have been incorporated into the syntax. The "meaning" of a sentence is a program in the procedural sense defined by Winograd (1972). Pronoun references are resolved using a context mechanism which saves the past history of the interaction. Depending on the semantic role of the pronoun, the system searches in reverse order through the history list to determine an appropriate referent. Similarly, the problem of finding referents for ellipses is handled by searching the history list for a semantic construct appropriately related to the elliptical phrases.

The natural language system for SOPHIE is both efficient (so that a typical statement of 8 to 12 words is processed in about 150 milliseconds) and friendly. The latter is, of course, difficult to measure but the results of several hundred hours of tests by participants in the project and realistic sessions with several dozen people, demonstrated a system able to handle most of the questions presented to it.

We have already noted the debt of the PLANES project to the semantic grammar of Brown and Burton and its influence is sure to be felt for years to come. It is likely that dialogue systems will take advantage of the flexibility and robustness offered by semantic grammars. An interesting question is how such grammars can be integrated into script or frame based systems.

III THE ARTIFICIAL INTELLIGENCE - LINGUISTICS CONTROVERSY

In section I.6 we discussed the notion of procedural semantics, a concept which has developed directly out of the AI experience. It has been explicitly articulated by Winograd (1976), Johnson-Laird (1977), and Wilks (1976b). Others have referred to a computational metaphor or the AI paradigm as a way of distinguishing a viewpoint on natural language which has emerged in AI in vivid contrast to the position held by the transformational stream in linguistics. A particularly sharp and lengthy attack was launched by Dresher and Hornstein (1976) against the 'supposed contributions of artificial intelligence to the scientific study of language'. The gist of their argument is that the transformationalist position promulgated by the Chomsky interpretivist school (CIS) is or defines the scientific approach to the study of language. Therefore by definition any deviation, especially the perceived gross one pursued within the AI community, is non-scientific and heretical.

Dresher and Hornstein were especially concerned with criticising Winograd, the Schank school, and the use of ATN's to model psychological processes in linguistics. Responses to this attack were made by Winograd (1977a) and Schank and Wilensky (1977); Dresher and Hornstein (1977a,b) issued their rejoinders, reiterating their original position. The mini-war continued in 1978 with another major volley by Fodor (1978) against the procedural semantics of Johnson-Laird (1977) followed immediately by Johnson-Laird's (1978) response. Why all this activity? Was the CIS feeling threatened by an emerging, challenging paradigm?

George Lakoff (1978), an important linguist, but certainly not a transformationalist offered his analysis of the sudden, vigorous attacks. He suggested that the competition from AI for research funds in natural language was making some linguists quite nervous. The focussing of the attack on the alleged unscientific nature of the AI approach was supposed to interest those agencies which primarily funded scientific research. Lakoff went on to criticize both sides but especially the CIS for failing to respond to recent developments in language acquisition and universal grammar.

It appears that some linguists including Fillmore and G. Lakoff, already alienated from the CIS, have become increasingly interested in the AI approach. This should bode well for future developments unless the exigencies of constructing practical working systems mitigate against a coherent, principled research strategy.

IV. Conclusions

These will be mercifully brief as we have already provided some conclusions at various points along the way. The problems we have been discussing in discourse analysis are many and complex. Insights and discoveries from a variety of disciplines will be needed. At the outset we suggested that, at present, such contributions may form a collection rather than a cohesive structure. Only the future will tell whether or not, under the computational paradigm offered by AI, they can be transformed into a comprehensive theory.

We should like to at least mention, some other important contributions to the study of discourse. The significant approach to discourse anaphora by Nash-Webber and Reiter (1977) and Webber (1978) (also known as Nash-Webber) should be noted. It is reprsentative of a formal treatment of the problems we have been studying and interestingly enough is consistent with a turn to logical formalisms by the CIS. There were two late arrivals by distinguished researchers, Philips (1978) and Hobbs (1979).

There are other surveys of text processing or discourse analysis worthy of the reader's attention. Among these are Damereau (1976), Davidson (1977), Kender (1977), and Young (1977). These vary in their emphasis and depth of treatment but together are complementary with the present discussion. The reader may have noticed several references to work done at the University of British Columbia, namely, Taylor and Rosenberg (1975), Rosenberg (1975),

McCalla (1977), Davidson (1977), and Hirst (1979). We trust the author may be forgiven for bringing to wider attention, work done at his institution.

ACKNOWLEDGEMENTS

This paper was written with the financial support of NSERC grant A5552.

REFERENCES

The following abbreviations for collections of articles will be used:

CSCSI-2 Proceedings of the Second National Conference of the Canadian Society for Computational Studies of Intelligence (Société Canadienne des Études d'Intelligence par Ordinateur), July 1978, Toronto, Ontario.

COLING 76 Preprints of the International Conference on Computational Linguistics, 1976, Ottawa, Ontario

TINLAP Schank, R.C. and Nash-Webber, B.L., Theoretical Issues in Natural Language Processing, June 1975, Cambridge, Mass.

TINLAP-2 Waltz, David L., Theoretical Issues in Natural Language Processing -2, July 1978, Urbana, Illinois.

IJCAI-4 Advance Papers of the Fourth International Joint Conference on Artificial Intelligence, September 1975, Tbilisi, Georgia, USSR.

IJCAI-5 Proceedings of the Fifth International Joint Conference on Artificial Intelligence, Aug. 1977, Cambridge, Mass.

IEEE-AI IEEE Transactions on Computers, April 1976, Vol. C-25, No. 4, Special Issue on Artificial Intelligence.

Allen, J.F. and Perrault, C.R. (1978), Participating in dialogues: understanding via plan deduction, CSCSI-2, pp. 214-223.

Anderson, John R. and Bower, Gordon H. (1973), Human Associative Memory, Wash., D.C., W.H. Winston & Sons.

Austin, J.L. (1955), How to Do Things with Words, Oxford University Press, 1973 (The William James Lectures).

Bartlett, F.C. (1967), Remembering, Cambridge at the University Press.

Bobrow, D.G. (1964), Natural language input for a computer problem-solving system. In Minsky (1968), pp. 135-215.

Bobrow, Daniel G. and Collins, Allan (1975), Representation and Understanding, New York, Academic Press.

Bobrow, Daniel G. and Winograd, Terry (1977), An overview of KRL, a knowledge representation language, Cognitive Science 1,1, pp. 3-46.

Bobrow, Daniel G., Kaplan, Ronald M., Kay, Martin, Norman, Donald A., Thompson, Henry, and Winograd, Terry (1977), GUS, a frame-driven dialog system, Artificial Intelligence 8,2, pp. 155-173.

Brachman, Ronald J. (1977), What's in a concept: structural foundations for semantic networks, Int. J. Man-Machine Studies 9, pp. 127-152.

Brown, Gretchen B. (1977), A framework for processing dialogue, MIT Laboratory for Computer Science, MIT/LCS/TR-182.

Brown, J.S., Burton, R.R., and Bell, A.G. (1974), SOPHIE: A sophisticated instructional environment for teaching electronic troubleshooting, Bolt Beranek and Newman Report No. 2790, Cambridge, MA.

Brown, John Seely, Burton, Richard R., and Bell, Alan G. (1975), SOPHIE: A step toward creating a reactive learning environment, Int. J. Man-Machine Studies, 7, pp. 675-696.

Brown, John Seely and Burton, Richard R. (1975), Multiple representations of knowledge for tutorial reasoning. In Bobrow and Collins (1975), pp. 311-349.

Bruce, Bertram C. (1975), Discourse models and language comprehension. In Diller (1975), AJCL Microfiche 35.

Buchanan, B.G., Sutherland, G.L., and Feigenbaum, E.A. (1969), Heuristic DENDRAL: a program for generating explanatory hypotheses in organic chemistry. In Meltzer, B. and Michie, D. (eds.) Machine Intelligence 4, Edinburgh University Press, 1969, pp. 209-254.

Bullwinkle, Candace L. (see also Sidner, Candace L.).

Bullwinkle, Candace L. (1977), Levels of complexity in discourse for anaphora disambiguation and speech act interpretation, IJCAI-5, pp. 43-49.

Burton, Richard R. (1976), Semantic grammar: an engineering technique for constructing natural language understanding system, Bolt Beranek and Newman, Report No. 3453, Cambridge, Mass.

Charniak, Eugene (1972), Towards a model of children's story comprehension, Ph.D. Thesis, M.I.T.(issued as Report AI TR-266).

Charniak, Eugene (1975), Organization and inference in a frame-like system of common sense knowledge, TINLAP, pp. 42-51.

Charniak, Eugene (1977a), Inference and knowledge in language comprehension. In Elcock and Michie (eds.) Machine Intelligence 8, N.Y. Halstead Press (J. Wiley), pp. 541-574.

Charniak, Eugene (1977b), Ms. Malaprop, a language comprehension program, IJCAI-5, pp. 1-7.

Charniak, Eugene (1977c), A framed PAINTING: The representation of a common sense knowledge fragment, Cognitive Science 1,4, pp. 355-394.

Charniak, Eugene (1978a), With spoon in hand this must be the eating frame, TINLAP-2, pp. 187-193.

Charniak, Eugene (1978b), On the use of framed knowledge in language comprehension, Artificial Intelligence 11, 3, pp. 225-265.

Chomsky, Noam (1965), Aspects of the Theory of Syntax, Cambridge, Mass., MIT Press.

Chomsky, Noam (1971), Deep structure, surface structure, and semantic interpretation. In Steinberg, Danny D. and Jakobovits, A. (eds.), Semantics, Cambridge at the University Press, pp. 183-216.

Clark, Herbert G. and Lucy, Peter (1975), Understanding what is meant from what is said: A study in conversationally conveyed requests, J. of Verbal Learning and Verbal Behavior 14, pp. 56-72.

Codd, E.F. (1970), A relational model of data for large shared data banks, Comm. ACM, 13,6, pp. 377-387.

Codd, E.F. (1974), Seven steps to rendezvous with the casual user, in Klimbie, J.W. and Koffeman, K.I. (eds.), Data Base Management, N.Y., North-Holland, 1974.

Codd, E.F., Arnold, R.S., Cadiou, J-M., Chang, C.L., and Roussopoulos, N. (1978), RENDEZVOUS Version 1: an experimental English-language query formulation system for casual users of relational data bases, Research report RJ 2144, IBM Research Laboratory, San Jose, California.

Cohen, Philip R. (1978), On knowing what to say: planning speech acts, Ph.D. Thesis, University of Toronto, Technical Report No. 118.

Cole, Peter and Morgan, Jerry, L. (eds.) (1975), Syntax and Semantics, Vol. 3, N.Y., Academic Press.

Corum, Claudia et al (eds.) (1973), Papers from the Ninth Regional Meeting of the Chicago Linguistic Society, Chicago.

Cullingford, R.E. (1976), The uses of world knowledge in text understanding, COLING 76, 36p.

Damereau, Fred J. (1976), Automated language processing. In Williams, Martha E. (ed.), Annual Review of Information Science and Technology, Vol. 11, Amer. Soc. for Inf. Sc., Wash., D.C., pp. 107-161.

Davidson, James Edward (1977), Topics in discourse analysis, Department of Computer Science, University of British Columbia, Technical Report 77-19.

Diller, Timothy C. (ed.) (1975), Proceedings, 13th Annual Meeting of the Association for Computational Linguistics, AJCL Microfiches 32 to 36.

Dresher, B.Elan and Hornstein, Norbert (1976), On some supposed contributions of artificial intelligence to a scientific study of language, Cognition, 4, pp. 321-398.

Dresher, B. Elan and Hornstein, Norbert (1977a), Reply to Schank and Wilensky, Cognition, 5, pp. 147-149.

Dresher, B. Elan and Hornstein, Norbert (1977b), Reply to Winograd, Cognition 5, pp. 379-392.

Erman, Lee D. and Lesser, Victor R. (1975), A multi-level organization for problem-solving using many, diverse, co-operating sources of knowledge, IJCAI-4, pp. 483-490.

Feigenbaum, E. and Feldman, J.(eds.)(1963), Computers and Thought, N.Y. McGraw-Hill.

Feldman, Jerry (1975), Bad-mouthing frames, TINLAP, pp. 92-93.

Fillmore, C.J. (1968), The case for case. In Bach and Harms (eds.), Universals in Linguistic Theory, N.Y., Holt, Rinehart and Winston, pp. 1-90.

Fillmore, C.J. (1971a), Some problems for case grammar. In O'Brien (ed.) Linguistics: Developments of the Sixties - Viewpoints for the Seventies, 22 Annual Georgetown Roundtable, Monograph Series on Languages and Linguistics, No. 24, Georgetown, pp. 35-56.

Fillmore, Charles J. (1971b), Santa Cruz Lectures on Deixis, reproduced by the Indiana Linguistics Club, Nov. 1975.

Fillmore, C.J. (1976), The need for a frame semantics within linguistics, COLING 76, (an invited address printed in SMIL; Statistical Methods in Linguistics, 1976, pp. 5-29).

Fodor, J.A. (1978), Tom Swift and his procedural grandmother, Cognition, 6, pp. 229-247.

Goffman, Erving (1974), Frame Analysis, New York, Harper Colophon Books.

Goldstein, Ira P. and Roberts, R. Bruce (1977), NUDGE, A knowledge-based scheduling program, IJCAI-5, pp. 257-263.

Gordon, David and Lakoff, George (1971), Conversational postulates. In D. Adams et al (eds.), Papers from the seventh regional meeting of the Chicago Linguistics Society, Chicago, pp. 63-84.

Green, B.F. Jr., Wolf, A.K., Chomsky, C., and Laughery, K. (1961), Baseball: an automatic question answerer. In Feigenbaum and Feldman (1963), pp. 207-216.

Grice, H.P. (1967), Logic and conversation. In Cole and Morgan (1975), (taken from William James Lectures, Harvard, 1967), pp. 41-58.

Grosz, Barbara J. (1977a), The representation and use of focus in a system for understanding dialogs, IJCAI-5, pp. 67-76.

Grosz, Barbara J. (1977b), The representation and use of focus in dialogue understanding, Stanford Research Institute, Technical Note 151 (Slightly revised version of the Ph.D. thesis, University of California, Berkeley).

Grosz, Barbara J. (1978a), Focussing in dialog, TINLAP-2, pp. 96-103.

Grosz, Barbara J. (1978b), Discourse knowledge. In Walker (1978), pp. 229-344.

Harris, Larry R. (1977a), ROBOT: a high performance language interface for data base query, Technical Report, TR77-1, Mathematics Department, Dartmouth College.

Harris, Larry R. (1977b), User oriented data base query with the ROBOT natural language query system, Int. J. Man-Machine Studies 9, pp. 697-713.

Harris, Larry R. (1978), The ROBOT system: natural language processing applied to data base query, Proceedings of the ACM Annual Conference, pp. 165-172.

Hawkinson, Lowell (1975), The representation of concepts in OWL, IJCAI-4, pp. 107-114.

Hemphill, Linda and Rhyne, James (1978), A model for the knowledge representation in natural language query systems, IBM Research Laboratory, San Jose, RJ 2304.

Hendrix, G.G. (1975), Expanding the utility of semantic networks through partitioning, IJCAI-4, pp. 115-121.

Hendrix, G.G. (1977), Human engineering for applied natural language processing, IJCAI-5, pp. 183-191.

Hendrix, Gary G., Sacerdoti, Earl D., Sagalowicz, Daniel, Slocum, Jonathan (1978), Developing a natural language interface to complex data, ACM Transactions on Database Systems, 3,2, pp. 105-147.

Hirst, Graeme (1979), Anaphora in natural language understanding: a survey, Department of Computer Science, University of British Columbia, Technical Report 79-2.

Hobbs, Jerry R. (1976), A computational approach to discourse analysis, Department of Computer Sciences, City College of New York, Research Report No. 76-2.

Hobbs, Jerry R. (1977), Coherence and interpretation in English texts, IJCAI-5, pp. 110-116.

Hobbs, Jerry R. (1979), Coherence and reference, Cognitive Science 3,1, pp. 67-90.

Johnson-Laird, Philip N. (1977), Procedural semantics, Cognition, 5, pp. 189-214.

Johnson-Laird, P.N. (1978), What's wrong with Grandma's guide to procedural semantics: a reply to Jerry Fodor, Cognition 6, pp. 249-261.

Kaplan, S. Jerrold (1978), Indirect responses to loaded questions, TINLAP-2, pp. 202-209.

Kaplan, S. Jerrold and Joshi, Aravind K. (1978), Co-operative responses: an application of discourse inference to data base query systems, CSCSI-2, pp. 196-205.

Katz, J.J., and Fodor, J.A. (1963), The structure of a semantic theory, Language XXXIX, pp. 170-210.

Katz, J.J., and Postal P. (1964), An Integrated Theory of Linguistic Description, Cambridge, Mass., MIT Press.

Kender, John R. (1977), An annotated bibliography of natural language and speech understanding systems, Department of Computer Science, Carnegie-Mellon University.

Kuno, S. (1967), Computer analysis of natural language. In Proceedings of Symposia in Applied Mathematics, Vol. XIX, Am. Math. Assoc. pp. 52-110.

Lakoff, George (1974), Interview with Herman Parret. In Herman Parret, Discussing Language, The Hague, Mouton.

Lakoff, George (1978), Some remarks on AI and Linguistics, Cognitive Science 2,3, pp. 267-275.

Lakoff, Robin (1973), The logic of politeness: or, minding your P's and Q's. In Corum et al (1973), pp. 292-305.

Larkin, Don and O'Malley, Michael H. (1973), Declarative sentences and the rule-of-conversation hypothesis. In Corum et al (1973), pp. 306-319.

Lehnert, Wendy (1976), Dynamic processing and question answering, COLING 76, 38 p.

Lehnert, Wendy (1977a), Human and computational question answering, Cognitive Science 1,1, pp. 47-73.

Lehnert, Wendy (1977b), A conceptual theory of question answering, IJCAI-5, pp. 158-164.

Lesser, Victor R. and Erman, Lee D. (1977), A retrospective view of the Hearsay II architecture, IJCAI-5, pp. 790-800.

Levin, James A. and Moore, James A. (1977), Dialogue games: metacommunication structures for natural language, Cognitive Science 1,4, pp. 395-420.

Lowerre, Bruce T. (1976), The HARPY speech recognition system, Ph.D. thesis, Department of Computer Science, Carnegie-Mellon University.

Mackworth, A.K. (1977), How to see a simple world. In Elcock, E.W. and Michie, D. (eds.), Machine Intelligence 8, N.Y., Halstead Press.

Mann, William C., Moore, James A., and Levin, James A. (1977), A comprehension model for human dialogue, IJCAI-5, pp. 77-87.

McCalla, Gordon I. (1977), An approach to the organization of knowledge for the modelling of conversation, Technical Report 78-4, Department of Computer Science, The University of British Columbia (based on Ph.D. thesis of the same title submitted in 1977).

McCalla, Gordon I. (1978), Analyzing conversation, CSCSI-2, pp. 224-232.

McCarthy, J.T. (1958), Programs with common sense. In Minsky (1968), pp. 403-417.

Minsky, M. (ed.) (1968), Semantic Information Processing, Cambridge, Mass., MIT Press.

Minsky, Marvin (1975), A framework for representing knowledge. In Winston, Patrick Henry, The Psychology of Computer Vision, New York, McGraw-Hill.

Moore, J.A., Levin, J.A. and Mann, W.C. (1977), A goal-oriented model of human dialogue, Amer. J. of Comp. Ling., Microfiche 67.

Nash-Webber, Bonnie (see also Webber, Bonnie Lynn).

Nash-Webber, Bonnie (1975), The role of semantics in automatic speech understanding. In Bobrow and Collins (1975), pp. 351-382.

Nash-Webber, Bonnie and Reiter, Raymond (1977), Anaphora and logical form: on formal meaning representations for natural language, IJCAI-5, pp. 121-131.

Newell, A., Barnett, J., Forgie, J.W., Green, C., Klatt, D., Licklider, J.C.R., Munson, J., Reddy, D.R., and Woods, W.A. (1973), Speech Understanding Systems, Final Report of a Study Group, N.Y. North-Holland/American Elsevier.

Norman, D.A. and Rumelhart, D.E. (1975), Explorations in Cognition, San Francisco, Freeman.

Palmer, Stephen E. (1975), Visual perception and world knowledge: notes on a model of sensory-cognitive interaction. In Norman and Rumelhart (1975), pp. 279-307.

Parkinson, Roger C., Colby, Kenneth Mark, Faught, William S. (1977), Conversational language comprehension using integrated pattern-matching and parsing, Artificial Intelligence 9,2, pp. 111-134.

Perrault, C. Raymond, Allen, James F., and Cohen, Philip R. (1978), Speech acts as a basis for understanding dialogue coherence, TINLAP-2, pp. 125-132.

Petrick, S.R. (1976), On natural language based computer systems, IBM J. Res. Develop. 20,4, pp. 314-325.

Philips, Brian (1975), Judging the coherency of discourse. In Diller (1975), ACL Microfiche 35.

Philips, Brian (1978), A model for knowledge and its application to discourse analysis, Amer. J. of Comp. Linguistics, Microfiche 82.

Propp, V. (1968), Morphology of the Folktale, Austin, University of Texas Press.

Quillian, M. Ross (1968), Semantic memory. In Minsky (1968), pp. 227-270.

Quillian, M. Ross (1979), The teachable language comprehender, Comm. ACM 12,8, pp. 459-475.

Reddy, D. Raj (1976), Speech recognition by machine: a survey, Proceedings of the IEEE 64,6, pp. 501-531.

Reddy, D.R., Erman, L.D., Fennell, R.D., and Neely, R.B. (1976), The Hearsay - I speech understanding System: an example of the recognition process, IEEE-AI, pp. 422-431.

Reichman, Rachel (1978), Conversational coherency, Cognitive Science 2,4, pp. 283-327.

Rieger, C. (1975), Conceptual memory. In Schank (1975).

Riesbeck, C. (1975), Conceptual analysis. In Schank (1975).

Roberts, R. Bruce and Goldstein, Ira P. (1977), The FRL primer, AI Laboratory, MIT, Memo 408.

Robinson, Arthur L. (1979a), More people are talking to computers as speech recognition enters the real word, Research News, Science, 203, pp. 634-638.

Robinson, Arthur L. (1979b), Communicating with computers by voice, Research News, Science 203, pp. 734-736.

Rosenberg, Richard S. (1975), Artificial Intelligence and Linguistics: a brief history of a one-way relationship, Proceedings of the First Annual Meeting of the Berkeley Linguistics Society, Berkeley, CA., pp. 379-392.

Rosenberg, Steve (1977), Frame-based text processing, AI Laboratory, MIT, AIM 431.

Rumelhart, David E. (1975), Notes on a schema for stories. In Bobrow and Collins (1975), pp. 211-236.

Rumelhart, David E., Linsay, Peter H., and Norman, Donald A. (1972), A process model for long-term memory. In Tulving, E. and Donaldson, W. (eds.) Organization of Memory, N.Y. Academic Press, pp. 197-246.

Sacerdoti, E.D. (1977), Language access to distributed data with error recovery, IJCAI-5, pp. 196-202.

Schank, Roger (1972), Conceptual dependency: A theory of natural language understanding, Cog. Psych. 3,4, pp. 552-631.

Schank, Roger C. (1973), Identification of conceptualizations underlying natural language. In Schank and Colby (1973), pp. 187-247.

Schank, R.C. (1975a), Conceptual Information Processing, Amsterdam, North-Holland.

Schank, Roger C. (1975b), Using knowledge to understand, TINLAP, pp. 117-121.

Schank, Roger C. and Abelson, Robert F. (1975), Scripts, plans and knowledge, IJCAI-4, pp. 151-157.

Schank, Roger C. and Abelson, Robert F. (1977), Scripts, Plans, Goals and Understanding, New York, Lawrence Erlbaum Associates (distributed by John Wiley & Sons).

Schank, R.C., and Colby, K.M. (1973), Computer Models of Thought and Language, San Francisco, Freeman & Co.

Schank, Roger C., Goldman, N.M., Rieger, C., and Riesbeck, C. (1975), Inference and paraphrase by computer, J. ACM 22,3, pp. 309-328.

Schank, Roger C. and Wilensky, Robert (1977), Response to Dresher and Hornstein, Cognition 5, pp. 133-145.

Schubert, L.K. (1976), Extending the expressive power of semantic networks, Artificial Intelligence 7,2, pp. 163-198.

Scragg, Greg W. (1975), Answering questions about processes. In Norman and Rumelhart (1975), pp. 349-375.

Searle, John R. (1970), Speech Acts, Cambridge University Press.

Searle, John R. (1975), Indirect speech acts. In Cole and Morgan (1975), pp. 59-82.

Shortliffe, Edward Hance (1976), Computer-Based Medical Consultations: MYCIN, New York, Elsevier.

Sidner, Candace L. (1978a), A progress report on the discourse and reference component of PAL, CSCSI-2, pp. 206-213.

Sidner, Candace L. (1978b), Use of focus as a tool for disambiguation for definite noun phrases, TINLAP-2, pp. 86-95.

Simmons, R.F. (1965), Answering English questions by computer: a survey, Comm. ACM 8,1, pp. 53-70.

Simmons, R.F. (1970), Natural language question-answering systems: 1969, Comm. ACM 13,1, pp. 15-30

Simmons, R.F. (1973), Semantic networks: their computation and use for understanding English sentences. In Schank and Colby (1973), pp. 63-113.

Taylor, B.H. and Rosenberg, R.S. (1975), A case-driven parser for natural language, American Journal for Computational Linguistics, AJCL Microfiche 31.

Thompson, Frederick B. and Thompson, Bozena Henisz (1975), Practical natural language processing: the REL system as a prototype. In Rubinoff, Morris and Yovits, Marshall (eds.), Advances in Computers, Vol. 13, N.Y. Academic Press, 1975.

Thompson, Bozena Henisz and Thompson, Frederick B. (1978), Rapidly extendable natural language, Proceedings of ACM Annual Conference, pp. 173-182.

van Dijk, T.A. (1972), Some Aspects of Text Grammars: A Study in Theoretical Linguistics and Poetics, The Hague, Mouton, 1972.

Walker, D.E. (1976), Speech understanding through syntactic and semantic analysis, IEEE-AI, pp. 432-439.

Walker, Donald E. (1978), Understanding Spoken Language, N.Y., North-Holland, 1978.

Waltz, David L. (ed.) (1977), Natural language interfaces, SIGART Newsletter, No. 61, pp. 16-64.

Waltz, David L. (1978), An English language question answering system for a large relational database, Comm. ACM 21,7, pp. 526-539.

Waltz, D.L., Finin, T., Green, F., Conrad, F., Goodman, B., and Hadden, G. (1976), The PLANES system: natural language access to a large data base, Coordinated Science Lab., University of Illinois, Urbana, Tech. Report, T-34.

Waltz, David L. and Goodman, Bradley, A. (1977), Writing a natural language data base system, IJCAI-5, pp. 144-150.

Webber, Bonnie Lynn (1978), A formal approach to discourse anaphora, Bolt Beranek and Newman, Report No. 3761, Cambridge, Mass.

Weizenbaum, J. (1966), ELIZA - a computer program for the study of natural language communication between man and machine, Comm. ACM 9,1, pp. 36-45.

Wilensky, Robert (1978), Why John married Mary: understanding stories involving recurring goals, Cognitive Science 2,3, pp. 235-266.

Wilks, Yorick (1975), A preferential pattern-seeking, semantics for natural language inference, Artificial Intelligence 6,1, pp. 53-74.

Wilks, Yorick (1976a), Frames, scripts, stories and fantasies, COLING 76, 27 p.

Wilks, Yorick (1976b), Natural language understanding systems within the AI paradigm: a survey and some comparisons, Amer. J. Comp. Ling., Microfiche 40.

Winograd, Terry (1972), Understanding Natural Language, New York, Academic Press, 1972.

Winograd, Terry (1976), Towards a procedural understanding of semantics, Revue Inter. Philosophie (3-4): 117-118, pp. 260-303.

Winograd, Terry (1977a), On some contested suppositions of generative linguistics about the scientific study of language, Cognition 5, pp. 151-179.

Winograd, Terry (1977b), A framework for understanding discourse. In Just, M. and Carpenter, P. (eds.), Cognitive Processes in Comprehension, N.Y., Lawrence Erlbaum Associates, 1977.

Woods, W.A. (1970), Transition network grammars for natural language analysis, Comm. ACM 13,10, pp. 591-606.

Woods, William A. (1975), What's in a link: foundations for semantic networks. In Bobrow and Collins (1975), pp. 35-82.

Woods, W.A., Kaplan, R.M., and Nash-Webber, B. (1972), The lunar sciences natural language information system: final report, Bolt Beranek and Newman, Report No. 2378, Cambridge, Mass.

Woods, William A. and Makhoul, J. (1974), Mechanical inference problems in continuous speech understanding, Artificial Intelligence 5,1, pp. 73-91.

Woods, W.A., Bates, M.A., Bruce, B.C., Colarusso, J.J., Cook, C.C., Gould, L., Makhoul, J.I., Nash-Webber, B.L., Schwartz, R.M., and Wolf, J.J. (1974), Speech understanding research at BBN, final report on natural communication with computers, Vol. I, Bolt Beranek and Neuman, Inc., Rep. 2976, Cambridge, Mass.

Young, Robert (1977), Text understanding: a survey, Amer. J. of Comp. Ling., Microfiche 70.

AN INTEGRATED THEORY OF NATURAL LANGUAGE UNDERSTANDING

by

F. M. Brown
University of Texas at Austin
C. B. Schwind
Technische Universität München

Abstract

We describe and exemplify the underlying structure of a new kind of theory of natural language understanding which would allow for a rich and smooth interaction between syntactic and semantic concepts.

The basic idea is to let the representation language in which the meaning of natural language text is expressed be the same language as the language in which the parsing and translation laws are expressed. This is done by supplementing a modal quantificational state logic with names of both natural language and logical expressions. Natural language expressions are then parsed and translated into logical expressions which in turn are translated into their logical meanings by use of a meaning function. Since both the laws of parsing, translation and meaning are themselves expressed in logic one can easily write such laws so as to interact with the meaning of the natural language text.

Key Words and Phrases: Natural Language Parsing and Understanding, Preference Semantics, Theory of Meaning, Modal Quantificational Logic, Quantified State Logic.

1. Introduction

Our research is aimed towards creating a theory of natural language understanding such that the representation language in which the meaning of natural language text is represented is itself the language in which that theory is described. This is, laws for the description of the syntax of natural language, laws for the translation of natural language into meanings, and the representation of those meanings are all written in a single representation language. We believe that a theory of this nature has important technical and methodological advantages over other types of theories of natural language understanding in that we will be able to precisely and concisely state laws involving all aspects of the process of natural language understanding. Because both syntactic and meaning concepts are represented in a single language we will call such a theory an integrated theory of natural language understanding.

Since not only must laws of natural language understanding be representable in our representation language, but the meaning of natural language text must also be representable, it is clear that this language must be a language of great representational ability. Partially, for this reason we will assume that the representation language is some logic at least as strong as modal quantificational logic.

2. Basic Structure of an Integrated Theory

As it is in the case of other theories of natural language as well as with practical natural language understanding systems, an integrated theory involves at least three basic processes: (see Figure 1).

1. The parsing of natural language expressions and their translation into meanings, which are expressed in the representation language.
2. The inference of meanings expressed in a representation language from other meanings expressed in a representation language.
3. The generation of natural language expressions from meanings which are expressed in a representation language.

In our case the representational language will be a modal quantificational logic supplemented by a theory of action. The parsing system as well as the translation system are described by axioms of our theory which are intended to be executed by an automatic theorem prover.

Theory	Example
Names of Natural Language Exp.	Name of (Kate is a doll)
↓	↓
1.1 Parsing and translation Laws	
↓	↓
Names of Logical Exp.	Name of (Doll Kate)
↓	↓
1.2 Meaning Laws	
↓	↓
Logical Exp.	(Doll Kate)
↓	↓
2. Inference using non-linguistic laws such as: $\forall$ x (Doll x) ⟶ (Beautiful x)	
↓	↓
Logical Exp.	(Beautiful Kate)
↓	↓
3.1 Inverse Meaning Laws	
↓	↓
Names of Logical Exp.	Name of (Beautiful Kate)
↓	↓
3.2 Generation Laws	
↓	↓
Names of Natural Language Exp.	Name of (Kate is beautiful)

Fig. 1. Basic Structure of an Integrated Theory

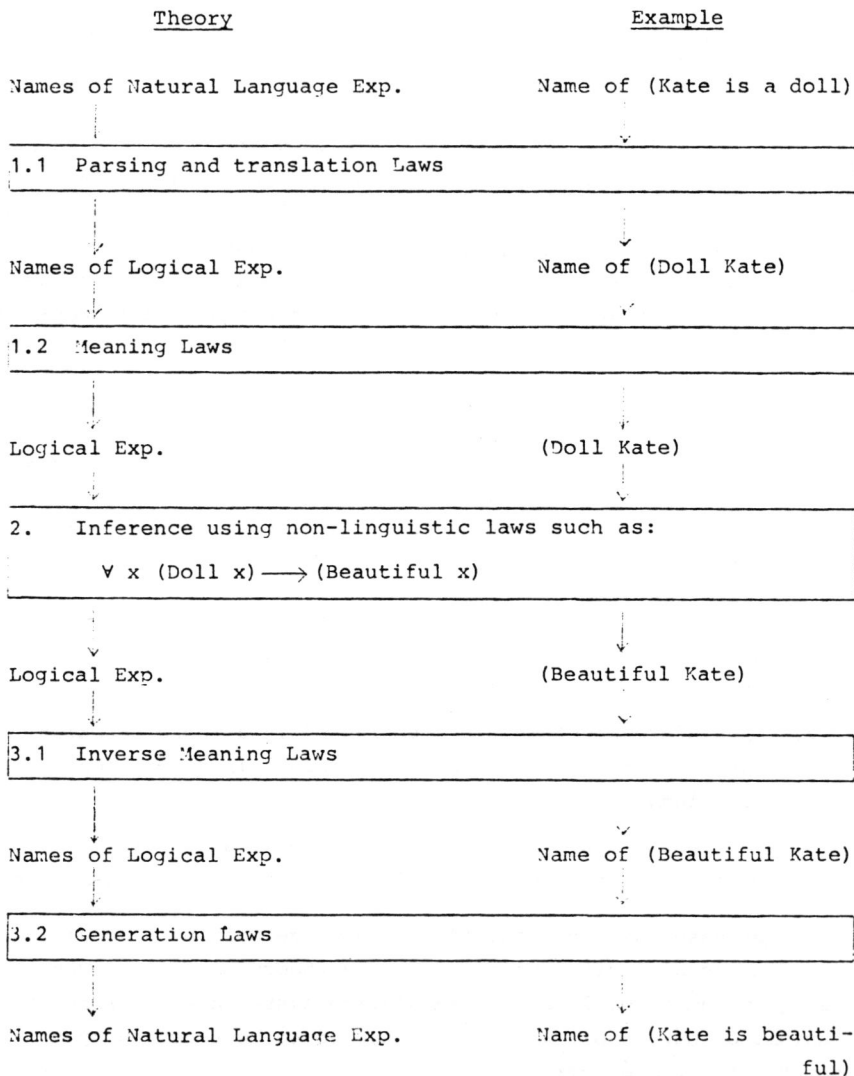

It is important to understand that natural language expressions are syntactic objects which are expressed in our system by names of such expressions whereas the meaning of such expressions is represented in our system, not by names of logical expressions, but rather by logical expressions themselves. For this reason we can divide each of the parsing and generation steps into two steps: (see Figure 1).

(1.1) A parsing and translation step which translates natural language expressions, which are represented by their names, into logical expressions which are represented by their names.

(1.2) A meaning step which translates logical expressions, which are represented by their names, into their meanings which are represented by logical expressions.

Likewise, the generation step can be divided into two steps: (see Figure 1).

(3.1) An inverse meaning step, which translates meanings represented by logical expressions, into those logical expressions which are represented by names of logical expressions.

(3.2) A generation step which translates logical expressions, which are represented by their names, into natural language expressions, which are represented by their names.

The inference step (2) allows the derivation of logical expressions by means of logical inference rules, axioms of logic, and non-logical laws pertaining to both linguistic subjects such as: parsing, generation and meaning; and non-linguistic subjects such as a model of various physical and social facts about the real world.

There are two basic reasons for using a representation language, and in particular for the use of logic as the representation language rather than using natural language itself as the representation language. The first reason is to simplify the description of both the linguistic and non-linguistic axioms, in that such laws will not have to be stated in terms of the complex syntax of natural language which is often very ambigious, but will be expressed in the much simpler syntax of logic. The second reason is that the inference laws for making logical derivations have been profoundly studied whereas there is no comparable body of knowledge about how inference in natural language might work. In particular efficient automatic theorem proving techniques have been developed for quantificational logic, and even modal quantificational logic [1], whereas no such comparable automatic inference techniques have been developed for natural language. Thus by using logic as the representation language we have the option of actually testing our theory by executing it on an automatic theorem prover.

2.1. Formal Orientation

We have indicated that an integrated theory is to be represented in a logic at least as strong as modal quantificational logic. The syntax of such a language includes:

(1) Logical connectives

$p \wedge q$	p and q
$p \vee q$	p or q
$p \rightarrow q$	if p then q
$p \leftrightarrow q$	p iff q
$\sim p$	not p
$\blacksquare$	true
$\square$	false

(2) Logical Quantifiers

$\forall x \phi x$	For all objects x, ϕ of x holds
$\exists x \phi x$	For some object x, ϕ of x holds
$\forall p \phi p$	For all propositions p, ϕ of p holds
$\exists p \phi p$	For some proposition p, ϕ of p holds

(3) Intensional and Extensional Equality

$x = y$	x intensionally equals y
$x \triangleq y$	x extensionally equals y

Intensional equality: = possesses substitution properties over all expressions including those containing modals symbols. Extensional equality does not possess substitution properties over modal symbols. Thus:

$$x = y \rightarrow (\varphi x \leftrightarrow \varphi y)$$

$$p = q \rightarrow (\Box p \leftrightarrow \Box q)$$

but $p \triangleq q \rightarrow (\Box p \leftrightarrow \Box q)$ does not hold.

(4) Description Operators

$\iota x \varphi x$	'iota' - operator:

where: $\Psi(\iota x \varphi x) \leftrightarrow \left(\begin{array}{l} (\exists y\ (\forall x(\varphi x \leftrightarrow x = y) \wedge \Psi y) \\ \vee \sim\exists y(\forall x(\varphi x \leftrightarrow x = y)) \wedge \Psi\ nil) \end{array} \right)$

the $x\varphi x$	the x such that φ of x

where: (the $x\varphi x$) $=$ df$\iota x(\varphi x \wedge \mathcal{F} x)$

where $\mathcal{F}$ is a special linguistic function which we will leave undefined.

(5) Modal Connectives

$\Box p$	p is logically true
$\Box p_q$	p entails y
$\Diamond p$	p is possible

The axioms of our modal logic are those of S5 modal logic plus Leibnitz's law which states that something is logically true if it is true in all possible worlds:

	MO:	from p infer $\Box p$
	M1:	$\Box p \rightarrow p$
	M2:	$\Box(p \rightarrow q) \rightarrow (\Box p \rightarrow \Box q)$
	M3:	$\Box p \vee \Box \sim \Box p$
Leib:	M4:	$(\forall w(\Diamond w \wedge \forall p\ \Box wp \vee \Box w(\sim p)) \rightarrow \Box wq) \rightarrow \Box q$

(6) Tense operators and other non-logical symbols

(present p) p holds in the present

(past p) p holds in the past

(7) Variables which range over various domains

Since the parsing and generation laws of an integrated theory refer to both natural language und logical expressions, it follows that the theory must also include names of these expressions. This is done first by including in the theory a name for each logical or natural language symbol and then by forming names of expressions by representing them as a list of the names of the subexpressions occurring in that expression.

Names of symbols are formed by simply prefixing to that symbol an accent sign ´. Thus ´∧ is a name of the ∧-symbol of logic, and ´and is the name of the and-symbol of English. The apparent visual similarity between a symbol such as ∧ and its name ´∧ is merely a pneumonic.

Lists are formed as in LISP by use of two symbols Nil and Cons in

Nil

(Cons x y)

where (Cons xy) is an ordered pair and Nil is not an ordered pair. A list $[x_1 \ldots x_n]$ of zero or more elements is then defined in terms of cons and Nil as follows

$$[x_1 \ldots x_n] = df\ (\text{Cons}\ x_1 \ldots (\text{Cons}\ x_n\ \text{Nil}) \ldots)$$

Note that [ ] is simply Nil. Sometimes we will also use the abbreviation [x,y] for (Cons xy).

Given these lists, and names of symbols we can now form names of arbitrary expressions. For example a name of the expression:

((all men) are mortal)

is

[[´all ´men] ´are ´mortal]

We will also use various selector functions which select subparts of a list, in particular:

(Car x) such that (Car(Cons x y)) = x

(Cdr x) such that (Cdr(Cons x y)) = y

(Cadr x) such that (Cadrx) = (Car (Cdr x))

The Modal Logic on which this theory is based is developed in more detail in [1,2]. The Tense logic used in this theory is described in[10,11]. The Syntactic devices are described in [2].

2.2. Parsing and Translation

The laws of parsing and translation in an integrated theory state how to translate expressions of natural language into equivalent expressions of logic. Generally such laws are equivalences between an atomic sentence and a conjunction of atomic sentences:

$$A \leftrightarrow (B_1 \wedge \ldots \wedge B_n)$$

For example a law of parsing might say that s is a sentence ($Sent_1$) iff the first part of s is a noun phrase (NP), the second part of s is a form of the verb "be" (VBE), and the last part of s is an adjective (ADJ).

(SENT1 s) ↔ (NP (first part of s))
∧(VBE (second part of s))
∧(ADJ (last part of s))

The "part of" idioms are handled in logic by representing each part of a sentence as the difference of two lists x_i, x_{i+1}. For example if

xo is ['The 'Tree 'is 'pretty]

x1 is ['Is 'pretty]

then the difference xo - x1 intuitively represents ['The 'tree].

Using these difference lists we can write the above parsing laws as:

(SENT1 xo-x3) ↔ ((NP xo-x1) ∧ (VBE x1-x2) ∧ (ADJ x2-x3))

Thus for example if we wish to parse the sentence

[´the ´tree ´is ´pretty]

we would try to prove

(SENT1 [´the ´tree ´is ´pretty]-[])

Then by using the above parsing law we could deduce

(NP [´the ´tree ´is ´pretty] - x1) ∧ (VBE x1-x2) ∧ (ADJ x2-[])

By using further parsing laws pertaining to noun phrases we would instantiate x1 to [´is ´pretty] thus finding that [´the ´tree] was a noun phrase. After this only two subgoals remain:

(VBE [´is ´pretty] - x2) ∧ (ADJ x2-[])

which are easily proven by using parsing laws pertaining to the verb be and to adjectives, in the course of which x2 will be instantiated to [´pretty].

As we parse a sentence we will also want to translate it into an equivalent logical expression. This is done by including in each atomic sentence an extra argument place for the logical expression which is roughly equivalent to the natural language expression contained in the difference list. For example the above parsing law might be modified to state that xo-x2 is a sentence translated as the logical expression [β α] iff xo-x1 is a noun phrase translated as α, x1-x2 is a form of the verb be, and x2-x3 is an adjective translated as β:

(SENT1 xo-x3 [β α]) ↔ ((NP xo-x1 α) ∧ (VBE x1-x2)
∧ (ADJ x2-x3 β))

Thus if a noun phrase [´the ´tree] is translated as the logical constant ´TREE21 and if the adjective [´pretty] is translated as the unary predicate ´PRETTY then the sentence [´the ´tree ´is ´pretty] will be translated as [´PRETTY ´TREE21].

We have just given a parsing law which states that something is a sentence iff it is a noun phrase followed by an intransitive verb followed by an adjective. But it is clear that this is not the only possible immediate constituent structure for a sentence of English. For example something could be a sentence if it begins with a noun phrase followed by a transitive verb. Thus what is needed is a distinct atomic name: SENT1, SENT2 ... for each parsing law about sentences, and then to say that something is a sentence iff it is a sentence of type 1 (SENT1), or a sentence of type 2 (SENT2) etc. Thus in general it is clear that we also need parsing laws in which the right side is a disjunction of atomic sentences:

$$A \leftrightarrow (A_1 \vee \ldots\ldots \vee A_n)$$

such as:

(SENT xo-x1 α) ↔ ((SENT1 xo-x1 α)∨(SENT2 xo-x1 α))

Disjunctive parsing laws are also used to express the lexicon. For example

(ADJ [x,y] -y z) ↔ ((x = ´pretty ∧ z = ´PRETTY)
∨ (x = ´red ∧ z = ´RED))

is used to express the fact that ´pretty and ´red are the only adjectives in the lexicon and that pretty and red are translated into logic as respectively the unary predicates

´PRETTY and ´RED. Note that [x,y] -y intuitively represents [x].

So far we have specified that atomic sentences are to have three arguments: two for the difference list representing a part of the sentence being parsed and one in which to specify the equivalent logical expression. Usually the atomic sentences will have several more arguments. For example often they will have two more arguments usually written v_i v_{i+1} which are essentially a difference list of variables of the logical object languages. It is clear that such variables are needed since a sentence like [´all ´trees ´are ´pretty] would be translated into logic as

[´∀´x [´tree ´x] → [´pretty ´x]]

where ´x is the first variable in the difference list for variables. Also it should be noted that some atomic sentences do not contain all the arguments specified here. For example the intransitive verb sentence does not contain an argument position for the equivalent logical expression, since there is none.

We say that z is a translation of the natural language sentence s iff z is a translation of the sentence s-[] using a sufficiently long difference list of variables v-[]:

(Trans s z) $\leftrightarrow$ (SENT s-[] v-[] z)

Then to find a translation of a sentence s we merely try to prove that there is an α which is its translation

$\exists$ z (Trans s z)

We now give in Figure 4 some parsing and translation laws for a very small subset of English in order to illustrate how both syntactic and meaning concepts interact in our theory. Figure 2 contains a description of the categories of expressions used in these laws. Figure 3 contains a summary of these parsing laws obtained by deleting all the arguments of the atomic sentences. Figure 3 is of no help in understanding the translation process but it will at least give one a general idea of the grammar used by these laws.

The example parsing and translation laws given in Figure 4 are derived from a larger parsing and translation algorithm, for both English and German, described in[8,9,10].

We also define a function tran which chooses any one translation z of the sentence S

trans S = (choice z (trans s z))

This function will be used in section 2.4. The choice function obeys the axiom:

Ax: $\exists x \varphi x \rightarrow (\varphi(\text{choice } \underline{z}\ \varphi z))$

for any property φ.

Basic Categories

DETD	definite determiner
DETQ	quantifier
N	noun
ADJ	adjective
PREP	preposition
VBE	the verb "to be"
VDO	the verb "to do"
VT	transitive verb
PRON	pronoun
RELPRON	relative pronoun

Derived Categories

SENT, SENT1, SENT2, SENT3, sentence
CLAUSE embedded sentence
NP, NP1, NP2, NP3, NP4 noun phrase
NG, NG1, NG2, NG3 noun group
PP prepositional phrase

Figure 2. Syntactic categories

(subst x for y in z) is a function the result of which is the expression obtained by replacing y in z by x.

Grammar:

SENT ↔ SENT1 ∨ SENT2 ∨ SENT3
SENT1 ↔ NP ∧ VBE ∧ Adj
SENT2 ↔ NP ∧ VT ∧ NP
SENT3 ↔ VDO ∧ NP ∧ VT ∧ NP

CLAUSE ↔ RELPRON ∧ VT ∧ NP

NP ↔ NP1 ∨ NP2 ∨ NP3 ∨ NP4
NP1 ↔ NG
NP2 ↔ DETQ ∧ NG
NP3 ↔ DETD ∧ NG
NP4 ↔ PRON

NG ↔ NG1 ∨ NG2 ∨ NG3
NG1 ↔ N
NG2 ↔ NG ∧ PP
NG3 ↔ NG ∧ CLAUSE

PP ↔ PREP ∧ NP

Lexicon:

DETD ↔ the
DETQ ↔ (a ∨ some ∨ all ∨ every)
N ↔ (tree ∨ trees ∨ garden ∨ gardens
∨ rose ∨ roses ∨ cone ∨ cones)
ADJ ↔ (pretty ∨ red)
PREP ↔ in
VBE ↔ is ∨ was
VDO ↔ do ∨ does ∨ did
VT ↔ (owns ∨ owned ∨ grow ∨ grows
∨ have ∨ has ∨ had ∨ grew)
RELPRON ↔ which ∨ that ∨ who
PRON ↔ somebody ∨ everybody

Figure 3. Summary of Parsing Laws

```
(SENT xo-x1 vo-v1 z) ↔ (SENT1 xo-x1 vo-v1 z)
            ∨ (SENT2 xo-x1 vo-v1 z) ∨ (SENT3 xo-x1 vo-v1 z)

(SENT1 xo-x3 vo-v1 [zo(subst [z2 y] for * in z1)]) ↔
∃x1∃x2((NP xo-x1 vo-v1 y z1) ∧ (VBE x1-x2 zo) ∧ (ADJ x2-x3 z2))

(SENT2 xo-x3 vo-v2
[(cadr zo) (subst(subst[(car zo)y1 y2] for * in z2)
  for * in z1)]) ↔
∃x1∃x2∃v1((NP xo-x1 vo-v1 y1 z1) ∧ (VT x1-x2 zo)
∧(NP x2-x3 v1-v2 y2 z2))

(SENT3 xo-x4 vo-v2
[?[zo(subst(subst[(car z3)y1-y2] for * in z2) for * in z1)]])↔
∃x1∃x2∃x3∃v1((VDO xo-x1 zo) ∧ (NP x1-x2 vo-v1 y1 z1) ∧
            (VT x2-x3 z3) ∧ (NP x3-x4 v1-v2 y2 z2))

(CLAUSE xo-x3 vo-v1 y1 [(cadr zo) (subst[(car zo) y1 y2]
 for * in z1)])↔
∃x1∃x2((RELPRON xo-x1) ∧ (VT x1-x2 zo) ∧ (NP x2-x3 vo-v1 y2 z1))

(NP xo-x1 vo-v1 y z) ↔ ((NP1 xo-x1 vo-v1 y z) ∨
(NP2 xo-x1 vo-v1 y z ) ∨(NP3 xo-x1 vo-v1 y z) ∨
(NP4 xo-x1 vo-v1 y z))

(NP1 xo-x1 vo-v1 y ['∃y[z '∧ *]]) ↔ (NG xo-x1 vo-v1 y z)

(NP2 xo-x2 vo-v1 y [(car z1) y [z2 (cdr z1)*]])↔
∃x1((DETQ xo-x1 z1) ∧ (NG x1-x2 vo-v1 y z2))

(NP3 xo-x2 vo-v1 ['the y z]*) ↔
∃x1((DETD xo-x1) ∧ (NG x1-x2 vo-v1 y z))

(NP4 xo-x1 [y.v1]-v1 y [z y *]) ↔ (PRON xo-x1 z)

(NG xo-x1 vo-v1 y z) ↔
((NG1 xo-x1 vo-v1 y z) ∨ (NG2 xo-x1 vo-v1 y z)
∨ (NG3 xo-x1 vo-v1 y z))

(NG1 xo-x1 [y.v1]-v1 y [z y]) ↔ (N xo-x1 z)
```

Figure 4. <u>The example Grammar</u> cont'd..

(NG2 xo-x2 vo-v2 y1 [z1 '∧ z2]) ↔
∃x1∃v1 ((NG xo-x1 vo-v1 y1 z1) ∧ (PP x1-x2 v1-v2 y1 y2 z2))

(NG3 xo-x2 vo-v2 y1 [z1 '∧ z2]) ↔
∃x1∃v1 ((NG xo-x1 vo-v1 y1 z1) ∧ (CLAUSE x1-x2 v1-v2 y1 z2))

(PP xo-x2 vo-v1 yo y1(subst [zo yo y1] for * in z1)) ↔
∃x1((PREP xo-x1 zo) ∧ (NP x1-x2 vo-v1 y1 z1))

Lexicon

(DETD [x.xo]-xo) ↔ x='the

(DETQ [x.xo]-xo z) ↔ (((x='a ∨ x='some) ∧ z=['∃'∧]) ∨
((x='all ∨ x='every) ∧ z=['∀'→]))

(N[x.xo]-xo z) ↔
(((x='tree ∨ x='trees) ∧ z='TREE) ∨ ((x='garden ∨ x='gardens)
∧ z='GARDEN)
∨ ((x='rose ∨ x='roses) ∧ z='ROSE) ∨ ((x='cone ∨ x='cones)
∧ z='CONE))

(ADJ[x.xo]-xo z) ↔((x='pretty ∧ z='PRETTY) ∨ (x='red ∧ z='RED))

(PREP[x.xo]-xo z) ↔ (x='in ∧ z='IN)

(VBE[x.xo]-xo z) ↔ ((x='is ∧ z='PRESENT) ∨ (x='was ∧ z='PAST))

(VDO[x.xo]-xo z) ↔ (((x='do ∨ x='does) ∧ z='PRESENT)
∨ (x='did ∧ z='PAST))

(VT[x.xo]-xo z) ↔
(((x='own ∨ x='owns) ∧ z=['OWN 'PRESENT]) ∨ (x='owned
∧ z=['OWN 'PAST]) ∨
((x='grow ∨ x='grows) ∧ z=['GROW 'PRESENT]) ∨ (x='grew
∧ z=['GROW 'PAST]) ∨
((x='had ∨ x='has) ∧ z=['HAS 'PRESENT]) ∨ (x='had
∧ z=['HAS 'PAST]))

Figure 4. The example Grammar cont'd ...

(RELPRON [x.xo]-xo) ↔ (x='which ∨ x='that ∨ x='who)

(PRON [x.xo]-xo z) ↔ ((x='somebody ∧ z='∃) ∨ (x='everybody ∧ z='∀))

Figure 4. The example Grammar

(A)

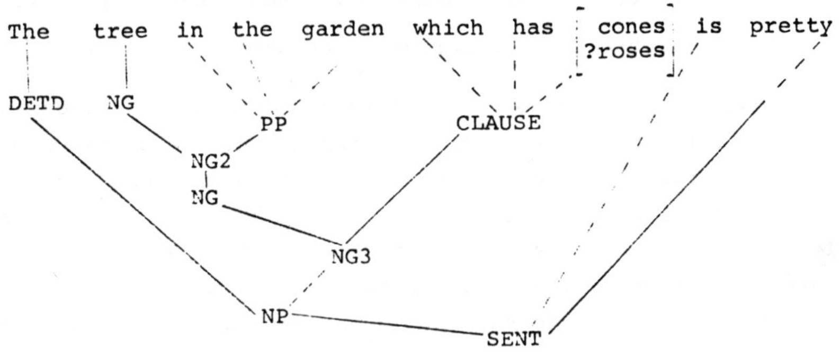

(B)

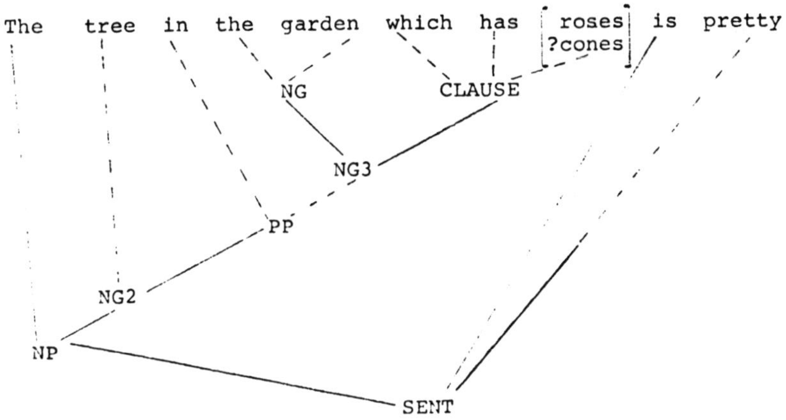

Figure 5. Syntactically ambiguous sentences

2.3. Interaction between Parsing and Meaning

In section 2.2 we described a syntactic parser which made no use what-so-ever of the meaning of the expressions it was parsing. One problem with such syntactic parsers is that there are generally many possible syntactically correct parsings of any given Natural Language sentence. For an example, there are two different syntactically correct parsings of each of the following sentences:

1. The tree in the garden which has cones is pretty.
2. The tree in the garden which has roses is pretty.

The possible parsings of each of these sentences is given in Figure 5. It should be clear that for semantic reasons we would like to parse the second sentence as parsing (B) and never as parsing (A) because it is false to claim that trees have roses. It should also be clear that for semantic reasons we would like to parse the first sentence as parsing (A) and not parsing (B), not because it is false to say that a garden has cones, but because it is more preferable to say that a tree or a plant has cones rather than to say that a garden or place has cones.

How can this semantic information about which possible parsings to reject be represented in our parser? If we look back at the parsings in Figure 5 and compare them we see that they differ in the parsing they give to the constituent:

"tree in the garden which has (cones/roses)"

for whereas the first parsing states that this is an NG3, the second states that it is an NG2. Clearly then what we need to do is to modify the NG axiom of Figure 4 so as to state that if both NG3 and NG2 parsings are possible then we want to reject one of them on semantic grounds. That is we want to say that the parsing accepted by the NG law should be the parsing produced by the NG2 law only if either there is no parsing produced by the NG3 law or if there is one and the meaning of the logical expression which is the translation of the natural language expression parsed by the NG2 law is more likely than the meaning of the logical expression which is the translation of the natural language expression which was parsed by the NG3 law. Likewise a similar rule should hold for the NG3 law. We modify the NG law as follows:

$$(NG\ xo\text{-}x1\ vo\text{-}v1\ y\ z) \leftrightarrow$$
$$((NG1\ xo\text{-}x1\ vo\text{-}v1\ y\ z) \vee$$
$$((NG2\ xo\text{-}x1\ vo\text{-}v1\ y\ z) \wedge (\forall z1(\sim\exists y(NG3\ xo\text{-}x1\ vo\text{-}v1\ y\ z1)) \vee$$
$$(LIKELIER(\sim(M['\sim z]))\ ('\sim(M['\sim z1]))))))$$
$$((NG3\ xo\text{-}x1\ vo\text{-}v1\ y\ z) \wedge (\forall z1(\sim\exists y(NG2\ xo\text{-}x1\ vo\text{-}v1\ y\ z1)) \vee$$
$$(LIKELIER(\sim(M['\sim z]))\ ('\sim(M['\sim z1]))))))$$

It is important to notice that the arguments to the propositional function LIKELIER are meanings of sentences of logic rather than the sentences themselves. Thus for example we are not saying that the NG2 parsing is to be used if a particular sentence is more likely than another but rather we are saying that it is to be used if a meaning of a sentence is more likely than another.

When would we like to say that one meaning is more likely than another? In accordance with the example parsings of our two sentences it appears to be reasonable to say that one meaning is more likely than another if the first meaning is consistent with our current knowledge of the world and the second meaning is not. This would allow us to reject the parsing which claimed that a tree has roses since we would expect

$$\neg\exists x\ \exists y\ [TREEx \wedge ROSEy \wedge HASxy]$$

to be deducable from general knowledge. Also in accordance with the example parsings producing the statements that a tree has cones, and a garden has cones, it appears to be reasonable to say that one meaning is more likely than another if the first meaning is consistent with the current world knowledge and entails a meaning which is more preferable than a meaning which is entailed by the second meaning. This would allow us to reject the parsing which claimed that a garden has cones, since trees are plants, gardens are places, cones are fruit and it is more preferable for plants to have fruit than it is for places to have fruit.

A definition of LIKELIER satisfying these intuitions is given below:

$(\Box_w \text{ (LIKELIER}xy)) \leftrightarrow_{df}$
$(\Diamond (w \wedge x) \wedge \sim\Diamond (w \wedge y)) \vee$
$(\exists P\ \exists Q(\Diamond (w \wedge x) \wedge \Box (w \wedge x \rightarrow P) \wedge \Box (w \wedge y \rightarrow Q) \wedge \Box_w \text{ (PREFER } P\ Q))$.

The symbol w represents a conjunction of the nonlogical axioms expressing facts of the current state of "real world". The PREFER symbol is either to be defined in terms of more elementary concepts or may be axiomatized by the inclusion of axioms like

$S\ \Box_w(\text{PREFER}(\exists x\exists y(\text{PLANT}x\wedge\text{FRUIT}y\wedge\text{HAS}xy))(\exists x\exists y(\text{PLACE}x\wedge\text{FRUIT}y\wedge\text{HAS}xy)))$

expressing that plants have fruits rather than places do. Since a tree is a plant, a garden is a place, and a cone is a fruit we can prove that it is more likely for trees to have cones than for gardens and hence we can reject the parsing which claims the latter.

2.4. Dialogue Control

The purpose of the dialogue laws are to state the basic social behaviour of a natural language understanding system. That is, such laws determine when and what the system is to communicate with the outside world, and how the world knowledge of the system is changed by such communications.

We represent such communication and world state by the use of three time predicates:

(In t) Input communication at time t
(Out t) Output communication at time t

The Input at any time t is defined by the person communicating with the system in the following manner by asserting:

(In t) = Σ

where Σ is a name of the input sentence. For example the input at time 0 is asserted to be: "all trees are pretty" as follows:

(In 0) = ['All 'Trees 'Are 'Pretty]

Once a sentence is given to the system the system will react in various ways depending on whether the input sentence is a declarative sentence or a Yes/No question sentence.

Since our parsing and translation laws return a list consisting of the symbol ? followed by a logical sentence in the case of a question sentence, and only a logical sentence in the case of a declarative sentence we use the atomic sentence (Isdel α) to determine the type of sentence. (Isdel α) is defined as follows:

(Isdel α) ↔df ∿(Car α)≏?

The system is also defined to react differently depending on whether the meaning of a declarative input sentence is consistent or contradictory with the system's state of knowledge. In all there are four social laws which govern the systems basic behaviour.

The first law states that if the meaning of a declarative input sentence is consistent with the systems beliefs then the meaning of that sentence is added to the systems beliefs and the next output is that the system believes that sentence:

C1:(⊐(Bel t) x≏(trans(Int))) ∧ (Isdel x) ∧ ◊ ((Bel t) ∧ (M x))
→ (Bel t+1) = ((Bel t) ∧ (M x)) ∧ (Out t+1) =['I 'Believe 'You]

The second law states that if the meaning of a declarative input sentence is inconsistent with the systems beliefs then the system remains the same and the next output is that the system disbelieves that sentence:

C2: (⊐(Bel t) x≏(trans(In t))) ∧ (Isdel x) ∧ ∿ ◊((Bel t) ∧ (M x))
→ (Bel t+1) = (Bel t) ∧ (Out t+1) =['I 'disbelieve 'you]

The third lay states that if the meaning of a Yes/No question is true according to the systems beliefs then yes is returned:

C3: $(\Box(\text{Bel } t)\ x \hat{=} (\text{trans}(\text{In } t))) \wedge \sim (\text{Isdel } x) \wedge (\Box(\text{Bel } t)$
$(\text{M}(\text{Cadr } x)))$
$\to (\text{Bel } t{+}1) = (\text{Bel } t) \wedge (\text{Out } t{+}1) = [\text{'Yes}]$

Finally the fourth law states that if the meaning of a Yes/No question is not true according to the systems knowledge then No is returned:

C4: $\Box(\text{Bel } t)\ x \hat{=} (\text{trans}(\text{In } t)) \wedge \sim(\text{Isdel } x) \wedge (\Box(\text{Bel } t)$
$(\text{M}(\text{Cadr } x)))$
$\to (\text{Bel } t{+}1) = (\text{Bel } t) \wedge (\text{Out } t{+}1) = [\text{'No}]$

It will be noted that the simple control laws described here make no use of any inverse meaning laws or generation laws as the outputs by the system are merely pre'stored canned phrases. In general this of course is not adequate and complex laws for generation would be needed. Laws for inverse meaning are essentially the same as the meaning laws but are intended to be used in reverse.

The control system is initialized by two axioms:

$(\text{Bel } 0) = \ast$
$(\text{Out } 0) = [\text{'Hello}]$

3. Examples

We will give two examples of the use of the laws given in section 2. The first example which is given in section 3.1. exemplifies how syntactic and semantic concepts can smoothly interact using the parsing and translation laws, and the meaning laws so as to handle syntactically ambiguous sentences. The second example which is given in section 3.2. exemplifies the dialogue theory, showing how the natural language system based on this theory might interact with its environment.

3.1. Example

In the following we shall show by a detailed example how the laws of parsing, translation and meaning work. We shall not show the entire search space for the whole sentence because this would be much too complex. The detailed parsings for the ambiguity branches are shown in Figures 7, 8 and 9. The "world" is given by the following nonlogical axioms:

A1 PLACEx ↔ GARDENx ∨ CITYx

A2 PLANTx ↔ TREEx ∨ FLOWERx

A3 FRUITx ↔ CONEx ∨ APPLEx

A4 ∼∃x ∃y (TREEx ∧ ROSEy ∧ HASxy)

w = A1 ∧ A2 ∧ A3 ∧ A4 ∧ L ∧ S

From the parsings as far as executed in Figures 7 and 8 we get:

(1) z ∧ (((NG2...z3) ∧ (LIKELIER('∼(M['∼z3]))('∼(M['∼z33]))))∨
((NG3...z33) ∧ (LIKELIER(∼∼(M['∼z33]))('∼(M['∼z3])))))

where

z3=['TREEy1 '∧ ['INy1 ['the y2 ['GARDENy2 '∧ '∃y3 ['CONEy3 '∧
'HASy2y3]]]]]

z33= ['TREEy1 '∧ ['INy1 ['the y2 ['GARDENy2]]] '∧ '∃y3 ['CONEy3
'∧ 'HASy1y3]]

It is easy to see that

□(w ∧ ∼ M['∼z3]) → ∃y2∃y3 (GARDENy2 ∧ CONEy3 ∧ HASy2y3) and
□(w ∧ ∼ M['∼z3]) → ∃y1∃y3 (TREEy1 ∧ CONEy3 ∧ HASy1y3) and since
□(w → A2) and □(w → A1) we get

(2) □ (w ∧ ∼ (M['∼z3])) ↔ ∃y2∃y3(PLACEy2 ∧ FRUITy3 ∧ HASy2y3)
and

(3) □ (w ∧ ∼ (M['∼z33])) ↔ ∃y1∃y3(PLANTy1 ∧ FRUITy3 ∧ HASy1y3)

□(w ∧ ∼ (M['∼z3])) is derivable as well as □(w ∧ ∼ (M['∼z33]))

The idea of that proof is to use axioms of the form $\Diamond$(px $\wedge$ qy) for all the nonlogical predicates p,q of the world. The reader may imagine that we cannot present that proof here since we would need such axioms for all combinations of our 11 nonlogical symbols. So we use that w is consistent with ∼M['∼z3] and with ∼M['∼z33] . If we instantiate the existential expressions of (2) and (3) to P and Q resp. we get LIKELIER (∼M['∼z33]) (∼M['∼z3]) by S and L. So, the NG2-branch of (1) evaluates to ⊓. Now we are able to finish the parsing and translation derivation and we get:

```
z=[zo z1 ['THE y1 ['TREEy1 '∧
      ['INy1['THEy2['GARDENy2 '∧  '∃y3 ['CONEy3
                              '∧ 'HASy1y3]]]]]]]
      ∧ ∃x1∃x2(x1= '(is pretty)) ∧ (VBE x1-x2 zo)
                                 ∧ (ADJ x2- [ ]z2)
```

Laws VBE, ADJ:

```
z='PRESENT['PRETTY['THEy1['TREEy1 '∧
                 ['INy1['THEy2['GARDENy2 '∧
                             '∃y3['CONEy3 '∧  'HASy1y3]]]]]]]
```

```
xo='(the tree in the garden which has cones is pretty) ∧ (SENT xo-[] z)
                         (o)

(o) ∧ z=[(zo(subst[z2 y] for * in z1)] ∧ ∃x1∃x2((NP xo-x1 y z1)∧(VBE x1-x2 zo)∧(ADJ x2-[]z2)),
                 (z)                                                          ••

(o) ∧ (z) ∧ ∃x1∃x2(y=['THEy1 z3] ∧ z1= * ∧ ∃x4(x4='(tree in the garden which has cones is
                                                                          pretty), ∧
                                                                (4)

((NG2 x4-x1 y1 z3) ∧ (∀z33(7∃b(NG3 x4-x1 b z33) v (LIKELIER∿(M['∿z3])('∿M['∿z33])))))
                                               S1

        ((NG3x4-x1 y1 z3) ∧ (∀z33(7∃b(NG3 x4-x1 b z33) v (LIKELIER'∿M['∿z3]))))),..)
                A2                               S2
```

Figure 7

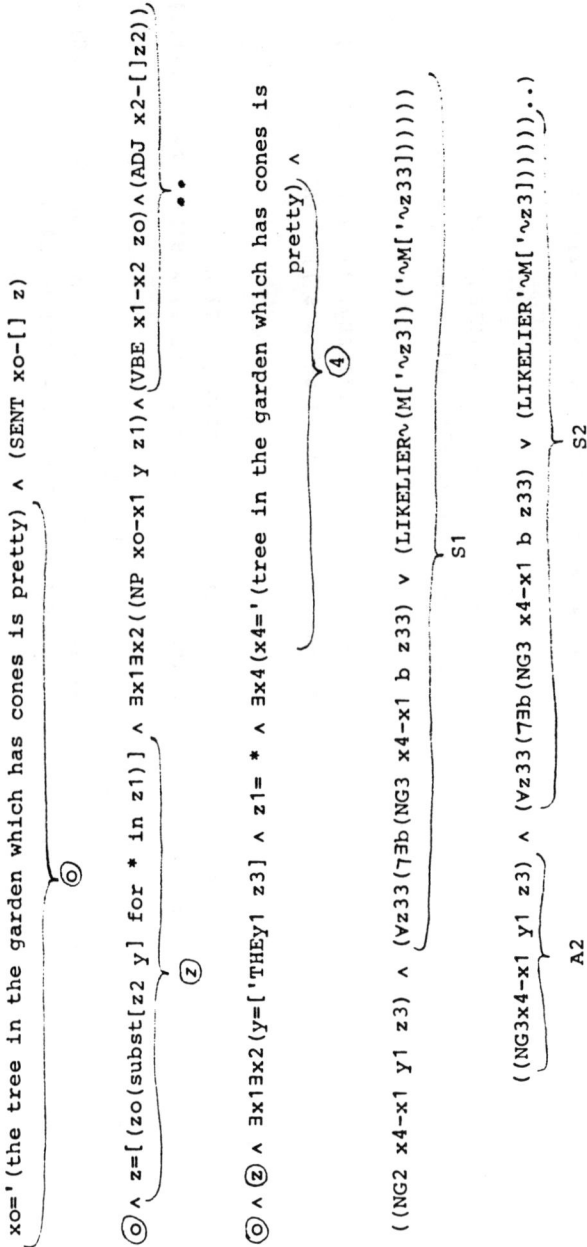

```
A1 ∧ S1:NG2
z=[zo z2 'THE y1 z3] ∧∃x1∃x2∃x4( (4) ∧  ((∃x5((NG  x4-x5  y1 z4) ∧ (PP  x5-x1 y1 y2 z5) ∧
      (z)                                 z3=[z4 '∧  z5] ∧ S1)) ∨ (A2 ∧ S2))..)

Laws NG, NG1, N:
z ∧ ∃x1∃x2((∃x5(x5='(in the garden which has cones is pretty) ∧ z4='TREEy1 ∧ z3=[z4 '∧ z5] ∧
                                          (PP  x5-x1 y1 y2 z5) ∧ S1) ∨ (A2 ∧ S2))..)

Law PP:
z ∧∃x1∃x2(((∃x6(x6='(the garden which has cones is pretty) ∧ z3=['TREEy1 '∧ (subst['INy1y2]
                                    for * in z6)] ∧ (NP x6-x1 y2 z6) ∧ S1)) ∨ (A2 ∧ S2))..)

Laws NP, NP3:
z ∧∃x1∃x2(((∃x7(x7='(garden which has cones is pretty) ∧ y2=['THE y3 z7] ∧
   z6=* ∧ (NG  x7-x1 y3 z7) ∧ z3=['TREEy1 ∧ (subst['INy1y2] in z6 ior*)] ∧ S1)) ∨(A2 ∧ S2))..)

Laws NG, NG3, NG, NG1, N:
z ∧∃x1∃x2(((∃x8(x8='(which has cones is pretty) ∧ z7=['GARDENy2 ∧ z8] ∧ (CLAUSE x8-x1 y2 z8) ∧
                               z3=['TREEy1 '∧ ['INy1['THEy2 z7]]] ∧ S1)) ∨ (A2 ∧ S2))..)

Laws CLAUSE, RELPRON, VT, NP, NP , NG, NG1, N:
z ∧∃x1∃x2(((x1='(is pretty) ∧ S1 ∧ z3=['TREEy1 '∧ ['INy1['THEy2['GARDENy2] ∧ 'PRESENT[∃y3
                                           ['CONEy3 ∧ HASy2y3]]]]] ∨ (A2 ∧ S2))..)
```

Figure 8

A2 ∧ S2: Law NG3:

Law NG3:

```
z=[zo z1 'THEy1z1]∧∃x1∃x2∃x4( (4) ∧((A1∧S1)v∃x5((NG4x4-x5 y1 z4)∧(CLAUSE x5-x1 y1 z5)∧
              (z)                                           z3=[z4 '∧  z5]∧S2))..)
```

Laws NG, NG2:

```
(z) ∧∃x1∃x2∃x4( (4) ∧((A1∧S1)v∃x5∃x6((NG x4-x6 y1 z6)∧(PP x6-x5 y1 y2 z7)∧z4=[z6 '∧ z7] ∧
                                 z3= x4 '∧ z5 ∧ S2 ∧ (CLAUSE x5-x1 y1 z5)))..)
```

Laws NG, NG1, N:

```
(z)  ∧∃x1∃x2(((A1 ∧ S1)v ∃x5∃x6(x6='(in the garden which has cones is pretty) ∧
  z3=['TREEy1'∧ z7 '∧ z5] ∧ (PPx6-x5 y1 y2 z7) ∧ (CLAUSE x5-x1 y1 z5) ∧ S2)) ..)
```

Law PP:

```
(z)  ∧∃x1∃x2(((A1 ∧ S1)v ∃x5∃x7(x7='(in the garden which has cones is pretty) ∧ S2 ∧
     z3=['TREEy1 '∧ (subst['INy1y2] for * in z8) ∧ (NP x7-x5 y2 z8)∧(CLAUSE x5-x1 y1 z5)))..)
```

Laws NP, NP3, NG, NG1, N:

```
(z)  ∧∃x1∃x2(((A1 ∧ S1) v∃x5(x5='(which has cones is pretty) ∧ (CLAUSE x5-x1 y1 z5) ∧
     z3=['TREEy1 '∧  ['INy1['THEy2['GARDENy2]]] '∧  z5] ∧ S2))..)
```

Laws CLAUSE, RELPRON, VT, NP, NP1, NG, NG1, N:

```
(z)  ∧∃x1∃x2((A1 ∧ S1) v (x1='(is pretty) ∧ S2 ∧

     z3=['TREEy1 '∧  'INy1['THEy2['GARDENy2]]] ∧ 'PRESENT ∃y3[ CONEy3 ∧ HASy1y3 ])... )
```

Figure 9

3.2. An Example Dialogue

We give below an example dialogue illustrating the four laws of social behaviour. It should be noted that this example uses an extended version of the grammar and lexicon that was described in Section 2.2.

$$0 - \begin{cases} O = \text{'Hello} \\ B = \blacksquare \\ I = \text{'(All Men are Mortal)} \end{cases}$$

At time 0 the beliefs of the system is simply ■. The system begins by saying "Hello" and inputs the first input which in this case is "All Men are Mortal". Since the meaning of the translation of this declarative sentence namely:

$\forall x(\text{Men } x \rightarrow \text{Mortal } x)$ is possible with respect to the current beliefs, this proposition is now assumed by the system using the social law C1

$$1 - \begin{cases} O & \text{'(I believe you)} \\ B & \forall x(\text{Man } x) \rightarrow (\text{Mortal } x) \\ I & \text{'(John is a Man)} \end{cases}$$

Again using the social law C1 we get:

$$2 - \begin{cases} O & \text{'(I believe you)} \\ B & (\text{Man John}) \wedge \forall x((\text{Man } x) \rightarrow (\text{Mortal } x)) \\ I & \text{'(Is John Mortal?)} \end{cases}$$

The Input at time 2 is an interrogative sentence whose translation is [? ['Mortal 'John]]

Since (Mortal John) is deducible from the beliefs at time 2 using social law C3 we get:

$$3 - \begin{cases} O & \text{Yes} \\ B & (\text{Man John}) \wedge \forall x((\text{Man } x) \rightarrow (\text{Mortal } x)) \\ I & \text{'(Is John Green?)} \end{cases}$$

The input at time 3 is an interrogative sentence, but since (Green John) is not true according to the systems it answers NO using social law C4.

	O	No
4	B	(Man John) $\wedge$ $\forall$x((Man x) $\rightarrow$ (Mortal x))
	I	'(No Man is Mortal)

Since the input at time 4 is a declarative sentence which contradicts the systems beliefs at that time, the system replies using social axiom C2

5	O	'(I disbelieve you)
	B	(Man John) $\wedge$ $\forall$x((Man x) $\rightarrow$ (Mortal x))

4. Theoretical Claims

We now compare various features of our theory of natural language understanding to related work in a number of subject areas.

We shall try to summarise our work by listing a number of theoretical claims about language understanding.

4.1. Relationship to Formal Grammar

A formal grammar is defined as a finite set o_N of nonterminal symbols, a set o_N of terminal symbols, a start symbol S such that $S \in o_N$, and a set of production rules which have the form p => q, where p and q are strings over $o_N \cup o_T$ and p contains at least one element of o_N, that is p = X N Y for $X,Y \in (o_N \cup o_T)$ * and $N \in o_N$. It is worth remembering that transformational grammars are equivalent to formal grammars.

As we stated in Section 2.2. our parsing laws have the form:

(A xo-xn) $\leftrightarrow$ $\exists$ x1... $\exists$ xn-1((B1 xo-x1) $\wedge$...$\wedge$ (B x(n-1) -xn))

This law roughly corresponds to the production rule:

A => B1 ... Bn

However it should be noted that this law does not exactly correspond to the production rule, and that the meaning of the law is quite different from the meaning of the production rule. Production rules form a device or algorithm to generate sentences and hence the meaning of such a rule is something like: Whenever A occurs within a sentence then replacing A by B1 ... Bn generates another sentence. On the other hand, the meaning of our parsing laws is like: a string xo-xn is an A <u>iff</u> xo-x1 is a B1 and ... x(n-1)-xn is a B.

This difference of meaning implies that a formal grammar cannot always be rewritten as a set of "corresponding" parsing laws as described above, but sometimes must be changed in order to describe the same set of sentences which the formal grammar generates. An example of such a case is given below:

(a) Formal Grammar:

R1: S => NP + VP + PP

R2: VP => VP + PP

R3: VP => V

(b) "Corresponding" Parsing Laws:

L1: (S xo-x3) $\leftrightarrow$ ((NP xo-x1) $\wedge$ (VP x1-x2) $\wedge$ (PP x2-x3))

L2: (VP xo-x2) $\leftrightarrow$ ((VP xo-x1) $\wedge$ (PP x1-x2))

L3: (VP xo-x1) $\leftrightarrow$ (V xo-x1)

The sentences which can be generated by this formal grammar are:

NP+V+PP, NP+V+PP+PP, NP+V+PP+PP+PP..

However the parsing laws describe all these sentences plus the sentence: NP+V which is obtained by applying the law L2 backwards to L1, and applying L3 in the normal manner.

We can of course rewrite a formal grammar as parsing laws. For example the above formal grammar is correctly described by the following parsing laws:

L1': (S xo-x2) $\leftrightarrow$ ((NP xo-x1)$\wedge$(VP x1-x2))

L2': (VP xo-x2) $\leftrightarrow$ (((VP xo-x1)$\wedge$(PP x1-x2))$\wedge$((V xo-x1)$\wedge$(PP x1-x2)))

This difference between parsing laws and generation rules can explain some apparent problems in formal grammars such as the deadlock problem. Consider for example the following grammar for arithmetic expressions:

P1: E => T	P4: T => T*F
P2: E => E+T	P5: F => (E)
P3: T => F	P6: F => V

where the syntactic categories are:

E Expressions

T Term

F Factor

V Variable

This grammar has what is called a deadlock: namely a sentence which can be generated by it can be analysed, by applying the rules in reverse only as in bottom-up parsing, to produce a sentence which cannot be generated by this grammar:

```
E       : P2
E+T     : P4
E+T*F   : P1
T+T*F   : P3
T+F*F   : P3
F+F*F   : P6
V+F*F   : P6
V+V*F   : P6
V+V*V
```

Thus V+V*V can be generated by these production rules. Analysing V+V*V we obtain:

```
V+V*V
V+V*F   : P6
V+F*F   : P6
F+F*F   : P6
T+F*F   : P3
T+T*F   : P3
E+T*F   : P1
E+T*T   : P3
E*T     : P2
```

E*T however cannot be generated from these production rules.

We point out that there is nothing really strange about the existence of such deadlocks, but rather that this is merely the consequence of writing grammars which don't really say what one thought they meant. This point is easily seen once we rewrite the production rules as the roughly "corresponding" parsing laws. In this case the parsing law for P2 states:

$$(E\ xo\text{-}x2) \leftrightarrow ((E\ xo\text{-}x1) \wedge (T\ x1\text{-}x2))$$

that something is an expression ift it consists of an expression followed by a term. But this parsing law is clearly false because an expression followed by a term is not always an expression, but is an expression only if the subexpression is not followed by *. This merely reflects the fact that times * binds more closely than plus +.

A correct version of the parsing law corresponding to P2 would be:

$$((E\ xo\text{-}x2) \wedge (x2=[\ ] \vee (Car\ x2) \neq *\ ))$$
$$\leftrightarrow (E\ xo\text{-}x1) \wedge (Car\ x1) = {}'+ \wedge (T(Cdr\ x1) - x2)$$

Since we require a grammar, (i e parsing laws) to specify what a sentence is and not merely how it might be generated we are constrained to write grammars which are not wrong.

Chomsky [4,5] claims that a grammar for a natural language should be a generating device, or rather a formal grammar, for producing the sentences of that language. Our purpose however is to write laws which tell us what a sentence is rather than merely to design an abstract machine which generates sentences. Although in a theoretical sense it could be argued that such a generating device does define what are the sentences of a language, we point out that it does so only by virtue of the overall interaction of all the production rules in the system. In a larger grammar, particularly for natural language these interactions will be so complex that it will in a practical sense be impossible for anyone to understand, correct or modify the grammar. Parsing laws by contrast have a clear and directly understood meaning in which each law can be understood purely in terms of the syntactic categories appearing within it.

A further problem with the use of grammars based on production rather than on parsing laws is that it is practically impossible to tell what aspects of the production rules make substantial claims about a natural language, and what are mere artifacts forced by the use of production rules. Indeed in a large grammar this situation is so bad that for example in the UCLA English Syntax Project grammar [13] the authors felt constrained to write (p -37):

> "In the development of the analysis we shall take pains to distinguish between complexity in the formulation that seems to have a substantive basis, and complexity that is attributable rather to some artifact in the general theory or in this particular implementation of it".

In other words the use of production rules forces the authors' formal system to make more claims than they actually wished to make, and they are therefore going to try to tell us in English what they really did not wish to claim.

We can summarize the relationship of our system to formal grammars by the following claim:

Claim 1: The laws of parsing bear a logical relationship between syntactic categories. They do not bear a generative production rule relationship.

4.2. Relationship to transformational grammar

Transformational grammar has three basic faults when applied to natural language understanding. Since these three faults do not occur in an integrated theory we shall simply list these faults in the form of theoretical claims made by our theory. We will not however argue why these claims are correct, as we believe this will be apparent to anyone with the least familiarity with this subject.

Claim 2: Recognition grammars are different from Generation grammars. Transformational rules such as those used in Transformational grammars are not really acceptable in a recognition grammar.

Claim 3: Parsing laws must include translation into some general meaning representation (such as a logic) in which inference may be able to be performed.

Claim 4: The laws of parsing must be able to refer to the meanings of the expressions being parsed, so that those meanings may interact with general world knowledge during the parsing process. That is, the theory must be capable of meta theoretic reasoning.

4.3. Relationship to Artificial Intelligence

Contemporary research in Artificial Intelligence on implementing Natural Language Understanding systems such as [17,3,6,16] shares with our theory, at least to some extent claims 2,3 and 4. However, most of this research differs from our theory in two important ways:

Claim 5: The Meaning Representation must be rich enough to allow every inference that the system might need to make. That is, we claim that the system must be a logic, and in view of claim 4, this logic must be capable of meta theoretic reasoning.

Claim 6: (Methodological). The theory must be capable of being easily modified and communicated to other researchers. This implies that the basic theory must be a logic, for logic due for example to the localness of its variables is easily modifiable and communicatable. Other languages such as programming languages like Algol are comparatively speaking difficult to modify or communicate.

5. Conclusion

We think that our natural language understanding system is an entirely new approach to the natural language understanding problem because it is an integrated theory. Most natural language understanding systems use several languages for their description: English, Programmar, Planner, Lisp, semantic networks. Approaches like [17], or [3] are wonderful programs but do not contribute much to our understanding of the processes underlying natural language understanding. Programs have built in more or less ad hoc devices which simulate special situations. They do not apply or know general laws underlying the natural language understanding processes. They do not allow to derive general statements about natural language understanding. Moreover we think that a theory which is baded on logic has immense advantages of expressional power and deductive capacity over theories using needleworked knowledge structures [6] the properties of which have not been investigated.

Problems of preference semantics [16] are very frequent in natural language understanding. Our theory suggests a very elegant and adequate way to solve them. Since our theory is formulated in the same language as the meaning of the natural language ambiguous sentences can be disambiguated during the syntactic analysis in a very natural way.

References

[1] Brown, F. " A Sequent Calculus for Modal Quantificational Logic", (1978). Proceedings of 3rd A.I.S.B./G.I. Conference, Hamburg, (1978).

[2] Brown, F. "The Theory of Meaning", (November 1976). D.A.I. Research Report No. 35, Department of Artificial Intelligence, University of Edinburgh.

[3] Charniak, E. "Ms Malaprop, A Language Comprehension Program (1977). Proceedings of 5th International Joint Conference on Artificial Intelligence, M.I.T. Press, Cambridge, Mass.

[4] Chomsky, N. "Syntactic Structures" (1957). (Janua Linguarum, 4) Mouton & Co., The Hague.

[5] Chomsky, N. "Aspects of the Theory of Syntax". (1965). M.I.T. Press, Cambridge, Mass.

[6] Schank, R.C. "The primitive acts of conceptual dependency". Theoretical Issues in Natural Language Processing, (1975), Cambridge, Mass.

[7] Schank, R.C., Abelson, R.P. "Scripts, Plans, and Understanding". (1977). (Lawrence Erlbaum Associates, Hillsdale, N.Y.)

[8] Schwind, C.B. "Ein Formalismus zur Beschreibung der Syntax und Bedeutung von Frage-Antwort-Systemen". TUM-INFO-771o. (1977) (Institut für Informatik, Technische Universität München).

[9] Schwind, C.B. "A Formalism for the Description of Question Answering Systems" in: Bolc, L. (Hg.) Natural Language Communication with Computers. (Springer-Verlag, Heidelberg) (1978)

[1o] Schwind, C.B. "The Translation of Natural Language Texts into State Logic Formulae. TUM-INFO-78o6. (1978)

[11] Schwind, C.B. "Representing Actions by State Logic" in: Proceedings of the AISB/GI Conference on Artificial Intelligence, Hamburg, S. 3o4 (1978)

[12] Shoenfield, J.R. "Mathematical Logic". (Addison Wesley Publ., Comp., London) (1967)

[13] Stockwell, Schachter, Partee. "The Major Syntactic Structures of English". (1973). Holt, Rinehart & Winston.

[14] Wilks, Y. "An Intelligent Analyzer and Understander of English". (1975) Comm. A.C.M. Nr. 18, S. 264

[15] Wilks, Y. "Making Preference more Active". DAI Research Report Nr. 32. (1977) (Department of Artificial Intelligence, University of Edinburgh).

[16] Wilks, Y. "Knowledge Structures and Language Boundaries". (1977). Proceedings of 5th International Joint Conference on Artificial Intelligence, M.I.T. Press, Cambridge, Mass.

[17] Winograd, T. "Understanding Natural Language". (1972). Academic Press.

THE REPRESENTATION AND USE OF KNOWLEDGE IN AN ASSOCIATIVE NETWORK FOR THE AUTOMATIC COMPREHENSION OF NATURAL LANGUAGE

by
Nick Cercone

Abstract

The systematic development of a representation for individual items of factual knowledge in a computer, where this knowledge is considered as being conveyed in natural language, is reported. The extended semantic network notation depicts the meaning structure of natural language utterances. The notation encodes any proposition that can be expressed in natural language, preserving distinctions between utterances with distinct meanings and between distinct readings of ambiguous utterances. Furthermore, judgments of truth and falsity about natural language utterances correspond appropriately to truth and falsity in the formal representation. The network notation is closely related to predicate calculus representations, but it provides readability and is suggestive of appropriate computer data structures.

States, actions, events, and intentionality are analysed in the context of a state-based theory as opposed to a formulation based on primitives (Cercone and Schubert, 1975). The recognition that all actions can be represented by a sequence of suitably defined states is crucial to the formulation. The arbitrary and unnecessary distinction between activities and states or between actions and events and the insistence on the use of primitive concepts often leads to inadequacies in the representation and manipulation of complex concepts. Schank's and Wilk's approaches to complex concepts are particularly troublesome, but the state-based representation offers solutions. The state-based representation permits efficient use of semantic preferences and is capable of accomodating unlimited amounts of information about complex concepts without loss of computational efficiency in the use of those concepts.

We discuss the representation in the semantic network notation of English adverbs and adjectives, and the use of such modifiers for natural language comprehension.

Topic access skeletons, which conform to general topic hierarchies in memory, are proposed to solve the problem of effectively accessing facts relevant to a query (Goebel, 1977).

Two mini-implementations have demonstrated the feasability of deriving meaning structures from surface text, making some common sense inferences, building hierarchies, and accessing information based on those hierarchies. Though not all of our ideas have been implemented, and programming invariably yields insight into theory, our emphasis on theoretical issues should ultimately prove wise.

Computing Science Department, Simon Fraser University
Burnaby, British Columbia, CANADA V5A 1S6

1. Introduction

The mystery and power of natural language understanding has long inspired theories about its operation. Mankind, unable to account for human use of natural language, has challenged machine intelligence with understanding natural language. Artificial intelligence research should develop a general theory of natural language understanding as a foundation for computer programs which understand natural language. Any theory of natural language understanding must account for the representation, organisation, and subsequent utilisation of knowledge (e.g. for making plausible inferences, associating meaningful pieces of discourse, etc.).

What follows are my ideas concerning knowledge representation, organisation, and use. A variety of representations and organisations of knowledge have evolved, their differences expose interesting issues which will be discussed. Cercone and Schubert (1975) derived a conceptual scheme for representing the meaning content of ordinary English utterances as a succession of states, the state based representation. The semantic network formalism was devised as a suitable notation for representing such knowledge (Schubert, 1976; Cercone, 1975). As initially conceived, semantic networks did not facilitate the use of knowledge. They lacked the organisational structure which would permit effective access of facts relevant to language comprehension. Organisation and hence comprehension were improved by according special pragmatic status to some propositions. Goebel (1977) innovated organisational hierarchies. These hierarchies are necessary for even the most elementary types of inferences. They permit us to distiquish groups of related propositions.

Three controversial philosophical issues emerge from our description of knowledge representation and organisation. Their resolution is of central importance to natural language understanding, so they are discussed.

Cercone´s and Schubert´s state based conceptual representation, semantic network notation, and Goebel´s organisational hierarchies were tested in mini-implementations. These mini-implementations revealed interesting features and shortcomings of the ideas of knowledge representation, organisation and use.

Future developments of ideas of knowledge representation and organisation should include the design and formation of adaptive topic hierarchies. These hierarchies should facilitate the inferential process necessary for natural language understanding and contribute to our progress towards the ultimate implementation goals.

1.1 Introduction to Knowledge Representations

The following is a cursory introduction to knowledge representations which will permit us to discuss representations. Usually knowledge is organised and represented in ways that are appropriate for the various uses that the processing system must make of the knowledge. For example, when knowledge is used for problem solving, we should recognize that the manner in which we represent the problem influences the way in which we formulate a solution. Often in working with a difficult integral a human problem solver might change representations several times, perhaps from trigonometric functions to rational functions and so on, to develop a solution. Different representations are adapted to different computational environments. A computer scientist might benefit from knowing about multiple representations such as a ring structure for storing sparse multidimensional arrays when storage is at a premium, and linear non-linked structures when execution time is of paramount importance.

Language processing systems make several distinct and interrelated uses of knowledge. Initially, in dialogue situations, processing systems must represent the meaning content of utterances for the purpose of comprehension. In order to establish these meaning representations for utterances, it is often necessary to draw inferences which will account for missing or incomplete information. Later, other inferences may be drawn to answer questions. These inferences are drawn from knowledge conveyed through the dialog and from general knowledge that is entered a priori in the processing system.

Some of the prominent approaches to representing knowledge in natural language utterances have used semantic networks (Quillian, 1968, 1969; Schank, 1972), logical statements (Sandewall, 1971; Moore and Newell, 1973), procedures, (Winograd, 1972; Hewitt, 1971), and descriptions, (Moore, 1973).

The predicate calculus or logical statement approach represents knowledge in the form of propositions. Conjunctive normal form is often used where each proposition is a disjunction of a set of literals. Literals are atomic formulae composed of predicates and terms where predicates are functions of variables over a domain of discourse. One significant advantage of the predicate calculus approach is having a uniform representation for all knowledge. This tends to make the control structure for programs manipulating knowledge quite simple, but the benefits of multiple representations are ignored. Using only first order predicate calculus, the expressive power is sufficient to represent almost anything that we can formulate precisely, such as most of mathematics. However, many problems can be conveniently and compactly represented by higher than first-order logic and by modal logic.

Knowledge can be stored in the form of programs rather than in the form of propositions. The knowledge embedded in procedures can be accessed using pattern directed procedure invocation (Hewitt, 1971). Advocates of knowledge representation through procedural embedding stress the parallel between their representation and intelligent human behaviour. A person has prescribed 'procedures' which control the performance of his activities. These procedures establish a kinship correspondence between a person's intelligent behaviour and the manner in which he uses his knowledge for his activities. Procedural knowledge representations, such as PLANNER data bases (Winograd, 1972) are very application dependent. I am concerned with a more general form for knowledge representation, application independent, which can use superimposed procedures as a heuristic device for a particular task.

The semantic network notation has been extended to improve its scope. Moore and Newell (1973) defined the scope of a representation as the range of knowledge that it can represent. The extended semantic network has expressive power sufficient to represent the propositional content of any English language utterance.

Currently no knowledge representation is capable of systematically acquiring knowledge in a general way. McDermott (1974) is concerned with adding factual knowledge to his data base such that it maintains integrity in the data base in the same way that people do, that is by altering belief structures.*1* Others, including Winograd (1972) have tackled the issue of knowledge acquisition, but no acceptable solution has been found.

We have observed that different representations are suitable for different uses in different computational environments. Finding the appropriate representation, or modifying the existing representation, is an important activity which requires attention. Multiple representations have never been incorporated within the same artificial intelligence system.

1.2 Some Motivational Problems in Representing Knowledge

Some constructions in ordinary discourse are particularly difficult to represent, such as quantification, modalities, ambiguities, etc. As we consider these problems, we will begin to appreciate the expressive power and visual clarity of extended semantic networks. Consider the sentence

"All people have some bad habits." (1.1)

To begin with, the sentence is ambiguous. Two possible meanings include:

"Each person has a particular set of bad habits and that set may differ from person to person."; and (1.2a)

"There is a particular set of bad habits that all people possess." (1.2b)

Also, it is doubly quantified. Johnson-Laird (1969) conducted experiments which suggested that doubly quantified sentences were predominantly interpreted with the greater scope belonging to the quantifier on the surface subject. Thus we would assign the sentence the meaning expressed by (1.2a). If we accept this for the moment, the problem remaining is how to represent the meaning. Predicate calculus easily represents the scope (logic definition) of universal and existential quantifiers, but the representation is problematic in semantic networks. We could adopt the convention that would include the scope of any quantifiers in a predicate within the scope of the subject quantifiers. Anderson and Bower (1973) in fact accomplish this, Bower(1973). The scope problem, however, remains. Consider the following pair of sentences:

"There is someone who is always there." (1.3)

"There is always someone there." (1.4)

Here the surface subject is identical for both sentences while the existential and universal quantifiers are interchanged before the predicate. As our description of the network will demonstrate, the semantic network formalism provides a solution to the fundamental problem of representing quantifiers.

Propositional attitudes and other modalities present special difficulties in ordinary discourse. For example, it is common to talk about certain information without explicitly stating that information. The utterance "I know John´s phone number" presents a problem in dealing with propositional attitudes. This sentence can be paraphrased as "There exists an x such that I know that x is John´s phone number". This is an example of a transparent modal context, i.e. we´re quantifying into the scope of "know".

Problems also arise with referentially opaque contexts. The sentence

"John wants to marry the prettiest girl." (1.5)

generates two possible interpretations or readings:

"John wants to marry a specific girl who also happens to be the prettiest girl."; and (1.6a)

"John has no particular girl in mind, but he wants whoever he does marry to be the prettiest girl." (1.6b)

The transparent reading is given by (1.6a) and the opaque by (1.6b). We will consider referential opacity in the context of modal operators.

Counterfactual conditional statements often occur in discussions. It is desirable to represent conditionals in a consistent manner; so that they are not confused with events that actually occur. These and other representational problems are resolved when we consider assertions, causality, and time.

2. The Semantic Network

Semantic networks and predicate calculus are both formal representations designed to paraphrase natural language utterances precisely and unambiguously. Natural language analysis with semantic networks emphasizes associative and other non-deductive processes. Predicate calculus has mainly been applied to resolution-based theorem proving. Theorem proving techniques could however be adapted to the semantic network representation, and nondeductive inference algorithms could be designed for predicate calculus.

The nonlinear fashioning of semantic networks presents special problems with respect to the representation of logical connectives, quantifiers, descriptions, modalities, and certain other constructions. These constructions are often useful and sometimes necessary to explicate the meaning of complex concepts. Schubert (1976) has proposed systematic solutions to these problems by extending the expressive power of (more or less) conventional semantic network notation. Woods (1975) independently made a series of similar proposals. The following is a digest of the detailed description of the network formalism presented in Schubert (1976).

2.1 Introduction to the Semantic Network Notation

Semantic network notation distinquishes between labels designating storage locations and labels designating pointers to storage locations. Quillian (1968) used the distinction to designate unique storage locations as "type nodes" and pointers to storage locations as "token nodes". The notation can be made uniformly explicit as in Figure 1 which diagrams "Vancouver is part-of British Columbia" and "British Columbia is part-of Canada". Here "part-of", which in some notations corresponds to a token node, designates a type node (as suggested by Winston, 1970). All encircled nodes correspond to storage locations and all arrows to addresses of storage locations. What were formerly called token nodes are now called "proposition nodes". They serve as graphical nuclei for propositions as a whole. Nodes may be labeled with names for the concepts they denote, e.g. John, book, book1, book2; ordinary attributive terms such as "book" are reserved for the corresponding universal concepts, while numerically suffixed words such as "book1" are used for particular instances of the concepts.

Occasionally the detailed use of arcs and nodes in the explicit notation of Figure 1 will clutter a diagram, reducing readability. Therefore, binary predicates will be represented as in Figure 2 with the understanding that the structure is built upon explicit propositions. In Figure 1, the arc labels ´A´, ´B´, and ´PRED´ are simply distinguishing marks. They are analogous to parentheses or commas in the predicate calculus in that they relate denoting terms syntactically; they are non-denotative themselves. Whenever possible they will be chosen to enhance readability and be suggestive of meaning, but numeric labels could also be used (McDermott, 1976).

One advantage of the explicit notation of Figure 1 is that it handles n-ary (n>2) predicates "Gives" is a three place predicate in "John gives the book to Mary". The sentence is diagrammed in Figure 3, which is appealing because of the significance we can attach to the labels - ´agent´, ´object´, and ´recipient´. Nevertheless, Figure 3 is not a graphical analogue of "case-structured" grammars. Cases are not viewed as "conceptually primitive binary relations" as Fillmore (1968) and researchers influenced by him, notably Schank (1972), view them. Cercone and Schubert (1975) and Bartsch and Vennemann (1972) discuss cases further. The "case" labels in Figure 3 are to be regarded as mere mnemonics, although indicative of more complex relations. To avoid confusion, predicate names will be designated in small letters and markers by capitals.

2.2 Notation for Logical Connectives

Logical connectives, ignored in most network formalisms, occur frequently in discourse and are necessary for truth-functional completeness. In the extended semantic network notation logical connectives are represented as explicit nodes for logical compounds of propositions (or open sentences), with graphical links to the components. Figure 4 "Mary is not at home; she is either at school, or on the playground, or at the zoo; if she is not at school, her mother will be angry" illustrates the formation of disjunctions by the use of graphical links to tokens of the disjunction operator. The operator-operand links of the logical operator are represented by broken lines in Figure 4. Observe that no distinguishing marks are needed on the links (disjunction is a symmetrical operator) and arrowheads can be dropped when there is no ambiguity. The use of "will be" as a modifier of "angry" is an evasive manoeuvre; it postpones discussion of time. Other logical connectives can be introduced in exactly the same way. For example, it would have been more natural to render "If Mary is not at school her mother will be angry" by means of implication (ignoring the implicit causal proposition) instead of disjunction.

In a semantic network containing logical compounds it is not suitable to regard all propositions in the network as asserted. In this formalism we adopt the convention that the complete semantic net ASSERTS EXACTLY THOSE PROPOSITIONS WHICH ARE NOT CONSTITUENTS OF COMPOUND PROPOSITIONS (i.e., operands of connectives or modal operators). Graphically this means that precisely those propositions are asserted which are not pointed to. In Figure 4, "Mary is not at home" and "Mary is at school or her mother will be angry" are asserted whereas "Mary is at the zoo" and "Mary is at school" are not.

We must devise a method for asserting a proposition which is also a constituent of a compound proposition. The assertion of a constituent simplifies any logical compound. For propositional attitudes, causes, intentions and the like, however, it may prove worthwhile to assert a proposition independently of the compound. In this case, we can use disjunction with a single operand, V --> p, as a way of saying "p holds" since the compound proposition established by the token V is not pointed to.

2.3 Representing Quantifiers in the Semantic Network

Any representation of natural language must include logical quantifiers such as "John sent the cards to all of his friends" and "several of my friends were at the game today". General knowledge relies upon quantifiers as in "It is always windy near tall buildings". Definite descriptions implicitly make use of quantification as the example "the people of China" shows. The meanings of complex concepts require quantification. Any complex action concept such as "walking" has associated with it, as part of its definition, assertions such as "at all times, some of the limbs of the individual engaged in walking support the individual".

Conceptual dependency theory provides three methods for expressing universal quantification. The first method involves the use of variables assumed to be universally quantified, as in "if ONE smokes this may cause ONE to get cancer." Here "one" stands for any person. It is unclear whether universal quantification over other non-human sets is approached similarly. In any case this device is inadequate, since it does not allow for multiple quantification, e.g. "Any politician can fool some of the people all of the time".

The inference rule governs the second method for expressing universal quantification. According to the inference rule, "If X is thirsty, infer that X will drink something", where X is a universally quantified object which stands for any person. A machine might easily answer a question like "John is thirsty. Will John drink something?"; however, the inference rule will not allow a machine to answer questions like "Will John drink something IF he is thirsty?" and "Do thirsty people drink liquids?", since no assertion to the effect that someone is in fact thirsty has been made. We lack access to a procedurally encoded piece of knowledge AS A FACT. In other words, knowing how to use a fact does not guarantee recognition of the fact.

Quantification can also be expressed by the conceptual tenses "timeless" and "continuing". Schank uses the timeless tense to designate "habitual actions", for example, "John sells cars". The continuing tense is closely related. It is used in the sense of activity as defined in Evans (1967). However, these special devices do not address the general problem of quantification.

Preference semantics expresses quantifiers in common sense inference rules (Wilks, 1973) or by relating them to a primitive semantic unit called "type indicator". Relating quantifiers to a semantic unit of the form "type indicator" is used purely as a device for translation.

Quantification challenges semantic network representations to indicate the "scopes" of universal and existential quantifiers. The notation used in the semantic network is analogous to quantifier-free normal form in predicate calculus. Propositions are in "prenex form" (i.e., quantifiers have maximum scope), existentially quantified variables are Skolemized, and universal quantification is implicit. To distinquish between them, we simply use "solid lines" for existentially quantified concept nodes (as in all previous figures), and "broken lines" for universally quantified nodes. Graphical Skolemization then links each existentially quantified node to all universally quantified nodes on which it depends (i.e., whose universal quantifiers precede the existential quantifier in prenex form). "Dotted lines" represent these dependency links to distinguish them from propositional and logical links. For example, "All dogs chase some cat" is represented as shown in Figure 5a. In predicate calculus notation this is

$$(Ax)\{dog(x) => (Ey)[cat(y)\&chase(x,y)]\}$$

or dog(x) => [cat(f(x))&chase(x,f(x))], Skolemized. Now if we can assume (Ey)cat(y), i.e., there is at least one cat (or alternatively, that there is at least one dog), then this becomes

cat(f(x)) & [dog(x) => chase(x,f(x))],

which corresponds to the slightly simpler diagram shown in Figure 5b. Here the "cat" proposition is no longer regarded as a consequent of the "dog" proposition. This type of simplification is often appropriate for encoding natural language statements, since we do not usually communicate in terms of propositions which are trivially true by virtue of the nonexistence of their referents (which is not to say that we do not communicate about nonexistent entities). The diagram for the proposition "There is a cat which all dogs chase" differs from Figure 5b only in the absence of the dependency link between the "cat" and "dog" nodes.

Time requires special treatment because of its central importance in structuring events. The notation uses "pairs of parentheses" instead of circles for moments of time and "pointers" to moments of time are marked "T". A name for a moment of time can be placed between the parentheses. "Intervals" of time are represented as pairs of square brackets. "Broken brackets" and "broken parentheses" indicate universally quantified time variables. Pointers to time nodes may be suppressed altogether by placing times directly alongside the predicate tokens to which they apply. With this notation, complex time relations can be represented quite conveniently. The sentence "There is always someone there" is diagrammed in Figure 6.

The proposed method of representing quantification is applicable only to propositions in prenex form. If we deal only with existential logic (one in which all propositional constructions are truth-functional), no generality is lost, though clarity is occasionally compromised. However, propositions involving (nonextensional) "modal" operators such as "necessarily" and "believes" cannot be converted to prenex form. The present notation is expanded to allow arbitrary embedding of quantifiers, so such propositions can be represented.

The notation already introduced expresses many higher-ordered constructions. For example, "John has all of his father's faults, and carelessness is one of them" is represented as shown in Figure 7a. Observe that both the abbreviated and unabbreviated notation for propositions have been used here. The higher-order predicate is "fault", and the universally quantified node should be read "for all predicates". Alternatively we might define the set of faults of John´s father and predicate each member of the set about John. "Careless" would be asserted to be a member of this set. Figure 7b illustrates this alternative formulation. Let "C" denote set membership. Conventions for abbreviating implication and equivalence assertions of the type appearing in Figure 7b will be mentioned shortly.

In the past, quantificational apparatus has not been adequate to support claims about equivalence of certain types of semantic network notation to second or higher ordered logic. Statements about predicates alone do not demonstrate a second-order capability. Since such statements can be made in a many-sorted first-order logic. Logical quantifiers remain unsuitable for expressing many natural language quantifiers such as "several", "many", "most of", "a few", "more than", etc. Natural language quantifiers not readily expressible in terms of the logical quantifiers can be handled systematically with (fuzzy) properties of set cardinality and relations between set cardinalities, plus standard set relations such as set inclusion.

We can classify natural language quantifiers according to their indication of set size from absolute to comparative, where comparative indicators are those comparing the size of one set to that of another set. The logical quantifier E (there exists) is an absolute indicator of set size since (Ex)P(x) tells us that the set of P´s contains "at least one" member. The quantifier A (for all), by virtue of its equivalence to ~E~, is also an absolute indicator. In the context (Ax)(P(x)=>Q(x)) however, where the number of P´s is finite, it can be considered a comparative indicator of set size. It tells us that the subsets of P´s that are Q´s is "as large as" the set of P´s itself. Common absolute quantifiers are "none", "one", "two", "three", ... , "several"; common comparative quantifiers are "all of", "most of", "a small fraction of", "a slight majority of", "one-half of", "two-thirds of", "as many as", "twice as many as", etc. Some quantifiers show both absolute and comparative attributes, especially "some" and "many". For example, in "Many artificial satellites are orbiting the globe" "many" is used absolutely - it appears to imply a cardinality of at least about a dozen. In "Many students attend John´s class" "many" is used in the sense "considerably more than attend the average class". This particular use of "many" is discussed quite satisfactorily in Bartsch and Vennemann (1972). They do not consider the absolute indicativeness of "many", however, nor of its comparative use in selecting a "subset" of another set, as in "Many of the world´s people are undernourished". Contrast the numerical indication here with that in "many of the apples in the basket were rotten".

Recognising the absolute/comparative behaviour of quantifiers, we can characterise them systematically by means of predicates on set cardinality and on pairs of set cardinalities as in Figures 8 and 9. In Figure 8b the convention for abbreviating implication is shown, i.e. single broken lines are used for the conjoined antecedents and solid lines for the conjoined consequences. Let "#" denote set size (cardinality). Equivalence of two sets of propositions is abbreviated in an analogous manner in Figure 9, the members of one set are attached to a node with double broken lines and the members of the other set with solid lines.

We regard "#" as a function from sets onto integers and "several" as a (fuzzy) property of numbers. If instead we accepted "several" itself as a possible value of set size, then it would be impossible to talk about "the" size of the set, as "#" would be many valued (eg., a 6-element set might have both size "6" and size "several"). In the next example "many" is expressed in two parts, the first being an "absolute" indicator of size (about a dozen or more), and the second comparing set size to an average set size, as in Bartsch and Vennemann (1972). In the construction "avg #" is regarded as a function on classes of sets whose value is the average cardinality of the sets in a given class of sets.

2.4 Representing Definite and Relational Descriptions

Natural language representations usually ignore the distinction between definite and indefinite descriptions, so the method for representing both types of descriptions is shown here. The expressive power of the semantic network formalism has not been extended in the area of descriptions. The representation of both definite descriptions ("the little old lady at the door") and indefinite descriptions ("a big apple") are based on the conventions for logical connectives and quantifiers already introduced rather than on a description operator such as Moore (1973) uses. Description operators appear to be useful only at a superficial level of language representation, and in the domain of pure mathematics.

The description "John's car" (Figure 13) conveys the presupposition that

John has exactly one car. This is true at least for certain discourse contexts for which the given sentence might occur. Figure 13b shows one method of representing "John´s car". It is preceded by the non-equivalent proposition that John owns a red car, and followed by an abbreviated version of Figure 13b. Observe that the uniqueness condition has been expressed in Figure 13b with the aid of equality. This convention also proves to be useful for definite descriptions of "sets", such as "the French-speaking people of Canada". This description is shown in full and abbreviated notation in Figure 11. The abbreviated notation may tempt one to incorrectly read the operands of the implicit equivalence operator as independently asserted propositions. In fact only the equivalence is asserted. If we use the abbreviated notation, we must add another universally quantified node to make statements about the members of the defined set. Any statements made about the node bearing the set definition will become part of the definition. Thus we could diagram "The French-speaking people of Canada are vivacious" as in Figure 12a. With the abbreviated implication convention Figure 12a is redrawn as shown in Figure 12b.

The notation for descriptions as introduced is inadequate for descriptions of predicative concepts which are expressed in terms of predicates of the same, rather than higher, type. For example, suppose we wish to say that the property "human" is the same as the property "rational animal"; note that the latter property is of type 1 and is expressed in terms of the type 1 properties "rational" and "animal". We cannot diagram this statement on the basis of the formula (Ax)[human(x) <=> rational(x) & animal(x)], since this merely asserts extensional identity (i.e., the set of human beings equals the set of rational animals). The desired statement of intensional identity can be made with the aid of Church´s lambda operator. This operator abstracts a predicate from an open sentence by designating certain variables of the sentence as arguments of the predicate. Thus we write

human = lambda x [rational(x) & animal(x)].

A more interesting example is provided by the sentence "Loving one´s neighbours is a virtue", which requires abstraction of the monadic predicate "loves one´s neighbours" from the dyadic predicate "loves". This is shown in Figure 13, using a graphical analogue of lambda abstraction.

Lambda conversion is accomplished by means of a (solid) "lambda link" from the proposition expressing that an individual "loves all of his neighbours" to the node for the individual. In general graphical lambda abstraction involves the construction of some open sentence (possibly with embedded lambda expressions), and lambda conversion of some of the variables of the sentence. Open sentences are formed exactly like propositions, except that some of the participating concept nodes are regarded as free variables. Lambda conversion is symbolised by lambda links from the node corresponding to an open sentence to free variables of the sentence. In the nonmonadic case lambda links are labeled lambda A, lambda B, etc., (or in some other systematic way) to distinguish the arguments of the abstracted predicate.

2.6 Including Time in the Representation

Time is regarded as the only situational or contextual variable (Cf. McCarthy and Hayes, 1969) that needs to be added to action propositions. This contrasts with Anderson and Bower (1973), Rumelhart et al. (1973), and Schank et al. (1973), who include time and locale as basic dimensions of events in their representation.*2* However, locale is not a property of events as a whole, but a (frequently time-dependent) property of the participants in an event. For example, in "John is watching a circling hawk" it is John and the hawk who have locations, not the event.

We use time in "instantaneous" and "interval" modes. In the instantaneous mode a proposition can have either a fixed or variable moment of time associated with it. In the interval mode the "moment" is replaced by a time interval. The interval can be omitted in particular contexts (where it would normally be given) to simplify propositions that describe states and events with more enduring properties (like being a girl, car, etc.). This omission is a matter of expediency; any change involving a metamorphosis (like a girl becoming a woman or a caterpillar becoming a butterfly) would require explicit recognition of time dependencies.

Within this framework, temporal relations including tenses (which can be built up from more elementary temporal relations) can be defined. If we restrict our view of time as consisting of a set of elements (time points) and a relation that partially orders them, we can define binary temporal relations similiar to those of Bruce (1972) or Schank et al (1973).*3*

Bruce (1972) has devised a systematic method for defining tenses. He maps various time relations given by auxiliary verbs and the form of the main verb and he defines seven binary ordering relations on time segments, e.g. "I had gone" - maps to "after". Thus a tense is an n-ary relation on time segments, e.g. "past" tense is one in which the relation "after" holds between two time segments.

Our modifications to some of Bruce´s binary ordering relations permit us to represent a sentence like "While he was in Rome, before he met his murderer, he first sang in La Traviata" as in Figure 14.

2.7 Conventions for Including Modal Operators

The semantic network must be extended to represent propositions involving modal operators such as the necessity operator, the belief operator, the causal operator, and the counterfactual conditional.*4*

The only apparent notational problem raised by the introduction of modal operators is that of distinguishing between "opaque" and "transparent" environments generated by such operators. A sentential environment is opaque if replacement of a term by a referentially equivalent term can change the truth value of the sentence, and transparent otherwise. For example, the necessity operator generates an opaque environment in the sentence "9 is necessarily greater than 8", as we cannot replace "9" by the referentially equivalent term "the number of major planets". Many English modal sentences, particularly those involving verbs of propositional attitude such as "wants" or "believes", admit both a transparent and an opaque reading.

A term in an opaque environment is locked into the "scope" of the modal operator (necessarily, wants, etc.). Since quantifiers in such terms cannot be extracted to convert the proposition to prenex form, the previous notation for quantifiers is inadequate. We need constructions that allow arbitrary embedding of quantifiers within the scopes of propositional connectives (extensional or otherwise). To see how the prenex restriction can be removed consider the following proposition: (Ax)(Ey)(Az){(As)P(s,x) => (Et)[Q(t,y,z) <=> (Au)(Av)(Ew)R(u,v,w)]}. We can completely specify the scopes of all quantifiers as follows. First, for each sequence of "adjacent" quantifiers, the notation specifies the dependence of the existentially on the universally quantified variables as before, i.e., y depends on x and w depends on u and v.

Second, the notation specifies which variables have their quantifier scopes nested just inside the scopes of which propositional connectives. Thus s and t depend on =>, and u, v, and w depend on <=> in this sense. Exactly the same kind of dotted dependency link can be used for this second type of scope relationship as for the first. The network representation of the above proposition is shown in Figure 15. By the transitivity of scope inclusion (Au), (Av), and (Ew) lie within the scope of =>, since the equivalence proposition is embedded within the implicative proposition. The assumption that all quantifiers have "maximum" scope compatible with the indicated constraints uniquely determines all scopes.

We now apply this notation to the representation of opaque constructions, beginning with the example involving necessity. The representations of the nonsynonymous sentences "9 is necessarily greater than 8" and "The number of major planets is necessarily greater than 8" are shown in Figure 16.

Counterfactual implication can be treated in much the same manner as necessity. In the sentence "If there were a major planet beyond Pluto, the number of major planets would equal 10", the term "the number of major planets" is nonreferential. [Neptune is presently beyond Pluto and will be for the next 20 years; this is due to Pluto's elliptic orbit and doesn't change the validity of the example.] The representation as shown in Figure 17 borrowed Lewis' symbol □=> to represent counterfactual implication (Lewis, 1973); however, any number of implicitly conjoined antecedents and consequents are allowed as operands, much as in the generalised form of material implication.

Propositional attitudes may involve quantification over propositions, as in "John knows everything", or in "John knows everything Mary knows". The most direct way of representing such propositions is by quantification over propositional variables, as in Figure 18.

In Figure 18a "John knows everything" has been interpreted as "John believes all true propositions". If we accept these representations, we must carefully distinguish between the universally quantified "proposition nodes" in Figure 18 and the proposition nodes previously introduced as points of attachment for the parts of an explicit proposition. These previous proposition nodes are not quantifiable. The propositions in which they participate "exist" simply by virtue of appearing in the semantic net. The universally quantified nodes in Figure 18, by contrast, are "concept" nodes denoting "complete" propositions. We could avoid using propositional variables by expressing "for all propositions" as "for all predicates P and all x such that P(x)", giving the new version of Figure 18a shown in Figure 19. This would avoid the use of propositions as concepts, but Figure 18 has the advantage of being more concise. Replacing quantification over propositions by quantification over predicates and variables can also be applied to existential quantification. For example, the sentence "There is a proposition x such that if x is true then mankind is doomed" can be paraphrased as "There is a predicate P such that if P(x) is true for all x then mankind is doomed".

The techniques for representing knowing and believing apply equally to other propositional attitudes such as remembering, supposing, intending, deciding, avoiding, hoping, imagining, pretending, and trying. Nonreferential terms within the scopes of such operators (whichever ones are deemed useful independently of the others) can be identified by means of scope dependency links as in Figures 16-19. The same applies to the denotic modalities such as obligation. It should be obvious, for example, how "John ought to marry the prettiest girl" would be represented.

Causal dependency is an important modality deserving attention. Causal explanations are rather closely related to counterfactual conditionals, as can be seen from the inference "B would not have happened if A had not happened", which is often reasonable given that "A caused B". "John asked Mary to dance because she was the only girl left without a partner" is an example of an opaque context generated by a causal construction. Substitution of the term "Mary" for its referential synonym "the only girl left without a partner" clearly fails. As in other modal constructions, therefore, we may need scope dependency links to express causal constructions.

3. The State-Based Representation

Conceptual dependency diagrams (Schank 1972) and preference semantics templates (Wilks 1973) are capable of expressing four sorts of assertions: (1) state attribution in which a modifier is ascribed to an object or set of objects at some time; (2) events in which a change of state is ascribed to an object or set of objects at some time; (3) actions; and (4) events.

However, a sentence such as

The sun was turning red and approaching the western horizon. (3.1)

raises many questions about Schank's and Wilks' formalisation of these distinctions. Utterances are classified into one of these types using the <actor-action-object> formalism espoused by both Schank and Wilks, which states that modes of behaviour which are expressed by actions MUST have actors whereas all other modes of behaviour CANNOT have actors. In (3.1) the motion of the sun MUST be done BY somebody or something whereas its change of colour CANNOT be done by somebody or something. In the case of the (apparently) moving sun in (3.1), one is hard pressed to identify the actor, as in the sentence "The breaker was moving toward shore". Consequently we are compelled to regard certain ongoing activities which intuitively just "happen" as instigated by someone or something (including natural forces in a vague unspecified sense).

Just as we are compelled to regard certain ongoing activities as instigated by somebody or something, Schank and Wilks deny us the option of regarding certain actions as having an agent. For example:

John was hurting Mary by pulling her hair. (3.2)

In (3.2) the "hurting", not being an action, has no actor whereas in

John was dragging Mary by pulling her hair. (3.3)

the "dragging", insofar as it involves PTRANS'ing DOES have John as an actor.

The criterion for distinguishing what an actor DOES and what he CAUSES becomes unclear. In (3.2), according to Schank, we are to regard the "hurting" as CAUSED BY the "pulling" action. But the same is true of PTRANS'ing in (3.3). Furthermore, even direct bodily action such as moving an arm can be viewed as caused by muscle contraction or, subjectively, as caused by an act of will, either of which again may have antecedent causes.

No structural primitives should be associated with actors at all. Instead I propose a neutral representation in which events are expressed as sequences of states of the participants, the state-based theory. The successive states simply express "what happened", without explicit commitment as to "who did it". The agent(s) in an event can be identified by supplementary propositions, so that the notion of an agent can still be used to aid interpretation and inference. However, it would be regarded as a rather "fuzzy" higher level concept, understood by the system in terms of the role of a supposed agent within a sequence of causally and teleologically related states. For example, in the sentence "John uprooted the sapling" the term agent would be considered highly applicable to John´s role in the event while in the sentence "The avalanche uprooted the tree" its applicability to the role of the avalanche would be considered relatively low. The notion of an "agent" depends in part on causal priority of a state of the supposed agent in the sequence of states under consideration, in part on the extent to which purposive behaviour can be ascribed to the supposed agent in general, and in part on the extent to which the particular sequence of states which he initiated can be assumed to be intentional on his part.

Similarly we propose to separate WHY something happened (causes enabling conditions, reasons, explanations, justifications, and the like) from WHAT happened. As with "agents", this does not prevent us from including causal propositions in the representation and relying heavily on them for interpretation and inference. However, time relations and changes of state, not causes, will give coherence to a set of propositions as an "event".

Schank uses instrumental case relations to attach supplemental conceptualisations to the main conceptualisation where the supplemental conceptualisation serves as a means toward the end expressed by the main conceptualisation. Schank´s "instrumental" relation between actions can and should be represented in terms of causation and intention. For example, if a system has a conceptualisation to the effect that John was PTRANS´ing the ball BY PROPEL´ing it, then this conceptualisation should also express that the PROPEL´ing was CAUSING the PTRANS´ing. In fact, phrases ostensibly expressing instrumental actions often express no more than causation. An example is the "by" clause in

The effluents were killing the fish by
raising the temperature of the water. (3.4)

When there is a difference, it lies in the intimation of PURPOSIVE causation. In

John woke Mary by blowing his trumpet. (3.5)

purposive causation is expressed, while in

Mary woke up because John was blowing his trumpet. (3.6)

it is not. Sentences (3.5) and (3.6) clearly show that the instrumental relation is composed of a causal relation supplemented by intentional states.

According to Fodor (1972), actions should be considered a proper subclass of events. Let us determine if this is the case for Schank's notion of an action, and what might justify the special status of actions as opposed to events. According to Schank, an action is something a nominal can be said to BE DOING AT SOME MOMENT (this is not a quote, but an interpretation of Schank's definition). A study of his proposed inferences shows that in itself an action does not express a definite change in a situation; rather it expresses existence of a situation which TENDS TO PRODUCE change, and all actual changes must be INFERRED. Formulas for actions in Wilks' theory are analogous although they are not described as explicitly as Schank's primitive action concepts. Actions, then, express MODES OF BEHAVIOUR which promote but do not guarantee the occurrence of events. For example, the actions PTRANS, INGEST, MOVE do not EXPRESS changes in location; instead those changes are primary inferences given that an actor is PTRANS'ing, INGEST'ing or MOVE'ing something. Syntactically, the relationship between an EVENT, say a change in location, and the ACTION, say PTRANS, whose primary inference is that event, corresponds quite closely to the relationship between VERBS and their PARTICIPLES respectively. For example to say that John was PTRANS'ing himself with the RESULT that his location changed is quite analogous to saying that he WAS GOING somewhere with the result that he went there. Unlike Schank we do not regard "he was going" and "he went" as equivalent; we claim that "he went there", unlike "he was going there", affirms that he DID arrive at his destination. It is decidedly odd to say "he went there but didn't get there." We should remember that though "action" normally connotes the occurrence of definite "events", to Schank it means the existence of a "dynamic" situation which TENDS TO GENERATE events. Schank's actions correspond more closely to states than to events! To say that A is PTRANS'ing B is merely to express a momentary truth about the system in which A and B participate, not a change in that system. The change in the system remains to be inferred. Recognising that "actions" in Schank's sense are essentially states rather than events is important, since it leads to a uniform view of all (true) events as sequences of states. The need for identifying "actors" of events does not arise.

The definition of events as sequences of states is compatible with the observation that many common modifiers express subtle blends of "passive" and "dynamic" attributes. The examples below bring to mind conceptual images that illustrate a gradually increasing emphasis on dynamics.

blue sky --> bright sun --> glowing (or luminous) candle -->
burning candle --> blazing fire --> billowing smoke

Schank's actions, and, as far as we can determine, Wilks', are "dynamic states", or "activities", or "modes of behaviour" which MEDIATE changes in certain attributes. Th PTRANS and MOVE mediate changes in location, INGEST and EXPEL mediate changes in containment relationships, and MTRANS mediates changes in awareness.

Expressions of time are crucial to the meaning of utterances, serving for example to structure events. Nevertheless in other representations, particularly Schank's (1972) conceptual dependency networks, aspects of time are handled as a quantificational apparatus. Problems with inference and aspect can arise if time is allowed to assume this protean character. For example, the use of the conceptual tense 'timeless' to denote "habitual actions" as in the statement "John sells cars" fails to acknowledge the progressive aspect "is selling" which is concerned with the state and not the disposition. For there may have been a time (surely) when John did not sell cars and a time when he may not sell cars. We fare no better, unfortunately, if we say "John now sells cars", reporting an incident of behaviour instead of an evolving pattern of behaviour, since "now" sets no temporal boundaries (vide Strawson, 1959). Within a particular approach to representation we can, however, artifically contrive temporal boundaries for "now".

We regard any condition which can hold momentarily (blue, moving, running, etc.) as A STATE. Accordingly, any atomic proposition which is based on a time-dependent predicate is a STATE PROPOSITION. Figure 20 shows two concurrent state propositions: something (the redness of the sun) was increasing throughout some time interval and something else (the distance between the sun and the horizon) was decreasing throughout the same time interval. Actually there are two additional state propositions concerned with the existence of unique values of redness and distance at all moments of time within the time interval of interest, these have not been made explicit since they can be taken to be implicit in the redness and distance relations.

EVENTS involve a change in state as "the last leaf fell from the tree" illustrates. The definitive characteristic of state changes is the following: if a system has property A at time t1, and property B at time t2, then A-->B is a change of state if and only if A and B are mutually exclusive properties, e.g. A=solid, B=liquid; A=round, B=rectangular. In fact a state attribute such as colour which can assume various values can consistently be defined as a set of mutually exclusive properties, each member of the set being regarded as a value of the attribute. This admits both qualitative attributes such as colour as well as quantitative attributes such as location. Figure 21 shows a simple event involving a single change of state of a "system" with one component (Mary). The time relation "then" implies immediate succession of the two time intervals. Figure 22 is our representation of one of Schank´s standard sentences. It is paraphrased as: "Some unknown mode of behaviour of John caused some object to move quickly toward Mary. Subsequently the object reached Mary and exerted a force on her." Note that we have a state and an event here, viz. John´s unknown state and the event of the object moving toward Mary and striking her. The causal connections between John´s state and the ensuing event does not make John´s state part of that event. Only exclusive and successive states of a particular system of objects form events. A natural inference in Figure 22 would be that John intentionally hit Mary, i.e., that the missing state of John is that he was trying to bring about the event in question. We would represent "trying" by the state predicate "x has active goal y at time t".

3.1 Embodying Complex Concepts in State-Based Theory

An important consequence of our very broad conception of states is that new complex states (modes of behaviour) can be defined in terms of events involving primitive or already defined states. The time of occurrence of these events can extend some distance backward and forward from the moment at which the new state is defined to hold. For example "walking" is defined in terms of successive states of motion and displacement of the walker´s feet and body over a "period of observation" encompassing (say) two steps, since an instantaneous "snapshot" of a person is insufficient for deciding whether or not that person is walking (although it may of course supply enough cues to prompt the inference that the person is walking). The constructions are necessarily as complex as the states they describe. Complexity can result from the intricate coordination of several simultaneous activities (e.g. "rolling" expresses rotation and translation at coordinated rates), or from complex time dependencies (e.g. flickering), or from both (e.g. "walking" or even "building a snowman").

According to Schank's (1973) dictionary, if X WALKS to Z (where X is human and Z is a location) then X PTRANS's X by X MOVEing the feet of X in the direction of Z. This formula disallows walking on one's hands and knees, or walking on one's hands (admittedly a rare skill). More importantly, the formula admits running, skipping, hopping, jogging, shuffling, and even skating. Presumably, the dictionary entry is not intended to capture the full meaning of "walking" as we understand it, but only those aspects which are most essential to language understanding and immediate inference.

Similarly Wilks' formulas are incomplete [Cf. Lakoff's (1972) lexical decomposition trees]. For example, it is correct to say that DRINK implies

((*ANI (SUBJ) (((FLOW STUFF) OBJE) ((*ANI
IN)(((THIS (*ANI (THRU PART)) TO)(BE CAUSE)))))

but not the converse (which could mean someone was receiving an enema). Wilks has selected only some of the linguistically important features.

It is important to formulate more complete meaning representations for two reasons. First, more information will be required for adequate comprehension of ordinary discouse. Secondly, MUCH more information will surely be required to match the human ability to describe concepts and reason about them. For example, suppose we ask a reasonably articulate person to describe human "walking" IN AS MUCH DETAIL AS POSSIBLE. We might elicit at least the following information: Each foot of the walker repeatedly leaves the ground, moves freely in the walking direction comparable to the length of the walker's legs (while staying close to the ground), then is set down again, and remains in position on the ground, supporting the walker, while the other foot goes through a similar motion. The repetition rate is about one repetition per second. The legs remain more or less extended. The body remains more or less erect and is carried forward at a fairly constant rate. Further details could be added about the flexing motions of feet, knees, and hips, the slight up-and-down motion of the body, typical arm motion, and forces exerted on the ground.

Figure 23 shows a network which describes "walking" (regarded as a state predicate with three arguments in addition to time) according to this description. A few propositions have been omitted so as not to clutter the diagram. These are that each foot is also above the ground (and close to it) while moving, that each foot is also supporting x while stationary; that the duration of each of the unlabeled time intervals [] is approximately half a second; and that the speed of motion of the walker's body is approximately constant. There is no difficulty in adding these state propositions, except that the last requires "moving" to have an additional argument, namely the speed of motion. Note that [ti] is the "time interval of observation" of the walker, and that it contains t, the time at which x is said to be walking. Thus "walking" is defined by behaviour in the temporal vicinity of the moment of predication, specifically about two seconds of motion allowing about three or four steps.

This representation of "walking" is limited in that it is not applicable to unusual modes of walking (e.g. on hands and knees) or to walking by animals. We wonder how many "kinds" of walking should be represented separately? We have attempted a representation which expresses the common features of all kinds of walking in Figure 24. The representation is based on the following characteristics of walking in general:

(1) it is done using the limbs that are a subset of the limbs of the individual involved in the walking;
(2) the number of limbs involved is greater than or equal to two;
(3) at all times some of the limbs used for walking are in nonsliding contact with the walking surface (this is not the same as saying some of the limbs are in contact with the surface at times);
(4) each limb used for walking is stationary on the walking surface at some time and subsequently is moving for some time; and
(5) the individual as a whole is in motion in the walking direction.

Quantification is used to indicate the role of any number of legs in the walking. Without quantification, describing the locomotion of say, a millipede, would be very tiresome. Unfortunately the "fuzziness" of many of the meaning components has been ignored in this representation of walking.

For example, it seems necessary to put some constraints on the length of stride (lest the walker be allowed to mince forward in millimeter increments), yet to give an exact distance would be absurd. Since conceptual fuzziness pervades the meaning representations for complex concepts, we can no longer draw a sharp boundary between extracting the meaning of an utterance and making probable inferences on the basis of the derived meaning structure. This is because we only find the probable meaning of an utterance. For example, the utterance "John built the house" probably means that he built a large, rigid-walled enclosure with a roof, separate rooms, etc.; but none of this is certain. The utterance "John was laughing" probably means that he was producing a series of voiced sounds by staggered exhalation of air, and that his facial expression was merry; but he might have laughed silently, or his facial expression might have been derisive or even hostile. It is not suitable to try to reduce semantic uncertainty by excluding from the "meaning" of a term all but its absolutely minimal content, and ascribe everything else to inference.*5* In the case of "house" all that would remain would be a "partial enclosure" - which accommodates a fenced-off field, a shipping crate, or a jacket. In the case of "laughing" we would perhaps be left with "spasmodic breathing and intent to convey amusement," which could suggest that John is asthmatic and dancing a jig. Currently, some progress is being made on this problem.

3.2 Consolidating Adjectives and Relative Terms

Bartsch and Vennemann (1972) outline a unified treatment of relative adjectives and comparatives, extending Montague´s (1970) treatment within the intensional logic framework. One criticism cautions against prima facie acceptance of their theory. The reference set is a set of objects whose members are used for comparison with some given object relative to some measurable attribute of the objects. This device is inadequate to solve the problem of comparisons. While it is possible to define a "reference set" for a phrase like "a large apple", it is not immediately apparent what the reference set would be if one were to ask a child to draw a large circle on a sheet of paper. Faced with the problem of how the reference set is determined, Bartsch and Vennemann raised the pertinent question of how the reference set is inferred from the context, especially extra-sentential context.

Parsons (1972) also falls victim to this "reference set dilemna". He represents adverbs as operators added to an ordinary first-order predicate calculus and also applies this representation to non-predicative (descriptive) adjectives. Accordingly, the phrase (Parson's example) "x is a small four-footed animal" has the following two representations:

small [four-footed(x) & animal(x)]; and
small [animal(x)] & four-footed(x).

Parson's interpretation for the former is "x is small relative to the class of four-footed animals", and of the latter is "x is small relative to the class of animals and is also four-footed". When we try to specify the operators at this more detailed level of analysis, we reach the "reference set dilemna". We might enumerate the rather large (but still finite) set of all four-footed animals but how would the operator be specified to account for a "small star" or a "small circle"?

The inadequacies of reference-sets convinced us that higher-order functions (or relations) are essential in the representation of natural language. We use functors which map generic concepts into generic concepts. Many adjectives must be regarded as higher-order functions. The sentence "Trigger is a tall pony" cannot seriously be represented as [[Trigger pony] & [Trigger tall]], since a tall pony is still a small horse. Superficially [Trigger (tall pony)], in which "tall" functionally transforms the generic concept "pony" into the generic concept "(tall pony)", is adequate.

A functor is a symbol which, occurring as the first member of a sequence of symbols of certain syntactic kinds, makes a sequence of the same or another syntactic kind, Cresswell (1973). The typical value functor applied to a concept with some measure attribute returns a value, e.g. the typical value of size for man. Note that this is not the same as the typical man's size. The typical man's size is not readily determinable since it is difficult to ascertain exactly what constitutes a typical man. A typical value functor is shown in Figures 27 and 28. We can abbreviate the typical value functor in a manner analogous to the collasping of predicates in the abbreviated semantic network notation.

Descriptive adjectives are treated as conjoined predications in most cases. In the diagram of "Judy ate a delicious spice cake", Figure 25 (abbreviated notation), spice is treated as a flavour of cake.

Regardless of their morphology, most adjectives appear to be comparative. For example, big, tall, slow, heavy, hard, and so on are relative adjectives based on some measurable attribute of the object of attention. The sentence "John is a bigger than Bill" is diagrammed in Figure 26. The explanatory paraphrase of Figure 26 is "John's size is greater than Bill's size". Often the comparative is implicit in the utterance. For example, in the sentence "John is a big man" the adjective "big" serves as a comparative. The meaning of "John is a big man" is diagrammed as Figure 27. The associated paraphrase is "John is a man and the size of John is greater than a typical value of size for a man". Notice the use of the typical value functor in this example.

Finally, Figure 28 illustrates a non-directly predicative, non-directly comparative use of a relative adjective of the type under discussion. The sentence "Big John drinks the whiskey" is paraphrased in the diagram as "John drinks the whiskey and John's size is greater than the typical value of size for something and John is an instance of that something". In Figure 28, the node immediately to the left of John represents John's size (size is used as a functor in the proposition containing John and size). The treatment of relative adjectives based on measurable attributes can be summarised as follows: The value of the "attribute" of "x" exceeds the value of the "attribute" which is typical for that concept (of which x is an instance).

Normal discourse admits constructions such as (3.7) through (3.10).

John is the perfect man. (3.7)
Mary is the worst conceivable baker. (3.8)
Mike is the ideal fat man. (3.9)
In order to form a more perfect union... (3.10)

Modifiers such as perfect, worst conceivable, and ideal are problematic to represent because of the way they operate on what they modify. For example, we might formulate (3.7) in logical terms as:

(AP)([(Ax)[man(x)&P(x)%=>y-approves[P(x)]]]=>P(John)) (3.7a)

Here y is the speaker. The formulation reads "John has all properties such that y would approve of any man's having them". We can then easily formulate an expression for "someone is not a perfect man" by utilising (3.7a) with the existential quantifier added (Ez)~ and replacing P(John) with P(z). Clearly, the method of handling comparative adjectives such as big does not work here.

At this time I make no definitive proposal for handling adjectives such as perfect, ideal, worst kind of, best conceivable, etc., at any adequately detailed level of analysis. However at a superficial level of analysis the sentence "John gave Mary the worst conceivable alibi" is rendered as shown in Figure 29. If we later find out that "John is a basketball player", this information can easily be added to the structure shown in Figure 29 by adding supplemental propositions to the node representing John. At a less superficial level of analysis one might render the sentence "Big Mike is the perfect fat man" as shown in Figure 30. Note that the predicate "fat man" is formed using lambda abstraction as discussed by Schubert (1976) and Cercone (1975, 1977). The predicate "fat man" is then operated on by the functor "perfect". In the case of descriptive adjectives (as opposed to the implicit comparative "fat" in the "fat man" example above) the best one could do, in absence of context, is to treat them as conjoined predications outside the scope of the functor operating.

3.3 Adverbials Defy Logic

Reichenbach's (1947) approach, seemingly accepted by Schank (1972) and Anderson and Bower (1973), is to regard adverbial modifiers as second-order predicates that impose constraints on a specific relation, thereby restricting the class of specific relations of which it may be a member. Montague (1972), Bartsch and Vennemann (1972), and Zadeh (1972) regard comparative adjectives and adverbs as operators which transform predicates. In particular, Bartsch and Vennemann's approach seems promising but has serious defects.

Schank (1972) diagrams adverbs as action modifiers without further analysis. Apparently he has not as yet concerned himself with the meanings of genuine manner adverbials (but see Schank, 1974 for a discussion of adverbs such as vengefully, thoughtlessly, etc.). For many adverbs (as for many adjectives) this neglect is probably justified, since most of the meaning content derives from perceptual processes. In the sentence "Mary walked gracefully" it is difficult to paraphrase "gracefully" in more elementary terms. Essentially we know gracefulness when we see it. Perceptual understanding needs to be supplemented only by a few facts for language comprehension purposes, such as the fact that graceful motion is generally pleasing, is more or less the opposite of awkward motion, is smooth and well-coordinated. Other adverbial modifiers, however, clearly require systematic analysis. An adequate representation of "quickly" should include the information that the word describes speed by comparing it to some standard.

Bartsch and Vennemann suggest that adverbial modifiers operate on verb meanings in the same manner that adjectival modifiers operate on noun meanings, i.e. they have semantic representations with functors f such that f is applied to term x to map x onto a new term f(x). The following example clearly illustrates one problem with this approach.

John owns a large car. (3.11)

John is running quickly. (3.12)

The reference set for large in (3.11) is the set of cars; John´s car is large in relation to the "average" for that set. "Running quickly" cannot be analyzed so easily. If the analogy were perfect then the reference set operated on by "quickly" would be the set of "runnings"; but clearly this set of runnings must be further restricted to the set of runnings which John is capable of performing. "Quickly" operates not on "running" alone, but on "John running".

The nature of the runner can be used to focus the reference set to which we apply a measure function. We could substitute "the cheetah" or "the ant" for John in (3.12) to change the reference set to which we apply a measure function. Unfortunately the reference set to which we apply a measure function can be affected by other factors, including locale. "Quickly" varies in meaning in examples (3.13) to (3.17).

John is running quickly on his hands and knees. (3.13)

John is running quickly on the moon. (3.14)

John is running quickly in Chile. (3.15)

The cheetah is running quickly in the dense forest. (3.16)

The cheetah is running quickly on the plain. (3.17)

The context which determines the meaning of an adverbial modifier cannot be absolutely circumscribed. Adverbials must be allowed to interact with any knowledge available about the participants in and the location of an action. Zadeh´s (1972) adverbial "hedges" specify weighted components of each fuzzy term on which a hedge may operate once and for all. Because he needs to specify these (weighted) components prior to using a particular hedge, his approach lacks generality. Our semantic network would represent "The cheetah is running" without the adverb as diagrammed in Figure 31. Figures 31a and 31b are based on alternative (but equivalent) representations of definite descriptions. Figure 32 represents the adverbial construction for "The cheetah is running quickly in the dense forest" in a manner consistent with Bartsch and Vennemann, but allowing the adverbial to interact with knowledge of the participants and situation of the action. The representation shows the explicit relationship between the speed of the cheetah's running as compared to the typical value of speed for something that is running, a cheetah, and in dense forests.

In our formulation we have applied the typical value functor to the lambda abstracted predicate

(LAMBDAx)[cheetah(x)&running(x)&in-dense-forests(x)].

The set of cheetahs running in dense forests, required for comparison, may well be empty. The "reference set" therefore, is not necessarily of this world but some imaginary world which is our conception of how hard cheetahs would find the going if they were to run through forests. The typical value functor does not presume the existence of a reference set.

4. Organising Propositional Knowledge for Comprehension and Inference

Schubert (1975) distinguished between the representational and the organisational aspects of semantic networks by demonstrating their different advantages. A logical representation couched in network form was as formally interpretable and expressively adequate as "classical" propositional representation, and would retain the methodological advantages of the associative network organisation. The network was an "intelligent" indexing scheme coupled with a data base of logical formulae.

We wish to emphasize the organisational aspects of semantic networks, in the tradition of Quillian (1968) and in the spirit of Hayes (1978B). As originally conceived by Quillian (1968), the characteristic concept-centred organisation of semantic networks did not address representation issues but rather focused primary concern with organising knowledge for effective use.

Subsequent semantic network notations have been developed in an independent and application specific manner, (eg. Anderson and Bower, 1973; Winston, 1970) often indicating a disdain for classical propositional knowledge representations such as the predicate calculus. The resulting efforts have generally been epistemologically inadequate (in the sense of McCarthy and Hayes, 1969) and expressively weak with respect to standard logical representations. Moreover, they have often disregarded the distinction between the representational and organisational aspects of network devices.

Early efforts by Shapiro (1971) to imbue networks with increased logical power explicitly documented this distinction by contrasting "system relations", "items", and "item relations". In Shapiro's mens (Memory Network Structure) data structure, system relations were user defined pointers which structured items and item relations into propositions and indexed propositions according to their item participants. The basic distinction between the propositional content of a knowledge database and the access mechanism to that content has recently been noted by Bobrow and Winograd (1977). They state "We believe that the presence of 'associative links' for retrieval is an additional dimension of memory structure which is not derivable from the logical structure being associated". The correspondence between semantic networks and logic has been established; the meaning of a given network is identical with the meaning of the equivalent logical expression. The object of our immediate attention is that structure which remains after paring the propositional content from a semantic network, i.e., the indexing structure which provides concept-based proposition access.

The design of the data base was strongly influenced by the nature of the information to be organised and the nature of retrieval requests. The information stored in semantic memory represents objects, concepts, relations, states, events, facts, propositions, and other items which serve ancillary functions to facilitate information retrieval. The memory system was designed for computer understanding of natural language for making logical deductions and common sense inferences, for solving problems ad formulating plans, for understanding verbal explanations of complex concepts, and for recreating past events for expository purposes. The structure of memory, that is, the relationships between propositional constructs in memory, must be built according to a formalism which can express all of the complex relationships between items of information which occur in natural language. The propositional constucts and the relationships between them have been adequately represented by predicate calculus and semantic networks.

In order to discuss the design of memory for a natural language understanding system, I must explain the terminology which I have adopted from a very divergent spectrum of terminology which has developed concerning memory. In an information processing sytem, memory is the part that can selectively retain information. "Lexical memory" represents knowledge about words and other symbols, the meanings of words and their referents, relations among words, in addition to rules and algorithms for manipulating the verbal symbols and relations. "Semantic memory" refers to the type of organisation of stored facts, (namely networks), and routines used to process these facts.

Propositional constructs are normally represented in memory as property lists attached to concepts. Elements of property lists may be pointers to other lists. For example, the propositions associated with a "drinking" action would be accessed via the property list for that "drinking" under the "propositions" indicator. Generally, the interrelationships among concepts could represent other concepts. A memory structured in this way becomes a network of interrelated property lists with pointers from words on many of the lists to words on other lists. Many word senses can be represented unambiguously since any word with more than one meaning would have more than one list attached. Property lists are indefinitely expandable, so there is no restriction on the amount of detail in the representation.

There is one meaning representation associated with each sense of open class category words.*6* The semantic network notation meaning representation for words includes both pragmatic and semantic information. Figure 33 depicts the ordinary sense of "drinks" in a network as "drink1". The figure is divided into a pragmatic section and a semantic section. The pragmatic section includes the template(s) that guides the parse of the utterance and two lists: the first list contains propositions that represent the implications that are likely to be needed for the comprehension of subsequent text; and the second list contains propositions representing critical implications that we expect to match in the surface structure. In Figure 33 this first list is (P5) and the second list is (P1,P2). The semantic section contains the network that represents the meaning of the word sense.

When the parsing programs were implemented, no method for structuring knowledge associated with generalisation hierarchies had been devised. Nor was quantification implemented. Thus all general knowledge was placed on the property lists of generic concepts. For example, the implication "AxEzAy[[[x drink1 y] => [[x ingest y z] & [z mouth-of x]]], which is part of the meaning of "drink1", is stored as a set of properties on the property list. The remaining implications of "drink1" are stored in the same way. These propositions will be integrated into the network for proper use by the inference processes.

Many senses of "drinks" (and "eats", "receiving an enema", etc.) all have the notion of "change in containment location" in common. This corresponds to a "general concept" that subsumes these narrower concepts. We can extract more general concepts from the specific concepts that they subsume, either totally or in part. When creating the meaning representations (networks) for concepts it is desirable to avoid the duplications of propositions in storage. We can avoid duplication by associating the common propositions with the more general concept. In a sense the work of both Schank (1972) and Wilks (1973a) supports the contention that the meaning of a concept is best represented by predications at the highest level of generality that adequately explain the term´s meaning. Thus we extract from "drinking" (and eating, etc.) the structure shown in Figure 34. It is important to note, however, that while Schank and Wilks might conclude that "ingesting" is a primitive action, I consider it a general concept. This applies to all primitive actions proposed by Schank and Wilks. Examining Figure 34 shows clearly that ingesting is ´not a primitive´ action but one whose meaning is expressed in terms of causes, motion, time, and other concepts.

The original representations for the various action senses of "drink" can be replaced with the more simplified diagram based on the general concept "ingest". Figure 35 shows the representation of "drink" as expressed in Figure 33 redrawn in terms of the general concept "ingest".

As described above, semantic networks are simply associative because they consider the relationship between concepts and property lists, and between property lists and property lists, but the network itself does not embody the more profound relationship between concepts and concepts. The design of the relationship structure between concepts must permit inference. It is typical that the particular relations which are established between concepts determine what class of inferences about those concepts is possible. Collins and Quillian (1972) suggest that frequently questions which could easily be answered on the basis of explicitly stored propositions are nevertheless answered through inference facilitated by a hierarchical organisation. It is doubtful that a person would store the fact that a rose is a plant, but rather that it is a flower and infer that it is a plant. The process of inference requires that they establish a relationship between concepts, in this case a subconcept-superconcept, or hierarchical relationship. Human beings frequently establish this type of knowledge organisation, with general concepts towards the top, and narrow concepts towards the bottom.

We need to understand the relationship between concepts in the semantic network because the process of comprehension, when we reason by analogy, speak metaphorically, or resolve anaphoric references, is really the process of matching, or establishing relationships, between concepts. A selective retrieval must search memory for concepts which will yield information about the new concept. Recognising this, Quillian (1968, 1969) developed the intersection technique which is an ordered serial search that looks for all possible intersections between the designated concepts. The search procedes outward along links from concepts denoted by words in the utterance. All connections found are checked to see if the relations between concepts meet syntactic and contextual constraints.

The following example demonstrates this type of comprehension. The sentence "The rain drums on the shelter" would probably be interpreted something like "The rain falls on the shelter and produces a hollow sound like someone beating on a drum". The intersection technique must yield an intersection between the concepts "rain" and "drum".

The hierarchical organisation of concepts facilitates comprehension by associating a less general concept with a more general concept. Within the semantic network, one concept is a superconcept of another concept if the set of properties attached to the former is a subset of the properties attached to the latter. "Mammal" is a superconcept of "elephant" since the set of "mammal" properties is a subset of "elephant" properties. The usefulness of concept hierarchies in comprehension and in inference can be demonstrated by asking questions about elephant's color, in particular Clyde's color, where Clyde is an elephant. After asserting "Clyde is an elephant", the colour of Clyde can be found as follows: the individual concept node "Clyde" is accessed, and the attached propositions are scanned sequentially for one which indicates the colour of Clyde. Should one not be found, Clyde's immediate successor in the subconcept-superconcept hierarchy is accessed (e.g., elephant), and its attached properties are again searched sequentially for a colour proposition. This process continues until either all the existing superconcepts' propositions have been checked, or a colour proposition has been found. Notice that the subconcept-superconcept structure simply guides an exhaustive seatch for a colour property attached to each of the superconcept classes of which Clyde is a member. It does not increase the efficiency of locating relevant information about the colour of Clyde. It would be more efficient to phrase the question: "Is there a colour proposition attached to Clyde?", and if the answer is no, proceed up the subconcept-superconcept hierarchy asking the same question of each successive superconcept.

Subconcept-superconcept hierarchies organise and formalise the relationships between concepts, but knowledge about concepts themselves remains unstructured. In order to answer questions about a subconcept, the information about the superconcept must be organised.

We propose that the direct knowledge about a concept, that is, the concept's associated attributes or properties, be classified by higher-order predicates called topic predicates. The topic predicates will establish subtopic-supertopic relationships between predicates. Topic hierarchies are designed to impose a classification on each network concept's associated knowledge in order to provide efficient access of topically relevant propositions for an arbitrary query.

An instance of the topic hierarchy called a topic access skeleton is attached to each individual or type concept in the network. Only those topics under which knowledge has been classified will be instantiated in any particular topic access skeleton. For example, Figure 37 gives the "APPEARANCE" topic access skeleton for "Clyde" after asserting "Clyde is pink" and "Clyde is spotted". Additions to a concept's topic access skeleton are signalled by the appearance of a topically classified predicate in an input proposition. When a proposition about "Clyde" involves a predicate appearing as a leaf of the "APPEARANCE" topic hierarchy, that proposition is inserted in the corresponding position in Clyde's "APPEARANCE" topic access skeleton.

Now, a search for the colour of Clyde begins by accessing the "Clyde" concept, but rather than looking at each proposition sequentially, the

"COLOUR" topic of Clyde can immediately be checked for a colour proposition. If this fails, each of Clyde's superconcept nodes (i.e., elephant, mammal, etc.) are searched in exactly the same fashion. If the topic access skeletons attached to each concept are approximately balanced, the access time for a classified proposition about a particular concept will be approximately proportional to the logarithm of the number of propositions "known" about that concept. The combined organisational power of the subconcept-superconcept hierarchy and the topic hierarchy should provide for a significant reduction in proposition access time.

In general, the topic organisation need not be strictly hierarchical, in order that predicates may be classified under multiple topics. In Figure 36, notice that the first order predicate "shiny" appears as an instance of both "texture" and "colour", providing two viewpoints of the same predicate.

Our first implementation of topic hierarchies (Goebel, 1977) permitted predicates to be ranked according to their "degree of relevance" to the topics under which they were classified. In an attempt to combine a fuzzy logic model of vagueness with a probabilistic mode of uncertainty, relevance rankings were specified as cumulative probability distributions over degrees of relevance. Although it is clear that some measure of relevance is useful in specifying which of several possible viewpoints is most relevant, we are now skeptical of the approach of Goebel (1977). An alternate approach for representing degrees of relevance is provided in Schubert (1978).

Schank (1975) objects to hierarchical organisation on the basis that the "organisation will not work for verbs or for nouns that are abstract or for nouns that do not submit easily to standard categories (such as teletypes)." We recognise that many relationships exist which are not strictly hierarchical, e.g., certain geometrical relations, causal relations, precedence relations, etc. Also, some categories (teletypes) may be difficult to fit into a single hierarchy, but they can be fitted into various hierarchies (machine, transducer, communications systems, etc.).

Schank believes that a canonical form is necessary for meaning representation, so he proposed conceptual dependency. This representation restricts the development of many and varied heuristic techniques for organising the propositional information. Our state-based representation in the semantic network notation permits use of the most suitable organisation for propositional constructs - the hierarchical organisation.

Semantic network representations and predicate calculus have been criticised as imposing only a local organisation on the world (Bobrow, 1975). Recently, organisational theories of knowledge have been characterised by clustering related knowledge into "chunks", in the belief that the "chunks" would reduce the computation required to isolate knowledge relevant in a particular context. Many of the recent higher-ordered knowledge organisation systems use the logical tools of predicate calculus and concept-centred organisation of networks, without becoming mere local organisers. For example, in reference to the GUS system (Bobrow et al., 1977), Kay (1976) reports "... now the contents of these slots in the dialog frames (and in slots of other frames that exist in the system) are typically other frames. These structures recurse to great depth. Of course they are not simply tree structures, but they are circular and point to one another; they're networks". Further, Hayes (1977a) provides a translation of the "main features" of KRL-0 into a many-sorted predicate logic, which he takes to be the "external meaning" of KRL expressions.

The remaining salient feature of frame-like systems is simply the idea of grouping pieces of knowledge which may be useful for understanding a particular concept or situation. Hayes (1977a) explains that a frame may be viewed as an n-ary relation between itself and its slots, which themselves may be viewed as binary relations and unary predicates (vide Bundy and Wielinga, 1978). One could therefore represent a frame within the semantic network notation. The major difference between the "frames" view of memory and the network view of memory is one of function versus structure, as noted by Schubert et al. (1978a): "A memory structure is regarded as a frame because of the kinds of knowledge and capabilities attributed to it, rather than because of any specific structural properties".

General properties of concepts must be structured to facilitate their inheritance by related concepts and individuals (Reiter, 1975; McDermott, 1975a; Moore, 1975; Mylopoulos et al., 1975). A newly instantiated individual must effectively access all known concept properties. Fahlman's (1975) example illustrates the problem. He asked how, when told a fact like "Clyde is an elephant", can a system quickly and efficiently provide access to all known elephant properties via the newly created object "Clyde"? We solved the problem with the concept and topic hierarchies.

Fahlman (1975) proposed that a network of parallel hardware elements could provide for efficient inheritance of properties. Each element represents either a concept (e.g., elephant) or a relation (e.g., "is-a") and is capable of storing "marker bits" which can be propagated through the network in parallel. The relations shared by two nodes can be found by "marking" the nodes in question, and then broadcasting the "markers" through the network and noting which relation nodes receive intersecting "marker" signals.

Those who have not despaired of a serial solution have concentrated on concept-based indexing to provide efficient access to concept properties. For example, McDermott (1975b) suggests organising concept properties into "packets" or "context" vis a vis the programming language constructs available in CONNIVER (Sussman and McDermott, 1974) or QA4 (Rulifson et al., 1972). When the assertion "Clyde is an Elephant" is made, a new index entry is created which links "Clyde" to the packet containing all known "Elephant" properties. Of course access to the "Elephant" packet does not ensure efficient access to an arbitrary "Elephant" property within the packet; McDermott (1975a) notes that the issue of how to access packets internally is related to the issue of "shallow" versus "deep" binding (vide Moses, 1970).

Moore (1975) proposes a scheme which structures asserted properties around a hierarchy of types (e.g., Elephant IS-A Mammal IS-A Animal ..., etc.). A list of subsuming types is attached to each instantiated constant or variable, e.g., the elephant named "Clyde" might have the attached type list

PHYSOB - ALIVE - ANIMAL - MAMMAL - ELEPHANT.

A type checker ensures that an individual matches only those properties which may be legally inherited from subsuming types. In this case, since "Clyde" is an instance of type "Elephant", he may inherit any property true of Elephants, Mammals, etc. The type checker works in conjunction with a pattern matcher. Moore recognises that the efficiency of the pattern matcher's operation depends on how the data base of properties is indexed. He tentatively suggests that assertions be grouped in hierarchical buckets indexed by type. This corresponds to the subconcept-superconcept organisation for networks, suggested earlier.

Cercone's (1975) and Goebel's (1977) mini-implementations have demonstrated the feasibility of using the state-based semantic network representation with organisational structures superimposed as topic hierarchies. After discussing additional representational and organisational issues, we will present the details and results of the implementations.

5. Some Pervasive and Controversial Issues

The designer of a natural language understanding system must face fundamental representation, organisation, and processing issues very early in his approach to design, and his choices are critical. The designer must decide what should be represented, that is, the content of the representation, the form of the representation, and the level to which the representation is restricted. In addition, since the representation strongly influences the organisation of knowledge, the appropriate organisational strategies and structures must be examined. On the basis of these considerations, we argue in favour of a non-primitive semantic network representation in which propositions are organised in normal form determined by the concept hierarchy.

5.1 Representational Form and Content

Is it sufficient to extract the propositional content of sentences and use that as the basis of representation, or should the representation also reflect aspects of meaning such as speaker intention, presupposition, connotation, and style? An example from Woods (1975) demonstrates the significance of these various aspects of meaning. He argues that the sentence

The dog that bit the man had rabies. (5.1)

should not have a representation identical to the sentence

The dog that had rabies bit the man. (5.2)

even though the propositional content for (5.1) and (5.2) is identical, i.e., there is a dog, there is a man, the dog had rabies, and the dog bit the man (ignoring, for simplicity, temporal considerations). He protests, correctly, that the differing descriptions of (5.1) and (5.2) are inappropriate criteria for accessing the memory node for the referent of either description. Woods further insists that (5.1) and (5.2) intuitively mean different things, so syntactic distinctions must be made between the meaning expressed in the relative clauses and the meaning expressed in the main clauses. Perhaps Woods derives this position because he believes that "intensional" and "extensional" entities must be represented by different sorts of nodes in a semantic network.*7* For example, Woods says that in some contexts "the prettiest blonde" refers to only "Sally Sunshine", yet in other contexts "the prettiest blonde" depends on the notion conveyed by the descriptive phrase. Woods believes that these contexts are distinquished by different sorts of nodes (or sub-networks). We believe that terms (or nodes) already encompass both extensions and intentions, and that a syntactic distinction is not appropriate to distinquish extensional and intensional nodes. It is appropriate to explain the conditions under which a term contributes to the truth value of a sentence through its intension rather than through its extension alone. Woods´ differentiation between intensional and extensional entities parallels the distinction between transparent and opaque readings which we illustrated with sentence (1.5) "John wants to marry the prettiest girl". The syntactic distinction lies in the relative scope of the "wants" modal operator and the existential quantifier of sentence (1.5). Many additional examples are lucidly illustrated in Schubert (1976).

We propose that a distinction be made between the propositional content of sentences and their pragmatic aspects. Their different pragmatic aspects generate the different meanings of sentences like (5.1) and (5.2). We agree with Woods that the internal meaning representation of a sentence should reflect both its propositional content and its pragmatic aspects, but the two sorts of information should not be inextricably mixed. Mingling propositional and pragmatic information would handicap comprehension processes which must utilise any acquired knowledge. Woods´ special syntactic representational device would also encumber the matching process since the matching processes seeking suitable referents for (5.1) and (5.2) would depend on the original text. In contrast, Schank (1975) has presented convincing reasons why an internal representation should be in a canonical form, relatively independent of the original English sentence. Mingling propositional and pragmatic information about utterances would disperse pragmatic information about a particular section of discourse over the propositional data base. Information about speaker intentions and assumptions would be buried with knowledge about dogs, people, etc. We maintain that a separate model for discourse status (speaker intentions and the like) is necessary. This model is the proper place for semantic information.

We limit our discussion of the form of representation to the issue of property inheritance. Our extended semantic network notation is capable of expressing any arbitrary proposition expressible in English. But any system designed for reasoning about the real world must also effectively exploit property inheritance within generalisation hierarchies. Conceptual entities typically consist of many components, the relationship between these components is valuable information. We require a mechanism which allows inheritance of the relationships from components to corresponding components within a conceptual entity. For example, the attachment relationships between the body parts of birds would require nontrivial inference processes to transfer to other similarly structured animals.

The method of "variable-sharing" was proposed by Hayes (1977) and adapted by Schubert et al. (1978) to solve this problem and allow for trivial transfer of relationships. We recommend that the knowledge associated with a generalisation hierarchy be stored as a set of implicative propositions which share one universally quantified node and any number of existentially quantified nodes dependent on the universally quantified node. The antecedents of the implications involve the universally quantified node as argument and correspond to concepts making up the generalisation hierarchy in the manner of hierarchies described above. Thus the implicants of a concept are accessible by topic rather than a long list of propositions involved in the concept. This mechanism facilitates addition of new information and we speculate that it is possible to organise other than monadic concepts, say relational concepts, hierarchically as well.

5.2 The Problem with Semantic Primitives

The expressive power and formal interpretability of the state-based representation contrasts with Schank´s conceptual dependency representation and Wilks´ preference semantics representation. To argue against the use of a small number of very general primitive predicates for representing meaning in natural language utterances, we contrast the methods of Schank (1972) and Wilks (1973) with the network oriented state-based representation.

Conceptual dependency evolved over approximately six years to the MARGIE system (Schank et al., 1973). The system is rich in semantic representation which was designed to facilitate paraphrase, inference, and machine translation. The following example of output illustrates Margie´s limited success in "paraphrase" and "inference" modes.

INFERENCE MODE

INPUT: John told Mary that Bill wants a book.

OUTPUT: A book about what?
Mary knows that Bill wants a book.
Bill wants to come to have a book.
Bill wants someone to cease to have a book.
Bill wants to read a book.

PARAPHRASE MODE

INPUT: John killed Mary by choking Mary.

OUTPUT: John strangled Mary.
John choked Mary and she died because she could not breathe.
Mary died because she was unable to inhale some air and she was unable to inhale some air because John grabbed her neck.

Schank represents meaning structures with a graphical notation which divides words into four conceptual categories. These categories are picture producers [PP], picture aiders [PA], action aiders [AA], and actions [ACTS] and they correspond closely to nouns, adjectives, adverbs, and verbs, respectively. Margie´s fundamental structural unit is the "conceptualisation" which is a graphical structure that links conceptual categories together. The conceptualisation symbols include conceptual tense markers (to indicate timeless or continuing conceptualisations), conceptual cases (analogous to and certainly influenced by the linguistic case structure of Fillmore, 1968), and primitive actions.

Schank currently uses four primitive conceptual cases as subgraphs in a conceptualisation graph. These cases include the "objective" case, which relates an objective PP to an ACT; the "recipient" case, which relates a donor PP and a recipient PP to an ACT; the "directive" case, which relates direction (to and from) to an ACT; and the "instrumental" case, which links conceptualisations instrumental to an ACT to a conceptualisation containing the ACT. In addition to primitive conceptual cases, Schank uses only fourteen primitive actions from which all other actions are derived. These primitive actions are: PROPEL, MOVE, INGEST, EXPEL, GRASP, PTRANS, MTRANS, ATRANS,

SMELL, LOOK-AT, LISTEN-TO, CONC, and MBUILD.

Wilks´ preference semantics also represents the meaning content of natural language utterances with a uniform structure of primitives. Wilks has concentrated on machine translation, from English to French, of small input paragraphs and has reported reasonably good translation.

Preference semantics represents each meaning sense of a word by a "formula". A formula is derived from the binary decomposition trees developed by Lakoff (1972). The formula is a tree structure of semantic primitives interpreted formally using dependency relations. A formula for the action of "drinking" follows

((ANI SUBJ)((FLOW STUFF) OBJ)(SELF IN)((THIS(ANI(THRU PART))) TO)(MOVE CAUSE))

The rightmost element is called the "head" and it represents the conceptual category to which the formula belongs. A sentence is represented by a network of formulas which is called a template. A template always includes an agent node, an action node, and an object node in addition to any other nodes that may depend on these three formulas. Formulas determine how other places in the template should be filled. Thus "drink" would "prefer" a "flow stuff" as object and an "animate" as subject. "Prefer" is the correct word to use because if either a non "animate" subject or a non "flow stuff" object is the only choice available, the utterance will still be recognised metaphorically. The template finally accepted for a fragment of text is the one in which the largest number of formulas have their preferences satisfied. This very simple device is able to perform most of the work of a syntax and word sense ambiguity resolving program.

After the local agent-action-object templates have been established for fragments of input text, preference semantics attempts to tie these templates together in an overall meaning structure for the input. "Paraplates" are attached to formulas for English propositions so that they range across two, not necessarily contiguous, templates. A semantic block is the structure of mutually connected templates. The representation of English in formulas, templates, and semantic blocks is accomplished in the "basic" mode of preference semantics. Whenever sentences cannot be resolved into a semantic block by the basic mode, Wilks employs the "extended" mode, which utilises common sense inference rules. The extended mode attempts to construct the shortest possible chain of rule-linked template forms from previous text containing one of its possible referents. This chain represents Wilks´ solution to the ambiguity problem.

After a semantic block is constructed, French generation proceeds by "unwrapping" the block. The generation routines do not deepen the representation.

Wilks is, perhaps, the most vocal advocate favouring the use of a small number of primitive predicates to represent meaning. Indeed his representation is based almost entirely on approximately sixty primitive predicates. In a recent position paper, Wilks (1977), appears to soften that stance, yet remains vague. In particular, Wilks cites Hayes (1974, 1977) for presenting a number of sophisticated (radical and non-radical) arguments against the use of semantic primitives as Schank and Wilks use them. Wilks writes:

> "One aspect of these criticisms is not radical - in the sense of questioning the very basis of primitives - but it is a demand by Hayes that primitive systems give a more explicit account of the rules regulating inferences concerning a primitive for substance, like STUFF. This demand for greater explicitness is a good one, though there is reason to doubt that any coherent and consistent metaphysics of substance can in fact be given. Two and a half millenia of philosophy have failed to provide one, yet through out that time everyday conversation about substances, such as coal, oil, and air goes on unimpeded. It is important to stress this fact, so as not to fall into the error of imagining that language about substances requires such a metaphysics of substances in order to function at all. It clearly does not."

Wilks misinterprets Hayes´ remarks when he ascribes to Hayes the belief that a coherent and consistent metaphysics for STUFF is necessary for all ordinary language comprehension. At the other extreme, embedding the minimal content of terms into a minimum conceptualisation does not facilitate the human interpretive process. The original term itself suggests what content we could infer in addition to the minimal content. This idea of inference can be efficiently programmed in a semantic structure by inserting probable inferences with direct reference to the word definitions. This is simpler than analyzing the minimal representation and then looking for applicable inference rules.

Wilks rejects Hayes´ criticism that there is no model theoretic semantics for primitive based systems. Wilks feels that Hayes´ demand for such a model theoretic semantics makes Hayes´ demand for a metaphysics of STUFF radical. Wilks emphatically rejects the application of model theoretic semantics (in the manner of the semantics that Tarski constructed for logic) to the analysis of natural language meaning. Wilks believes that preference semantics evolves inevitably into a "natural language" itself. However, Wilks misconstrues "truth conditions" as serving to determine the ACTUAL truth of sentences in the object language, and gives the example of the inappropriateness of computing over a possible world. Nevertheless, possible worlds are not intended to be computational domains, but as part of an abstract conception of meaning and truth. Truth is thus only relevant to truth-determination. Model theoretic semantics does, in fact, provide a practical means for deciding truth-determination, e.g., checking whether an inference mechanism is truth-preserving.

Wilks also chides Bobrow (1975) for arguing that a primitive expansion or "paraphrase" requires a more complex match than does the original English word that the paraphrase is for. He disputes the complexity of the matching, however, since preference semantics does not operate in paraphrase mode, he uses Schank´s arguments about the paraphrase mode of Schank´s primitive based system to reject Bobrow´s critique. Examining Schank´s defense of primitive-based systems, we find the following list of advantages:

(1) Paraphrase relations are made clearer.
(2) Similarity relations are made clearer.
(3) Inferences that are true of various classes of verbs can be treated as coming from the individual (primitive) ACTs. The inferences come from ACTs and states rather than from words.
(4) Organisation in memory is simplified because much information need not be duplicated. The primitive ACTs provide focal points under which information is organised.

The increased clarity of paraphrase and similarity relations derives from Schank´s use of canonical form rather than his basing his meaning representation on primitives, (see Schubert et al. 1978 for detailed arguments). Neither can the last two advantages be traced to the use of semantic primitives. The sharing of inferences within classes of verbs can be accomplished without restating words in terms of primitive ACTS. See Cercone (1975) for the detailed example which demonstrates that both "eats" and "drinks" as sentential forms share in the implications that a single primitive "ingests" would store but they are conservative of storage space and computation time. Also, argument constraints for predicates may be shared by related "nonprimitive" predicates through a constraint inheritance mechanism analogous to the property inheritance method illustrated in section 4.

Moreover, while we see no disadvantages of non-primitive based representations, point (4) shows a major disadvantage in their elimination, namely the resultant need for matching complex primitive representations instead of originally simple propositions Examining a typical "restaurant script" such as Schank proposes for "John dined at a restaurant" convinces us of the complexity of matching. Schank's method stores John's actions in the restaurant as a sequence of scenes, partially obtained from the restaurant script, which represent several successive conceptualisations about "restaurant dinings". An inquiry such as "Did John dine at a restaurant" requires another construction of the complex succession of conceptualizations about "restaurant dining". Then the succession of conceptualizations would have to be matched. The task is not trivial. Wilks entire primitive-based system is spared this complication since the system was designed for sentence by sentence translation and not question answering.

Elsewhere we (Cercone and Schubert, 1975) present arguments which illustrate the need for a meaning representation more detailed than the oversimplified meaning formulas of both Schank and Wilks. We maintain that no representation of meaning is adequate until it captures many of the same notions that people realise when they comprehend language utterances. Our version of what walking means to people is at least an order of magnitude more complex than the definitions Schank and Wilks allow for walking, since their formulas also admit other complex concepts such as running, skipping, skating, shuffling, and hopping under the same meaning formula. Our illustration demonstrates that the semantic network formalism was equal to the representation task and also dramatised the acutal complexity of ordinary concepts when expressed in the primitive-based representations of Schank and Wilks. The meaning formulas of primitive-based representations do single out those properties most frequently needed for comprehension and simple inferences. This is their remaining salient feature. The primitive-based representations do capture major properties of the defined concepts and we have only added minor details to them. But to rely on meaning caricatures as Schank and Wilks do, ensures that comprehension will remain of a crude sort. Non-primitive based representations can be equipped with the advantages of the Schank-Wilks approach, simply by providing lists of the most frequently needed properties for comprehension of each predicate and allowing the significant properties of concepts to become independently accessible without invoking the full meaning representation defining the concept. The complexity of a concept does not interfere with its matchability since it is retrieved by its name. Considerations of storage economy and the computational complexity of pattern-directed retrieval convince us of the limited value of primitive-based representations.

5.3 Networks or Frames

We discuss the relative advantages of semantic network organisations when compared to the organisation of frames, by considering first the effective retrieval time of topically organised networks, and that of unmodified nets. Then we consider the inherent retrieval problems associated with framelike organisations.

The expense incurred to retrieve facts relevant to an arbitrary query appears to be inversely proportional to additional storage that topic hierarchies require. Further examination reveals that the time required (cost) to access relevant facts depends directly on how effectively a topic hierarchy reduces the number of propositions that need to be accessed in a given inference task. Normally it is only necessary to access propositions at one leaf of a topic access skeleton where previously a complete scan of all propositions attached to a concept was required. The topic hierarchy allows that only the propositions at one leaf of a topic access skeleton need be accessed, instead of requiring a complete scan of all propositions attached to a concept.

In a full access skeleton with N propositions distributed somewhat uniformly over the K terminal topics of a topic hierarchy, the number of propositions scanned is reduced by a factor of 1/K. In a sample hierarchy with K=40, this would represent a significant reduction.

The descent time in the access skeleton is directly proportional to its depth and its branching factor. In a typical hierarchy with average depth of about four levels and average branching factor of about four branches per node, the depth is less than or equal to logNmax/log4 where Nmax is the maximum number of propositions attached to any concept, assuming that the access skeletons are approximately balanced. Even when hundreds of propositions are attached to a concept, the depth is not very great. By decreasing the branching factor on the nodes to less than four, and deepening the topic hierarchies, we reduce the number of propositions at any leaf of an access skeleton.

The depth of the most "populous" access skeleton is applied to all access skeletons, so the descent time will be proportional to log Nmax even for nodes with [illegible] much less than Nmax. Schubert et al. (1978) suggest path contraction, that is, elimination of all single-branch nodes, to remedy this disadvantage. Path contraction may not yield dramatic savings in access time but will reduce required storage significantly. Even without path contraction, the topically relevant access skeletons have much more rapid access than the unmodified semantic networks. We are currently developing "adaptive" topic predicates to accelerate access and reduce storage.

We must compare the information retrieval capabilities of frames and our version of semantic nets. In a network a concept is an access point for at least some of the relevant information about that concept. This is a concept-centred organisation, and the essential characteristic of the network is its structure. In a frame, information about a stereo-typed situation is grouped together, the fundamental organisation of the representation is based on the function of the items of knowledge in each separate stereo-typed situation. Frames, or frame related structures such as scripts, or nets, exhibit a form of procedural embedding of knowledge within their frame structure. The following pair of sentences illustrates the associative access of frame slots:

John unlocked his car. (5.3)

He used his key. (5.4)

It is clear that "his key" is the key for unlocking John's car door. Replace (5.3) with

John graded the exam. (5.5)

Now "his key" is understood differently. Frame theorists postulate the activation of frames for "unlocking car doors" and "grading exams" to comprehend (5.3) and (5.5). The frames contain slots for car keys and examination keys respectively, or slots for other frames to explain car keys and examination keys. They also contain information about the kind and use of keys. Frame advocates rely on clever access mechanisms to select the appropriate slots on the basis of the description "his key".

In Scragg´s (1975) network, "car" and "exam" are identified as "key nodes" with "weak links" to their descriptions, i.e., their parts and other information about these concepts such as their purpose. These "weak links", distinct from propositional links within a semantic network, gather information useful to a particular concept into a "plane". This serves the "activation" role of frames for networks. Unfortunately, the access mechanism is the Achilles heel of Scragg´s proposal.

Possible meanings of the word "key" are determined and all inverse weak links from nodes representing these meanings are followed. So "car" will be reached from "carkey" and "exam" will be reached from "examinationkey". Since "car" and "exam" are consider "key nodes" in this example, the access mechanism succeeds. But the access mechanism starts its search outside the active plane and fumbles its way back. This is probably more efficient than forward fumbling from an active key node to a key of some kind. But one shudders at the thought of tracing inverse weak links from events in which, say men and women participate.

We speculate whether or not semantic networks can be enhanced by attaching procedural knowledge so as to equip them with frame-like potential. See Schubert et al. (1978) for details.

In a semantic network, the complexity of propositional retrieval depends directly on the number of propositions relevant to a query, which in turn depends directly on how the propositional knowledge is organised. The complexity of retrieval in frame systems is not so easily determined. We must determine the effect on computational complexity of increasing the number of frames. Unfortunately, frame theorists have not as yet decided what number of frames is adequate or even when a subframe is not further divisible into other subframes. If we postulate a system of N predicates, with a typical frame in the system involving M of these N predicates such that M is much less than N at a given time, allowing that the same predicates might appear in several frames; the number of frames present in the system could be on the order of N predicates taken M at a time. For values of M and N that any realistic domain of discourse would require, the number of frames is significantly greater than N. Most authors of frames systems, including Charniak (1976), Hobbs (1977), McCalla (1977), and Havens (1977), have not concerned themselves with the computational complexity that framelike capabilities inflict on a system. They have been concerned with what sorts of triggering mechanisms are necessary for predicate instantiation. Perhaps computational complexity will be investigated when frames and framelike systems mature beyond the embryonic stage.

6. Mini-Implementations

The objective of the first implementation (Cercone, 1975) was primarily to create the semantic network from English utterances. During the first implementation we were exploring how to structure the generalisation hierarchies and the knowledge associated with them. The first implementation was programmed without quantifiers, so all general knowledge was omitted from the network. General knowledge was included on property lists of generic nodes. The second implementation (Goebel, 1977) tested the organisation of network propositions for inference purposes.

6.1 Cercone´s Mini-implementation

We explain how English is parsed in the mini-implementation which uses the lexical structure described in Cercone (1978). A semantic structure expressing a particular utterance is formed according to simple structural rules. The central role of verbs is acknowledged and preferred semantic categories for the subjects and objects of verbs guide each choice in the creation of meaning structures. Word sense disambiguation for verbs, modifiers, and nominals follows naturally in this approach, vide Cercone (1975). Extensive trial and error searches are eliminated since the interpretation takes on a "slot and filler" character. The approach to interpretation is almost completely semantically oriented and syntax is used only when meaning analysis alone fails.

Initial Classification

Initially the text is read (either in discourse mode or from an external file for longer text) and broken into clauses (at present this process is unsophisticated). Each clause is then "classified" in the following manner. Words in each clause are morphologically analyzed and, based on that analysis, are classified to determine all of their possible syntactic functions. For example, the form "drinks" of the root word "drink" can only be used nominally or as an action. The root form is located in the lexicon and using affix information from the morphological analysis, all of the possibilities for the word are extracted. When all words in the clause are classified, the next phase, parsing, begins.

Parsing

Traditionally, the purpose of parsing sentences has been to output syntactic trees. These trees served as input to semantic routines which generated meaning structures. Winograd (1972) and Woods (1970) tried, with limited success, to integrate the two processes and have each guide the other. Schank (1972) and Wilks (1973) stressed that syntactic processing was secondary to meaning analysis and should be necessary only if the resolution of ambiguity and meaning analysis alone had failed. Their parsing phase is almost completely semantically oriented. One important by-product in our parsing method is the detection of the correct "sense" of nominals and actions and, although not yet implemented, modifiers as well (I am restricting utterances to active voice).

Parsing begins as words in a "classified" clause are scanned from left to right in search of a suitable candidate for an action. When the action candidate is identified the sentence is separated into ((FIRST PART)(ACTION CANDIDATE)(SECOND PART)). The action candidate contains, among other things, a list of possible action "senses" that this particular root form may have. These senses are ordered by a local and global frequency count scheme, to be described later. Templates are associated with word senses as described in Cercone (1975). For example the sense *GIVE1 of the root form "give" has a template X GIVE Y Z and an alternative (ALTERN) template X GIVE Z TO Y. The template is used to guide the parsing. In this example X, Y, and Z are variables representing the arguments of the predicate "give" that we expect to find in the surface utterance, in the given order. If an argument is not present in the utterance, the implication template can be used to infer arguments. More detailed information concerning the arguments is obtained by examining the network propositions; for the sense of "give" in question, those which involve the arguments. Thus X would represent an ANIMATE nominal capable of "giving".

This is similar to what Schank does when parsing in conceptual dependency theory. If the words in the surface utterance do not satisfy the constraints for arguments, one of four reasons is likely. First, alternate syntactic constructions could exist. Second, a different "sense" of the action is "correct". Third, the particular action-candidate is not the valid action of the clause. Finally, some other reason, like slang expressions or a metaphor might be the cause.

Whenever arguments fail to satisfy a predicate, a search for alternative implication templates begins. If this fails the list of senses for the root form is further examined. If other senses of the action candidate exist, they are examined further to see if arguments in the surface utterance match variables in the template. This procedure is repeated until the correct sense of the action candidate is found or the list of senses is exhausted. If the sense list is exhausted, scanning continues in the surface clause for another suitable action candidate and the process is repeated.

The matching of predicates´ arguments in surface text to variables in implication templates also requires finding the correct sense of nominals and modifiers. The sentence "A drinker drinks many drinks" has as the second argument of the predicate "drinks" the word "drinks". Possible nominal senses for that "drinks" include an alcoholic beverage, a body of water (throw Howard into the drink), or a thirst quencher. Thus, if the first sense of a nominal fails as argument, all other senses must be examined before deciding not to accept it as argument. This reasoning applies with respect to modifiers in a similar but not identical fashion. For instance, a "yellow cake" is a type of cake much like a chocolate cake, whereas a "yellow car" is something that is yellow and something that is a car. Using these methods, sentences such as "A ´drinker´ ´drinks´ many ´drinks´" and "The pilot ´banked´ his plane near the river ´bank´ over the ´bank´ that he ´banks´ on for good ´banking´ service" present little difficulty.

Morphological analysis is important since only those forms that can authentically be considered as actions need be examined. In the example, "A drinker drinks many drinks" morphological analysis eliminates "drinker" immediately as an action candidate, permitting us to identify the correct action candidate.

The way that Schank and Wilks defined and used semantic "primitives" indicates how they used their intuitions to establish meaning representations. One way in which my intuition has shaped the experimental program can be shown with the following superficial scheme for choosing word senses.

```
                          "bank"
                            |
                            |
     |-------------|--------------|--------------|
     |             |              |              |
  (g1,l1)       (g2,l2)        (g3,l3)        (g4,l4)
  (16,0)        (92,0)         (47,0)         (12,0)
```

Each sense of a word has associated with it, gi´s and li´s which denote frequency counts for "global" and "local" usage of the ith meaning sense of the word. Whenever a term is encountered, the local frequency counts are first examined to see if any context has been established in the dialogue thus far. They are all zero in the example, so no context has been established; then the global frequency counts are examined. According to highest frequency of use the second sense is selected as the most likely candidate. If it fails, then the third, first, and fourth senses would be selected in that order. If the third sense turns out to be correct, the local frequency count is set to one, and, whenever the term "bank" is encountered, the third sense will be selected first and its local frequency count will be incremented by one (if it is the correct sense). This would continue until the third sense fails to be correct. At this point we would examine the second, first, and fourth senses until we arrive at the correct meaning sense (i.e. the ith term). The l3 is added to g3, li is set to one (non zero), l3 is reset to zero, and the ith meaning sense is selected whenever the term "bank" is encountered.

The parsing phase also generates a list of modifiers found in a clause. The modifiers are classified as to function, and associated with correct predicate arguments they modify.

Once the parsing phase has been completed, the meaning representation is built for the clause, and that structure is integrated into the semantic network, vide Schubert (1976). The first step involves building an intermediate structure based only on the predicate of the clause and its arguments. This initial structure may be altered to accomodate other information detected in the parsing phase. This information mainly includes modifiers. Though only some adjectival modifiers are now analyzed, however adverbial and quantificational are planned.

Appendix A presents the clause by clause results of the parsing phase, under the heading +++ ASSOCIATED <ACTION-ARGUMENT-VARIABLE> TRIPLES +++. The example includes the list of modifiers, further classified according to function, and associated with the correct predicate arguments they modify. The semantic network is then generated as the meaning representation of the input sentence.

6.2 Goebel's Mini-implementation

Goebel's (1977) mini-implementation refined, complemented, and extended the Cercone's earlier mini-implementation. The system was programmed in the "C" programming language and runs under the UNIX operating system on a PDP 11/45 with 64k bytes of mainstore. Goebel (1977) supplied parts of the following description of his mini-implementation.

This mini-implementation was primarily designed to test the topic hierarchy schema, so input to the program took the form of "English-like" predicate calculus formulae.

Each node in the semantic network is represented by a unique record consisting of various fields depending on the type of node (proposition, predicate, constant, or variable) being represented. All links to other nodes are represented by a LINK record consisting of type and pointer fields.

Proposition nodes have a field for assertion time and fields for links to conceptual constituents (predicate or operator, and arguments), scope links to quantified nodes within the scope of the predicate or operator, and links to superordinate (embedding) propositions. For propositions representing logical conjunctions or disjunctions, the conjuncts or disjuncts are sorted by the index of the first predicate node found in each constituent. For example, if the predicates "dark" and "horse" appear in the internal dictionary in that order, the asserted conjunction

[[Jack horse] & [Jack dark]]

will be stored as

[[Jack dark] & [Jack horse]].

So inference is not necessary to determine whether two differently ordered conjunctions or disjunctions are equivalent.

A functional notation is provided which permits reference to an individual concept by its participation in an atomic network proposition. For example, the expression

(father-of Fred)

is a functional reference to Fred's father, whoever he may be. This facility works only for existing nodes; unresolved functional references do not cause the creation of new nodes. We should be cautious about creating new nodes since indiscriminant creation of new nodes could quickly lead to data base inconsistency. For example, if the proposition

(Sally sister-of Fred)

has been asserted, the functional references

(father-of Sally), (father-of Fred)

refer to the same father, but reasoning is required to recognise this fact in order to refrain from creating two new individual concepts.

The implementation explicitly inserted subtopic-supertopic relations to form arbitrary topic hierarchies. For example, the "APPEARANCE" topic hierarchy of Figure 8 would be defined as follows:

[APPEARANCE supertopic-of COLOUR TEXTURE PATTERN]
[COLOUR supertopic-of yellow pink green]
[TEXTURE supertopic-of shiny rough smooth]
[PATTERN supertopic-of striped spotted checked].

The experimental implementation uses a simple proposition classification scheme based on the recognition of individuals (e.g., Clyde, peanut37) and type concepts (e.g., elephant, mammal, animal) in input propositions. For example, the assertion "Elephants are grey" would be classified under the "COLOUR" topic in the "APPEARANCE" topic access skeleton for the "elephant" concept. Schubert et al. (1978) present a detailed description of an automatic classification mechanism based on the logical form of propositions.

A retrieval request for topically classified propositions takes the form of a concept name followed by a topic name. The request

Clyde;APPEARANCE

would retrieve all the classified "APPEARANCE" propositions about "Clyde". Clearly, this facility can support a sophisticated question-answering system.

The prototype propositional data base model had been programmed to demonstrate the programmability of the topic hierarchy organisation. Procedures for defining and superimposing a topic hierarchy organisation on the propositional data base were implemented and examples are given in the latter half of Appendix A. Propositions were classified by a focus-finder routine, an argument-topic-access-skeleton routine, and an assert-proposition-in-category routine.

Cumulative credibility distributions were attached to propositions and topic definitions but were not used by system. Since the time of the implementation, the use of these credibility distributions has undergone significant change.

Internally, topic structures were represented as linked lists of integer indices. This may present difficulties when we attempt to implement a larger, more comprehensive system. Appendix A reproduces an essentially unaltered listing of a terminal session with the mini-implementation.

7. Concluding Remarks

7.1 Critical Assessment

The advantages of a non-primitive based representation for natural language utterances have been demonstrated by the two mini-implementations. Primitive representations for factual knowledge are cumbersome since the further the reduction to primitives is carried, the more computation bound the resulting representation becomes. Our state-based representation, easily encoded in the extended semantic network notation, has the added advantages of intuitive clarity and formal interpretability (in the Tarskian sense). The network formalism is regarded as a computer-oriented logic distinguished by the addition of associative access paths from concepts to propositions; this device is a clever indexing scheme.

Specific proposals were made for representing logical and natural language quantifiers. These proposals are aimed at enhancing the expressive power of semantic networks; they may not be computationally optimal. The semantic network representation easily expresses intentionality, which has proved problematic in many representations, and other propositional attitudes. The arbitrary (and unnecessary) distinction between actions and states, and between intentional action and purposive causation was examined in detail. Our representation remedied logical inadequacies that have appeared in other representations, especially inadequacies with quantifiers and connectives.

The handling of vagueness, the lexical meanings of complex concepts, and overall knowledge organisation all raise additional notational problems in the representation of informal knowledge. Beyond these relatively static issues lie the more dynamic issues of actual language interpretation and generation, plausible inference, learning, and the interplay between procedural and factual knowledge. We have speculated on solutions to these problems in the context of the state-based representation.

While we feel it is important to recognise the distinction between representations and organisations, we note that the distinction has a fuzzy boundary. The topic hierarchy is simply a relational structure which can be represented within the proposition network, permitting a system to reason ABOUT topics. We believe that existing knowledge representations which do not initially (or ever) distinguish between representation and organisation (e.g.,

McCalla, 1977) can avoid needless complexity by representing their relational structures within proposition based networks.

One cannot overstate the advantages of a logical approach to investigating and developing knowledge representation and organisation. Contrast the clarity of Reiter's (1975) approach to the inheritance of properties to the approaches of McDermott (1975b) or Moore (1975). The second order nature of topic organisations introduces the idea of "knowledge about knowledge", and this inspires speculation about methods for identifying and using different "levels" of knowledge.

Topic hierarchies are suitable for organising other kinds of knowledge, in addition to knowledge of attributes or properties. Topic hierarchies can be constructed for knowledge about actions. Schank (1972) used an organisation similar to a topic hierarchy to organise primary inferences associated with his primitive action concepts. For example, Schank's abstract transfer primitive "ATRANS" may be viewed as a supertopic of the first order predicates "buy", "sell", "trade", etc.. One of the "pieces" of knowledge associated with "ATRANS" which is inherited by the first order concepts is the fact that some object has changed possession.

Hopefully, the logical nature of the topic hierarchy approach will provide a unifying framework in which to view current and future organisations of propositional knowledge.

7.2 Plans for Future Research

Three distinct areas present challenges for continued progress. A more complete implementation should include a larger vocabulary within a question-answering framework. The mini-implementations described in section 6 will be coalesced and extended.

We will develop special purpose representations to integrate with the state-based representation. These special purpose representations will efficiently compute numerical and spatial aspects of linguistic processes. The representation must also be extended to include vague information.

Our present approach to parsing frustrates our ambition for language comprehension. Parsing can be improved by expanding the present capabilities to bring major implications of action concepts into direct focus. This interpretative phase must be able to accept a larger class of English utterances and perform computations such as anaphoric disambiguation routinely.

The organisation of knowledge presents perhaps the most severe challenges. The topic hierarchies require refinements and we are experimenting with "adaptive" topic hierarchies to test some non-hierarchical organising algorithms. We would also like to systematically include the procedural attachment of knowledge in a nontrivial way.

Acknowledgements

This research has been reported at various stages of its development and represents a collective of ideas from Len Schubert, Randy Goebel, and myself. Without the clear insight and depth of perspective which Len and Randy provided, this paper would not be possible. Errors of ommision and commision, however, remain my responsibility. Len Schubert was instrumental through all the design and development of the research reported; Randy Goebel, with Len, developed the notion of the topic hierarchy and topic access skeleton and provided a second mini-implementation to test our theory. The style and readability of this paper owe much to the persistent and tenacious editing of Carol Murchison. Her devotion to this project from the beginning was a source of constant inspiration to me. This research was supported by the National Science and Engineering Research Council of Canada under Operating Grant no. A4309.

Footnotes

1 His data base is procedure oriented in the same fashion as Winograd (1972), with Conniver (see McDermott and Sussman, 1972) replacing Microplanner (see Sussman et al, 1971).

2 Whenever a proposition is regarded as true only within a particular situational context, that context can be made an explicit premise instead of an argument of the predicate. Thus "Mary is livelier with her lovers than with her parents" (Bartsch and Vennemann, 1972) would be rephrased as "For all times t and all times s, if Mary is with a lover at time t and if Mary is with her parents at time s, then Mary is livelier at time t than she is at time s".

3 We would modify some of the binary ordering relations defined by Bruce to use endpoints of time segments (his definition) in the following way.

Instead of defining after(X,Y) iff x2<y1 where X, Y are time segments with endpoints (x1,x2) and (y1,y2) respectively, we would choose to define after(X,Y) as after(X,Y) iff (Ax∈X)(Ay∈Y)[x GE y]. This allows the event associated with time segment X to terminate at precisely the same time as the event associated with time segment Y initiates.

4 Note that it is only the representation, not the manipulation or formal semantics of modal constructions that is at issue here. However, it is reassuring that the "possible worlds" semantics devised in recent years by modal logicians appears to provide an adequate basis for the formal semantical analysis of modal constructions.

5 It would seem that the human interpretative process does not proceed on the basis of the minimal conceptualisation formed by embedding the minimal content of terms into the conceptualisation. Rather the "original term itself" suggests what we could infer in addition to the minimal content. This seems like a reasonable view on the basis of efficiency considerations as well. It should be much simpler to insert probable inferences in a semantic structure by direct reference to the word definitions instead of analyzing the minimal representation and then looking for applicable inference rules.

6 Lexical items are items of vocabulary, ususally, but not necessarily, words. According to the traditional, Aristotelian view, they have both lexical (material) and grammatical (formal) meaning. This distinction between the two meanings of lexical items is useful in representing lexical items because we can divide lexical items into those best defined by material meaning, and those best defined by formal meaning. Those items whose meaning is best represented by their formal meaning belong to the closed class of lexical items. Typically, closed classes have a strictly limited membership which cannot be increased by adding new formations or adopting words from another language. Those items whose meaning is best expressed by their material meaning, expressed by synonyms, belong to the open class of lexical items. Open classes of lexical items have a large, readily increasing membership. The division of lexical items into classes is used in parsing. The representation of an appropriate lexical item can be selected from the lexicon using categories. Rather than expressing a particular sytagmatic relation among lexical items in an utterance, lexical categories are identified with classes of lexical items.

7 Extension and intension are the terms used to distinguish that to which a designator refers or applies and its meaning.

References

Anderson, J. and Bower, G. (1973) HUMAN ASSOCIATIVE MEMORY. Washington D.C.: Winston and Sons.

Bartsch, R. and Vennemann, T. (1972) SEMANTIC STRUCTURES. Frankfurt: Athenaum Verlag.

Bobrow, D. (1975) "Dimensions of Representation", in REPRESENTATION AND UNDERSTANDING. Bobrow, D. and Collins, A. (eds.), New York: Academic Press.

Bobrow, D. and Winograd, T. (1977) "An Overview of KRL, a Knowledge Representation Language", Cognitive Science, 1, 3-46.

Bobrow, D., Kaplan, R., Kay, M., Norman, A., Thompson, H. and Winograd, T. (1977) "GUS, A Frame Driven Dialog System", Artificial Intelligence, 8, 155-173.

Bruce, B. (1972) "A Model for Temporal References and its Application in a Question-Answering Program", Artificial Intelligence 3, 1-26.

Bundy, A. and Stone, M. (1975) "A Note on McDermott´s Symbol-Mapping Problem", SIGART Newsletter 53, 9-10.

Cercone, N. (1975) "Representing Natural Language in Extended Semantic Networks", Ph.D. Thesis, Technical Report TR75-11, Department of Computing Science, University of Alberta, Edmonton, Alberta.

Cercone, N. and Schubert, L. (1975) "Toward a State-Based Conceptual Representation", Advance papers of the Fourth International Joint Conference on Artificial Intelligence, 1, Tbilisi, USSR, pp 81-90.

Cercone, N. (1978) "Morphological Analysis and Lexicon Design for Natural Language Processing", Computers and the Humanities, 11, 235-258.

Charniak, E. (1976) "Inference and knowledge II", in COMPUTATIONAL SEMANTICS. Charniak, E. and Wilks, Y. (eds.), Amsterdam: North-Holland.

Cresswell, M. (1973) LOGICS AND LANGUAGES. London: Methuen.

Evans, C. (1967) "States, Activities, and Performances", Australasian Journal of Philosophy, 45, 293-308.

Fahlman, S. (1975) "A System for Representing and Using Real World Knowledge", AI Lab Memo 331, MIT, Cambridge, Massachusetts.

Fillmore, C. (1968) "The Case for Case", in UNIVERSALS IN LINGUISTIC THEORY. Bach, E. and Harms, R. (eds.), New York: Holt, Reinhart, and Winston.

Fodor, J. (1972) "Troubles About Actions", in SEMANTICS OF NATURAL LANGUAGE. Davidson, D. and Harman, G. (eds.), Boston: D. Reidel Publishing Company.

Goebel, R. (1977) "Organizing Factual Knowledge in a Semantic Network", TR77-8, Department of Computing Science, University of Alberta, Edmonton, Alberta.

Hayes, P. (1974) "Some Issues and Non-Issues in Representation Theory", in Proceedings of the AISB Conference, University of Sussex, Sussex, U.K.

Hayes, P. (1977) "In Defence of Logic", Proceedings IJCAI5, Cambridge, Massachusetts, pp 559-565.

Hewitt, C. (1971) "Description and Theoretical Analysis of PLANNER: A Language for Proving Theorems and Manipulating Models in a Robot", Ph.D. Thesis, MIT, Cambridge, Massachusetts.

Hobbs, J. (1977) "Coherence and Interpretation in English texts", Proceedings IJCAI5, Cambridge, Massachusetts, pp 110-116.

Johnson-Laird, P. (1969) "On Understanding Logically Complex Sentences", Quarterly Journal of Experimental Psychology, 21, 1-13.

Kay, M. (1976) "Xerox's GUS (Genial Understander System)", Proceedings Symposium on Advanced Memory Concepts, SRI, Menlo Park, California, microfich 5, pp 351-360.

Lakoff, G. (1972) "Linguistics and Natural Logic", in SEMANTICS OF NATURAL LANGUAGE. Davidson, D. and Harman, G. (eds.), Boston: D. Reidel Publishing Company.

McCalla, G. (1977) "An Approach to the Organization of Knowledge for the Modelling of Conversation", Ph.D. Thesis, Department of Computer Science, University of British Columbia, Vancouver, British Columbia.

McCarthy, J. and Hayes, P. (1969) "Some Philosophical Problems from the Standpoint of Artificial Intelligence", in MACHINE INTELLIGENCE. Meltzer, B. and Michie, D. (eds.), New York: American Elsevier.

McDermott, D. and Sussman, G. (1972) "The Conniver Reference Manual", AI Lab Memo 259, MIT, Cambridge, Massachusetts.

McDermott, D. (1974) "Assimilation of New Information by a Natural Language Understanding System", AI TR-291, Artificial Intelligence Laboratory, MIT, Cambridge, Massachusetts.

McDermott, D. (1975) "Symbol-Mapping: a technical problem in PLANNER-like systems", SIGART Newsletter 51, 4-5.

McDermott, D. (1975) "A Packet Based Approach to the Symbol Mapping Problem", SIGART Newsletter 53, 6-7.

McDermott, D. (1976) "Artificial Intelligence Meets Natural Stupidity", SIGART Newsletter, 57.

Montague, R. (1970) "The Proper Treatment of Quantification in Ordinary English", Department of Philosophy, University of California, Los Angeles, California.

Montague, R. (1972) "Pragmatics and Intensional Logic", in SEMANTICS OF NATURAL LANGUAGE. Davidson, D. and Harman, G. (eds.), Boston: D. Reidel Publishing Company.

Moore, R. (1973) "D-SCRIPT: A Computational Theory of Descriptions", AI Lab Memo 278, MIT, Cambridge, Massachusetts.

Moore, J. and Newell, A. (1973) "How Can Merlin Understand", Department of Computer Science, Carnegie-Mellon University, Pittsburgh, Pennsylvania.

Moore, R. (1975) "A Serial Scheme for the Inheritance of Properties", SIGART Newsletter 53, 8-9.

Moses, J. (1970) "The Function of FUNCTION in LISP", AI Lab Memo 199, MIT, Cambridge, Massachusetts.

Mylopoulos, J., Cohen, P., Borgida, A. and Sugar, L. (1975) "Semantic Networks and the Generation of Context", Proceedings IJCAI4, Tbilisi, USSR, pp 134-142.

Parsons, T. (1972) "Some Problems Concerning the Logic of Grammatical Modifiers", in SEMANTICS OF NATURAL LANGUAGE. Davidson, D. and Harman, G. (eds.), Boston: D. Reidel Publishing Company.

Quillian, M. (1968) "Semantic Memory", in SEMANTIC INFORMATION PROCESSING. Minsky, M. (ed.), Cambridge: MIT Press.

Quillian, M. (1969) "The Teachable Language Comprehender", CACM 12, 459-475.

Quillian, R. and Collins, A. (1972) "How to Make a Language User", in ORGANIZATION OF MEMORY. Tulving, E. and Donaldson, W. (eds.), New York: Academic Press.

Reichenbach, H. (1947) ELEMENTS OF SYMBOLIC LOGIC. New York: New York Free Press.

Reiter, R. (1975) "Formal Reasoning and Language Understanding Systems", Proceedings TINLAP Workshop, Cambridge, Massachusetts, pp 175-179.

Rulifson, J., Derksen, J. and Waldinger, R. (1972) "QA4: A Procedural Calculus for Intuitive Reasoning", AI Technical Note 73, Computer Science Department, Stanford University, Stanford, California.

Rumelhart, D., Lindsay, P. and Norman, D. (1972) "A Process Model for Long Term Memory", in ORGANISATION OF MEMORY. Tulving, E. and Donaldson, W. (eds.), New York: Academic Press.

Sandewall, E. (1971) "Representing Natural Language Information in Predicate Calculus", in MACHINE INTELLIGENCE, 6. Meltzer, B. and Michie, D. (eds.), New York: American Elsevier.

Schank, R. (1972) "Conceptual Dependency: A Theory of Natural Language Understanding", Cognitive Psychology, 3, 552- 631.

Schank, R. (1973) "The Fourteen Primitive Actions and Their Inferences", Stanford AI Project, Memo AIM-183, Stanford University, Stanford, California.

Schank, R., Goldman, N., Rieger, C. and Riesbeck, C. (1973) "Margie: Memory, Analysis, Response Generation and Inference on English", Proceedings IJCAI3, pp 255-261.

Schank, R. (1974) "Adverbs of Belief", Lingua, 33, 45-67.

Schank, R. (1975) "The Role of Memory in Language Processing", in THE STRUCTURE OF HUMAN MEMORY, Cofer, C. (ed.), San Francisco: W. H. Freeman.

Schubert, L. (1975) "Extending the Expressive Power of Semantic Networks", Advance papers of the Fourth International Joint Conference on Artificial Intelligence, 1, Tbilisi, USSR, pp 158-164.

Schubert, L. (1976) "Extending the Expressive Power of Semantic Networks", Artificial Intelligence, 7, 163-198.

Schubert, L. (1978) "On the Representation of Vague and Uncertain Knowledge", COLING 78.

Schubert, L., Cercone, N. and Goebel, R. (1978) "Organising Semantic Net Propositions for Comprehension and Inference", To appear in ASSOCIATIVE NETS - THE REPRESENTATION AND USE OF KNOWLEDGE BY COMPUTERS. Findler, N. (ed.).

Schubert, L., Cercone, N. and Goebel, R. (1978) "The Structure and Organization of a Semantic Net for Comprehension and Inference", TR78-1, Department of Computing Science, University of Alberta, Edmonton, Alberta.

Scragg, W. (1975) Ph.D. Thesis, University of California, San Diego, San Diego, California.

Shapiro, S. (1971) "A Net Structure for Semantic Information Storage, Deduction, and Retrieval", Proceedings IJCAI2, London, England, pp 512-523.

Strawson, P. (1959) INDIVIDUALS. London: Metheun.

Sussman, G., et al. (1971) "Microplanner Reference Mannual", Artificial Intelligence Laboratory, MIT, Cambridge, Massachusetts.

Sussman, G. and McDermott, D. (1974) "CONNIVER Reference Manual", AI Lab Memo 259A, MIT, Cambridge, Massachusetts.

Wilks, Y. (1973) "Preference Semantics", Stanford AI Project, Memo AIM-206, Stanford University, Stanford, California.

Wilks, Y. (1977) "Good and Bad Arguments About Semantic Primitives", D.A.I. Research Report 42, University of Essex, Colchester, U.K.

Winograd, T. (1972) UNDERSTANDING NATURAL LANGUAGE. New York: Academic Press.

Winston, P. (1970) "Learning Structural Descriptions from Examples", Ph.D. Thesis, MIT, MAC-TR-76, Cambridge, Massachusetts.

Woods, W. (1970) "Transition Networks for Natural Language Analysis", CACM, 13, 591-606.

Woods, W. (1975) "What's in a Link: Foundations for Semantic Networks", in REPRESENTATION AND UNDERSTANDING. Bobrow, D. and Collins, A., (eds.), New York: Academic Press.

Zadeh, L. (1972) "A Fuzzy-Set-Theoretic Interpretation of Linguistic Hedges", Journal of Cybernetics, 2, 4-34.

FIGURES

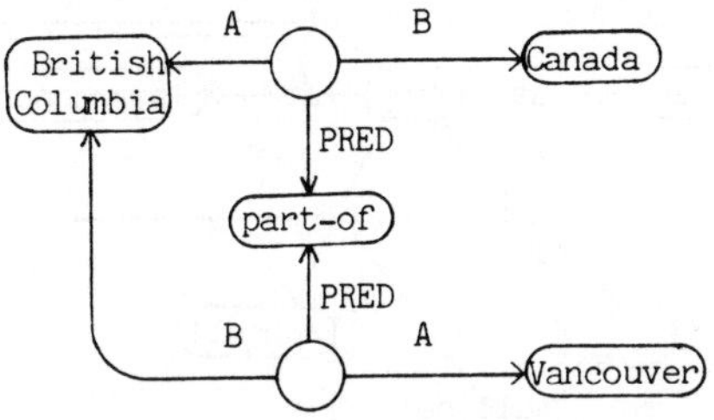

Figure 1. "Vancouver is part-of British Columbia"
"British Columbia is part-of Canada"

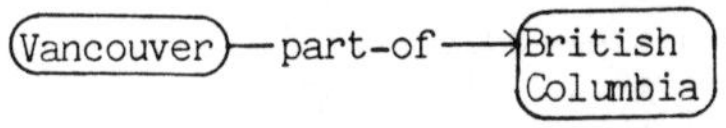

Figure 2. "Vancouver is part-of British Columbia"

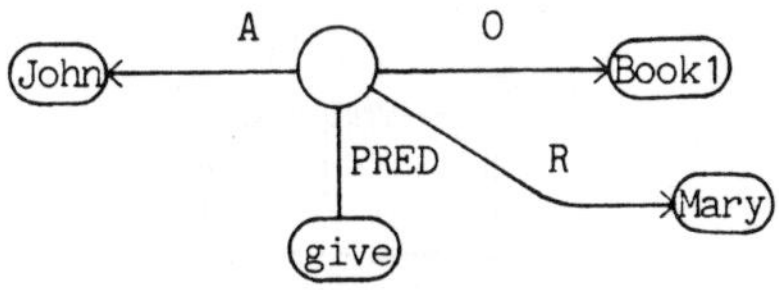

Figure 3. "John gives the book to Mary"

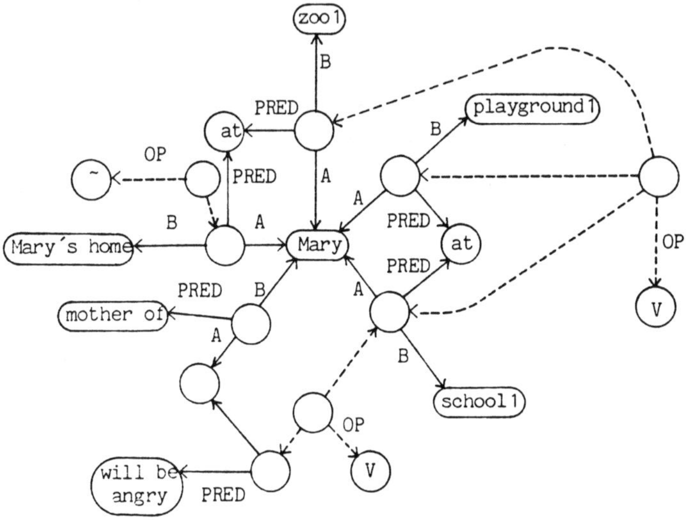

(a) Full Notation

Figure 4. "Mary is not at home; she is either at school, or on the playground, or at the zoo; if she is not at school, her mother will be angry"

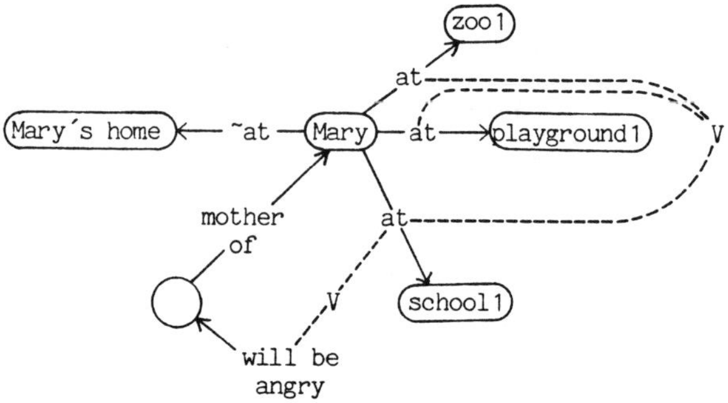

(b) Abbreviated Notation

Figure 4. (continued)

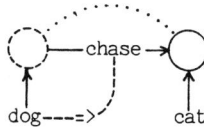

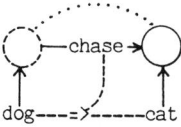

(a) (b)

Figure 5. "All dogs chase some cat"
(a) (Ax){dog(x) => (Ey)[cat(y)&chase(x,y)]}
(b) cat(f(x)) & [dog(x) => chase(x,f(x))],

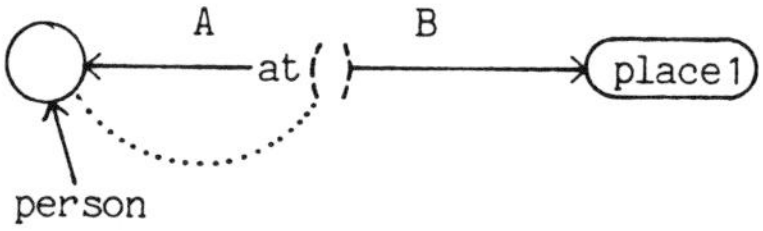

Figure 6. "There is always someone there"

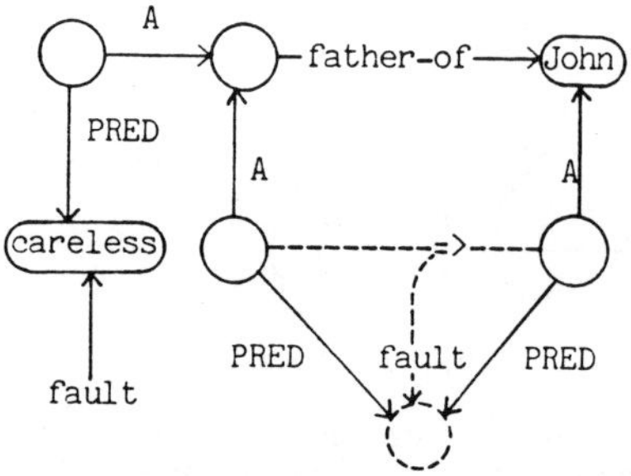

(a)

Figure 7. John has all of his father´s faults, and carelessness is one of them

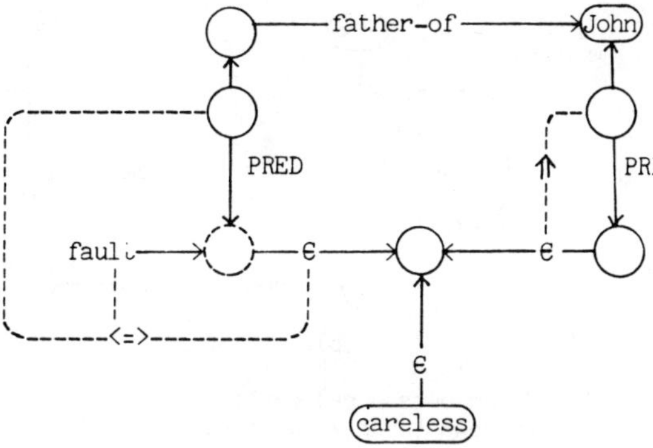

(b)

Figure 7. (continued)

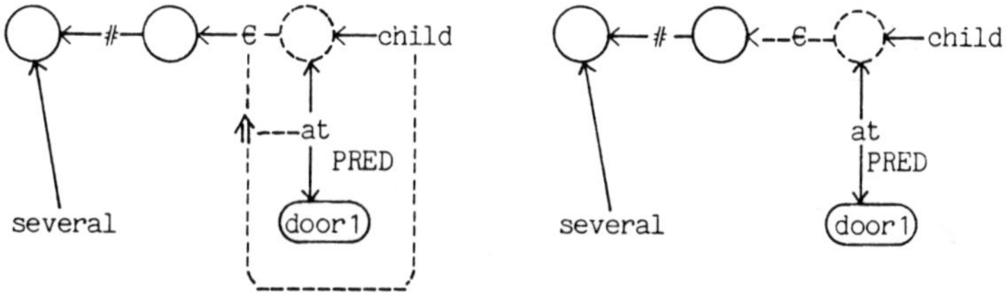

(a) (b)

Figure 8. "Several children were at the door"

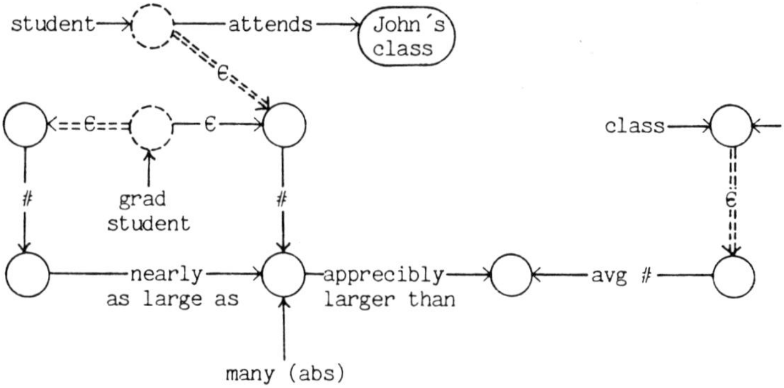

Figure 9. "Many students attend John's class.
Most of them are graduate students."

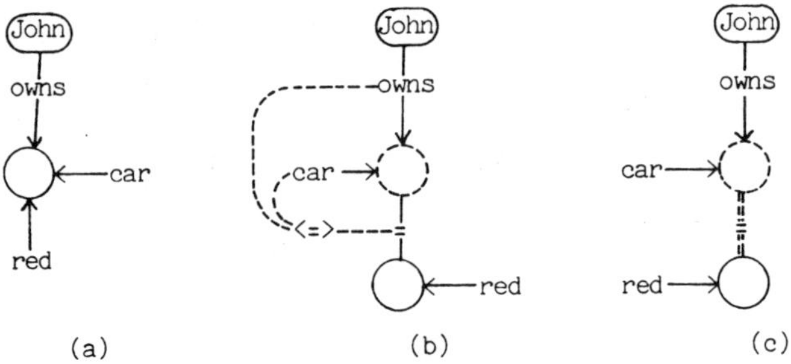

Figure 10. (a) "John owns a red car";
(Ex)[owns(John,x) & car(x) & red(x)]
(b)&(c) "John´s car is red".
(Ex)(Ay)[owns(John,y)&car(y)<=>x=y]&red(x)

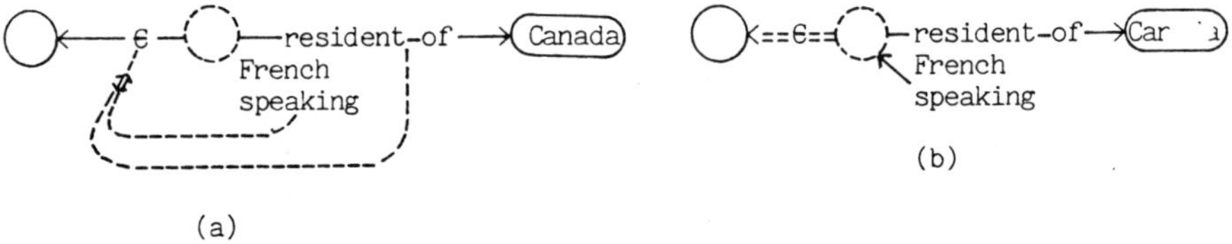

Figure 11. "The French-speaking people of Canada"
(ES)(Ax)[member(x,S) <=>
French-speaking(x)&resident-of(x,Canada)]

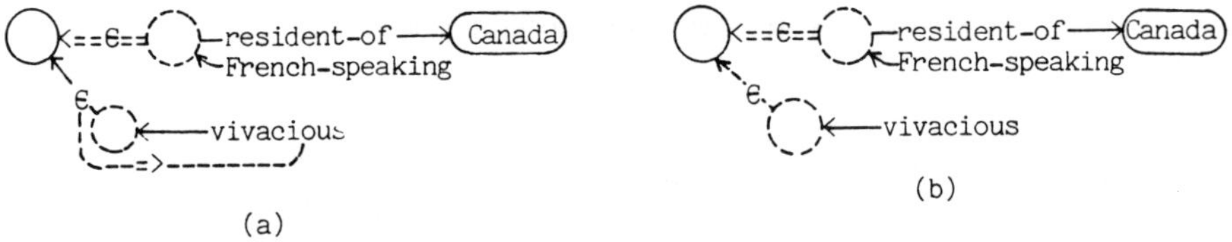

Figure 12. "The French-speaking people of Canada are vivacious"

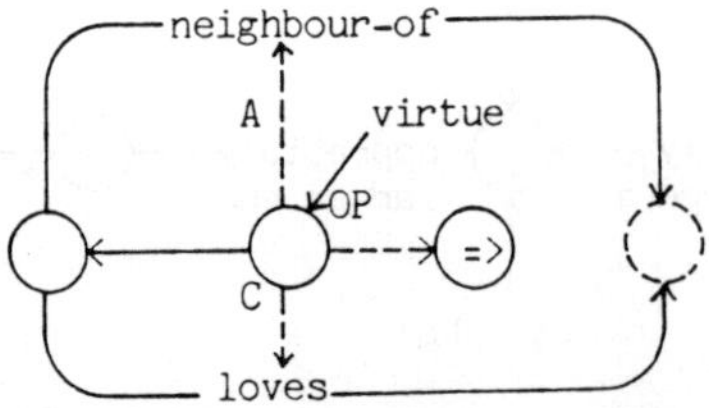

Figure 13. "Loving one´s neighbours is a virtue"
virtue{lambda x[(Ay)[neighbour(x,y)=>loves(x,y)]]}

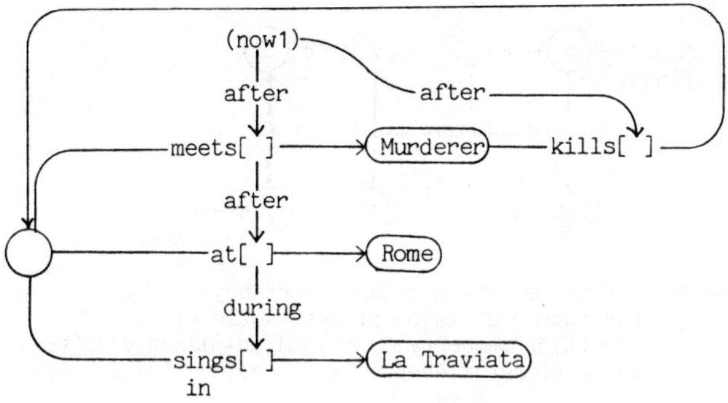

Figure 14. "While he was in Rome, before he met his murderer, he first sang in La Traviata"

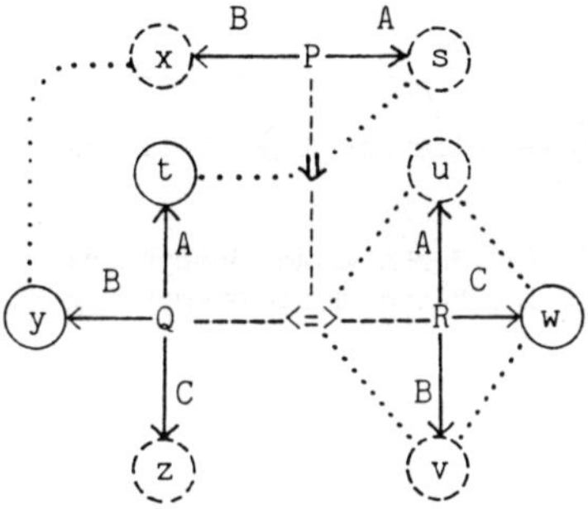

Figure 15. Indicating quantifier scopes
(Ax)(Ey)(Az){(As) P(s,x) =>
(Et)[Q(t,y,z) <=> (Au)(Av)(Ew) R(u,v,w)]}

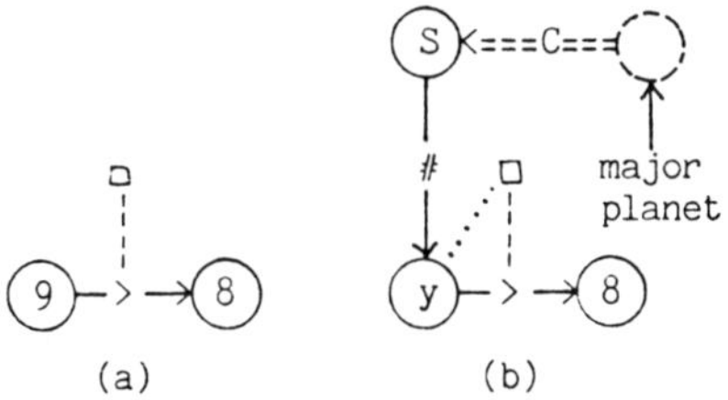

Figure 16. (a) "9 is necessarily greater than 8"
□(9>8)
(b) "The number of major planets is necessarily greater than 8"
(ES)(Ax){member(x,S)<=>major-planet(x) & □(Ey)[#(S,y) & y>8]}

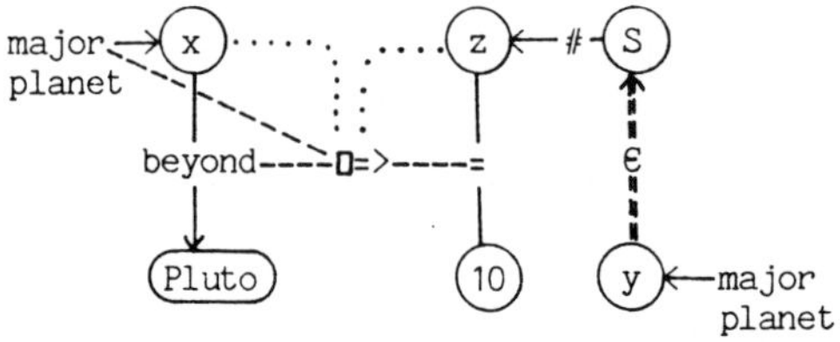

Figure 17. "If there were a major planet beyond Pluto, the number of major planets would equal 10"
(ES)(Ay){[member(y,S) <=> major-planet(y)]&[(Ex) major-planet(x)&beyond(x,Pluto)] =>(Ez)[#(S,z)&z=10]}

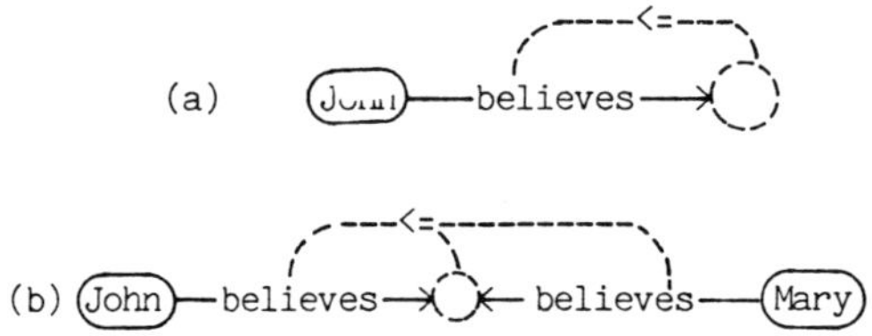

Figure 18. (a) "John knows everything"
(b) "John knows everything Mary knows"

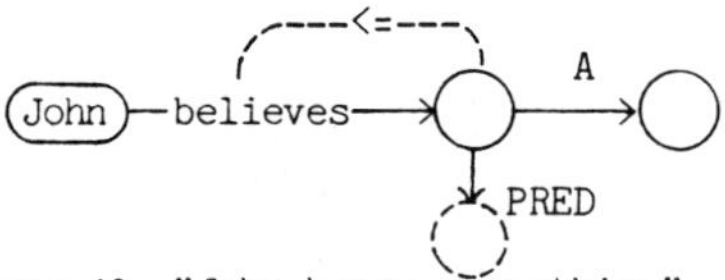

Figure 19. "John knows everything"

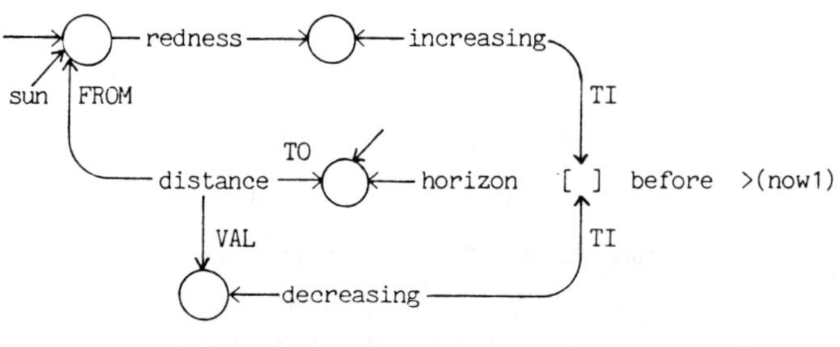

Figure 20. "The sun was getting redder and approaching the horizon"

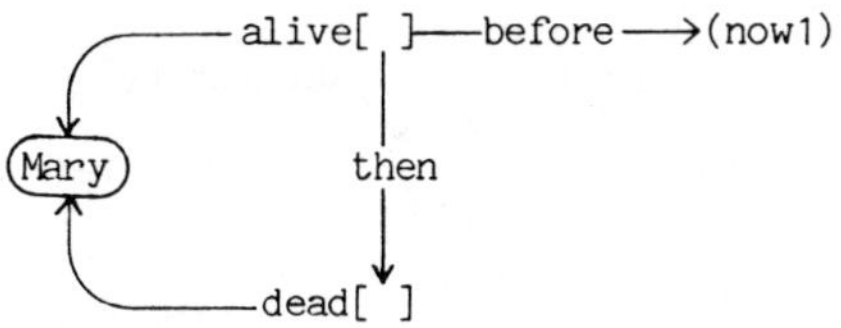

Figure 21. "Mary died"

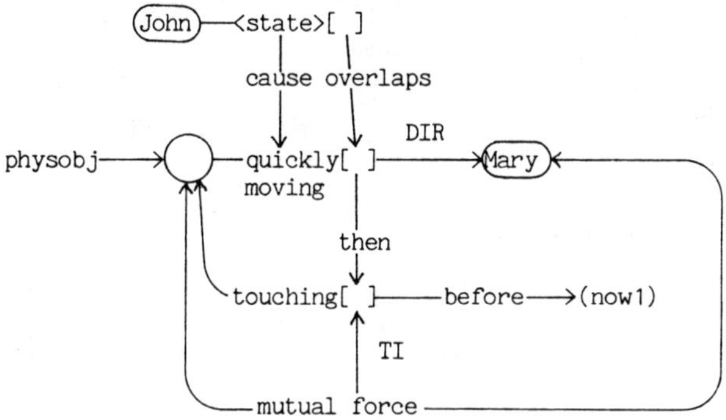

Figure 22. "John hit Mary"

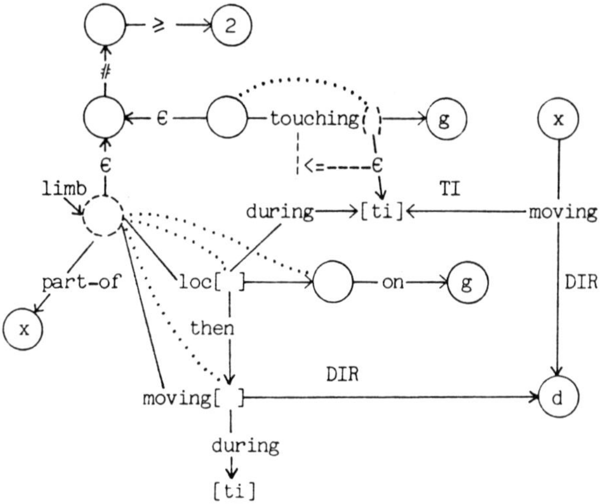

Figure 24. "x walking at time t in direction d on surface g"

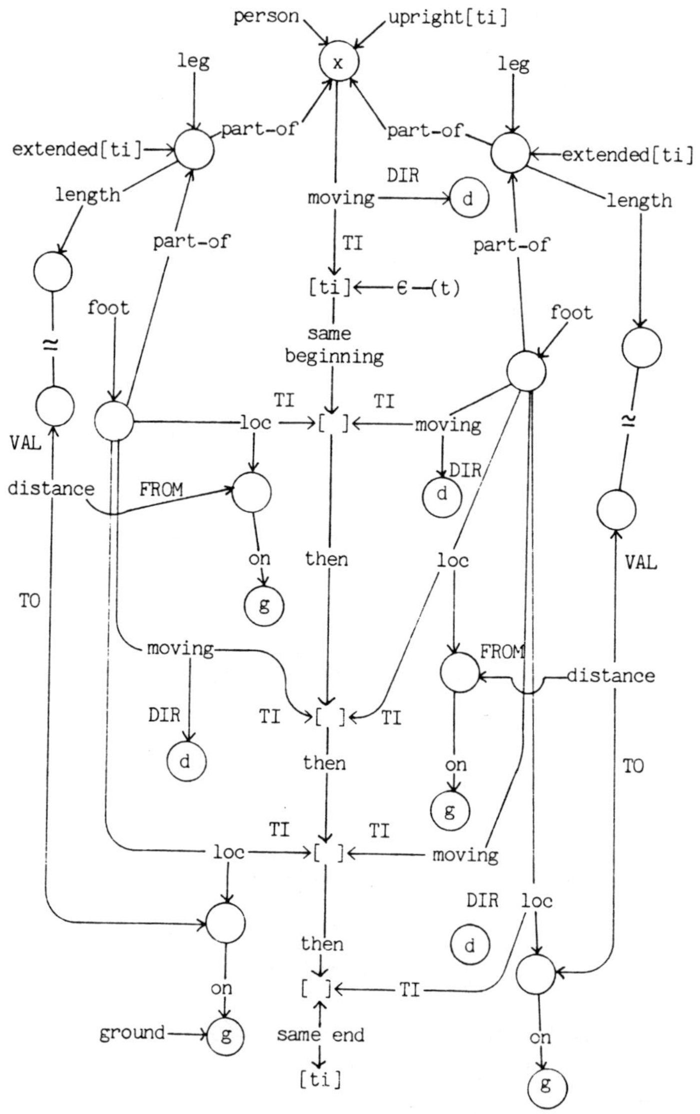

Figure 23. "Person x walking at time t in direction d on ground g."

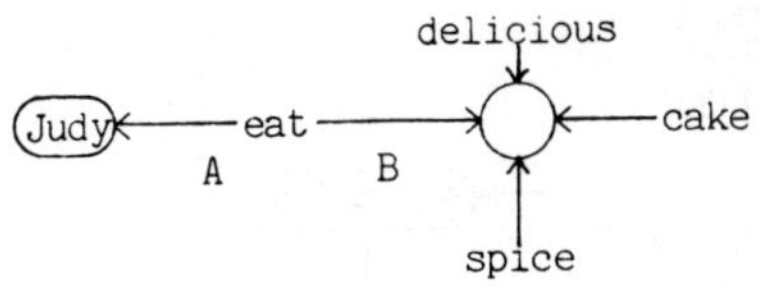

Figure 25. "Judy ate a delicious spice cake".

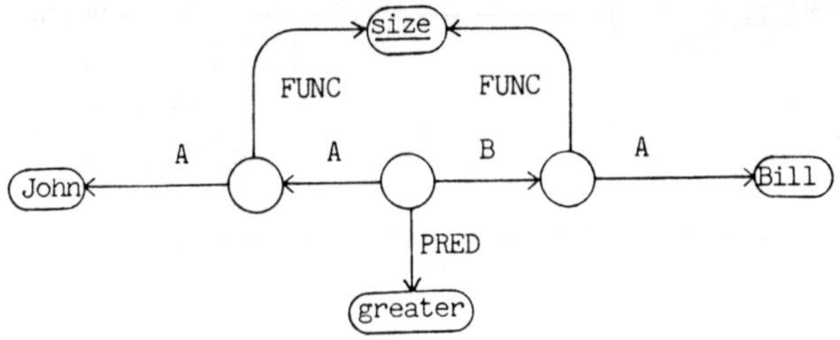

Figure 26. "John is bigger than Bill"

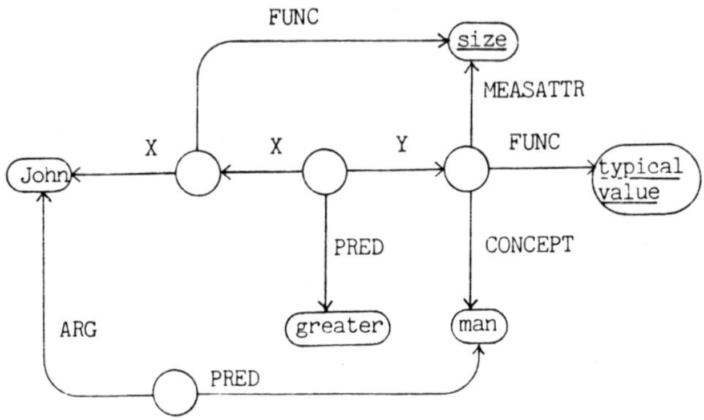

Figure 27. "John is a big man"

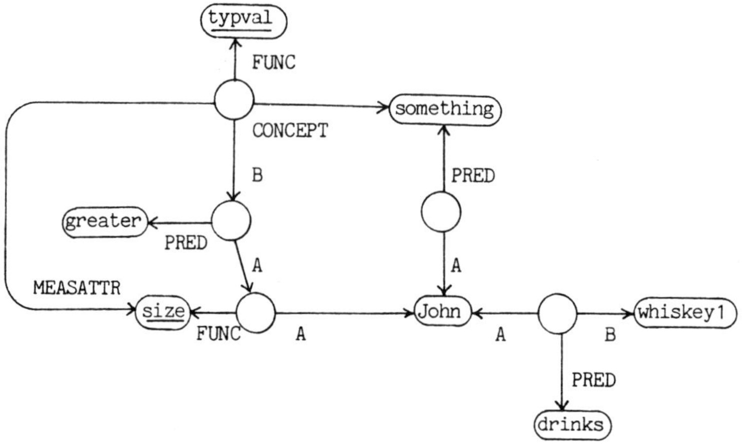

Figure 28. "Big John drinks the whiskey"

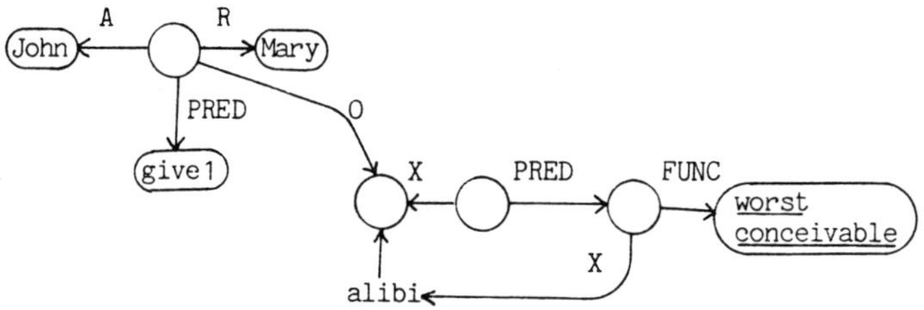

Figure 29. "John gave Mary the worst-conceivable alibi"

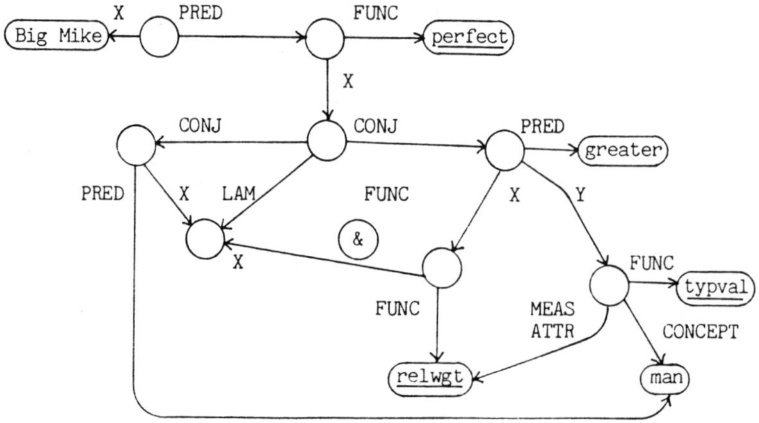

Figure 30. "Big Mike is the perfect fat man"

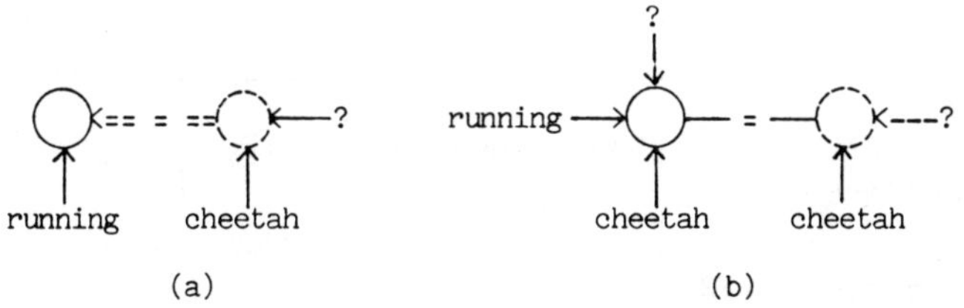

Figure 31. "The cheetah is running"
(a) (Ex){(Ay)[cheetah(y) & ?(y) <=> x=y] & running(x)}
(b) (Ex){running(x) & cheetah(x) & ?(x) & (Ay)[cheetah(y) & ?(y) => x=y]}

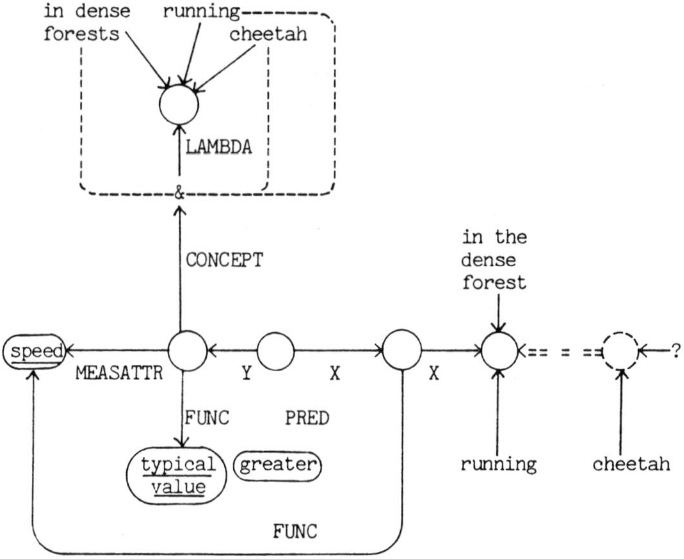

Figure 32. "The cheetah is running quickly in the dense forest"

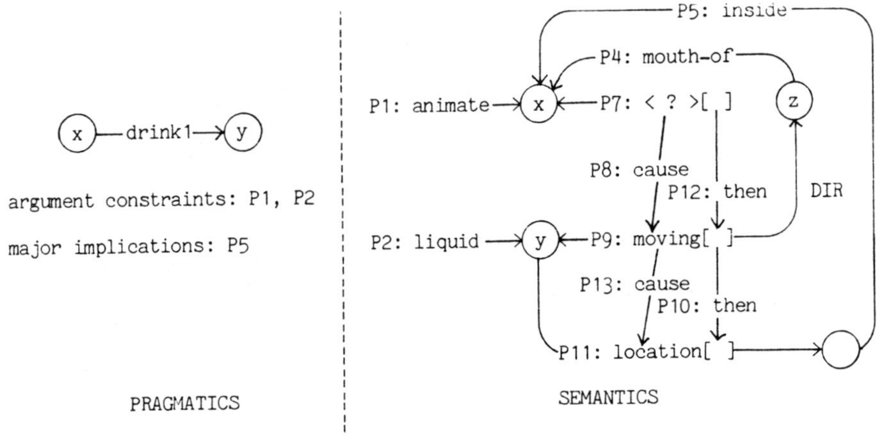

Figure 33. The ordinary sense of drinking called drink1 (as in "John drinks water").

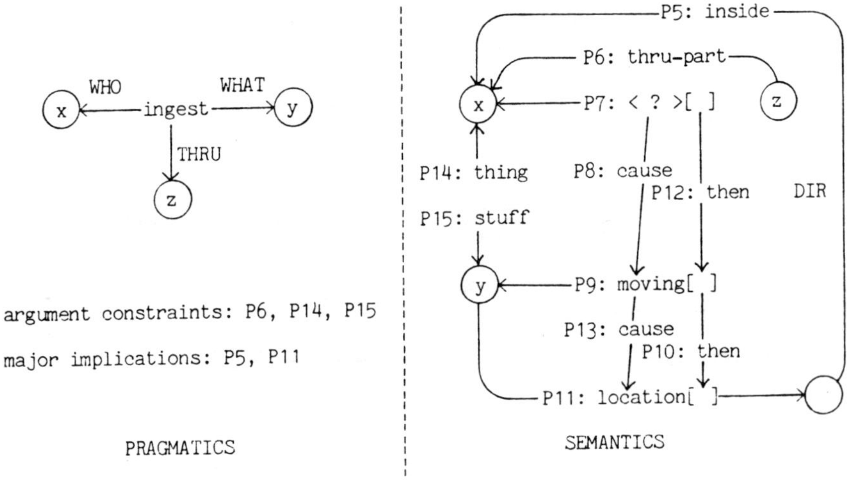

Figure 34. The properties of "ingest" (as in "John ingests medication" or "the car ´drinks´ gasoline").

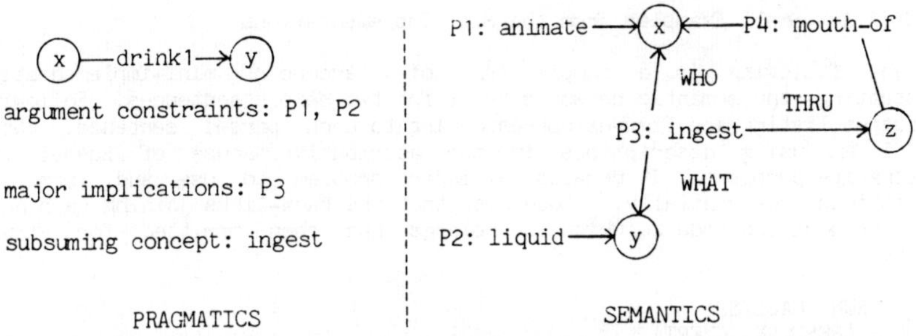

Figure 35. The properties of "drink1" (as in "John is drinking water" or "Mary drinks soda pop") using the more general concept "ingests".

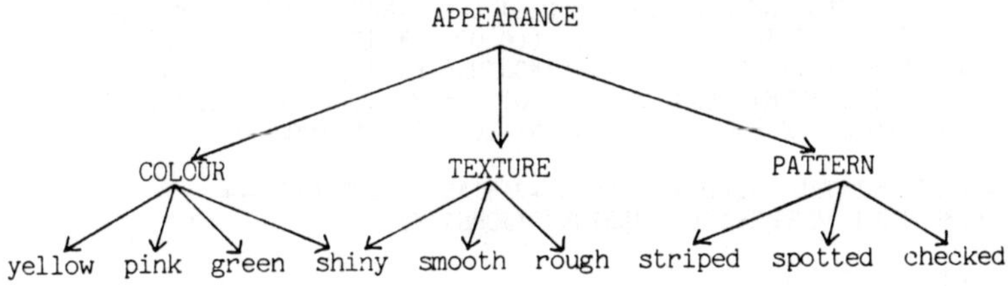

Figure 36. The "APPEARANCE" topic hierarchy.

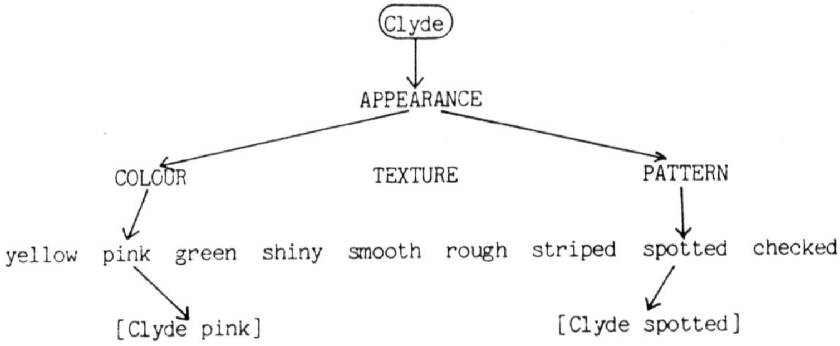

Figure 37. Clyde's partial topic access skeleton.

APPENDIX A - Small Examples from the Mini-Implementations

The following is a sample run of Cercone's mini-implementation illustrating the semantic networks built for two sample sentences. Following the output listing are figures corresponding to each parsed sentence. Note that I am using descriptions in the attributive sense of Russell for illustrative purposes. It remains a major problem to use and formulate descriptions referentially. Note also that the back-links joining each node to the proposition node to which it belongs has been ommitted for visual clarity.

```
#RUN *MACLISP
= (RESTORE 'CHKPT)
= (UNDERSTAND)
  READY
= John is drinking the delicious brown coffee. Big
= Bill drank the perfect red whiskey.

 +++ THE CLASSIFIED UTTERANCE IS +++
 ((N (NS ((0 0) (/*JOHN1)))) (A (IREG PRES ((0 0) (/*EQ1))))
  (N (NS ((0 0) (/*DRINK6))) A (PART ((0 0) (/*DRINK1 P1 P2)
 ) ((0 0) (/*DRINK1A P1 P2)) ((0 0) (/*DRINK3 P1 P2))) NM (ADJ
 CLASF ((0 0) (/*DRINK2 P1 P2)) ((0 0) (/*DRINK4 P1 P2)) ((0
  0) (/*DRINK5 P1 P2)) ((0 0) (/*DRINK6 P1 P2)))) (DET ((NS
 NP COLL)) (/*THE)) (NM (ADJ ((0 0) (/*DELICIOUS1)))) (NM (ADJ
 CLASF ((0 0) (/*BROWN1)))) (N (NS ((0 0) (/*COFFEE1)))))

 +++ ASSOCIATED <ACTION-ARGUMENT-VARIABLE> TRIPLES +++
  ((*DRINK1 *COFFEE1 Y) (*DRINK1 *JOHN1 X))

 +++MODIFIERS+++
  ((NM (ADJ CLASF ((0 0) (*BROWN1)))) Y)
  ((NM (ADJ ((0 0) (*DELICIOUS1)))) Y)

 PREDICATIVES->
 ADJECTIVES->
  ((NM (ADJ ((0 0) (*DELICIOUS1)))) Y)
  ((NM (ADJ CLASF ((0 0) (*BROWN1)))) Y)
 EXPLICIT-ADJECTIVES->
 IMPLICIT-ADJECTIVES->
 OPERATORS->

      +++ THE SEMANTIC NET +++
   *ATOM*       *VALUE*       *PROPERTY*
 PROP0001     *JOHN1        X
 PROP0002     *COFFEE1        PRED
 PROP0002     INST0003        ARG
 PROP0004     INST0003        ARG
 PROP0004     *UNS0005        PRED
 PROP0001     INST0003        Y
 PROP0006     *DELICIOUS1       PRED
 PROP0006     INST0003        ARG
 PROP0007     *BROWN1       PRED
 PROP0007     INST0003        ARG
 PROP0001     *DRINK1       PRED
```

```
+++ THE CLASSIFIED UTTERANCE IS +++
((NM (ADJ CLASF ((0 0) (/*BIG1)))) (N (NS ((0 0) (/*BILL1))
)) (A (IREG PAST ((0 0) (/*DRINK1 P1 P2)) ((0 0) (/*DRINK1A
P1 P2)) ((0 0) (/*DRINK3 P1 P2)))) (DET ((NS NP COLL)) (/*THE)
) (NM (ADJ ((0 0) (/*PERFECT1)))) (NM (ADJ CLASF ((0 0) (/*RED1)
))) (N (NS ((0 0) (/*WHISKEY1)))))


+++ ASSOCIATED <ACTION-ARGUMENT-VARIABLE> TRIPLES +++
 ((*DRINK1A *WHISKEY1 Y) (*DRINK1A *BILL1 X))

+++MODIFIERS+++
 ((NM (ADJ CLASF ((0 0) (*RED1)))) Y)
 ((NM (ADJ ((0 0) (*PERFECT1)))) Y)
 ((NM (ADJ CLASF ((0 0) (*BIG1)))) X)

PREDICATIVES->
ADJECTIVES->
 ((NM (ADJ CLASF ((0 0) (*RED1)))) Y)
EXPLICIT-ADJECTIVES->
IMPLICIT-ADJECTIVES->
 ((NM (ADJ CLASF ((0 0) (*BIG1)))) X)
OPERATORS->
 (((NM (ADJ ((0 0) (*PERFECT1)))) Y))

     +++ THE SEMANTIC NET +++
  *ATOM*       *VALUE*      *PROPERTY*
PROP0008       *BILL1       X
PROP0009       *WHISKEY1    PRED
PROP0009       INST0010     ARG
PROP0011       INST0010     ARG
PROP0011       *UNS0012     PRED
PROP0008       INST0010     Y
PROP0013       *RED1        PRED
PROP0013       INST0010     ARG
PROP0008       *DRINK1A     PRED
PROP0014       *GREATER1    PRED
INST0015       *SIZE1       MEASATTR
INST0015       *TYPVAL*     FUNC
INST0015       *SOMETHING1  CONCEPT
PROP0016       *SOMETHING1  PRED
PROP0016       *BILL1       ARG
PROP0014       INST0015     Y
PROP0014       INST0017     X
INST0017       *SIZE1       FUNC
INST0017       *BILL1       X
PRED0018       *PERFECT1    FUNC
PRED0018       INST0019     X
INST0019       *AND1        FUNC
INST0019       INST0010     LAMBDA
PROP0008       PRED0018     Y
INST0019       PROP0013     CONJUNCT
INST0019       PROP0011     CONJUNCT
INST0019       PROP0009     CONJUNCT
```

The following is a sample run of Goebel's mini-implementation illustrating the special input syntax which is described in Goebel (1977), Appendix 2.

```
*enter pdb system
*pdb empty
*enter input mode
*input clear.
*?  A*x[[x DOG] => E*yE*t[[y CAT] & [x CHASES<t> y]] =X]
*PDB insert UNNODE0000
*PDB insert internal dictionary WORD0068->DOG
*PDB insert CONCEPT000->dog
*PDB insert EXNODE0001
*PDB insert EXNODE0001
*PDB insert internal dictionary WORD0005->CAT
*PDB insert CONCEPT0001->CAT
*PDB insert EXNODE0002
*PDB insert internal dictionary WORD0035->CHASES
*PDB insert CONCEPT0002->CHASES
*PDB insert PROP0000
*PDB insert PROP0001
*PDB insert PROP0002
*PDB insert PROP0003
*PDB insert PROP0004
*insert A*x[[x DOG] => E*yE*t[[y CAT] & [x CHASES<t> y]] =X]
*CONCEPT FOCI:  DOG  EXNODE0001  EXNODE0002  CHASES
*assert A*x[[x DOG] => E*yE*t[[y CAT] & [x CHASES<t> y]] =X]
*input clear.
*?  [[Fred DOG] & [Fred BELIEVES :X]]
*PDB insert EXNODE0003
       .
       .
*?  save fred
*pdb saved in file->fred.pdb
*?  empty
*PDB empty
*?  input
*enter input mode.
*input clear.
*?  {appearance SUPTOP colour, texture, pattern}
*PDB insert TOPIC->appearance
*PDB insert internal dictionary WORD0092->appearance
*PDB insert internal dictionary WORD0091->APPEARANCE
*PDB insert CONCEPT0000->APPEARANCE
*PDB insert TOPIC->colour
       .
       .
appearance SUPER-TOPIC-OF colour
Enter values for truth distribution:
prob at 0.0?  0
prob at 0.1?  0
prob at 0.3?  0
prob at 0.5?  0
prob at 0.7?  0
prob at 0.9?  0
appearance SUPER-TOPIC-OF texture
```

```
Enter values for truth distribution:
      .
      .
appearance SUPER-TOPIC-OF pattern
Enter values for truth distribution:
prob at 0.0?  0
prob at 0.1?  0
prob at 0.3?  0
prob at 0.5?  0
prob at 0.7?  .2
prob at 0.9?  .2
*input clear.
*?  {colour SUPTOP grey, dark, shiny}
*PDB insert TOPIC->grey
*PDB insert internal dictionary WORD0059->grey
*PDB insert internal dictionary WORD0058->GREY
*PDB insert CONCEPT0004->GREY
*PDB insert TOPIC->dark
      .
      .
*?   {texture SUPTOP tough, smooth , shiny}
      .
      .
*?   {pattern SUPTOP spotted, striped}
      .
      .
*?   A*x[[x ELEPHANT] => [x GREY]]
      .
      .
*PDB insert PROP002
      .
      .
*?   {Clyde SHINY}
*PDB insert EXNODE0001
*PDB insert internal dictionary WORD0053->Clyde
*PDB insert PROP0003
      .
      .
*?  Clyde;colour
*TOPIC categories scanned: colour grey dark shiny
*relevant propostions: PROP0003
*input clear.
*?  Clyde;appearance
*TOPIC categories scanned: appearance colour texture pattern
       grey dark shiny rough smooth spotted striped
*relevant propositions: PROP0003
*input clear.
*? ELEPHANT;texture
*TOPIC categories scanned: texture rough smooth shiny
*no relevant propositions
*input clear.
*?  ELEPHANT;appearance
*TOPIC categories scanned: appearance colour texture pattern
       grey dark shiny rough smooth spotted striped
*relevant propositions:  PROP0002
*input clear
```

```
*?  A*x[[[x TOE] & [x PART-OF Clyde]]=> [x SHINY]]
       .
       .
*PDB insert PROP0008
       .
       .
*? Clyde;appearance
*TOPIC categories scanned: appearance colour texture pattern
       grey dark shiny rough smooth spotted striped
*relevant propositions: PROP0003   PROP0008
```

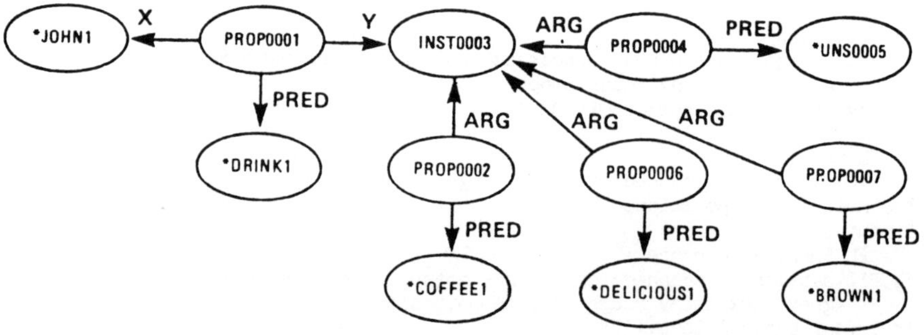

John is drinking the delicious brown coffee.

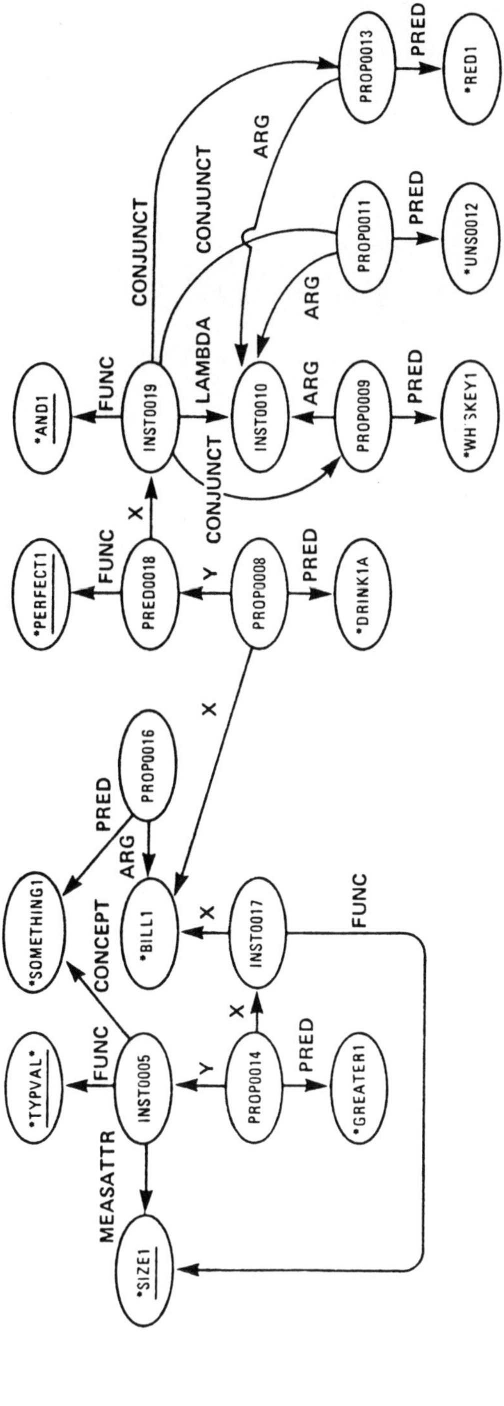

Big Bill drank the perfect red whiskey.

SYNTACTIC-SEMANTIC ANALYSIS OF GERMAN SENTENCES

by

Dietrich Koch
Winfried Heicking

Zentralinstitut für Kybernetik und Informationsprozesse
Akademie der Wissenschaften der DDR
119 Berlin, Rudower Chausee 5

1. Introduction

It is not a simple matter to present a work on one's own mother tongue in another language — in this case English. On the one hand, we believe that it is necessary to explain even very trivial phenomena in order to be understood in the world of another language , and on the other hand we are unable to discuss the really serious problems arising in German because of the incompatibilities of the two languages and of our inability to write in English. We have tried to make a compromise between a simple introductory description of our system, especially intended for those who are not familiar with German, and a more detailed description to indicate the more demanding parts of the system. We fear, however, that the latter will be insufficient for German-speaking colleagues, yet hard to understand for others. Perhaps we can help the first category by referring them to our other papers /1, 2/, but for the second category (always assuming that our apprehension is right) we can only apologize for our inability to explain ourselves sufficiently.

We shall now make a few remarks on some of the limitations of the system.

1. It is not a language understanding system in the sense specified by Schank, Winograd or Woods. We are restricting ourselves to pure linguistic phenomena, and "sematics" is to be understood only as an internal matter of the language i.e. without considering a special discourse or application. We believe some authors have exaggerated the disadvantages of this point of view and have simultaneously neglected the means supplied by the language itself.

2. The semantic network, as briefly outlined in Chapter 14, is not the background of the system, but is rather generated by analysis, sentence by sentence, and forms the deep structure of the analysed text.

3. We have not treated conjunction constructions. It appears to be sure that this problem gives rise to new ideas and cannot be solved by adding to an ATN grammar more nodes and arcs.

We think Woods' facility SYSCONJ is a good starting point in principle, but it has some disadvantages which we cannot tolerate, mainly the necessity to use all "configurations" is, in our opinion, too expensive.

4. The analysis is not complete in all parts, i.e. not all meanings of a sentence can be found because backtracking only corrects decisions expressible by paths through the net and not decisions inside submoduls.

The system was implemented in a LISP version developed by H. Stoyan /9/ for computers of the ESER series (the German abbreviation for the Unified Computer System of the Council of Mutual Economic Assistance).
This LISP is not interactive. Perhaps our aims and opinions may be influenced by this restricted form of programming and testing.

We are indebted to Professor J. Kunze, Dr. M. Bierwisch, and Dr. J. Busse for their suggestions and helpful discussions. We would like to thank Mrs. G. Kawretzke and Mrs. U. Koch for their work in typing and preparing this manuscript, and Mr. J. Wüst for his assistance in translating this paper.

2. Modification of ATN Formalism

We presume that the ATN formalism, as introduced by Woods /11, 12/, is well known. Consequently, we can confine ourselves to explanations concerning the modifications made by us. In this context we refer the reader to the syntax of ATN given in fig. 1.

First of all we shall discuss a small set of deviations without great consequences for the whole strategy.

1. The arc set is not parenthesized. The nodes form natural parentheses for the arc sets.

2. An arbitrary number of tests can be written. All of them are to be understood as conjunctively connected. When only the trivial test T is involved it will be better to omit the parentheses. The ATN compiler is then able to produce a more effective program.

3. Likewise, the arc-type CAT can be used in our system, but the interpretation of such an arc is always as a TST arc, i.e. (CAT <class> (...) ...) ⟶ (TST ((CAT <class>) ...) ...). CAT is a user function and not a system function since CAT depends on the lexicon structure.

4. Actions and term actions at POP arcs are not expressed in our syntax, but they can be used nevertheless. Therefore, one can return to a point of the higher level net that differs from the point from where the subnet was called. We have not used this facility up to now.

We are coming to the important modifications.

a) Blocks with variable exits

In contrast to Woods' further developments, which carry forward the responsibility of advancing the input pointer from the term actions to the arc type, and which reduce the term action types to one, we obtained, indeed, an inflation of term actions. There are two main types, as in the first work by Woods:

```
<network>        ::=  ( <arc set>*)
<arc set>        ::=    <node>  <arc>*
<node>           ::=    <LISP-atom>
<arc>            ::=  (PUSH <node>{( <test>*)/T}[<atom>]
                        <preaction>* <action>*<term-action> )/
                      (POP <form> {( <test>* )/T } [<atom>] )/
                      (TST {( <test>*  )/T}[<atom>] <action>*
                        <term action> )
<preaction>      ::=  (SENDR  <register>  < form > )
<action>         ::=  (LIFTR  <register>  < form > )/
                      (SETR   <register>  < form > )/
                      (ADDR   <register>  < form > )/
                      (SETR1  <form>      < form > )/
                        LISP-form
<term-action>    ::=  (TO  <node>  )/
                      (JUMP  <node>  )/
                      (JUU   <node>* )/
                      (TOO   <node>* )/
                      (JU    <node-variable>  )/
                      (ZO    <node-variable>  )/
<register>       ::=   <LISP-atom >
<node-variable>::=     <LISP-atom >
<test>           ::=  (CAT  < word class name >  )/
                      (WRD  <word form >  )/
                      (GETR <register >  )/
                       <LISP-form >
```

Fig. 1 Syntax of ATN

JUMP	TO
JUU	TOO
JU	ZO

The functions in the first column work without advancing the input pointer, and the functions in the second one work with advancing.
JUMP corresponds to GO. JUU is a little more complicated. It has an arbitrary number of argumentswich have to be names of nodes. The first node will be activated first. The further nodes will be used as values of the node variables declared before. For instance, if the sequence of node variables MK1, MK2, ..., have been declared, then MK1 will take on as value the second argument of JUU, MK2 the third argument of JUU, a.s.o. These variables can be used as arguments of JU (ZO resp.). JU is similar to JUMP, but it initiates branching to the value of its argument, i.e. to the node set by JUU. It is customary, but not necessary, to use the node variables in the term actions of the arcs which have been reached immediately by JUU (or TUU). Such an arc set is called a block with variable exits. This is illustrated by a short section of an artificial network:

```
(TST ... (TOO BLOCK A ABB C D))
(PUSH .. (JUU BLOCK ABB R Q S))
.
.
.
ABB
(TST ((NULL T)) ...)
A
.
.
.
BLOCK
(TST ((WRD /.)) ... (JU MK1))
(TST ((WRD /,)) ... (ZO MK2))
(TST ((WRD : )) ... (ZO MK3))
(TST T (JU MK4))
```

Fig.2 An example of the use of blocks with variable exits

We have used the tests of syntax signs in the block because this was the reason for introducing this facility . According to past design philosophy it was necessary to request a syntax sign at each node, or at least at a large number of nodes. Next to the multiple encoding of arcs for syntax signs, there is yet another disadvantage: If there is a situation similar to the one drawn here

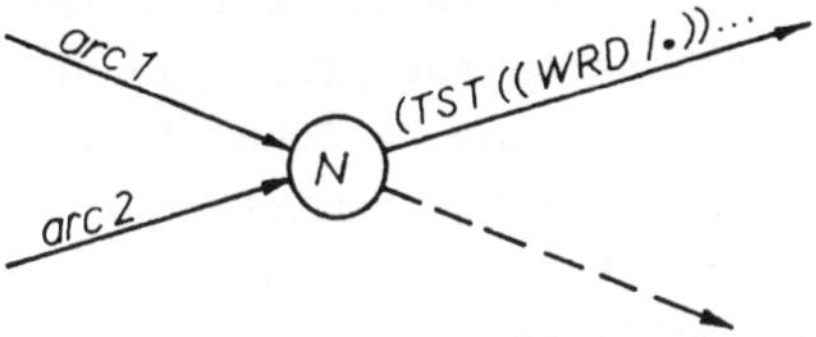

one does not know whether the node N has been reached through arc1 or arc2. This knowledge, however, could exert a major influence on further branchings. In our system it is possible to state what is to be done if, for example, a dot follows arc1, and what is to be done if a dot follows arc2. Entry into a (programmed) dead end (cf. ABB in fig. 2), or other things, can be planned. It should be noted at this point that a dead end reached in this manner contains a lot of information since the context is well known. In practice we have found it necessary to encode two blocks to handle syntax signs. One block with an arc for comma test, and one block without such an arc. The reason for this is that a comma in German is a sign for the start and end of a subclause. Consequently, it is also a sign for continuing the matrix sentence. When advancing in the input sequence after the first occurrence of a comma in a subclause, the comma vanishes, i.e. one cannot use it as a sign to continue or start the next subclause. But the PUSH arc to which one is returning is aware of this technical disappearance since the return (POP) was only possible when a comma was present. Consequently, if there is a second block without comma test one can jump to it and its trivial TST arc can be interpreted as a comma test, i.e. its exit had to be selected in a suitable manner as a start comma or as a continuation comma. Of course, the applicability of this facility is not restricted to syntax signs. In our system, however, other applications do not exist.

b) Generalized backtracking

It is well known that in a left-to-right analysis strategy the dead ends cannot be avoided and backtracking has to be possible. But backtracking always diminishes the efficiency of the system. Every state (configuration) has to be stored, and when a dead end occurs one has to restore the last decision point and seek another path. That is the well-known method of blind backtracking by the principle of the least changes. Certainly, all paths can be found in this manner, but the question is: - Are all paths linguistically interesting or, more precisely worded, is it possible to design an ATN grammar in such a way that the building of false end structures can be avoided if all paths can be followed or if one can try to follow all of them? Therefore, we see two main disadvantages in the old technique: wastage of storage and run time, and an increase of the danger to build up false structures. Both of them can be restricted if the following is considered: - Not all decision points are linguistically critical <u>and</u> dead ends are not informationless.

The first step has to be the implementation of the technical suppositions, while the next one is to find the relationship between the kind of risk in decision points and the information contained in dead ends (or more precisely: contained in the situation causing the dead end). The creation of sufficient facilities to implement intelligent backtracking is very simple. Firstly, the snap shot facility has to be placed in the hands of the user who now has two possibilities for storing the state ("configuration" in the language usage of Woods):

1. Determined snap shot. An arc can be declared as being always critical. For this reason the optional atom is immediately after the test part of the arc (cf. fig. 1). This atom, arbitrarily chosen by the user, is simultaneously a label for the snap shot, i.e. it will be stored together with the current values of system variables. The reason for this will become evident later on.

2. Non-determined snap shot. The user can define any test function as critical, i.e. the positive test in some branches of the test function can be assured by a snap shot. In such branches it is only necessary to encode a statement of the kind (SETQ BTR ' <atom>). If all tests of the arc were positive, then the system will perform a snap shot provided that this statement was previously evaluated and that it was not followed by another statement to the contrary effect (that is possible with (BTRAUS)!). The atom in (SETQ BTR ' <atom>) will again bc used as label for the snap shot.

The snap shot stack has the following structure:
(<atom> <n-th snap shot> ... <atom> <1-st snap shot>).
Every snap shot contains the values of the following variables:

- All registers
- SATZ, the input pointer
- MARKE, the label of the next possible arc at the critical decision point
- MKEL, the stack of return addresses used by POP
- ANAERG, a global list of all intermediate structures
- Global variables declared by the user before ATN compiling

The system knows the list of corresponding variables in the same order as built in a snap shot. Therefore, it is not necessary to use an a-list for the snap shot. It is sufficient to store only the values.
In the event that a dead end occurred a snap shot can be preferred by its label. Before running into a dead end there has to be a statement like (BCK ' <atom>). Then the system will seek a snap shot labelled with the same atom as used as the argument of BCK. (BCK ...) can be encoded as test form (always true) or as action. If (BCK ...) has not been encoded the last snap shot will be restarted, likewise if the label is not found. The last snap shots will not be destroyed by using a former one.

We can state:

1. This backtracking is recursively complete. All critical decision points can be restarted, independent of whether they are lying in the same level, or in any lower or higher level. The time for restarting is the same in all cases of distance.

2. Purposeful backtracking by means of label search does not violate completeness because the later snap shots will not be erased. This technique should not be considered as heuristic. It should be only a tool for search optimalisation.

3. The user is responsible for linguistical completeness. Technical completeness can be reached by very simple redefining of two system functions. The ability to implement this borderline case justifies the use of the term "generalized backtracking".

This chapter ends with some brief remarks on implementation.

We have developed a two-pass ATN compiler with the target language LISP. A grammatical function (the immediate translation of ATN grammar) and a control function are generated. The grammatical function, generated by the first pass, is very similar to the ATN grammar. The nodes have vanished and have been replaced by labels for each arc. A module for restarting the snap shots is attached. The PUSH arcs are split into two parts - PUSH1 and PUSH2. PUSH1 is activated for the subnet call, and PUSH2 after the POP evaluation belonging to that PUSH. Each node can be used as start node of a subnet without previous declarations. The jumps are global jumps. The second pass replaces the arc functions by its procedure body connected with partial evaluation, and the global jumps are substituted by local jumps. A more detailed description of our ATN compiler is given in /12/.

We have just seen that Burton and Woods have also built a compiler for ATN /13/. It appears to contain similar ideas. Deviations are probably caused by different LISP systems. In our system, for instance, there is no function like BRANCH. It could not be established whether Woods can compile his generated LISP function with his LISP compiler. We have great trouble with this problem. Up to now we have only been able to interpret this function. The use of label variables (necessary for POP, blocks with variable exits, and back-tracking) is responsible for this. But we hope to overcome this problem.

3. General Approach

German, like other inflexional languages, has to be analysed by ATN formalism in a style differing from that employed in English. The application of ATN for our language to build a complete syntax tree in a straightforward manner is very dangerous. Many false decisions would be made. The reasons for this are:

1. The ordering of phrases in sentences is very free. Inflexional ambiguities cannot be resolved by the position of phrases. The consequence is often an ambiguity of the whole sentence. Often, it is impossible to distinguish between the genitive attribute (in English usually expressed by "of" phrases) and the dative object, particularly if the noun is feminine. In the German language there are position preferences, too, but they depend generally on difficult context conditions hidden in previous or subsequent sentences. An analysis that is restricted to sentences has to take all customary positions of verb arguments into account.
2. Only when the main verb has been discovered will it be possible to find the grammatical function of NPs or PPs. The main verb of a German sentence, however, is rarely detectable at an early point in the sentence. In subclauses generally, and in main sentences containing more than one verb, the verb group with the main verb is located at the end.

Summa summarum, the practically free arrangement of phrases in the sentence and the late detection of the verb group, especially the main verb, have induced us to use ATN formalism in a weaker sense than proposed by Woods. Our ATN grammar had to provide only an intermediate syntactical structure without full subordination or function definitions of phrases. The parsing tree supplied by the ATN step has to fulfil the following conditions:

1. The main verb is explicitly given and the analysed syntactical features (tense, voice, etc.) of the verb group are correct.

2. Simplest constituents are separated and arranged in the correct sentence level. The only point not clarified is whether the constituents are immediate or mediate arguments of the verb, and which function they have.

3. Each subclause has its correct position in the tree. This is possible because of the strict punctuation rules in German, and because the position of subclauses gives sufficient reason for subordination. There are exceptions to these rules. Up to now, it has been impossible to resolve these problems by the known syntactical or semantical means. Our language has to be restricted in this point (andin other points, too, of course).

4. Infinitives with "zu" ("to"), extended or not, have to be represented by subclauses (more precisely: by the syntactical structure of the equivalent subclauses). Therefore, at least a preference proposal for the subject generally deleted in "zu" phrases has to be made.

5. Many transformations have been carried out. There are only active formats after ATN steps. This appears to be in contradiction (as in "zu" clauses) with our remark that grammatical functions are not defined - in contradiction because the grammatical subject and the agent have to be known for passive-active transformations. For this purpose, however, we are analysing a list of candidates that are morphologically possible, and one of them is preferred for the active structure. The other are retained for the event that the preferred candidate produces a failure.

Further transformations will be discussed in the text below.

We had the intention to outline only the situation after the ATN step. The next step, called semantic interpretation (abbrev. SI), has to overcome the deficiency of this intermediate structure, but without constructing the full syntax tree. That is unneccessary in our opinion. It is well known that a correct syntax tree can be constructed only by means of semantic features and rules. However, why should it not be possible to build a semantic representation (e.g. like Fillmore's case structure) immediately? We believe that a complete syntactic (surface or deep) structure is unneccessary - perhaps for synthesis, but not for analysis.

If the main verbs and simple constituents with their correct sentence levels and their syntactical features are known, then there would be little purpose to process further the sequence of constituents in any left-to-right manner. The main verb is able to control the flow of analysis. After binding the verb valences by means of searching for suitable constituents, taking into account the strong affinity of the verb to its arguments, we shall be able to continue to seek for the correct subordination of the other constituents with less risk. We are now preferring in the second step a mixed strategy not classifiable by the well-known notations of bottom-up or top-down.

In SI we are now going beyond the sentence domain. A short-time memory (e. g. 5 sentences backward) helps determine the pronominal references, and a long-time memory (called semantic network) is the basis of determining more complicated references, e.g. references by subordinated notions (building → cottage, man → little man, etc.) or functional references created by transformations (John sells a book → The seller of a book ...).

The following block diagram (fig. 3) gives a survey of the main modules of the system and their functional dependencies. The modules in the areas bounded by dash lines are not activated during sentence analysis. The system could be completed by a deduction and synthesis program. The first one was produced by our colleagues Geske and Werner /14/, but it has not yet been connected with the language processor. We have simplified the deduction problem for reference determination.

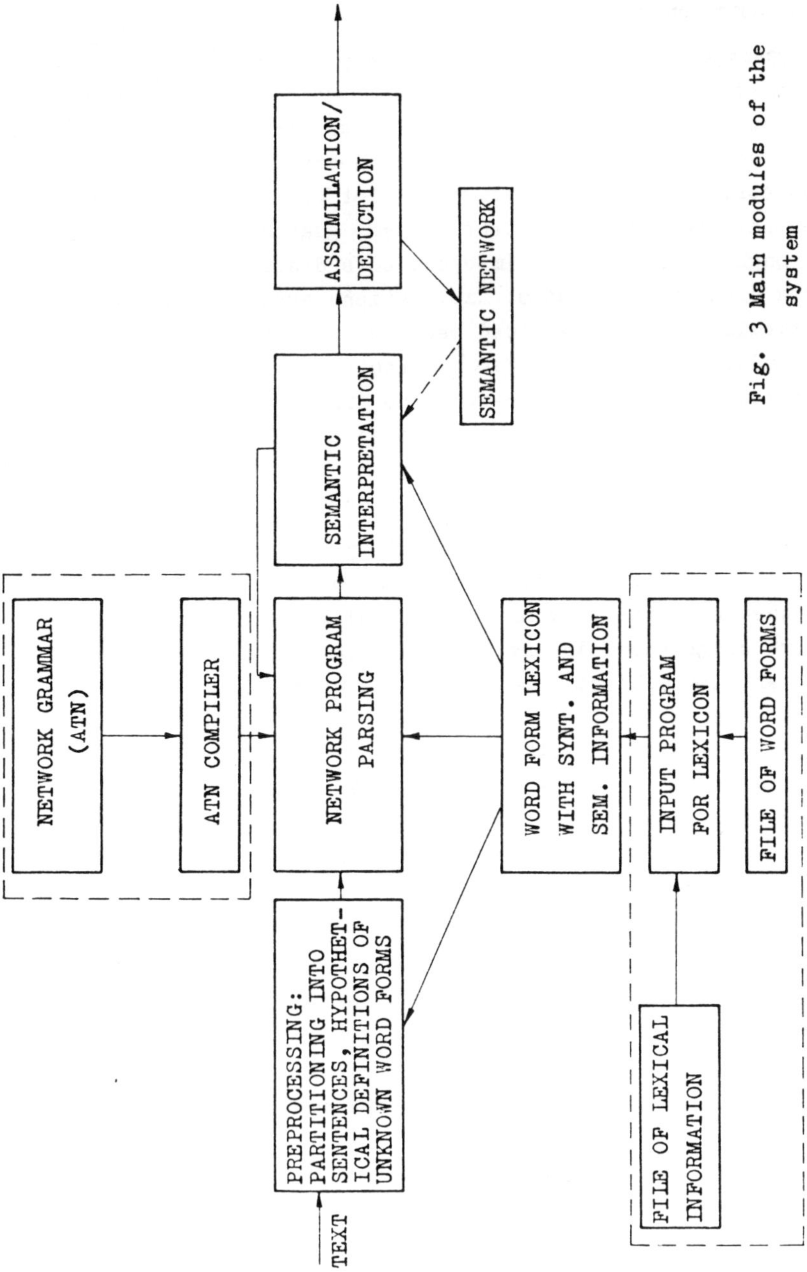

Fig. 3 Main modules of the system

4. Congruences

An ATN grammar can be interpreted as a procedurally connected set of hypotheses about the ordering of word classes in well-formed sentences. Hence, the constituents can be considered as hyper word classes. But these hypotheses are too weak to make up correct output structures. A lot of linguistic sub-modules have to refine the test system, guaranteeing a correct run through the net. It is impossible to describe all kinds of tests used in the system. Explanations about global tests, in particular, will be avoided because such tests are only understandable if the full flow of control is known. Such an instruction, however, goes beyond the framework of this paper. Instead, we shall limit ourselves to an explanation of two essential linguistic facilities in greater detail, namely the congruence and the verb group rules (abbrev. VGR).

The first one can be hardly explained by English examples because of the minor importance of congruences in English - a consequence of the lack of inflexional forms! Of course, there are congruences in English (see e.g. congruence between finite verb and subject), but it is not worth while taking them into account to the same extent for testing the correct paths as in German (and other inflexional languages). Congruence in NPs or PPs - the main field of use of congruences in German - is very weakly expressed by English forms. Because of this situation we shall start with a formal definition of congruences, possibly applicable to other languages, and then we shall give an example later on.

A word form is characterized by a set of binary vectors. In their implementation these vectors are LISP numbers. Each component of the vectors has a well-defined meaning, the same one for each vector. The meanings are values of categories, such as plural, singular of the category number, nominative, etc., of the category case. The exact definition of the components and conditions to be fulfilled to construct permissible vectors will be given after defining congruences (cf. table 1).

The projection function P_n is defined by

$$P_n(\tau) = \begin{cases} 1 & \text{if the value of the nth component of } \tau \text{ is 1} \\ 0 & \text{else} \end{cases}$$

We need a little other form of P_n, namely P_i^k defined by $P_i^k = P_{4k+i}$. k will be interpreted as category, and i as i-th value of the category k. It holds $0 \leq i \leq 3$. The division of the vectors in segments of the length 4 has a simple reason. There are not more than 4 values for each category (generally fewer values; only the category case has 4 values) and the hexadecimal numbers are then simply readable. This coincidence is random, of course, but useful. Another circumstance, likewise random, is very fortunate: the bit length numbers (32 bit) is sufficient for storing all values. Otherwise, we would have had to introduce very complicated procedures.

We define a special set C of binary vectors:

$$C = \{\tau \,/\, \forall k \; \exists i \;\; (P_i^k(\tau) = 1)\}$$

i depends on k. i must not be greater than the maximal number of values of the corresponding k (subtracted by 1, since we are starting with 0). $\langle k \rangle$ denotes the domain of i. k is not greater than 7 (for German), therefore, there are 8 categories.

w and w' should be two words, C_w and $C_{w'}$ are attached sets of binary vectors called inflexional components.

$C_{w,w'} = C_w \times C_{w'}$ is the cartesian product.

We denote by $\varkappa(\tau, \tau')$ the logical conjunction of the vectors τ, τ', i.e.

$$P_i(\varkappa(\tau, \tau')) = \begin{cases} 1, \text{ if } P_i(\tau) = P_i(\tau') = 1 \\ 0, \text{ else} \end{cases}$$

It is possible that $\varkappa(\tau, \tau')$ is incomplete, i.e. $\varkappa(\tau, \tau') \notin C$. The completeness for all categories is seldom of interest. The notation $\varkappa_A(\tau, \tau')$ should express that the resulting vector is complete with respect to a subset A of the category set. For the next steps we need the extended map $\varkappa_A^o$:

$$\varkappa_A^o(C_{w,w'}) = \{\vartheta \,/\, \vartheta = \varkappa(\tau, \tau') \wedge \tau \in C_w \wedge \tau' \in C_{w'}$$
$$\wedge \forall k(k \in A \rightarrow \exists i(i \in \langle k \rangle \wedge P_i^k(\tau) = 1))\}$$

Now, we are ready to define the congruence between word forms: Two word forms w and w' are congruent with respect to the set of categories A, if a congruence with respect to A is defined between the word classes of w and w' and if it holds

$$\varkappa_A^o(C_{w,w'}) \neq \emptyset$$

We give the extension of this definition for chains of word forms:
A chain of word forms $w_1, \ldots, w_n$ is congruent with respect to A if congruence is defined for the chain of the corresponding word classes and if the following sets inductively defined are not empty:

1. $C'_{w_1} = C_{w_1}$

2. $C'_{w_{i+1}} = \varkappa_A^o(C'_{w_i} \times C_{w_{i+1}})$

We can transfer these definitions to constituents. The notion "word class" has to be replaced by "type of constituent".

We distinguish between 4 types of constituents:

SS - sentence
NP - nominal phrase
PP - prepositional phrase
AD - adverb phrase

The corresponding inflexional components C_k are defined as follows:

$C_{SS} = C_{fin}$ $\quad$ C_{fin} is the inflexional component of the finite verb of SS

$C_{NP}=C_{PP}=C'_{w_n}$ $\quad$ w_n is the last form of the nominal phrase

$C_{AD} = \emptyset$

The inflexional component of NP and PP is the same because the resolution of the ambiguity caused by the preposition is transferred to the subordinated NP.
We have yet to define the meaning of each component of τ . This follows with the help of the table on the next page. Each vector, used as inflexional vector of word forms, has to fulfil the following conditions:

1. Condition of completeness
   τ has to be an element of C, i.e. at least one value of each category has to equal 1.

2. Condition of compatibility
   This condition can be precisely defined. We shall only give some plausible explanations. If some categories of a vector contain more than one value equalling 1, then the word form connected with this vector has to be able to actualize each combination of these values, i.e. all values specified by 1 have to be mutually compatible. The effectivity of the system is increased if the sets C_w are small, i.e. as many values as possible should equal 1. The condition 2 limits the possibility to reduce the sets C_w.

Finally, we give an example (cf. table 2). We have numbered the vector components from right to left. The chain "der guten Menschen" ("of the good human beings") is to be treated. The sets C_w are given for each word form. The categories ending with "2" are ignored because these do not have to be used for this congruence.

k	category name	i	value name
0	CASE	0	NOMINATIVE
		1	GENITIVE
		2	DATIVE
		3	ACCUSATIVE
1	NUMBER1	0	SINGULAR
		1	PLURAL
		2,3	not defined
2	GENUS1	0	MASCULINUM
		1	FEMININE
		2	NEUTRUM
3	PERSON1	0	1. PERSON
		1	2. PERSON
		2	3. PERSON
4	NUMBER2	0	stem-inflexion of possessive pronouns
		1	
5	GENUS2	0	
		1	
		2	
6	PERSON2	0	
		1	
		2	
7	TYPE OF INFLEXION	0	WEAK
		1	STRONG

Tab. 1 Definition of the vector components

29	28 ...	14	13	12 ...	10	9	8 ...	5	4	3	2	1	0	
0	1	1	0	0	0	0	1	0	1	0	0	0	1	
0	1	1	0	0	1	1	1	1	0	0	0	1	0	der
0	1	1	0	0	0	1	0	0	1	0	1	1	0	
0	1	1	0	0	0	0	1	0	1	1	1	1	0	
0	1	1	0	0	1	1	0	0	1	0	1	1	0	
0	1	1	0	0	1	1	1	1	0	1	1	1	1	guten
1	0	1	0	0	1	0	1	0	1	0	0	1	0	
1	0	1	0	0	1	1	1	1	0	0	1	0	0	
1	1	1	0	0	0	0	1	0	1	1	1	1	0	Menschen
1	1	1	0	0	0	0	1	1	0	1	1	1	1	

Tab. 2 The inflexional components of "der", "guten" and "Menschen"

The congruence is defined with respect to A = {case, number 1, genus 1, type of inflexion} . Application of $\varkappa_A^o$ supplies

1. $\varkappa_A^o\ (C_{der} \times C_{guten}) =$

   0 1 1 0 0 1 1 1 1 0 0 0 1 0

   0 1 1 0 0 0 1 0 0 1 0 1 1 0

2. $\varkappa_A^o\ (C'_{guten} \times C_{Menschen}) =$

   0 1 1 0 0 0 0 1 1 0 0 0 1 0

We see the word form "der" is ambiguous to the degree 7, "guten" to the degree 24, and "Menschen" to the degree 8, but the whole phrase is unique. Of course, the example is extreme, but we have to take into account that the forms "guten" and "Menschen" represent large classes and "der" is very often used.

A complete list and description of congruences in the German language can be found in the important work by J. Kunze "Abhängigkeitsgrammatik" /3/.

5. Verb Group Rules

We pointed out that the main task of the ATN step is to separate the simple constituents and to recognize the main verb. Apart from taking the word classes into account, we have got the congruences as a powerful means of separating the constituents and, simultaneously, of analysing the internal structure of the constituents, and we have a very exact mechanism called verb group rules (abbr. VGR) for handling the verb group. Both means, embedded in ATN grammar as tests and suppliers of syntactical information, limit the danger of false decisions. Because of the similarity of building up verb groups in English and German we shall start with an example to illustrate the method based on VGR. Let us look at the verb group:

"has been beaten"

If a "have" form is (immediately) followed by a perfect participle, then we say that the "have" form rules the perfect participle, and that yields PERFECT. Furthermore, if a "be" form rules a perfect participle, then PASSIVE is obtained. Therefore, the afore-listed chain yields:

PRESENT of PERFECT of PASSIVE

Further rules are: "will/shall" rules infinitive forms with the value (simple) FUTURE, "be" forms rule present participles with the value CONTINUOUS, and "should/would" rules infinitive with the value CONDITIONAL. Further rules can be built up with "to" forms. They will generally describe modalities ("have to ...", "be to ..."). These are the essential rules in simple verb groups, i.e. groups with one full verb. The handling of these groups in such a way is based on a suggestion of M. Bierwisch. The complex verb groups (as with more than one full verb or with some attached modal verbs) can be handled in a similar manner, except that the results cannot be interpreted in a similar obvious way. But they can give us information on the kind of ruling, particularly the argument of the ruling verb that is to be used as the subject of the ruled verb. For German there is a complete theory worked out by the Danish linguist G. Bech /4/ which we have used extensively, but it is impossible to take all the side effects and special cases described by him into account.

We shall now give a formal description of VGR, followed by its application in German. We see that the formalism of congruence cannot be used for VGR. It is neither required for the identity of features, nor are the obtained results used for the next rules. Besides the inflexional component of the finite forms, the verb needs two components for VGR. The first component is the ruling component, and the second the ruled component. We call these components the (syntactic) a-component and the e-component, respectively. The a-component of a verb w describes which features the e-component of the verb w' has to possess at least if the verb w' is the immediate successor to w. The a-component and the e-component can be defined as binary vectors, and it is sufficient to choose one vector for each component. We denote the vectors by ${}^{a}\mathfrak{w}$ and ${}^{e}\mathfrak{w}$. The logical conjunction $\varkappa$ is used without restrictions in respect to categories.

We define: A verb w_i rules a verb w_{i+1} if for the corresponding vectors ${}^{a}\mathfrak{w}_i$ and ${}^{e}\mathfrak{w}_{i+1}$

$$\varkappa({}^{a}\mathfrak{w}_i, {}^{e}\mathfrak{w}_{i+1}) \neq \vec{o}$$

holds where $\vec{o}$ is the zero vector.

Generalisation: A verb group $w_1 \ldots w_n$ is correct, if we have for all i = 1, ... n

$$\varkappa({}^{a}\mathfrak{w}_i, {}^{e}\mathfrak{w}_{i+1}) \neq \vec{o}.$$

For German we have to reverse the order. The definition has to base on the normal ordering of verb groups in subclauses with the finite verb in the last position and the main verb in the first position.

Therefore, if we use the ordering w_n ... w_1 the above-mentioned definition can be used without further changes.

Additional difficulties arise in German. Firstly, the verb group in main sentences is generally split in the following way:

... w_1 ... w_n ... w_2 ("... ist ... geschlagen worden") and a lot of other constituents can be arranged between w_1 and w_n. Secondly, the ordering of verb groups containing more than two verbs can be changed systematically:

...., daß man ihn hier liegen bleiben lassen kann
...., daß man ihn hier kann liegen bleiben lassen
...., daß man ihn hier kann lassen liegen bleiben

Thirdly, there are great problems in handling sentences with coherent ordering of complex verb groups because of the uncertainty about the arguments of the subordinate simple verb groups, although the correctness of the verb group can be proved better in the coherent case than in the incoherent case:

...., da er versucht, den Feind zu schlagen (incoherent)
(as he tries to beat the enemy)

...., da er den Feind zu schlagen versucht (coherent)
(not exemplifiable by translation)

A thorough treatment of these problems is given in /4/.
Tab. 3 gives the definition of the vectors $^{a}\mathfrak{v}$ and $^{e}\mathfrak{v}$ for German. Fo (w) means the set of all forms of w.

i	$P_i({}^{e}\varkappa_w)=1$, if w is	$P_i({}^{a}\varkappa_w) = 1$, if
1	infinitive	w ∈ Fo (werden)\{worden, geworden}
2	perfect participle and the perfect is built by "sein" forms	w ∈ Fo (sein)
3	perfect participle and the perfect is built by "haben" forms	w ∈ Fo (haben)
4	state passive participle	w ∈ Fo (sein)
5	motion passive participle	w ∈ Fo (werden)\ { geworden }
6	infinitive with "zu" (for analytical "zu" forms the 1-bit will be created during the analysis)	w ∈ Fo (sein)
7	"	w ∈ Fo (sein)
8	"	w ∈ Fo (haben)
9	infinitive	w is a modal verb
10	infinitive	w ∈ Fo (lernen) ... further full verbs ruling pure infinitives
11	infinitive	w ∈ Fo (sehen) ... and further full verbs ruling infinitives with accusative
12	infinitive with "zu"	w is a modal verb ruling infinitive with "zu".
13	infinitive with "zu"	w is a verb ruling an infinitive with "zu" and transferring the subject, e.g. "versuchen" ("try")
14	"	w is a verb ruling an infinitive with "zu" and transferring the prepositional object, e.g. "appellieren an" ("to appeal to")
15	"	w is a verb ruling an infinitive with "zu" and transferring the dative object, e.g. "helfen" ("help")
16	"	w is a verb ruling an infinitive with "zu" and transferring the accusative object, e.g. "bitten" ("beg")

Tab. 3
(see previous page)

6. Structure of the Lexicon

The structure of the internal lexicon is essentially influenced by the LISP-system. The object list is used for fast access to the items containing the information. There is, however, no immediate access to all items from the object list. The reason for this is the ambiguities of words and word forms. It would be possible to list all meanings of the items in the property list of the corresponding atom, but we have decided to generate a particular atom for each meaning of the string of signs. All these atoms have the same print names, but only one address of these atoms is in the object list and is immediately accessible. This atom is the carrier of the other atoms of the same print name, and it does not carry a linguistic meaning. The secondary items (or entries) are to be found by means of analysis, the primary one will be found by the LISP-system. We have to distinguish between two levels of ambiguities: Firstly, ambiguities of the word class of word forms (syntactical level) resolved by the ATN step, and secondly, the ambiguities of words without ambiguities in the word class (semantical level) resolved by the second step SI. Therefore, the atom with unique word class can be the carrier of a list of atoms with the same print name, but with different meanings. These are then the tertiary items. The primary entry is the same as the secondary one if the form is unique with respect to the word class, and the secondary entry is the same as the tertiary one if the word is semantically unambiguous. The reason for representing ambiguous forms by unique atoms (and not by lists of meanings of one atom) is the intention to represent the content of texts by means of a semantic network.

The drawing on the next page gives the LISP structures of the different levels of the lexicon.

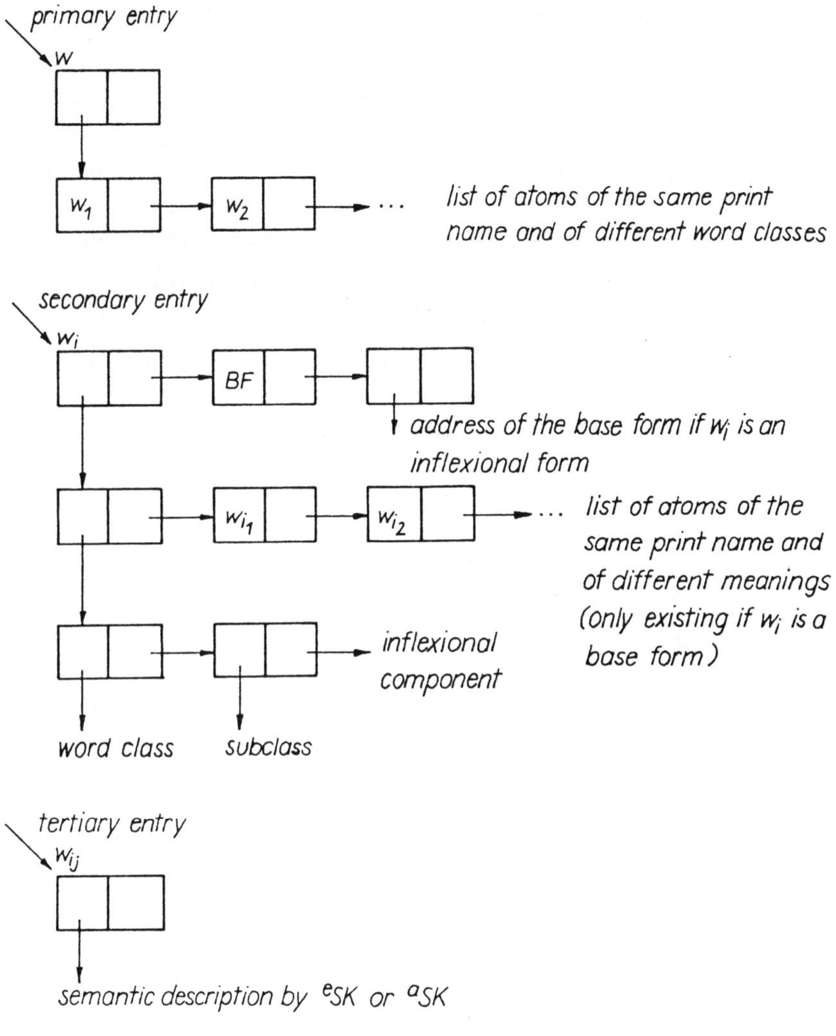

Fig. 4 Lexicon structure (see text)

7. Syntactic Intermediate Structure

The constituents of the sentence, and the sentence itself, are represented by GENSYM atoms. The value cells of these atoms contain the syntactic features, as generated by congruences and verb rules. Further syntactic features are the values of the following indicators:

PTYP - value: type of the constituent, explained in ch. 4

SC - value: HS (main sentence), NS (subsentence)
FS (question), BS (imperative sentence)

SUBS - value: subjoiners which are not constituents of the subclause but only connectors, cf. "daß" ("that"), "obgleich" ("although")

The meaning of the indicators responsible for the subordination is as follows:

V - main verb

MV - modal verbs

SP - list of constituents belonging to the main verb, mediately or immediately dependent

PREP - preposition

NP - nominal phrase

MODS - relative clause

REFR - at GENSYM referring to another GENSYM; value is the referred GENSYM

For illustration we give an example.

SYNTACTIC STRUCTURE OF THE SENTENCE:

"Da er dem Techniker erlaubt zu arbeiten, wird das Verfahren bald verbessert werden".
("Since he permits the technician to work the method will be soon improved").

```
G694  (V VERBESSERN SP (G693 G692 V G689) PTYP SS SC HS
      SPECIAL (1471F 4 1 8))
G693  (N  XY PTYP NP SPECIAL (4731))
G692  (N VERFAHREN ART DEF PTYP NP SPECIAL (4418))
G689  (V ERLAUBEN SUBS DA SP (G690 V G686 G685) PTYP SS SC NS
      SPECIAL ( 471F))
G690  (V ARBEITEN SUBS DASS SP (G691 V) PTYP SS SC NS
      SPECIAL (   3773F))
G691  (REFR G686 PTYP NP SPECIAL (4111))
G686  (N TECHNIKER ART DEF PTYP NS SPECIAL (4114))
G685  (PERSP ER PTYP NP SPECIAL (4111))
```

With the help of tab. 1,3 the hexadecimal numbers as values of SPECIAL (value cell) can be decoded.

8. Main Strategies of ATN Grammar

We have tried to clarify the aim of the ATN step. We are unable to explain all paths, tests, and actions of the program. It seems to us to be more useful to restrict ourselves to the essential aspects, particularly to the design philosophy. As pointed out earlier, each node can be used as entry node of a subnet. Nevertheless, we can still distinguish between two subnets that are not connected by term actions and which are to accomplish fixed tasks: The S-net for recognizing and building up the constituents of the type SS (main clauses and subclauses), inclusive the analysis of the verb group and the K-net for the other constituents, i.e. NP, PP, AD.

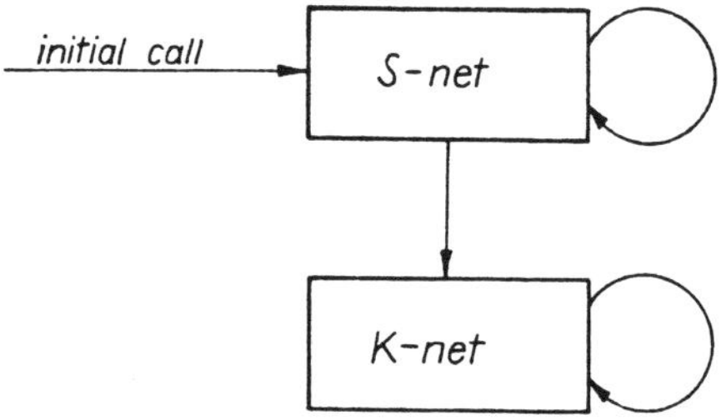

Fig. 5 Global Structure

The drawing shows the global structure of the net, the arrows denote recursive calls. We have to point out that the handling of the recursivity of sentences is not performed by the recursivity of ATN, except in the case of embedding recursivity. The S-net works only on two levels if there are no embeddings: the level of the main sentence (top-level) and the level of subclauses (only one level deeper). The correct subordination is performed by a set of functions being placed in test or action parts of suitable arcs. The advantages of this strategy are the following:

1. Avoidance of false recursive calls; 2. relief of the push-down stack; 3. (most essentially) the possibility of handling projective and non-projective structures on the same manner, i.e. additional difficulties with non-projectivities do not arise.

In recalling the most essential aim of the ATN step (analysis of the verb group and segmentation into simple constituents), we might consider the following net as a simple expression of this idea.

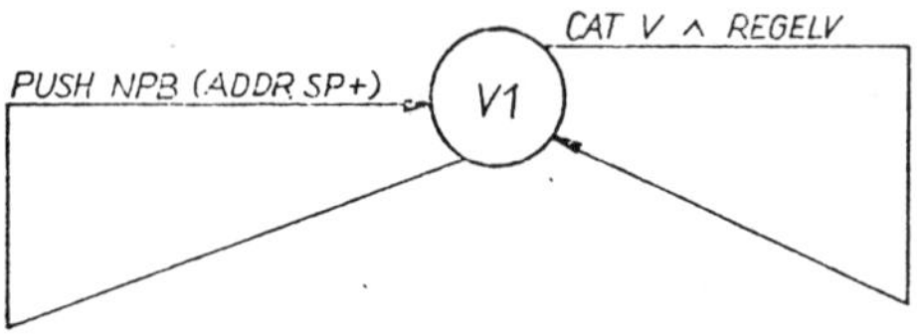

Fig. 6 Simple-S-net to illustrate the basic strategy

NPB is the main entry of the K-net, "+" the address of the structure of the constituent analysed by the K-net. Of course, this S-net is not sufficient. Besides additional arc sets for handling complex sentences, there are no features for simple discontinuous verb groups. Furthermore, there are no switchers for the event that the verb group must not be interrupted, or that the chain of "verbless" constituents must not be interrupted. We shall expand the net a little further.

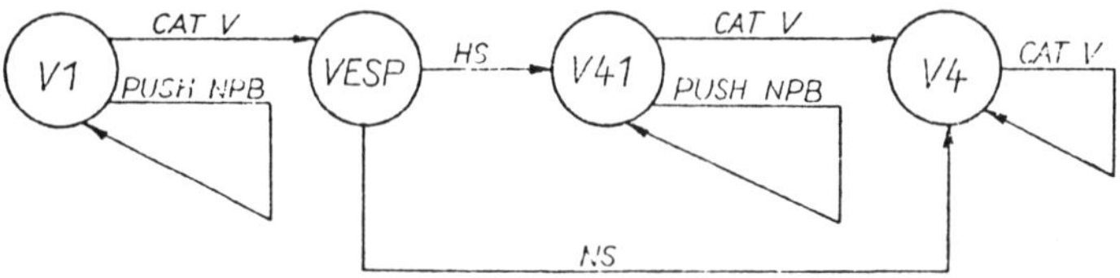

Fig. 7 A more realistic S-net to illustrate the basic strategy

There is no possibility to interrupt the verb group cycle by PUSH arcs at the node V4 because the second part of the verb group of the main sentence, and the whole verb group of subclauses, are continuous. Exceptions, sometimes met in belletristic literature, cannot be analysed. The test of the sentence type at VESP is a simple level test connected, if necessary, with the test of the status of the foregoing verb (i.e. finite or infinite). Consequently, if the first verb of the top level is an infinite verb, then the path is a dead end.

We shall now discuss a set of enrichements of this structure for a better understanding of the more complicated branches of the S-net (drawn in fig. 8) which corresponds to our implemented S-net, except for some minor details that have been left out here for reasons of greater clarity.

1. We have to enrich the arcs with calls of blocks discussed above (ch. 2).

2. The node V1 is to be used in all sentence levels. Therefore, it cannot be the start node. V1 will be reached by different ways, depending on the type of sentence.

3. The verb cycle at V4 has to be expanded with arc sets to test the verb group rules. An embedding of this test in the same arc as a CAT test would be disadvantageous for the recognition of the reason of dead ends.

4. We have to introduce an arc set to handle the situation after a comma, i.e. its use as an end comma. The arcs of the node NAKOM are responsible for this. There are five possibilities of continuation after a comma:

- Beginning of a relative clause
- Beginning of a subclause with one or more subjoiners
- Beginning of a "zu" phrase
- Continuation of the main sentence after the finite verb
- Continuation of the main sentence before the finite verb

A 6th possibility, namely the beginning of the main sentence, is handled by another node - see (PUSH NS) at node S.

5. The verb arc has to be split into two arcs, the first one treats the pure verb forms, the second one the infinitives with "zu" ("to"). These can appear in analytical ("<u>zu</u> rufen") and synthetical ("hervor<u>zu</u>rufen") forms. Therefore, the second arc has to consume sometimes two words. The procedure IZU looks first at the synthetical form and then, if this fails, at the form "zu" and the successor with combined

test for verbs standing in the infinitive. A special action is responsible to consume "zu", and the term action consumes the infinitive. An analysis with more arcs for this case (namely, one for "zu" and one for the infinitive) has the drawback of unnecessary dead ends.

6. The German full verb can be split, but only in main sentences, see for instance: "anrufen": "wir rufen an". Various other constituents can appear between the root of the verb and its separable prefix. Such a prefix has a well defined position in the sentence (before a comma, dot, or sometimes the conjunction "wie"). Immediately after the first verb one has to ask for a verb prefix (see fig. 11, node V41 and test VZ). In the presence of a verb prefix, further verbs on the same level are impossible.

Let us now make some technical remarks on the S-net drawn in fig. 8. The block call is symbolized by rectangles. Hence, the call of BLOCK1 is indicated by [X Y] and BLOCK2 by [//// X] . The arrow after the rectangles shows the branching if there is no syntax sign when BLOCK1 was called, or if the comma was consumed shortly before BLOCK2 was called. Rectangles without node names are used if branching to a block is mediated by a simple JUMP. In the block, then, the values of the node variables put somewhere before will be used. We remind you in this context that the node variables are registers, i.e. they cannot be changed by JUUs used in a level other than the current one. This supplies in a simple manner the possibility to handle the German frame sentences created by bipartite verb groups or separated prefixes in the main sentences.

We note that the first argument of POP arcs is not used to build up tree structures. These are constructed with actions at arcs immediately branching to the end node. The form of POP is always the variable "+" which addresses the tree previously constructed.

We shall not describe the K-net shown in fig. 10 because it gives, on the one hand, little new information, the only innovation being apparently the joining of different constituents into one subnet. On the other hand, the K-net is very complicated, especially when handling the embedded complex attributes and bipartite prepositions, but there would be no limits to such an explanation for us, particularly since we have to talk about specific features peculiar to German and not to English and, additionally, this would have to be accomplished with our limited abilities to express ourselves properly in English.

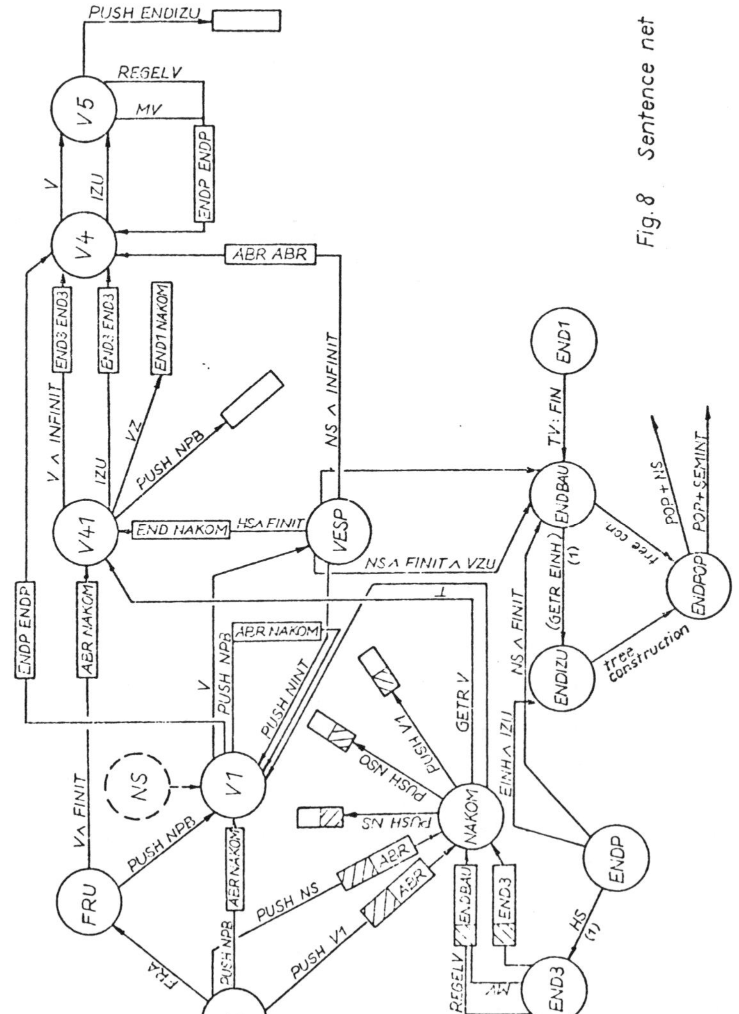

Fig. 8 Sentence net

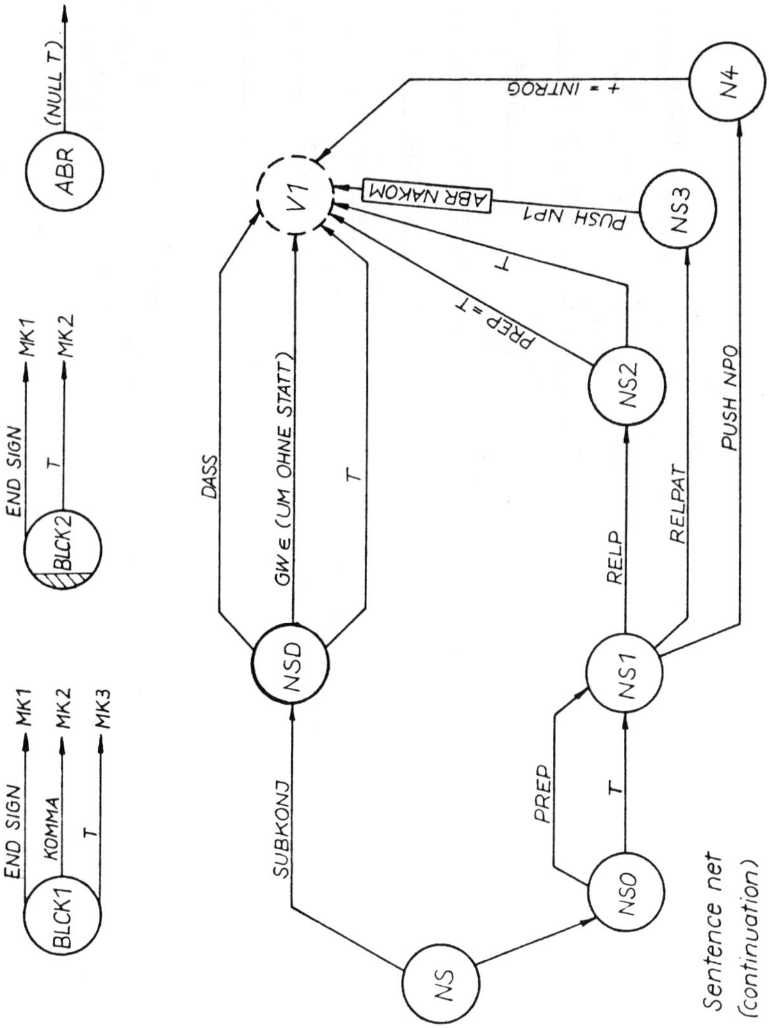

Fig. 9 Sentence net (continuation)

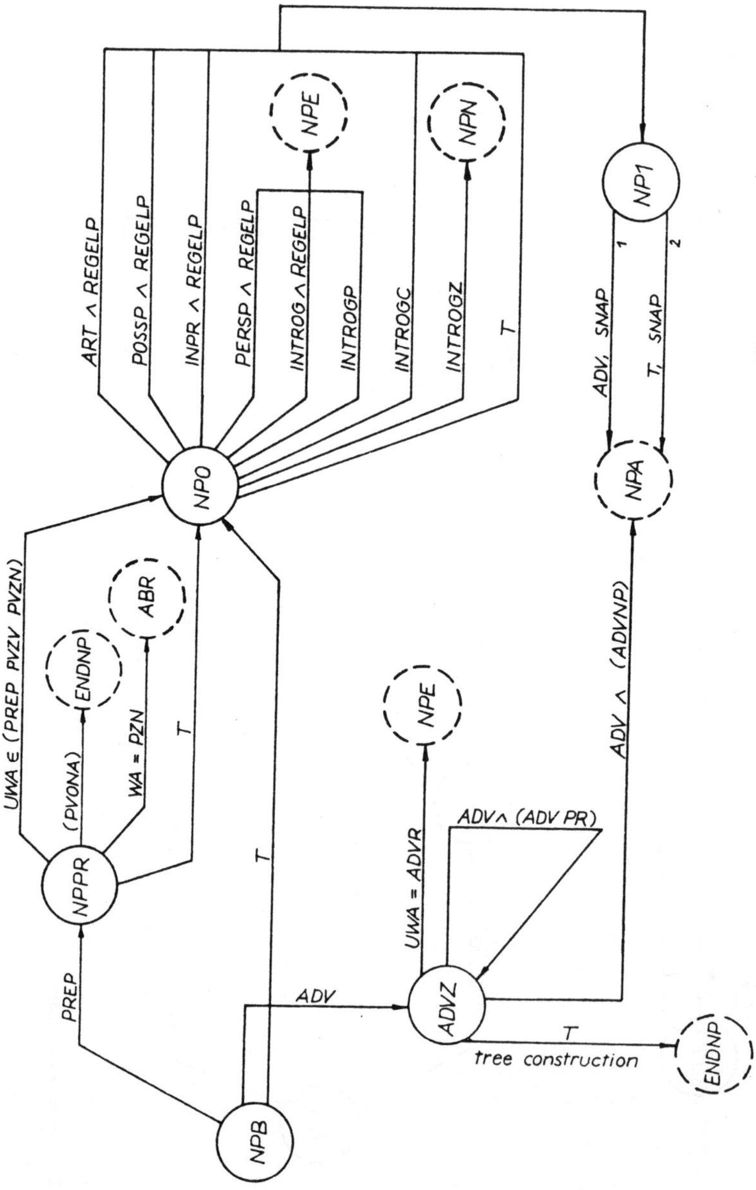

Fig. 10 Constituent net

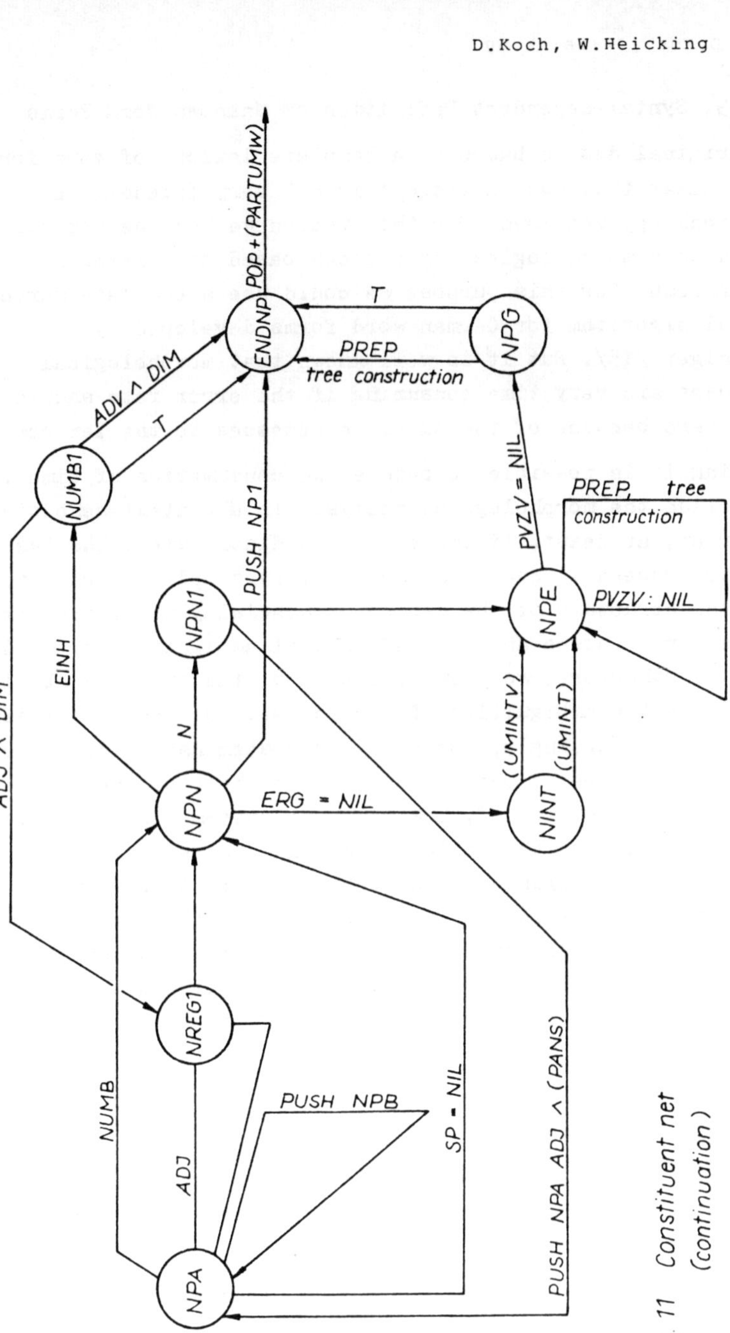

Fig. 11 Constituent net (continuation)

9. Syntax-dependent Definition of Unknown Word Forms

The original design bases on a complete lexicon of word forms. It is clear that such a concept is not very friendly in practical applications. For this reason we had the intention of adding a morphological preprocess based on a lexicon of morphems. For this purpose we could use a complete morphological algorithm for German word forms developed by B. Rüdiger /15/. But it is well known that morphological processes are very time consuming if the error rate should be about zero because of the multiple accesses to the lexicon.

We think it is possible to reduce the consumption of time if we accomplish the morphological analysis in a context-sensitive manner or, at least, if the costs are distributed. The basic idea to proceed in such a manner is very simple. We call to mind the structure of the lexicon, especially the representation of the word classes and the inflexional ambiguities of word forms. Furthermore, we draw attention to the system's ability to resolve the ambiguities if, of course, the sentence itself is unique. Accordingly, the analysis system had to discover the actual values of categories with the help of the syntactic and semantic context. If, however, the system possesses such capabilities, then the following assumption seems to us to be promising: - One trusts the system's ability to resolve ambiguities and defines - in a process taking place before the analysis of the sentence - all word forms not contained in the lexicon as totally ambiguous within limits that will be characterized below. We can then count on the following effects in the ATN step:

1. At least one result of analysis is correct and contains the actual word classes.

2. The inflexional ambiguities are reduced, but not to the same extent as would be the case on the basis of a lexicon that is "a priori" complete.

We think that this is a good basis for an aimed morphological analysis which has to verify or falsify the results syntactically found, and to detect the basic form. If the basic form is unknown too, then the error rate will grow because we now have to define the semantic information of the guessed basic form in the same manner, namely to assign all semantic features. This can be easily effected for the selective e-component ^{e}SK, but it is very difficult for case frames - the component ^{a}SK of verbs (cf. ch.10). It would be senseless to assign all possible case frames to the undefined word; the system would become ineffective and would have a high error rate. Hitherto, there has been only a good chance to guess the semantic classification of nouns not derived from verbs, or to guess deverbatives without arguments in the considered sentence so that the case frame of these deverbatives is not used. Such a classification would be incomplete, but sufficient in the given environment.

We now give the limits in which ambiguity definition is necessary. Of course, only the open word classes are interesting. The others are tolerably finite and, therefore, completely definable. We exclude the following subclasses among the verbs from guessing:

- Modals and auxiliaries because of their functional tasks in the verb group (see ch. 5).
- All irregular inflexional verb forms because the morphological analysis is too complicated. This class is small (about 150 basic forms) if we do not add the verbs which are derivable with affixes from the root.
- All participles building the active voice with "sein" forms. If we do not do this there would not be a possibility to distinguish between the state-passive (Zustandspassiv) and active voice.

From among the nouns and adjectives we exclude from guessing:

- Irregulary inflexional forms
- Forms ruling an infinitive with "zu" (frequently words derived from a verb ruling the same construction)

From among the adverbs we exclude from guessing:

- All original adverbs
- All adverbs with irregular comparison (perhaps a subclass of the first one)

We define the hypotheces for unknown forms built before the real analysis process starts and outline, thereby, the meaning of "distributing the cost of morphological analysis", noted above. For this purpose the sign string of the unknown form will be denoted by X, and a variable substring by x or y. The restrictions of the kind "if X = xaby" then mean that a simple morphological preprocess has to verify whether the string contains "ab" in the denoted position. Only such hypotheses are assumed which fulfil (simultaneously!) the given restriction.

Hypothesis 1

word class: N (noun)

$C_X \quad \{\mathfrak{n}\}$, except $P^1_{Person}(\mathfrak{n}) = P^2_{Person}(\mathfrak{n}) = 0$

$\mathfrak{n}$ denotes the vector only containing 1

Hypothesis 2 if $X \neq$ xlich / xbar / ...

word class: V (verb)

$C_X = \{\vec{o}\}$

$$P_i(a_w) = \begin{cases} 1, & \text{if } i = 13 \\ 0 & \text{else} \end{cases}$$

$$P_i(e_w) = \begin{cases} 1, & \text{if } i = 1,3,4,5,9,10 \\ 0 & \text{else} \end{cases}$$

Hypothesis 3 if X = xlich/xbar/... (alternative to hypothesis 2)

word class: V

$C_X = \{\vec{o}\}$

$a_w = \vec{o}$

$$P_i(e_w) = \begin{cases} 1, & \text{if } i = 6,7,8 \\ 0 & \text{else} \end{cases}$$

Hypothesis 4 if X = xe/xen/xer/xem/xes

word class: ADJ (adjective)

C_X available from the analysed end string

Hypothesis 5 if X = xzuyn

word class: IZU (synthetic infinitive with "zu")

$C_X = \{\vec{o}\}$

$a_{16} = \vec{o}$

$$P_i(e_{16}) = \begin{cases} 1, & \text{if } i = 12,13,14,15,16 \\ 0 & \text{else} \end{cases}$$

Hypothesis 6 if X = xig/xlich/xbar/ ...

word class: ADV (adverb)

$C_X = \emptyset$

As can be easily seen, the set of hypotheses are limited by the morphological restrictions previously tested. The syntactic analysis chooses one of the hypotheses automatically, and some of the inflexional possibilities. A morphological post-process has to verify (or falsify) the first one, to define more sharply the second one, and to search for a suitable basic form. All these procedures are closely connected, of course. The verification supplies no certainty and a multi-path-analysis by means of backtracking had to falsify the others. In general, we cannot expect a very low error rate. In any case, it does not appear to be responsible for updating the lexicon with the guessed features. For this reason we have designed a learning mechanism. As it has not yet been implemented we shall not describe it here. It should be noted in this context, however, that on this basis it is reasonable to guess (and to learn) also case frames because the learning process can be seen as a lexicon-generating process running before the real application.

10. Semantic Features

Up to now the following problem has not been solved, properly:- how many features and which features are necessary in order to analyse all sentences. There are well known examples showing that linguistic features are insufficient to clarify the correct subordination. For instance, let us consider the example of Winograd: "He drives down the street in the car". We cannot believe that the proportions of the concrete things are a matter of linguistics. This, and many other examples, show that a pure linguistic analysis has unsurmountable limits. This situation has created the modern trend of avoiding classical linguistic methods and of usin' 'frames', 'planes', 'scripts', 'demons' and perhaps a few other magical tricks. Of course, languages understanding is not reducible to linguistic analysis, and notions like the ones above can become important in the future, but in our opinion, the possibilities of a purelinguistic way are not yet exhausted.

How to design an experimental system without the backing of a linguistic theory that supplies the semantic features required for analysis without considering the knowledge on discourse? We think that the best way is to select a declarative description of semantic features, and to program the procedures independent of the features currently chosen. Then, a simple updating of the lexicon will induce a changed behaviour of the system. The same is valid of the semantic relations constituting the structure of sentences. We will not deal with the philosophy of semantic relations. Apart from the self-defined relations, we have taken over ideas from the works of Fillmore /5/, Chafe /6/, Lehmann and Zänker /7/, and Helbig /8/.
This experimental situation should be kept in mind if one considers critically the following sample of semantic features and relations. We had some success with this sample, but we were dissatisfied in many cases.

We have to point out that features are not a mean for generating correct sentences or for accepting only such sentences that are grammatical. These criteria are too strict for an analysis system. But there is a complementary principle: The more an analysis system accepts ungrammatical sentences, the higher the number of false structures of grammatical sentences it will supply, i.e. grammatical sentences take on an ambiguity of not being actual. We believe that this assumption is intuitively evident, but proof to this effect can be given only by a complete linguistic theory.

For an automatic system it seems to us very important to limit the set of features, i.e. to ask for an optimal set. This optimal set has to fulfil the following tasks:

1. Resolution of the ambiguity of expressions if the syntactic means are insufficient.
2. Distinction of different semems of a word.

These conditions for the selection of features are not independent. Each of them can be seen as a consequence of the other. We implied that the procedural scheme, using the semantic features, was intuitively clear. The question is the well-known selectional relations. This mechanism, and some procedures differing from the general formalism for the control of the semantic compatibility, will be discussed in ch. 13. As opposed to the demand of the pronounced validity of the selectional relations, it appears to state that there are violations of selection which do not make a sentence ungrammatical. In general, this is the case with the metaphoric usage of some words. Such sentences or phrases would be rejected by a system that demands the strict observance of the selectional relations. A way out could be to define a further semem of the word that affords metaphoric usage. We think that this course is justifiable if the metaphoric usage is fixed in the language or if, in a certain discourse, this usage prevails or is exclusively presented.
Let us consider the verb "rufen" ("to call"). This verb originally demands a subject with the feature HUMAN:

(1) Der Junge ruft mich.
    (The boy calls me.)

Now there is a limited class of abstract nouns as subjects:

(2) Die Pflicht (Duty) Die Arbeit (Work) Die Freiheit (Freedom)	ruft [mich] (calls)

We think that it is impossible to classify all abstract nouns in such a way that the set of potential subjects of "rufen" is determined by this classification. Of course, it is senseless to define tautologically a class that contains the abstract nouns which may be the subjects of "rufen". However, a refinement of the feature ABSTRACT for the definition of metaphoric semems would be necessary in many cases if the fact that the system accepted too many incorrect sentences was to be avoided. Hence, we have the discouraging alternative to make the acceptability too weak or too strict. It seems to us to be more reasonable to prefer the stricter version if there is no fixed discourse, and only then to introduce "metaphoric semems", i.e. to lexicalize the metaphor if this metaphor has been generalized or fixed by common usage in the language, or in certain discourses. For instance, in the field "Computer Science" the subject of "call" is generally a noun denoting a program. Here, we could introduce the special feature PROGRAM, or also the use of the more general feature MEANS OF INFORMATION.

In the latter instance we would have to accept sentences like "The newspapers call ...". Since this constellation will hardly occur in the discourse "Computer Science" additional ambiguities are therefore excluded. The situative metaphorism should be recognized procedurally in our opinion, i.e. if the analysis of a sentence is only then possible when one or more selectional restrictions are violated, then this should be taken as an indication of a metaphoric usage and the conditions of selection should be suppressed. We wish to point out that our system does not yet contain such procedures.

Our sample of semantic features is given in Table 4.

During the determination of the features we have treated mainly the selectional relations between the verb and its obligatory and facultative arguments, and those relations that are present in chains of NPs and PPs (abbrev. nominal complexes). Part of the latter relations are created by nominalized verbs (deverbatives). Consequently, they can be derived from the verb-argument relations. These are binary-selectional relations in the original sense. By contrast, other relations are not ruled by this general scheme. We want to explain the difference with two simple examples:

(3) der Käufer des Buches
(the buyer of the book)

(4) das Buch des Käufers
(the book of the buyer)

In (3) there is a selectional relation which we will denote as OBJ (object). It originates from the verb "kaufen" ("to buy"), and expresses itself in the transformation form as g e n i t i v u s o b j e c t i v u s. The object relation is explicitely and obligatorily demanded by the verb "kaufen" and can be therefore optionally manifested by the form (3). The genitive attribute in (4), however, does not depend on the lexem "Buch" ("book") in this specific way. Here, there is a general rule which operates on the features belonging to the occurring lexems (book, buyer).

For clarification we use the notations introduced by Kunze /3/:

$^{a}SK_{w}$ - selectional a-component of the word w. It contains, roughly speaking, the features which a word w' has to possess so that a relation denoted in $^{a}SK_{w}$ can be established between w and w'.

$^{e}SK_{w}$ - selectional e-component. It contains the features characterising the word w itself.

The formerly introduced vectors $^{a}\mathfrak{w}$ and $^{e}\mathfrak{w}$ have a similar task on the syntactic level and inside the verb group.

Tab. 4 The feature vector $^e\sigma$ of nouns

i	abbr.	interpretation	example
0 - 3		not occupied	
4	LOC	concrete things which, without these, are specified as LOCD	house, country, England
5	TIME	nouns describing time pionts or segments	year, minute, Monday
6	LOCD	concrete and abstract which can be used as "diffused situative places"	in the rain on the party
7	TIMED	similar to LOCD	after the rain during the run
8	MAT	materials for producing artefacts and which are subordinated to the artefact by the prep. "aus" ("of")	the table of wood
9	MENT	mental states	anxiety, fear, disguest
10	INSTR	concrete things used as instruments or tools	hammer, car
11	NMAT	negation of MAT	
12	NMENT	negation of MENT	
13	NINSTR	negation of INSTR	
14	BPART	parts of human beings	eye, leaf
15	NBPART	negation of BPART	
16	INANIM	negation of FLOW, BEST HUM	
17	FLOW	flowers	
18	BEST	beasts, bestial peoples	
19	HUM	human beings and institutions	
20	MTRANS	means of transport	car, bicycle
21	NMTRANS	negation of MTRANS	
22	INF	means of information	newspaper, book, radio
23	NINF	negation of INF	
24	GAS	gaseous substances	air
25	FLUID	fluid substances	water
26	SOLID	solid substances	
27	CONT	continuativa	
28	NCONT	negation of CONT (discontinuativa)	
29	CONCR	concrete things	
30	ABSTR	negation of CONCR (abstracts)	

We can outline the problems with the examples (3) and (4) in the following way: In case (3) a procedure works which uses the components

$^{a}SK_{buyer} \hat{=}$ buy and $^{e}SK_{book}$

and in case (4) a procedure works which uses the components

$^{e}SK_{buyer}$ and $^{e}SK_{book}$

The procedure working in (3) cannot be activated in case (4) because the lexem "book" does not possess an a-component.

And now let us turn our attention to the constructions that are not tested by semantic compatibility. The question is the relationship between the adjectives and nouns on the one hand, and between the verbs and the adverbs on the other. Hence, the system accepts the following expressions:

(5) ? Er schreit stumm.
(He cries dumbly)

(6) ? Er hört schnell.
(He hears quickly)

(7) ? die dicke Höhe
(the thick height)

(8) ? der grüne Schlaf
(the green sleep)

(9) ? der liebreiche Kasten
(the loving box)

etc.

Of course, the acceptance of these expressions which do not actually occur is not interesting when the neglectance of the compatibility tests does not lead to false structures for correct sentences. We give an example containing an ambiguity - due to this neglectance - that is not real:

(10) Er beobachtet stumm schreiende Kinder.
(He observes dumbly [-] crying children.)

"stumm" (dumbly) can be seen here as an attribute of "schreiend" ("crying"). (10), therefore, has two meanings:

(10_1) Er beobachtet stumm Kinder, die schreien.
(He dumbly observes crying children.)

(10_2) Er beobachtet Kinder, die stumm schreien.
(He observes children dumbly crying.)

We return to the feature components ^{a}SK and ^{e}SK. We reserve the notation a-component and e-component (^{a}SK and ^{e}SK, respectively) for verbs and nouns. Accordingly, the verbs possess primarily only an a-component, and the nouns only an e-component. The a-component of the derived nouns is taken from the corresponding verbs during analysis. Hitherto, we have renounced the explicite description of semantic verb classes as action verbs, state verbs, punctual verbs or also more defined classes. Such a description, however, becomes important when we can test, by means of this one, the compatibility of complex sentences. The mechanisms necessary for this purpose have not yet been treated.

The semantic characterization of functional words (prepositions, subjoiners) is formally similar to the a-component, but it must be interpreted in a slightly different way (see below, ch. 12).
We shall now turn our attention to the proper selectional components.

11. Definition of the Selectional Components

^{e}SK is defined as a set of binary vectors $^{e}\mathcal{G}$. Each position (component) of the vector $^{e}\mathcal{G}$ corresponds with a feature that can be existent (the value is 1) or not (the value is 0). Each vector defines one semem of the word. In the implemented lexical structure we have defined a secondary entry (cf. Ch. 5) for each semem. Consequently, the word is described by a set of these secondary entries, and these are characterized by exactly one vector. This actual situation is immaterial for the formal description, and we prefer the mentioned definition that the word is semantically described by a set of binary vectors:

$$^{e}SK = \{ {^{e}\mathcal{G}} , \ldots \}$$

(The same remark is valid for the a-component, mutatis mutandis).

We noted that each vector component corresponds with a semantic feature. But we can also say that the interpretation is imputed to each component. This means that the interpretation of the position is meta-theoretical and does not play a role in the system or in processing. Every user is free to interpret these components. This interpretation is only a support for the user's intuition when defining the lexems relevant to the user. If another interpretation is employed, as in our case, then the user has to know exactly the mechanism applying to the vectors.

Table 4 shows that, for each feature, there is a position containing the negation of this feature, or positions which can be interpreted as negations of another position. This principle has to be observed. We note that the components 5 to 11 possess a particular status. This will be dealt with in Ch. 12. The components 0 to 3 are not occupied by semantic features. They must not be used for additional semantic features.
We shall now define the selectional a-components. Their elements are also called <u>case frames.</u> A case frame describes a semem. We have to distinguish between obligatory and facultative valences of the verb. Therefore we define ^{a}SK as a set of ordered pairs:

$$^{a}SK = \{ ({^{a}sk_{obl}}, {^{a}sk_{fac}}), \ldots \}$$

Both components of the pair are structured analogously. We note that a difference is made between facultative arguments and free arguments. The latter can occur in the environment of nearly all verbs and are, therefore, not demanded explicitely by the case frame of a verb. Such a lexicalized information on free arguments of the verb would be redundant and storage wasting. Of course, there is some arbitrariness in the division into facultative and free arguments. Exact boundaries cannot be drawn.

^{a}sk is defined as a set of triplets and of relational vectors:

$$^{a}sk = \{(^{a}\sigma\ , r, P), \ldots, \sigma_V, \ldots\}$$

where $^{a}\sigma$ is a binary vector of the kind defined above. For the notion 'relational vector' see next chapter. The interpretation of the components of $^{a}\sigma$ has to be synchronous with that of $^{e}\sigma$. r is an element from an arbitrary set of relation names, and P a set of prepositions. P can be empty since not all arguments have prepositions. Contrary to $^{e}\sigma$, the first four components of $^{a}\sigma$ are occupied. They contain the inflexional case which the verb demands. E.g. the verb "kaufen" ("buy") demands a human agent (AGT), a concrete object (OBJ) that is not a human being (slave trade exempted) and, optionally, a beneficiary of the bargain (BENF) which has to be a human being. The beneficiary can be expressed either as dative object or as prepositional object. Both possibilities can be taken into account by defining the corresponding triplets in the facultative part of the case frame. If we demand from an actual structure that two arguments should never depend on the verb with the same relation then confusion will be avoided. The outlined case frame of "kaufen" has the following form:

$$^{a}sk_{kaufen} = (\{ (\sigma_1, \text{AGT},) \ (\sigma_2, \text{OBJ},) \},$$
$$\{ (\sigma_3', \text{BENF}, \{ \text{FUER} \}), (\sigma_3, \text{BENF},) \})$$

σ_3 and σ_3' differ only in the surface case positions. You can define the vectors with the help of tab. 4. If the positive features are specified by 0 then their negations have to be specified by 1. The inverse is not valide: Both features can be specified by 1. In this case the verb demands nothing with respect to these features.

The determination of the inflexional case of σ_i is ruled by the situation in active sentences. The passive-active transformation was done in the ATN step in such a way that the form of arguments contained in the syntactic structure is not in contradiction with the case frame. But it would be possible, and more correct, to do this transformation in the semantic step by means of procedural (and temporary) redefinition of the case frame if the ATN step supplies the mark PASSIVE. The case frame of "kaufen" would then take on the following form:

$$
\begin{aligned}
{}^{a}sk = (\{(\sigma'_2, \text{OBJ},)\}, \{ & (\sigma'_1, \text{AGT}, \{\text{VON}, \text{DURCH}\}) \\
& (\sigma'_3, \text{BENF}, \{\text{FUER}\}) \\
& (\sigma_3, \text{BENF},)\})
\end{aligned}
$$

$$
\begin{aligned}
\text{with } & P_0(\sigma'_2) = 1,\ P_3(\sigma'_2) = 0,\ \text{else } P_i(\sigma'_2) = P_i(\sigma_2) \\
& P_0(\sigma'_1) = 0,\ P_2(\sigma'_1) = 1,\ \text{else } P_i(\sigma'_1) = P_i(\sigma_1)
\end{aligned}
$$

With this method we could handle the well-known passive-active ambiguity "wird vergessen" ("is forgotten"), in German: future active or present passive. We only outlined the main case of passivization. A detailed treatment of this problem is beyond the scope of this paper.

12. The Semantic Characterization of Prepositions and Subjoiners

If some prepositions are demanded by the triplets of the case frame then their semantic characterization is not interesting. They, themselves, act like features. In general, the verb demands explicitely only NPs and prepositional objects. The application of the same technique to local adverbials leads to a large set P. This consumes storage place and time for examination. Additionally, most local adverbials are free arguments which are not defined in the case frame. Hence, there must be a mechanism for generation of local relations on the basis of their internal structure (preposition + noun), and only these relations should be demanded by elements of ^{a}SK (this is the task of the relational vectors σ_V) or should be subordinated as free arguments or prepositional (adnominale) attributes. For this purpose we shall procedurally reinterpret some components of the vector $^{e}\sigma$. They now additionally represent relations. We come to the details.
Firstly, let us consider the feature LOC. Names of things which can be places are conceived - in texts! - dynamically (directions: goal and origin) or statically. These are faculties of the inflexional case (in German!) and of the used prepositions. They do not belong to the original features of the nouns. For this reason the local feature (LOC) is split into 3 features during the analysis, and the preposition (and surface case) resolves the ambiguity of the noun with respect to these three features. Consequently, we need two further components in the vector $^{e}\sigma$. These features will be interpreted as relations, too. Secondly, we split the feature TIME into 6 features to which 6 different time-relations belong: the point (segment) of time itself (MOM), and before (ANTE), after (AFTER), since (SINCE), until (UNTIL), and during (DUR) the point (segment) of time. We can say that the features LOC and TIME become markers of relations by these splittings. We also interpret three further features as relations, namely INSTR, MENT, and MAT. If nouns with these features are ruled by some prepositions, then free arguments or adnominal attributes come into being, and the marking of their subordination is exclusively

determined by the preposition and the noun; for instance: "with the hammer" (INSTR), "for fear" (MENT), "of wood" (MAT). Once more we note that these decisions are context-sensitive. For instance, the OBJ relation can also characterize the subordination of the phrase "with the hammer", namely: "I am dealing with the hammer.". In this case the adverbial "with the hammer" is a prepositional object and is ruled by the case frame of the verb "to deal".
In the considered positions the relational vector of the prepositions and σ_V from the case frame has to be defined analogous to the split $^{e}\sigma$ -vector. Apart from the discussed relations, prepositions create a set of other relations which are independent of the features of nouns, i.e. almost all nouns can be chosen. The relation is exclusively determined - but not always unambiguously - by the preposition. For instance, let us consider the preposition "wegen" ("because of"), which is a relator connecting a fact with its cause (relation CAUS). The following examples show that the features of the nouns are of no consequence for this decision:

wegen des Jungen
(because of the boy)

wegen des Steines
(because of the stone)

wegen des schlechten Wetters
(because of the bad weather)

wegen der politischen Situation
(because of the political situation)

etc.

Features of the preposition which do not refer to features of nouns are called here *relational preselections* (in German: relationale Vorgaben), the other features introduced in the beginning of this chapter are called *relational features.* Therefore, the relational vector of prepositions (and verbs) contains components meaning relational features, and components meaning relational preselections. The interaction between them is explained in the next chapter (13 b).

The number of relational vectors of a preposition tallies with the number of inflexional cases which the preposition can rule and when a change of meaning is connected with it; static = DATIVE, dynamic = ACCUSATIVE. Uncertainties in language usage (see the preposition "wegen": GENITIVE, DATIVE) are expressed by one vector.

We demand from the part which represents the relational preselections that only one component be occupied by 1, i.e. this part has to be unique. The part of relational features can be ambiguous. Tab. 5 gives a survey. The relational vectors of subjoiners have the same interpretation, only the first 4 positions are neglected and the whole vector is seen as preselections.

Finally, we define in what manner the vector ${}^e\sigma$ of the noun is to be transformed dynamically in ${}^e\sigma'$ if the relation should be created by the preposition and the noun:

$$P_i({}^e\sigma') = \begin{cases} 1, \text{ if } 4 \leq i \leq 6 \wedge P_4({}^e\sigma)=1 & \text{(LOC} \rightarrow \text{LOC, DIR, ORIG)} \\ 1, \text{ if } 7 \leq i \leq 12 \wedge P_5({}^e\sigma)=1 & \text{(TIME} \rightarrow \text{MOM, AFTER, SINCE, UNTIL, ANTE, DUR)} \\ 1, \text{ if } 13 \leq i \leq 17 \; P_{i-7}({}^e\sigma)=1 & \text{(shifting of MENT, INSTR, MAT, ZEITD, ORTD)} \\ 0, \text{ else} & \end{cases}$$

Tab. 5 The relational vector of prepositions and subjoiners

i	abbr.	interpretation	example
0	NOM	nominative	
1	GEN	genitive	
2	DAT	dative	
3	ACC	accusative	
4	DIR	direction of the goal	into the house
5	LOC	static location	on the place
6	ORIG	original direction	from the house
7	DUR	duration of a time segment	during the Monday
8	UNTIL	until the time point	until the Monday
9	SINCE	since a time point	since the Monday
10	AFTER	after a time point	after this day
11	ANTE	before a time point	
12	MOM	at a time point (segment)	on Monday
13	LOCD	split into 4 - 12 during	in the rain
14	TIMED	the analysis	before the rain
15	MAT	of some materials	of wood
16	MENT		for fear
17	INSTR		with the hammer
18	CAUS	reason of actions or states	because of ...
19	PURP	purpose of an action	for the improvement
20	METH	method of an action	by means of ...
21	MOD	modale circumstantial	with zeal

13. Procedures for Testing Semantic Compatibility

As an introductory remark it must be stated that the procedures handled can be misunderstood if they are not seen together with the general strategy using them. It is only the general strategy that decides whether the procedures may be used or not. We hope that ch. 14 give some insight into the general frame work.

a) Test and fixation of the selectional relations

The test takes place between a triplet of the case frame and the e-component of a constituent k (that is the e-component of the top node of the constituent).

Definition:

$({}^{a}\sigma, r, P)$ and ${}^{e}SK_k$ are compatible, iff

1. If k is a PP then the preposition of k is an element of P

   If k is not a PP then $P = \emptyset$

2. Congruence:

   $\varkappa^{q}_{\{CASE\}}(\{{}^{a}\sigma\} \times C_k) \neq \emptyset$

3. $\exists^{e}\sigma \; ({}^{e}\sigma \in {}^{e}SK_k \wedge \varkappa({}^{a}\sigma, {}^{e}\sigma) = {}^{e}\sigma)$

If all three conditions are fulfilled then the node k can be subordinated to the verb with the relation r.

b) Creation of relations by preposition and noun

$SR = \{\sigma_P, \ldots\}$ and ${}^{e}SK = \{{}^{e}\sigma, \ldots\}$ are the sets of the relational vectors of the preposition and the feature vectors of the noun, respectively. C_{PP} is the inflexional component of the prepositional phrase. The creation of a relation for the PP subordination proceeds in the following steps:

1. Seek a vector σ_P from SR which has the same inflexional case as any vector from C_{PP}. There is only one vector with this case.

2. Define the vector ${}^{e}\sigma'$ with the help of ${}^{e}\sigma$ for each ${}^{e}\sigma \in {}^{e}SK$ in the manner described at the end of the previous chapter.

3. Test whether there is any ${}^{e}\sigma'$ with

(a) $\exists i \quad (4 \leq i \leq 12 \vee 15 \leq i \leq 17 \wedge P_i\ (\varkappa(\sigma_P, {}^{e}\sigma')) = 1)$
(local or time relation)

or

(b) $\exists i \quad (13 \leq i \leq 14 \wedge P_i\ (\varkappa({}^{a}\sigma, {}^{e}\sigma')) = 1$
(diffused local or time relation)
In this case the TIMED or LOCD features is split in the same way as TIME and LOC, and (a) is tried once again.

If the vector $\sigma_{PP} = \varkappa(\sigma_P, {}^{e}\sigma')$ does not equal $\vec{0}$ then the vector is unique (only one position is 1) and the corresponding relation is chosen.

4. If $\sigma_{PP} = \vec{0}$ then the relation is chosen from the part of relational preselections of σ_P.

We call the relational vector derived from the parts of PP briefly σ_{PP}.

The subordination of PP, marked by the relation encoded in σ_{PP}, can be a result of the application of a case frame, or it can be done by the control program on the strength of the analysis situation or the created relation.

c) Demand of relational vectors by the case frame

σ_{PP} can be ambiguous if the phrase is demanded by a relational vector σ_V of the case frame. The actual relation between the verb and PP is defined by

$$\sigma_R = \varkappa(\sigma_V, \sigma_P)$$

Subordination is possible if σ_R is not the zero vector, and σ_R is unique. In the current system the uniqueness is assured because the original vectors are unique. We note here that modal adverbs cannot be required by the case frame. In general, modal adverbs are free arguments and if a verb obligatorily demands a modal adverb then this cannot be expressed in the case frame. The consequence is again: incorrect sentences are accepted; for instance: ? "Er fühlt sich". ("He feels.")

d) The subordination of subjoined clauses

We noted in the syntactic part of our paper that the ATN step performs the unmarked subordination of the subclauses, where the subordination criterion bases on the ordering of clauses. This pure syntactic criterion is not always sufficient. But we do not know good semantic criteria to restrict the remaining ambiguities. The semantic step only has to mark the subordination. It is evident that, for this purpose, no com - patibility criteria can be used since such criteria would be a tool to find out the correct unmarked subordination. Marking, therefore, must be immediately supplied by the subjoiners, i.e. they must be characterized by relational vectors built in the same way as the relational vectors of prepositions except, of course, the positions for the inflexional case. The vector has to be completely unique. Ambiguous subjoiners have an arbitrarily preferred meaning.

e) The subordination of genitive attributes

This theme will be only roughly outlined. The problem is rather complicated, and the development of the program has not yet been completed. In ch. 10 we made some remarks about this in connection when discussing the examples (3) and (4). Let us consider two nouns N_1, N_2 (or NPs) that are suspected to be connected by a genitive:

N_1 des N_2

(N_1 of the N_2)

If N_1 is derived from a verb then we try to use the selectional mechanism on the basis of

$$^{a}SK_{V(N_1)} \text{ and } {}^{e}SK_{N_2}$$

where $V(N_1)$ means that ^{a}SK ist taken from the corresponding verb. The selectional mechanism is somewhat modified for this transformation. If the selectional mechanism is not applicable, either because no triplet is compatible with $^{e}SK_{N_2}$ or because N_1 is not derived, then a procedure is called which inquires

$$^{e}SK_{N_1} \text{ and } {}^{e}SK_{N_2},$$

and which derives selected relations from the identity or non-identity of some features. The following table gives a survey of which relation can be inferred which feature situation.

$^eSK_{N_1}$	$^eSK_{N_2}$	Relation	Example
HUM+NBPART	HUM+NBPART	SOCREL	der Vater des Jungen (the father of the boy)
BPART	~INANIM	WHOLE	das Bein des Jungen (the leg of the boy)
NBPART+CONCR +INANIM	HUM	POSS	das Auto des Jungen (the car of the boy)
CONCR+INANIM	CONCR+INANIM	WHOLE	das Bein des Tisches (the leg of the table)
ABSTR	CONCR	FEATC	die Macht des Vaters (der Wellen etc.) (the power of the father) (of the waves etc.)
ABSTR	ABSTR	QUAL	Jahre der Not (years of want)

Tab. 6 Derivation of relations represented by genitive attributes by means of selectional e-features of the nouns

To avoide mistakes we repeat once again that these relations are only derived if no selectional relations can be found. For instance "the application of the law" would not be interpreted by the last line of the table as QUAL but as OBJ because of the derivation: apply → application.

14. General Strategy of the Semantic Interpretation

We shall forgo the abstract description of the program and explain the most important parts by an example. Since the unmarked subordination of subjoined clauses is performed by the ATN step we restrict ourselves to one sentence level.

> John kaufte am Freitag das Fahrrad des Nachbarn für seine Schwester
> (John bought on Friday the bicycle of the neighbour for his sister)

Following elements of the syntactic structure are essential for the explanation of the semantics program:

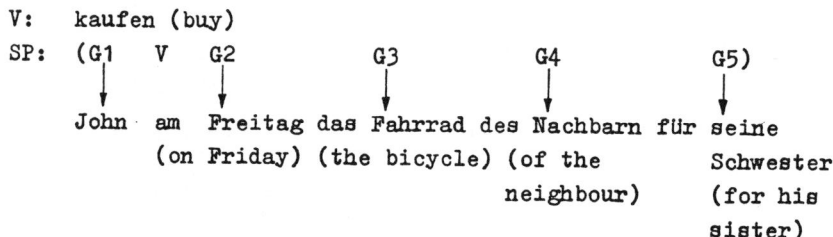

V: kaufen (buy)

SP: (G1 V G2 G3 G4 G5)

- G1 → John
- V → am
- G2 → Freitag (on Friday)
- G3 → das Fahrrad (the bicycle)
- G4 → des Nachbarn (of the neighbour)
- G5 → für seine Schwester (for his sister)

Here, we repeat the only case frame of "kaufen":

$$(\{ (\sigma_1, \text{AGT}, \ ) (\sigma_2, \text{OBJ}, \ ) \} , \{ (\sigma_3', \text{BENF}, \{ \text{FUER} \}) \; \sigma_3, \text{BENF}, \ ) \})$$

The proper constituents are sought in steps in SP by means of the triplets. When a compatible one is found then it is marked by the relation name given in the triplet by which subordination of this constituent is prevented later on.

1. (σ_1, AGT,) is compatible with G1, SP is transformed into

   SP: (AGT G1 V G2 G3 G4 G5)

2. (σ_2, OBJ,) is compatible with G3, consequently:

   SP: (AGT G1 V G2 OBJ G3 G4 G5)

All obligatory elements are satisfied, therefore the case frame is applicable.

3. (σ_3', BENF, {FUER}) is compatible with G5:

   SP: (AGT G1 V G2 OBJ G3 G4 BENF G5)

If the triplet (σ_3, BENF,) would be in the first position then this triplet is not applicable and the next step will use the FUER-triplet. The ordering of triplets plays some role because false decisions can be avoided by skilful ordering. For instance, the phrase "das Fahrrad der Tante" ("der Tante": GENITITVE and DATIVE) would cause such a false decision if (σ_3, BENF,) stands in front of (σ_3', BENF, {FUER}) since "der Tante" is a semantically and syntactically possible beneficiary.
The subordination of G2 and G4 is still pending. It is not controlled by the verb. Therefore, G2 and G4 are either free arguments of the verb or attributs of other constituents.

4. "am Freitag" ("on Friday") supplies by means of ch. 13 b) a time relation, namely MOM. The constituent follows the finite verb immediately and, for this purpose, it cannot be ruled by another constituent. Consequently it is a free argument of the verb:
SP: (AGT G1 V MOM G2 OBJ G3 G4 BENF G5)

5. As the verb does not demand a genitive object, G4 can only be a genitive attribute of G3. The program for the analysis of genitive attributes finds out the relation POSS (owner) by means of the features of G3 and G4. G4 is erased in the SP-list and subordinated to G3:

   SP: (AGT G1 V MOM G2 OBJ G3 BENF G5)
   G3: (N FAHRRAD POSS G4)

6. The sign V in SP is erased. The indicator SP, and its value of the p-list of the sentence node (for instance G6), is also erased and the p-list of G6 is lengthened by the SP-list built above:

   G6: (V KAUFEN AGT G1 MOM G2 OBJ G3 BENF G5)

7. The next steps belong to the assimilation phase. We give a short outline.
Each node is treated, whether it refers to an aforementioned individual or to an event. The definite pronouns (articles) and the attributes of phrases (adjectives, relative clauses, genitive and prepositional attributes etc.) are taken into account.

Let us examine the single nodes:

G1: We examine whether "John" was mentioned before. In this case an individual node (e.g. I1) was attached to "John". If the specifications of G1 are more restricted or are other than that of I1, then our "John" is interpreted as a "John" different to the one mentioned before, and a new individual node is created. G1 is replaced by the new or old individual node, as the case may be.

G2: We suppose that "Friday" was mentioned earlier. Then this atom possesses a conception node and at least one individual node. If any of those individual nodes do not fulfil the specification condition listed above (G1), then a new individual node (accordingly "Friday the 13 ...") is generated and attached to the conception node.

G3: With attribute G4 one seeks for individual nodes of more restricted specifications than G4 (e.g. "left neighbour"). If there is nobody then a new individual "bicycle" with the specification G4 is generated.

G5: To find out or newly generate an individual, the determination of the reference of "sein" ("his") is important. "Seine" coincides grammatically with "John". Consequently, he is considered as the possible social partner (SOCREL) of sister. There remains the determination of the individual node of "John's sister". This node (new or old) has the structure:

I15: (IST B7 SOCREL I1 ...)

B7: (N SCHWESTER ...)

During this process the graph is simulaneously symmetrized, i.e. each arc is to possess the inverse arc. We use the same name for that, and the CAR and CDR of the value of the corresponding indicator supply the two directions.

We show - a little shortened - the structure of the analysed sentence. With the numbering I1, I15, I25 we want to assign the fact that the individuals were mentioned before, while I74 and I75 are new. We give the linear structure of I74 and I75 for illustration:

I75: (V (KAUFEN) AGT (I1) OBJ (I74) BENF (I15))
I74: (IST (B7) POSS (I25) OBJ (NIL I75))

The explanation of the complicated connections between individuals and conceptions is beyond the scope of this paper. A sophisticated description of the semantic network will follow in a later paper.

Conclusions

The weakest point of these described system is its complete restriction to subjoined structures. Co-ordination in all its forms is the subject of our current work. The difficulties of this phenomenon are well known and we fear that a good solution will cost a lot of time. Likewise, the comparation problem is not solved by the system. But the new release will not only contain an approach to these problems, but also a new analysis strategy with more closed interactions of syntactic and semantic procedures.

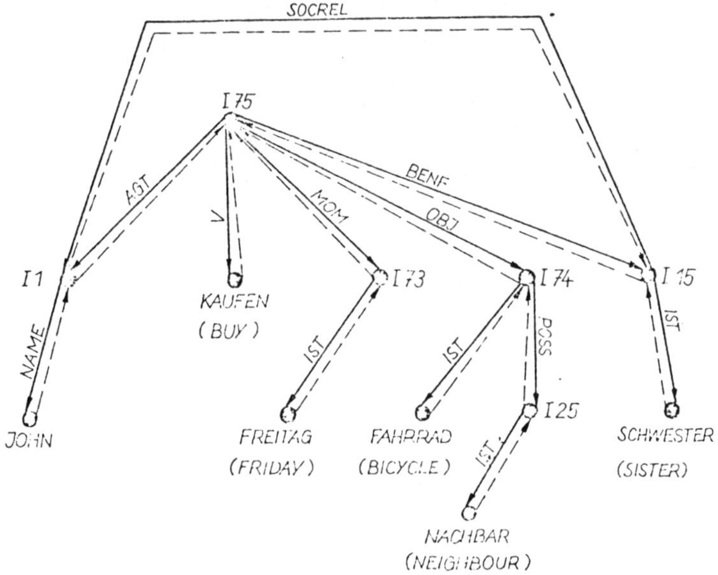

Fig. 12 Semantic network structure of the sentence "John kaufte am Freitag das Fahrrad des Nachbarn für seine Schwester." (John bought on Friday the bicycle of the neighbour for his sister.")

REFERENCES

/ 1/ Heicking, W. "Semantische Interpretation syntaktischer Strukturen", Diss. in prep.

/ 2/ Koch, D. "ATN-Analyse koordinationsfreier deutscher Sätze", Linguistische Studien, Berlin 1979

/ 3/ Kunze, J. "Abhängigkeitsgrammatik" studia grammatica, Berlin 1975

/ 4/ Bech, G. "Studien über das deutsche Verbum infinitum" KDVS 35/2, 1955, 1-222

/ 5/ Fillmore, C. J. "The case for case", in E. Bach and R. Harms (eds.) Universals in Linguistic Theory, Holt, Rinehard and Winston, 1968, 1-90

/ 6/ Chafe, W. L. "Bedeutung und Sprachstruktur" Berlin 1976

/ 7/ Lehmann, E. and Zänker, F. "Fakteneingabesprache für ein Frage-Antwort-System" VEB Robotron, Dresden 1974

/ 8/ Helbig, H. "Ein Repertoire von Darstellungsmitteln zur semantischen Repräsentation von Wissen in einem Frage-Antwort-System", VEB Robotron ZFT, Dresden 1978

/ 9/ Stoyan, H. "LISP-Programmierhandbuch", Berlin 1978

/10/ Woods, W. A. "Transition Network Grammars for Natural Language Analysis", CACM 13, 1970, 591-606

/11/ Woods, W. A. "An Experimental Parsing System for Transition Network Grammar", BBN Rep. No. 2362, 1972

/12/ Koch, D. "Zur Analyse der natürlich-sprachlichen Eingabe für ein FAS", Rep. 1975, Zentralinstitut für Kybernetik und Informationsprozesse der AdW der DDR

/13/ Burton, R. and Woods, W. A. "A Compiling System for Augmented Transition Networks", Proc. International Conference on Computational Linguistics, Ottawa 1976

/14/ Geske, U. and Werner, W. "Deduktionen im FAS", Rep. 1977, Zentralinstitut für Kybernetik und Informationsprozesse der AdW der DDR

/15/ Rüdiger, Barbara "Flexivische und Wortbildungsanalyse des Deutschen", Diss., Linguistische Studien, Berlin 1975

PLAIN - A PROGRAM SYSTEM FOR DEPENDENCY ANALYSIS AND FOR SIMULATING NATURAL LANGUAGE INFERENCE

by

Peter Hellwig

ABSTRACT

This article is a presentation of PLAIN, a new language processing system developed at the University of Heidelberg, Germany. The system uses lists as a disambiguous representation of natural language input. These lists are isomorphic to tree diagrams as produced by a dependency grammar. Every list element simultaneously expresses a lexical meaning, a logico-semantic role, and the morpho-syntactic features of an input segment.

The analysis component is characterized by its extremely lexical approach to syntax. The system contains neither phrase structure rules nor transition networks. Lexical descriptions are the only basis of the analysis. Syntactic completion patterns for lexical items are part of the lexicon. Complex expressions are formed by a bottom-up process of inserting lists into slots of other lists. The lexicalization of grammar makes it very easy to draw up and test dependency descriptions of any input language. Together with the dependency relationships, the phrase structure of the input is depicted in the list representations as well. The problem of integrating constituency and dependency structures within one notation is definitely solved.

The deduction component transforms analyzed sentences into other sentences in order to simulate inferences. There are two types of rules which guide the transformations. Rules of the first type are analytically valid and serve to turn input sentences which denote general relationships in the object domain into rules of the second type. Rules of the second type are empirically valid like the sentences they are derived from. They are stored in a data base together with the primitive sentences entered into the system. The empirically valid rules allow the compilation of all of the sentences which follow from a given sentence according to the data base or which are suitable for proving a given sentence as true according to the data base. Thus the problem of searching the data base for theorem proving is solved in a goal oriented way. The contents of the data base themselves guide the process. Rules apply to sentences according to the role indications that are included in the list representations. Since role indications belong to the syntax of the system's language and since a disambiguous representation can be provided for any syntactic construction of the input language by means of role markers, any inferential relationships between sentences of the input language can be dealt with. There is no need to translate the natural language input into a remote system of logic such as, for example, model theory.

Examples of analysis and deduction are discussed.

1. AIMS

The system PLAIN (Program for Language Analysis and Inference) resulted from linguistic research on the syntax and semantics of the German language. It is meant, so to speak, for two generations of users. The users of the first generation are linguists who advocate dependency descriptions in grammar and who are interested in modeling the logico-semantic relationships between the expressions of a language by means of syntactic transformations. For these users PLAIN is a research tool. At a later point, when adequate linguistic descriptions for one or more languages have been developed with the help of PLAIN, it will be possible to use PLAIN as part of an information system with natural language input and output. Then it will be at the disposal of users of the second generation, i.e. persons who would like to carry on a dialogue in a natural language with a computer. At present, PLAIN is oriented towards automatic question answering. A further conceivable application would be within the framework of a document retrieval system or, in case of sufficient research of two languages, as an automatic translation procedure.

PLAIN functions on the basis of two data sets that must be set up by the user: a description of the language that is to be used for the input and the actual input in this language via which a "world" is described. The language description data include the definition of morpho-syntactic categories, a morpho-syntactic lexicon, a valence lexicon, and analytically valid deduction rules.

The world description data are sentences stored in a data base. According to the analytically valid rules PLAIN converts some of the sentences into empirically valid inference patterns. Careful attention was paid to keeping the programs of PLAIN independent of the contents of the two data sets. Thus the program system can be used to describe any input language and any object domain. The data sets only need to be exchanged for the system to accept a different input language or to deal with another object area. However, at all times PLAIN functions on a single language basis. The examples in this article will be from German, since this is the language to which PLAIN is currently being applied.

The acronym "PLAIN" was chosen to allude to the simplicity of the basic ideas. The program system is also supposed to help bridge the gap that exists between computer science on the one hand and traditional linguistics on the other. Linguists who are used to expressing their empirical findings in natural language should not be frightened off by too much mathematics. At the same time, the notation system should be flexible enough to allow the formulation of as many empirical statements as necessary. Observations on syntax that, for example, do not fit into the mold of a phrase structure grammar should not be left untreated. Sentences which are difficult to translate into existing logic should still permit the deduction of other sentences. In any case, the differentiated know-how of traditional linguistics is to be made more productive for automatic language processing than has been the case so far. In the near future, a comprehensive transfer of non-formal German grammars and lexicons into PLAIN format is planned.

On the other hand, feedback from computer linguistics into ordinary linguistics is just as desirable. Therefore, the language descriptions that can be tested with PLAIN purposely have a format which enables a more general public to read and understand them. Thus these descriptions can serve other purposes besides those of automatic information processing. PLAIN can test valence dictionaries that are used in teaching. The expiriments with the deduction component of PLAIN may contribute to an argumentation theory of natural languages. To know more about reasoning in a natural language is also important for language education.

Chapter 2 of this paper describes the syntax of an artificial language which is used for data representation in the system. In chapter 3 the device is explained that pairs expressions of the input language with expressions of the artificial representation. Chapter 4 shows how the analyzed input can be further processed.

For the most part I shall forgo comparisons with other program systems and approaches to grammar and logic. Such a discussion would go beyond the scope of an introduction to the system PLAIN. I have discussed the pros and cons of PLAIN's linguistic concept in comparison to other grammatical theories elsewhere.[1] In Germany, as far as the aims are concerned, PLAIN is in competition with the system SATAN (within the framework of SUSY) of the special research project 100 at the university of Saarbrücken, with the system PLIDIS at the Institutefor the German Language in Mannheim, with the system BEAST at the Institute for Applied Computer Science at the Technical University of Berlin, with the system CONDOR of the Siemens Company in Munich. The reader will easily recognize the differences.[2]

2. ARTIFICIAL LANGUAGE

PLAIN works with three languages: the natural input language (NL), an artificial language (AL) for describing the input language and for representing analyzed input in a legible form, and finally a computer-internal coding of the artificial language expressions (IR). The natural language is given. The computer-internal coding is of interest only to the programmer. The current artificial language has to be designed by the linguist using PLAIN. The constraints he must take into account while doing so are described below.

---

1 In detail in HELLWIG 1978, briefly in HELLWIG 1977.

2 Research reports on the mentioned systems are continuously being published; several systems are described in KRALLMANN 1978; for BEAST see also HABEL/SCHMIDT/SCHWEPPE 1977, for CONDOR see BANERJEE 1977, for PLIDIS see BERRY-ROGGHE/WULZ 1978.

2.1. General Format

PLAIN is essentially a program for list processing. A "list" is defined in the system as a bracketed expression (with parentheses) which ends with a semicolon (or is followed in the input by an empty record) and which does not contain more closing than opening brackets. If there are fewer closing than opening brackets, PLAIN adds the missing brackets to the end of the expression. A "list element" is any sequence of characters enclosed directly by a pair of brackets. From here on I shall refer to a list element as "term".

Every term in the artificial language of PLAIN consists of a maximum of three "fields". The fields are separated from one another by ':'. The following expression is a list made up of three terms; only one field is used in each term:

(A) (B) (C);

An example of a list of one single term but with three fields used is the following:

(A : B : C);

A term "dominates" another when the brackets around the former enclose the brackets around the latter. A term dominates another "directly" when there are no unpaired brackets between the opening bracket around the former and the brackets around the latter. A term is "subordinated" to another when the latter dominates the former. A term is "directly subordinated" to another when the latter directly dominates the former. A term is "collateral" to another either when both are not subordinated to any other term or when both are directly dominated by another term.

A configuration of terms is a "tree" if one term directly or indirectly dominates all of the other terms and if there is no further term which is likewise subordinated to the dominating term in the bracketed expression. A term which does not dominate another term is also to be referred to as a "tree". Trees which are not made up of one single term contain in turn trees. These trees, with respect to the whole expression, are called "subtrees". I have chosen the term "tree", because bracketed expressions that fit the given definition are isomorphic with directed tree diagrams. Accordingly a list in the sense given above is the same as a sequence of tree diagrams with multiple labeled nodes. A list can also consist of just one tree (and correspondingly just one term).

According to the convention, the following expression is well-formed:

```
(A:(B:C:D)E(FGHI: JK LM NO : 1 2 3 4)(::x));
```

The above is a list which is, in its entirety, a tree. The list is made up of four terms, one of which directly dominates the other three. The first term contains in its first field the character 'A'. The second term contains characters in three fields, namely 'B', 'C', and 'D'. The next letter in the formula, 'E', belongs to the dominating term and fills the second field of this term. (In principle, subordinated terms can enter at any point into the string of symbols that make up the dominating term.) The third term embraces the fields 'FGHI', 'JK LM NO', and '1 2 3 4'. The fourth term only contains a character in the third field: 'x'.

PLAIN includes subroutines which compare expressions in artificial language with one another. Of the structural features, domination/subordination is checked but not the sequence of terms. Thus the following four lists are deemed to be equal.

```
(A (B) (C));
(A (C) (B));
((C) A (B));
((B) (C) A);
```

One of two expressions which are to be compared is viewed as a "pattern". If the other expression corresponds to the pattern, then it constitutes an "instance". There are two options with which the user can guide the comparison: EQUAL and INCLUDED. If, for the moment, we disregard variables within expressions, then the pattern and the instance must be isomorphic and must be labeled with identical characters in the fields of the terms in order to fulfill the option EQUAL. If INCLUDED is specified, then all of the terms and the structure of the instance must have a correspondence in the pattern. However, in the pattern there can be additional collateral terms which are not present in the instance. Example:

EQUAL	pattern:	(A (B) (C));
	instance:	((B) A (C));
	not an instance:	(A (B));
INCLUDED	pattern:	(X) (A (B) (C)) (Z);
	instance:	(A (B));
	not an instance:	(B);

In addition to EQUAL and INCLUDED the option LOCATE can be specified. In this case the uppermost term of the pattern does not have to correspond to the uppermost term of the instance, but to any term, i.e. it is now being determined whether and where within the instance a term configuration exists which coincides with the pattern:

LOCATE	pattern:	(B (C) (D));
EQUAL	instance:	(A (B (C) (D)));
	not an instance:	(A (B (C)));
LOCATE	pattern:	(B (C));
INCLUDED	instance:	(A (B (C) (D)));
	not an instance:	(A (B) (C));

Several patterns can be grouped together into one single pattern. This is done by means of the system-defined terms (,) and (&). The first denotes an alternative with respect to a list structure, the second denotes the co-occurrence of collateral terms.

Examples:

EQUAL	pattern	(A (,(B) (&(C) (D))));
	instances:	(A (B));
		(A (C) (D));
	not instances:	(A (C));
		(A (B) (C) (D));

Patterns can contain variables. Depending on the type, a variable is congruent to various sections of a list which functions as an instance. Certain characters are reserved to represent variables; they also indicate the type. (The standard representations can be altered by the user.) Variables of the same type which correspond to different expressions in an instance are distinguished by numerical indices. Variables, like other character strings, are noted in the fields of terms. The remaining fields can be filled by constants or they can also contain variables. Types of variables are established according to the different parts of a list which fit the variable. So far, comparison routines exist for the following types:

1) Variables in the first field of a term:

Type 11	(*)	congruent to any character string in the first field of a corresponding term.
Type 12	(-)	congruent to any sequence of collateral trees with any character strings in the terms. A term with this variable does not necessarily have to find a correspondence in the instance.

2) Variables in the second field of a term:

Type 21	(#)	congruent to any character string in the second field of a corresponding term.
Type 22	($)	congruent to a tree with any character string in the second field of the dominating term. The characters in the remaining field of the dominating term must be compatible with the remaining specifications in the pattern.
Type 23	(-)	congruent to any sequence of collateral trees with any character strings in the second field of the dominating terms. The characters in the remaining fields of all dominating

terms must be compatible with the remaining specifications in the pattern. A term with this variable does not necessarily have to find a correspondence in the instance.

Examples:

pattern:	(*:A (-));
instances:	(X:A);
	(X:A (B) (C));
not an instance:	(X:B);
pattern:	(*:#);
instances:	(X:A);
	(Y:B);
not an instance:	(X:A (B));
pattern:	(X:$:Z);
instances:	(X:B:Z);
	(X:A:Z (B) (C));
not an instance:	(Y:A:Z);
pattern:	(A (X:-));
instances:	(A);
	(A (X:B) (X:C) (X:D));
not an instance:	(A (X:B) (Y:C) (Z:D));

Patterns are not only used to check given expressions but also to construct new expressions. When an expression matches a pattern, PLAIN stores the names of the variables and the locations of the corresponding list segments in a register. A new expression can be formed, if a further pattern is available. The variables of this construction pattern which have names identical to those stored in the register are replaced by the segments of the original list. Constants as well as variables that do not appear in the register are taken over from the construction pattern, i.e. they can be different from those that have occured in the comparison pattern or in the initial instance.

A "rule" is an expression that contains a pattern for the comparison with a given expression as well as patterns for the construction of a new expression. The patterns are grouped together in a tree by superordinating a term with a rule symbol. The semantic differentiation between rules and the choice of a rule symbol is up to the user. However, for every new rule symbol the type of the rule which is to be indicated by the symbol must be explicitely defined. Types of rules result from the different operations that the program system carries out in processing a rule. In defining a rule symbol the user can select a corresponding operation from a number of possibilities.

The simplest operation in PLAIN is replacement. The section of an expression that fits the comparison pattern of a replacement rule is replaced by an expression built according to the construction pattern of the rule. If a replacement rule is applied from left to right, then the comparison pattern is the first subtree directly subordinated to the term with the rule symbol; the construction pattern is the second subtree. Example:

```
replacement rule:              (:⇒(*1:A (*2:#))
                                   (*1:# (*2:B)));
application instance:          (X (Y:A (Z:C)));
correspondences of variables:  *1 = Y, *2 = Z, # = C
result:                        (X (Y:C (Z:B)));
```

Other operations for which rules can be set up are discussed below in connection with the deduction component of PLAIN.

It may be necessary to say a few words about the artificial language of PLAIN in comparison to the programming language LISP which is most often used for list processing. Outwardly the expressions of PLAIN differ from those of LISP in that PLAIN also brackets terms which are neither subordinated to any other term nor dominate any other term. The additional parentheses in PLAIN are needed to group together the various character sequences that can make up one list element. The internal coding by means of cells and pointers is similar in PLAIN and LISP. The essential difference is that the expressions of PLAIN do not consist of recursive functions which can be directly evaluated. This might bother those who are used to thinking in LISP, especially when it comes to inferring. Doubtlessly, deduction problems can be more elegantly formulated and solved in LISP than with PLAIN, where programs, separate from the data, test and apply one rule at a time and thus transform one expression into the next, step by step, until the desired result is reached. However, my friends in computer science must not overlook the fact that the two fascinating characteristics of LISP, the integration of data and algorithms and the recursivity, lead to a type of description that differs quite fundamentally from the way in which most linguists formulate their findings. Thus only a small group of specialists qualify as authors and recipients of descriptions of natural languages in LISP, whereas PLAIN is to be accessible to many linguists.

2.2. Dependency Structures

It is well known that all kinds of quirks in natural language stand in the way of automatically carrying out deductions in the same manner as they are accomplished in human question answering and human reasoning. This begins with the morphological confusion - just think of German's strong and weak conjugations, its declensions with and without Umlaut, etc. - and it ends with the fact that the hierarchical syntactic structure of utterances appears only indirectly in the linear sequence of speech. This is why virtually all systems of computerized language processing use an artificial representation into which the natural language input is translated.

Within the framework of the format described in the previous chapter, the linguist as a user of PLAIN can construct his own artificial language. It is sensible to lay down the following postulates for this language: the artificial language (AL) should be more explicit and simpler than the natural language (NL), but both languages should resemble each other structurally as much as possible.

AL should be more explicit than NL. It is a prerequisite for computer processing that the syntactic structure of the expressions be known. This means that the syntacmatic relationships between the constituents of a complex expression are represented formally and do not, as is often the case in NL, become clear only from the implicit features of the elements. A result of the explicitness of the syntagmatic relationships is that there can be no structural ambiguities in AL.

AL should be simpler than NL. Superficial peculiarities of NL such as coincidences in the morphology should be eliminated in AL in order not to make the further processing unnecessarily difficult.

The expressions of AL and NL that are to be mapped together should be structurally similar. The number and type of basic elements of AL and NL and the number and type of the syntagmatic relationships should differ as little as possible.[3] To meet this requirement an individual AL must be developed for each natural input language. Many other systems differ from PLAIN in this respect. However, there are several reasons for retaining the postulate of structural similarity:

1) Translating NL into AL and vice versa is easier under this condition.

2) For practical application in information systems it is desirable that the storage requirements of AL structures do not substantially exceed those of plain text in NL.[4]

3) AL is a model for NL. Experimenting with AL can provide insights into NL. This is the reason why ordinary linguists (the users of PLAIN of the first generation) are interested in language processing systems. However, the benefit to linguistics is the greatest when the model and the model object are related by a maximum of analogy.

4) Natural language is unsurpassed as a medium for reasoning and problem solving. All conceivable worlds can be described in NL. All logical connections can be expressed in it. The most complicated logical calculi are usually illustrated in natural language. This suggests the supposition that in the long run a precise reproduction of an NL will lead to the most effective system of computer intelligence. Of course, nothing stands in the way of a

---

3 The stronger demand for isomorphy of AL and NL does not seem to be practicable without endangering the postulates of explicitness and simplicity.

4 PLAIN meets this requirement. Only 5 bytes are needed to code one term of AL including structural information. In the AL I designed for German there are 1 to 3 terms (thus 5 to 15 bytes) generated per input word.

later translation from the various artificial languages into a universal interlingua.

In my opinion the type of AL described below comes fairly close to satisfying the mentioned postulates. The expressions of the language are tree diagrams whose labeled nodes form the lexical units of the language; the arcs of the trees represent the syntagmatic relationships between the lexical units of the expression; the syntax is constrained by the fact that the number and type of all of the subordinated elements are determined by the lexical unit represented by the dominating term. I call such expressions "dependency trees" becuase I feel that they very well correspond to the intuitive dependency concept as it appears in traditional grammar or in the theory of L. TESNIERE, whereas several formal definitions of dependency grammars, e.g. those of D.G. HAYS and H. GAIFMAN, seem to miss an essential part of this concept.[5] In the AL format of PLAIN the arcs of dependency diagrams are represented by bracketing, the nodes by terms, and the labels by character strings in the fields of the terms. Every label of a dependency tree, i.e. every term of a bracketed expression, contains a specification of a "role" and a "lexeme".

The role specification indicates at the same time a unit within the syntactic construction and a logico-semantic function. When inferring, the program uses the roles markers to identify the structures to which a certain rule is applicable. Thus the roles that one must distinguish depend on the syntactic structure of the NL expressions which are to be mapped into AL as well as on the units that prove to be constitutive in inferences. In part, the roles will be congruent with traditional distinctions such as "subject", "predicate", "object", "adverb", etc.; in part, they will have to be further differentiated. In chapter 4.1. I shall deal in greater detail with setting up roles. Roles are noted in the first field of every term.

A lexeme stands for a lexical meaning. It satisfies our postulate of structural similarity of AL and NL that all terms of AL

---

5 See TESNIERE 1959, HAYS 1964, GAIFMAN 1965. The mentioned formalizations fail to sufficiently constrain the syntax of dependency trees. The necessary restrictions can be achieved only with a lexical approach to syntax. See HELLWIG 1978, pp. 79ff.

are labeled with lexemes and consequently superordination and subordination only exist between lexical units. This separates our AL from all representation systems that use phrase markers with nodes for non-terminal constituents. Lexemes are noted in the second field of every term.

If roles and lexemes are aptly selected, it is likely that a dependency tree will be available as a substitute for every natural language expression. However, further means of representation are needed. Strictly speaking, one must distinguish between a model language for the NL and a meta-language in which statements are made about the correlation of the model with the object and about the operations that can be carried out upon the model. Nevertheless, I combine both languages into one notation system and for simplicity's sake I shall continue to refer to it as the AL.

A natural language input is formally an unstructured character string except for word boundaries and punctuation marks. One of the tasks of the AL is to expose the hierarchical structure which is implicitly extant in the NL. In general, segments of the input string are paired with AL trees. In this process, the smallest segments of NL do not necessarily have to be associated with terms. The possibility of lexical decomposition also exists, i.e. an elementary segment of NL can correspond to a more or less structured tree.

I call a segment of NL that corresponds to an NL tree a "constituent". Since trees are in turn made up of trees all the way down to the terms, the expressions in our AL imply, at the same time, a constituent structure of NL. It is characteristic for dependency trees that non-terminal constituents are represented indirectly by the tree as a whole, whereas in phrase structure trees constituents of all levels are paired with a node of their own.

It is important to emphasize that the dependency trees of our AL are not projective with respect to the strings of NL, i.e. the sequence of terms in a bracketed expression is completely independent of the sequential order of the corresponding segments in the input string. Hence, the above definition of "constituent" does not exclude discontinuous constituents, because the terms that are included in a tree do not necessarily have to be associated with segments that are adjoining in the linear sequence.

In order to have the appropriate translation of NL into AL carried out by computer, the segments of NL must be described in greater detail. Here, morphology can no longer be ignored. The linear sequence of the segments in the input string must also be accounted for. For this purpose we expand our AL by adding complex morpho-syntactic categories and we note these in the third field of the terms. Thus a term now contains a maximum of three entries: a role, a lexeme, and a category.

A category is made up of a main category and any number of subcategories. Since categories in the terms of AL always occur together with lexemes which, in turn, represent lexical meanings, all main categories denote word classes or, in the case of compounds, morpheme classes. (Of course, categories do not make sense at all for terms that originate from lexical decomposition.) The restriction of categories to morpheme and word classes does not contradict the constituent concept just explained. Commutation tests show that most of the slots in a syntactic construction, e.g. in a sentence, can be filled with one single word. Therefore, it is reasonable to use the respective word class to characterize the slot. If a syntactic slot is occupied by a more complex construction, then the uppermost term of the corresponding AL tree serves as a substitute for the whole tree. If certain complements are crucial in a slot, for instance, if a noun as a filler must be accompanied by an article, then this can also be viewed as a morpho-syntactic feature of a word class and can be accounted for by a subcategory. It is true that this solution results in unusual word classes and lexemes such as, for example, "relative clause/hypotaxis", "main clause/assertion", "main clause/question", etc. This lexicalization of clause types, however, is surprising only at first glance. In the written input language one can attach the respective interpretations to punctuation marks such as commas, periods and question marks. In speech it is often the intonation that conveys the clause meaning. As A.V. ISACENKO and H.-J. SCHÄDLICH have pointed out for the German language, intonation, too, is segmentable.[6]

---

6 See ISACENKO/SCHÄDLICH 1966. The units of intonation which are significant for clause meaning are tone switches.

Subcategories denote feature types such as gender, number, case, relative position, etc. Every feature type encompasses a number of features, the "values" of the subcategory. For example, in German the features nominative, genitive, dative, and accusative belong to the feature type case.

The format for noting complex morpho-syntactic categories in PLAIN comes from K. BROCKHAUS[7], although the use of this notation in PLAIN differs from its use within the framework of BROCKHAUS' phrase structure grammar. A main category is made up of four characters. Each subcategory is three characters long. The features of the corresponding feature type are numbered through and in this form are placed after the subcategory in angled brackets. A noun in the genitive would, for example, be described as

nomn cas<2> .

If several features of the same type apply to a segment of NL, such as nominative, dative, accusative for the German expression 'BUCH ' (but not genetive which is 'BUCHES '), all of the appropriate values are listed and kept separate from each other by commas, for instance:

nomn cas<1,3,4> .

Further details about the notation and interpretation follow below.

By means of complex categories, the word order, too, can be described. This is especially noteworthy, because the problem of integrating dependency and phrase structure descriptions can now be definitely solved. The relative position of each constituent, represented by a tree, with respect to the segments corresponding to superordinated, subordinated and collateral terms is considered to be a syntactic feature and as such is noted in the form of subcategories. Instead of the one adjacency relationship that phrase markers are able to account for, in non-projective dependency trees any position parameters can be included as feature types. Compare the analysis example given in 3.5. Variable word order can easily be dealt with by alternative values of position subcategories. The actual linear structure of an utterance can be calculated from the intersection of the various position conditions for the segments associated with trees. Discontinuous

---

7 See BROCKHAUS 1971, pp. 74f. Also compare KRATZER/PAUSE/VON STECHOW 1974, pp. 5ff.

constituents can be explained as the result of position prescripts for segments whose corresponding terms are on different levels in the dependency tree.

To come back to the above cited postulates, the following can be stated: an AL of the suggested type is more explicit than the NL because in it the syntactic structure is represented formally by the bracketing and functionally by the role labels. The AL is simple because the morpho-syntactic categories can be eliminated from the lists as meta-linguistic relicts after they have done their duty during the translation of NL into AL. In further processing AL, one need only pay attention to roles and lexemes. AL and NL are structurally similar in that both languages represent non-terminal units by nothing but the elements these units consist of.

It is a recognized principle that the syntax of an artificial language is to be constrained in such a way that it includes no more than exactly the structures onto which expressions of the NL are to be mapped. The syntax of our AL is constrained by the stipulation that the number and type of subordinated terms are determined by the directly dominating term. This is, of course, not any different for the generation of a phrase structure tree. The characteristic trait of our syntax is, however, that each term contains a lexeme. Consequently, the syntactic structure of a compound expression is not determined on the basis of abstract constituents alone, i.e. by units that can be thought of as a combination of our roles and categories; the syntactic structure is constrained right from the start by concrete lexical units. It is not class-to-class relationships that make up the principle of this syntax but term-class relationships. This, it seems to me, is the fundamental concept of the linguistic valence theory.[8]

---

8 It is true that the valence idea has not yet been formalized by the established valence theory in a consistent way. L. TESNIERE, who introduced the notion of "valence" in chapter 97 of the "Eléments", does not comment on his lexical approach to grammar. However, this approach can be derived from all of the examples he gives in his book. Most of the subsequent theoretical presentations of valence theory presuppose a generative grammar into which valence descriptions are somehow to be integrated, e.g. the lexically determined disposition for completion is not dealt with as the basic principle of syntax but rather as

PLAIN is an attempt to formalize and apply the valence idea exhaustively. It is not important that many linguists limit the concept of valence to verbs and sometimes even to the "actants" as opposed to the "circonstants"[9], or that W.G. ADMONI and B. ABRAMOW on the other hand distinguish a completion potential ("Fügungspotenz") along the lines of domination and another along the lines of subordination.[10] Without any difficulty, one can extend the valence concept to cover all syntactic relationships, and the exclusiveness of "downwards" directed valence is only a technical means that does not exclude the implicit treatment of "upwards" directed syntactic disposition.

Assigning an AL representation to a given expression of NL is done by PLAIN on the basis of two data sets: a morpho-syntactic lexicon (in short "base lexicon") and a valence lexicon. Both lexicons must be drawn up, tested, and improved for each individual input language.

The base lexicon connects the basic segments of the NL with terms of the AL. For every word of the input, one or more AL trees are taken from the base lexicon. Every tree contains a specific lexeme and a morpho-syntactic categorization of the NL segment in question. Details will follow in section 3.2.

The valence lexicon provides information on the combining power of the terms and thus indirectly on the syntagmatic structure of compound expressions in NL. Two types of entries in the lexicon must be distinguished: "valence patterns" and "valence references". Valence patterns are dependency trees containing slots. Slots are terms with variables for which trees can be substituted. Valence patterns thus indicate which type of terms can potentially

---

a supplement. Compare, for example, HELBIG 1971 pp. 47ff. and the contradictory discussion in ENGEL/SCHUMACHER 1976 pp. 12ff. That term-class relationships are fundamental to the valence idea also follows from the fact that, up until now, the practical results yielded by valence theory were dictionaries and not abstract completion rules of the type introduced, e.g., in GAIFMAN 1965.

9 This distinction, which was introduced in chapter 48 of TESNIERE 1959, has given rise to extensive discussion. See HELLWIG 1978, pp. 122ff.

10 ADMONI 1966, see the example on p. 84; ABRAMOW 1971, pp. 52ff.

be dominated by a given term within a list. A valence pattern can be directly associated with a lexeme from the base lexicon. In this way, idiomatic expressions can be taken care of. In general, however, a valence pattern is linked to a base lexeme by means of a reference.

Each reference consists of two subtrees. The first subtree is a pattern of the expression to which the reference applies. Let it be called the "application part" of the reference. The second subtree denotes an expression which is referred to. Let us call the expression to which a reference refers the "referent". The referent can be the dominating term of a valence pattern or an expression which forms the application part of a further reference. Many different references can point to the same valence pattern. Also, in a single expression, one can refer to several alternative patterns or to various sequences of further references. When an initial tree, taken from the base lexicon, corresponds to the application part of a reference, then any valence pattern which is pointed to is added to the initial structure. References are thus a means of subordinating slots under terms. I will describe this device in greater detail in chapter 3.3.

Dependency trees and references to valence patterns are the most important formal innovation of PLAIN as opposed to customary valence dictionaries, which presuppose a phrase structure or transformational grammar.[11] In PLAIN a syntactic component besides the two lexicons is superfluous since the non-terminal categories generated by phrase structure rules are no longer needed in order to describe the valence of lexemes. By making all syntagmatic relationships dependent on lexemes, the separation of grammar and lexicon is totally dispensable. Our grammar is a lexical description or, if one prefers to see it the other way around, our lexicon is a grammar.

Designing an AL and correlating it to an NL in the form of two lexicons is left up to the linguist as a user of PLAIN. In doing so, the linguist does not have to define the roles and lexemes he is going to use. Whenever a new role or lexeme symbol appears in

11 Compare HELBIG/SCHENKEL 1973, SOMMERFELDT/SCHREIBER 1974, ENGEL/SCHUMACHER 1976, SOMMERFELDT/SCHREIBER 1977.

a lexicon entry or in a deduction rule it is automatically entered into the role inventory (ROLEF) or into the lexeme inventory (LEXF). The record keys of these two data sets, at the same time, form the basis for the internal coding of roles and lexemes in lists.

There are also a few system-defined lexemes which play a specific part in the operations that can be associated with rules. Their internal coding is always the same. Their AL representation can be changed via parameters. The following is a list of the parameter names, the default representations, and the meanings of the system-defined lexemes:

NON	'¬'	negation
VEL	'|VEL|'	logical disjunction
ET	'|ET|'	logical conjunction
TRUE	'|TRUE|'	logically true
FALSE	'|FALSE|'	logically false
CONFER	'+>'	rule symbol for valence references
REPLACE	'=>'	rule symbol for replacements
EXPAND	'|'	rule symbol for inference and proof expansion[12]

Morpho-syntactic categories belong to the meta-linguistic part of the AL. Their meaning does not originate from the translation of NL into AL. Therefore, morpho-syntactic categories must be explicitly defined before they can be used in AL expressions. (PLAIN refuses undefined categories in the input.) In chapter 3.1. I shall explain how such a definition is to be made.

---

12 On the use of replacement and expansion rules see chapter 4. In contrast to the other system defined meanings, the user can define several alternative rule symbols for every rule type. The different symbols will be kept apart by the program. Therefore they can be used for semantic differentiation.

3. ANALYSIS

An artificial language within a language processing system like PLAIN is a model. The model object is a specific natural language. The correspondence between the object and the model is determined by the function

$$f: NL \rightarrow AL,$$

the correspondence between the model and the object is determined by the function

$$f': AL \rightarrow NL.$$

An analysis program is a mechanical device for evaluating the function f for every expression of NL. Likewise a synthesis program is a device with which f' can be calculated for every expression of AL. A synthesis program for PLAIN does not yet exist. The analysis procedure is explained below.

I would recommend that the reader first look at the example in 3.5. including the explanations given there before he continues with the following chapters. Although the example will not yet be completely understandable, it is surely useful to have a practical application in mind while reading the following.

3.1. Description of Morpho-syntactic Categories

The criteria which determine whether or not a segment of NL receives a morpho-syntactic characterization are manifold. To determine if an expression is a neutrum or if it immediately precedes another or if it is the first among several constituents or if it is accompanied by another expression, etc., one must carry out heuristic operations that do not fit a single formal mold. If, on principle, one wants all empirically verifiable findings of traditional linguistics to be included in the descriptions, the analysis program must have access to an open number of special routines which check the decisive criteria for each feature. If a new feature is empirically discovered which can not be processed by any of the extant routines, a new "specialist" has to be written. The modular structure of PLAIN allows a new feature routine to be linked to the system at any time. Special routines are activated via a number associated with them.

The use of morpho-syntactic categories must be described. The description is stored in the data set CATF and is continuously consulted during the processing of lists. In a category description the following must be specified:

1. the name of the main category (4 characters long),
2. the name of the subcategories (each 3 characters long),
3. the number of "values" of each subcategory,
4. the number of the "authorized" special routine for each subcategory.

Main categories are morpheme or word classes. Of course, one is not bound to traditional classifications when setting up the main categories. The analysis program checks all main category symbols only with regard to identity or non-identity.

Subcategories are feature types such as case, gender, number, position, etc. Within each feature type the actual features are numbered through, e.g. 1 = nominative, 2 = genitive, 3 = dative, 4 = accusative for the feature type case. The number of values of the corresponding subcategory is 4.

Morpho-syntactic features are characteristics of individual languages. So far, nine special routines for subcategories were needed for the part of German I have studied. It is an empirical question whether further "specialists" will become necessary in the future. Before I give a general description of the 9 procedures let us make the following convention: HEAD is to be the dominating term in a tree with slots. SLOT is to be a term which represents a slot and FILLER is to be the uppermost term in a tree that is a candidate for occupying a slot. Category specifications occur in HEAD and SLOT as well as FILLER. It is possible to leave subcategories unspecified in a term by not listing them at all. The effect varies and, where it is important, will be indicated below. Finally, there is a special symbol 'C' which can take the place of subcategory values. Its interpretation will also be indicated separately for each subroutine. Examples refer to the analysis in chapter 3.5.

Procedure 1: The number of values and the interpretation of the subcategories, for which this procedure is authorized, is arbitrary. If a subcategory of this type is left out of a term, all of the values are considered as being present. 'C' can appear as a value in SLOT; it then signifies that congruence between HEAD and FILLER must exist. When 'C' occurs, the values of the respective subcategory of HEAD are first copied into SLOT. The procedure forms the intersection of the subcategory values in SLOT and FILLER. If 'C' was specified in SLOT, the intersection of the values is subsequently transferred to HEAD as well. If the intersection of the values of SLOT and FILLER is the empty set, then FILLER is turned down as an unsuitable substitute for SLOT. (Example: feature type case, subcategory cas, 4 values. Compare 'cas<1,4>' in list 6 as FILLER, list 7 with 'cas<1,3,4> ' in HEAD and term 3 with 'cas<C>' as SLOT and the result in list 16 with 'cas<1,4>' in HEAD and the filled slot.)

Procedure 2: The number of values of the subcategories of this type is arbitrary. The interpretation of the values is free except for the last one which indicates that none of the features of the type under consideration are present. If the subcategory is left out of SLOT, this means that none of the values are required. If the subcategory is unspecified in FILLER, this means that none of the features are present in FILLER. 'C' in turn requires congruence. A calculation is the same as in procedure 1 except that the absence of any features is itself a value. (Example: feature type strong/weak inflection of adjectives and determiners, subcategory fle, 3 values. Compare in list 6 'fle<2>' for 'ein' as FILLER, in list 7 'fle<C>' as SLOT 3, and in list 16 'fle<2>' in FILLER and HEAD. In list 16 one could still insert an adjective with 'fle<2>' in slot 9 such as *gutes* in *ein gutes Buch* but no longer one with 'fle<1>' such as *gute* in *das gute Buch*. If a noun has neither been completed with a determiner nor with an adjective, then it has the value 'fle<3>'. It is then unsuitable for some slots, e.g. as a genitive attribute.)

Procedure 3: Number of values and interpretation of values as in procedure 2. If the subcategory in SLOT is not specified, the value of FILLER is automatically transported to HEAD and the union of the previous values of HEAD with the new value is formed. In this way features can be passed upwards, bypassing various terms. If a value is specified in SLOT, an intersection with FILLER is formed and the passing on of the feature is stopped. (Example: Occurrence of a relative pronoun or a W-pronoun, subcategory rel, 6 values. Value 5 means W-pronoun. Compare 'rel<5>' for 'wie' in list 2, insertion and transfer of the feature to HEAD in list 20, passing on to HEAD in list 21, required by slot 6 in list 1, passing on ended in list 22.)

Procedure 4: 4 values, fixed interpretation: 1 = The constituent that corresponds with the tree under FILLER in NL precedes the segment that belongs to the term HEAD but not immediately. 2 = The FILLER-tree-constituent immediately precedes the HEAD-term-segment. 3 = The FILLER-tree-constituent immediately follows the HEAD-term-segment. 4 = The FILLER-tree-constituent follows the HEAD-term-segment but not immediately. Values can be specified in HEAD or in SLOT. Leaving out a subcategory for which procedure 4 is responsible means that all positions of the FILLER-tree-constituent with respect to the HEAD-term-segment are possible. 'C' indicates that the values of HEAD are to be copied into SLOT before comparing SLOT with FILLER. The actual position of FILLER relative to HEAD in the input is determined. Then the intersection of the values of SLOT and FILLER is formed. If it is the empty set, then the position of FILLER does not satisfy the requirements. (Example: subcategory pos. In list 1 'pos<3>' for main titles, 'pos<4>' for subtitles, if any. In list 7 'pos<3,4>' is specified in HEAD and 'pos<C>' in term 20, i.e. the slot for a prepositional phrase with 'ueber'. Since the position regularity is noted in HEAD and transferred to SLOT by copying, one single pattern is sufficient for a prepositional complement of a noun (= pos<3,4>), of a verb in the imperative (= pos<3,4>), of infinitives or participles (= pos<1,2>), and of finite verbs (pos unspecified).

Procedure 5: 3 values, fixed interpretation: 1 = The constituent that corresponds to the tree under FILLER in NL is the first among all of the constituents that correspond to other subtrees under HEAD. 2 = The FILLER-tree-constituent is the last among all the other constituents. 3 = No stipulation. Non-specification is identical to value 3. Values can be required by SLOT; they also can be assigned to certain words in the lexicon. The actual position of FILLER with respect to the other complements of HEAD is looked up. If this position matches the specification in SLOT and is congruent to the lexical predetermination of FILLER, FILLER is substituted for SLOT and at the same time the initial or final position is blocked for all future complements of HEAD. (Example: verb complements, subcategory vps. In list 2 'vps⟨1⟩', i.e. the first position among all of the verb complements, is prescribed lexically for 'wie'. The adverbial slots of 'entstehen' do not actually require this feature. However, after 'wie' has been assigned to slot 6 in list 20, the clause can no longer be expanded beyond 'WIE '. Also compare 'nps⟨1⟩' for the determiner in slot 3 of list 7.)

Procedure 6: 3 values, fixed interpretation: 1 = The segment belonging to the t e r m of FILLER occupies the first position within the constituent that corresponds to the t r e e under FILLER. 2 = The FILLER-term-segment occupies the second position within the FILLER-tree-constituent. 3 = The FILLER-term-segment occupies the last position within the FILLER-tree-constituent. Values can be required by SLOT. If this is the case, the actual position of the FILLER-term-segment within the FILLER-tree-constitutent is determined; the respective value is used to form the intersection with the values in SLOT. (Example: initial, second and final position of finite verbs in clauses, subcategory ord. Compare in list 11 'ord⟨3⟩' in slot 2 and the satisfying of this condition in list 20, so that list 21 can be formed.)

Procedure 7: 2 values, fixed interpretation: 1 = The constituent that corresponds to the tree dominated by FILLER is continuous. 2 = No stipulation. Non-specification of the feature is identical to value 2. If value 1 is required in SLOT, the continuity of the segments represented by the FILLER tree in the input string is checked. (Example: constituents that are clauses, subcategory con. See in list 11 the requirement 'con⟨1⟩' for the slot 2 with the role PRAED. It signifies that a list with a dominating verb can not be subordinated as a prediacte to the term that represents the period at the end of the sentence as long as this list corresponds to discontinuous sections of the input.)

Procedure 8: 2 values, fixed interpretation: 1 = The occupation of SLOT by FILLER maintains the continuity of the segments which were represented until now by the tree under HEAD. 2 = Filling SLOT with FILLER results in a discontinuous constituent as a correspondence to the tree under HEAD. With value 1 in SLOT the attempt towards discontinuous analysis can be suppressed. Non-specification in SLOT means skipping the feature. (Example: continuity of noun phrases, subcategory ctn. All of the slots in list 7 that do not have the feature 'pos<2>' or 'pos<3>', which prescribe immediate adjunction anyway, require continuity of the complements ('ctn<1>'). An exception is slot 13 for a relative clause, since relative clauses do not have to immediately follow their antecedents.)

Procedure 9: 3 values, fixed interpretation. 1 = HEAD must be completed by a specific type of term by means of subordination. 2 = HEAD itself is a term of the required sort or already dominates such a term. 3 = HEAD is not allowed to be completed by a term of the specific sort. The subcategory contains the val 'C' in all of the slots whose filling would represent a satisfactory completion. If such a slot is actually filled, then HEAD receives the value 2. (Example: determination of nouns, subcategory dte. See slot 3 in list 7 with 'dte<C>'. After this slot in list 16 is filled by 'ein', HEAD has the value 'dte<2>'. This value in turn is the prerequisite for list 16's being able to be entered as a subject into slot 8 of list 8. Filling slot 4 or 5 in list 7 (as in *sein Buch, Goethes Buch*) would have had the same effect, because here 'dte<C>' is also specified. In contrast to the singular, all nouns in the plural have the feature 'dte<C>' inherently (through specification in the base lexicon) so that *Wie Bücher entstehen* is accepted, whereas **Wie Buch entsteht* is not.)

As an example of what a category description could look like, I have listed the categories of the word class verb as I currently use them:

```
verb  num 2 1  fin 4 1  aux 2 1  per 3 2  rel 6 3
      pos 4 4  vps 3 5  ord 3 6  con 2 7  ctn 2 8
```

The first integer after each subcategory name is the number of values, the second is the number associated with the corresponding subroutine. The subcategories symbolize feature types as follows: num = number, fin = finite form or infinitive, present participle, past participle, aux = perfect formation with *haben* or with *sein*, per = person, rel = completion with relative or W-pronoun, pos = general position regularities, vps = initial and final position of the constituents dominated by the verb, ord = initial, second, and final position of the verb itself, con = continuity of the verb phrase, ctn = continuity of the verb complements.

Checking morpho-syntactic features during the syntactic analysis can be suppressed via the option CATEGORIES=OFF. In doing so, one can, for example, determine what is due to morphology and word order when generating an unambiguous reading and what is not. Also, someone might prepare a more semantically oriented description by refining the role repertory to such an extent that roles can serve to type lexemes in the base lexicon and, at the same time, to determine the admissible term combinations in the valence patterns.

3.2. Base Lexicon

Theoretically the base lexicon is a set of pairs: a term or tree is noted for every expression from NL that cannot be further split up. Thus for the elementary segments of the input language, the function f: NL $\rightarrow$ AL can be evaluated simply by looking up these segments in the base lexicon. Simple words including their inflection morphemes as well as the parts of compounds that have lexical meaning are considered to be elementary. Words are character strings that end with a blank or are followed by a punctuation mark.

In practice, there are reasons against organizing the base lexicon as an unstructured list of pairs. The terms of AL are made up of roles, lexemes, and categories in various different combinations. It is natural to treat these three types of information also separately when pairing segments from NL with terms from AL. In the majority of cases in NL roles can only be distinguished within the framework of a construction. Consequently role indications are above all a matter of the valence lexicon and of the analysis. In the base lexicon usually a variable will occupy the role field. Lexemes are associable with the word stems of NL. The morpho-syntactic features of a word often depend on the ending.

Endings, in turn, form paradigms as they are known from the inflection tables in traditional grammar. It would be uneconomical to list the morphological features for each word form separately, since they are the same for many different words. The base lexicon of PLAIN is therefore divided into various chapters, called "sections". The necessary information about each word is compiled from the various sections of the lexicon.

One of the sections contains word stems as well as non-inflected words. For example, if German is the input language, the lexicon contains 'ENTSTEH', the stem of *entstehen*:

```
'ENTSTEH'
(*: entstehen);
CONTINUATION: SECTION  101
```

The AL term '(*:entstehen)' is assigned to the segment 'ENTSTEH'. In addition, one finds a reference to the section of the base lexicon which contains the endings that fit the stem 'ENTSTEH'. When we are locking up the AL representation of the word 'ENTSTEHT ', we must, after having arrived at 'ENTSTEH', read on in section 101. To illustrate this we have PLAIN print out this section in its entirety:

```
------------------------------------------------------------
*** PUTIX - LEXICON SECTION NO. 101:
Verben, Praesens Indikativ, Imperativ, Infinitiv,
Partizip Praesens
------------------------------------------------------------

''
komp kty<1>

' '
((MODUS: imperativ_sg+));
verb per<2> num<1> fin<4>

'E'
komp kty<1>

'E '
((TEMPS: praesens+) (MODUS: indikativ+));
verb per<1> num<1> fin<1>

'E '
((MODUS: imperativ_sg+));
verb per<2> num<1> fin<4>

'EN'
CONTINUATION: SECTION 194

'EN '
((TEMPS: praesens+) (MODUS: indikativ+));
verb per<1,3> num<2> fin<1>

'EN '
verb fin<2>

'END'
CONTINUATION: SECTION  86

'ST '
((TEMPS: praesens+) (MODUS: indikativ+));
verb per<2> num<1> fin<1>

'T '
((TEMPS: praesens+) (MODUS: indikativ+));
verb per<3> num<1> fin<1>
verb per<2> num<2> fin<1>

'T '
((MODUS: imperativ_pl+));
verb per<2> num<2> fin<4>
```

Every one of the entries in section 101 contains a possible continuation of the character sequence of the stems linked to this section. In the first entry this is the empty string, i.e. the stem can occur on its own as an elementary segment of German. The associated term of the AL has the category 'komp kty<1>', i.e. the segment is suitable as a constituent of a compound like 'ENTSTEH' in 'ENTSTEHWEISE '. By the way, a separate AL list arises from every morpheme in a compound when the starting lists for the syntactic analysis are compiled. A term with a role variable and a lexeme was already taken from the stem section. The syntactic category of the input word is now included in this term.

Along with several of the endings in the section, further terms appear, e.g. together with the ending 'T ' we find ((TEMPS: praesens+) (MODUS: indikativ+)); in one entry and ((MODUS: imperativ_pl+)); in the other. It is stipulated that lists with an additional pair of brackets (i.e. trees with an empty dominating term) are to be subordinated to the term already found in the stem section. Thus for 'ENTSTEHT ' we end up with two trees:

```
(*: entstehen
     (TEMPS: praesens+)
     (MODUS: indikativ+));
```

and

```
(*: entstehen
     (MODUS: imperativ_pl+));
```

Hence, in our AL there is a lexical decomposition of the words into one term that represents the stem and into other terms that are common to all of the words with the same ending. In the case at hand the terms that are to be subordinated have fixed role markers, namely TEMPS for tense and MODUS for mode. Tense and mode cannot be treated like morpho-syntactic features because they are semantically relevant, which means that later, when the morpho-syntactic categories have been eliminated, they still must be available for the further processing of the analysis result.

In the first entry on 'T ' we find two morpho-syntactic categories. The first means "finite verb in the third person singular", the second "finite verb in the second person plural". Since each term in AL has but one field for a category indication, this leads to two alternative initial lists in the analysis. Thus, we find in the base lexicon a total of three readings for our test word 'ENTSTEHT ':

```
(*: entstehen: verb per<3> num<1> fin<1>
     (TEMPS: praesens+)
     (MODUS: indikativ+));

(*: entstehen: verb per<2> num<2> fin<1>
     (TEMPS: praesens+)
     (MODUS: indikativ+));

(*: entstehen: verb per<2> num<2> fin<4>
     (MODUS: imperativ_pl+));
```

The first of these three versions is the correct one for the analysis example in 3.5.

Let us have one more look at another entry in the above printed section of the base lexicon. For the ending 'EN' we are requested to read on in section 194. This contains the following:

```
-----------------------------------------------------------

*** PUTLX - LEXICON SECTION NO. 194:
Nominalisierter Infinitiv, wie 'das Uebersetzen'
-----------------------------------------------------------

' '
((FOCUS: abstrakt+) (DERIV: verb>subst+));
nomn gen<3> num<1> cas<1,3,4> flk<1>

'S '
((FOCUS: abstrakt+) (DERIV: verb>subst+));
nomn gen<3> num<1> cas<2> flk<1>
```

The continuation in the first entry consists of affixing a blank as the word boundary. The category here says "noun neuter singular in the nominative, dative or accusative, strong inflection". If the continuation is 'S ', then we have "noun neuter singular in the genitive, strong inflection". When one ends up in this section, e.g. when looking up 'ENTSTEHEN ' or 'ENTSTEHENS ', the terms to be subordinated show that this is a noun derived from a verb; the meaning of this noun focuses on the abstract verb content (as opposed to the agent or the object of the verbal content). Likewise, other derivations, such as participles used as nouns or adjectives and adjectives ending in '-LICH', '-ISCH', etc., can be treated by way of transitions between the sections of the base lexicon.

If a word stem itself is subject to changes when combined with inflectional endings (e.g. Umlaut), the various stem forms must be listed separately. Thus, in addition to 'ENTSTEH', there is also an entry 'ENTSTAND' in the stem section. In both cases the AL lexeme is the same. Along with the second entry, however, the ending section of the strong inflected past is referred to for continuation. In cases where one word stem can lead to several ending paradigms, one can set up a section that works like a switch. In the base lexicon of German the following section carries out such a function:

```
------------------------------------------------------------
*** PUTLX - LEXICON SECTION NO.  10:
Schwache Verben, Perfekt mit 'haben' und auf 'ge-'
------------------------------------------------------------

''
CONDITION:     -EMPTY CATEGORY-
CONTINUATION:  SECTION 101

''
CONDITION:     -EMPTY CATEGORY-
CONTINUATION:  SECTION 111

''
CONDITION:     -EMPTY CATEGORY-
CONTINUATION:  SECTION 115

''
CONDITION:     -EMPTY CATEGORY-
CONTINUATION:  SECTION 121

''
CONDITION:     komp kty<6>
CONTINUATION:  SECTION 124
```

All entries contain the empty string as a segment and, furthermore, the specification of a section in which a continuation of the character sequence of the word being looked for can be expected under certain conditions. Section 10 itself does not contribute to the analysis of the word in question; it lists only the various alternatives for the subsequent looking up process. The sections referred to are:

101 = the section of endings already discussed above for the indicative present, the imperative, the infinitive and the present participle, along with transitions to sections of adjectival and substantival derivations.

111 = the present in the subjunctive.

115 = the weak inflected past in the indicative.

121 = the weak inflected past in the subjunctive.

124 = the weak inflected past participle, used for perfect formation together with the auxiliary *haben*, as well as certain nominal derivations.

In the case of a weak inflected verb like *machen* the reference to section 10 from the stem 'MACH' suffices to have access to the whole conjugation of this verb including all of the derivations such as *(das) Machen, (der) Macher, gemachtes, machende*, etc.

When a past participle like 'GEMACHT ' is looked up, a loop arises while the program is going through the sections. The prefix 'GE' is also listed in the section of the stems where it is labeled with the category 'komp kty<6>'. The reference from 'GE' then leads back to the beginning of the same section so that, at last, one ends up with 'GEMACH' in section 10. Since it is crucial to know whether 'GE' has occurred or not, the continuations from section 10 are each restricted by a condition. In the first four cases, the condition is that no categories are allowed to have occurred previously. This applies to simple stems. The continuation in section 124, however, depends on the previous occurrence of category 'komp kty<6>', i.e. the presence of the prefix 'GE'. Later the category of 'GE' is rewritten by the final category of the word form.

A loop also arises when the program is looking up compounds. If a segment to which a term is assigned is reached before the input word is finished, the lexicon routine goes back to the beginning of the stem section. Hence, compiling terms for words from the base lexicon leads, at the same time, to a segmentation of the input words into elementary units. While the word *dreiundzwanzigtausendvierhundertundsiebzehn* is being looked up, the initial section is run through ten times.

Sections of the base lexicon can be restricted to text types. The number of such a section can be specified via the parameter SECTION before the start of the analysis. This section is then made into the starting point of the looking up procedure. The punctuation marks and words that have a specific meaning in each type of text are listed in a separate section. For example, when dealing with bibliographies the semicolon and the period have a specific function. One can also set up sections for language varieties. For example, the German word *Gruppe* has a different meaning in ordinary language, in the technical language of mathematics, and in the terminology of sociology. Depending on the subject domain of the input, one of three different sections can be made the starting point for analysis; each section contains another term associated with 'GRUPPE '. Every section bound to a text type also contains a switch which leads into the generally applicable part of the lexicon. In this way the particularities of many types of texts can be kept apart, whereas what is held in common by all remains accessible from every type of text.

A few more details about the base lexicon ought to be briefly mentioned. Each variant of homonyms receives its own entry. In the analysis this leads to the setting up of alternative lists for the same NL segment. The morpho-syntactic categories of non-inflected words or of irregularly inflected word forms can be listed right away together with the lexeme in one term, e.g. 'IST ' (an inflectional form of 'SEIN ') is associated in the stem section with

```
(*: sein: verb per<3> num<1> fin<1>);
```

For portmanteau morphs the AL representation is specified as a list of collateral terms whose lexemes separately map the morphemes contained in the portmanteau morph. For example, the following is registered for the preposition 'IM ' (which means the same as 'IN DEM '):

```
(*: in: prpo cas<3>)
(REFER: @_d: dete gen<1,3> num<1> cas<3>);
```

Thus if the segment 'IM ' appears in the input, the exact same terms are assigned to it as to the two words 'IN ' and 'DEM '. (The lexeme '∂_d' covers all of the inflectional forms of the definite article.)

To summarize, it can be said that the base lexicon resembles one single directed diagram; there are branchings and loop-forming arcs; some of the branchings lead to identical nodes. The specification of the morphology of an object language which is achieved with this organization has the character of a finite-state analysis. A specific route through the diagram corresponds to each word form. Our dictionary has the advantage of a word form lexicon because it makes morphological rules superfluous.[13] It saves time by providing direct access to every word through several references. It saves space by listing each piece of information only once. And last but not least it is legible and, consequently, can be used for non-computer purposes as well.

There is a special main procedure in PLAIN to draw up and update the lexicons. An item is incorporated into the base lexicon by specifying the section and entering the NL segment as well as a series of key words and data. The key words are the following:

TERM	A term follows.
GENERATE	Generate a term. (A variable is inserted into the role field; the symbolization of the lexeme is identical to the NL segment.)
CATEGORY	A morpho-syntactic category follows.
CONDITION	A morpho-syntactic category follows as a condition for proceeding to an ending section.
SECTION	The number of a section follows which indicates a possible continuation of the segment.
ADD	An alternative set of specifications for the same segment follows (used in case of homonymy).
DELETE	Delete the segment.

13 For the opposite, see "word syntax" in addition to "sentence syntax" in the program system SALAT; SFB 99 FORSCHUNGSBERICHT 1976, pp. 3 - 69.

SCRATCH	Scratch an alternative set of specifications for a segment.
REWRITE	Rewrite a set of specifications.
DISPLAY	Display the specifications for the segment that exist so far.

Determining pertinent ending sections for each word stem that is to be entered into the lexicon requires great effort. PLAIN makes it possible to do the main part of this work automatically as well. The principle is taken from traditional linguistics. In school one learns the inflection of certain lexical units, e.g. the so-called irregular verbs, by memorizing a few characteristic forms. All of the remaining word forms can be derived from the characteristic forms. To imitate this procedure, one must merely determine a minimum set of characteristic forms for each declension and conjugation, set up patterns for these forms, and finally, for each pattern, indicate the sections which are to be referred to from the stems that fit the pattern. Once one has this, one need only enter the characteristic forms of each word. The entry in the base lexicon is made automatically.

The patterns for the characteristic forms are stored in the data set PATF. The format of the entries must meet the following stipulations:

1. Each entry is made up of two lines. The first line contains a pattern of characteristic forms. The second contains references to sections in the base lexicon.

2. Any constants can appear in the pattern: words, prefixes, suffixes.

3. The alternating parts of characteristic forms are represented by a variable. Of the characteristic forms, one is always the basic form. The basic form must appear as the first of the characteristic forms. The stem of the basic form is represented by the variable '_' in the pattern.

4. The changes that the stem of the basic form undergoes when the other characteristic forms are derived (Umlaut, Ablaut, etc.) are indicated in the pattern in the following way. ('_' represents the stem of the basic form, 'a' and 'b' can be any character strings.)

_(a/b)	The character string a in the stem of the basic form is replaced by the character string b in the derived form.
_(a+b)	The character string a in the stem of the basic form is expanded by the character string b in the derived form.
_(/b)	Any character string in the stem of the basic form is replaced by the character string b in the derived form.
_(+b)	Any character string in the stem of the basic form is expanded by the character string b in the derived form.

A series of changes can be shown by several bracketed expressions after the variable.

5. In order to link the alternating stems of a word that fits a pattern of characteristic forms with the appropriate sections, the corresponding parts of the pattern are repeated in the reference line of PATF together with the numbers of the sections.

A few examples will illustrate the above. The inflection of a German verb is completely derivable when one knows the infinitive, the second person singular present indicative, the third person singular imperfect and the third person perfect with the auxiliary verb. Below I give an example for an input, a pattern from PATF that fits this input, as well as the reference line that goes with the pattern.

MACHEN	MACHST	MACHTE	HAT GEMACHT
_EN	_ST	_TE	HAT GE_T
_ 10			
LAUFEN	LAEUFST	LIEF	IST GELAUFEN
_EN	_(A/AE)ST	_(A/IE)	IST GE_EN
_ 33	_(A/AE) 34	_(A/IE) 29	_ 31
GREIFEN	GREIFST	GRIFF	HAT GEGRIFFEN
_EN	_ST	_(EI/I)(F+F)	HAT GE_(EI/I)(F+F)EN
_ 26		_(EI/I)(F+F) 29	_(EI/I)(F+F) 32

In the case of *machen* the stem 'MACH' is entered into the stem section and linked with section 10. As we have seen above, section 10 is a switch from which all inflectional forms of weak verbs are reached.

In the case of *laufen* the stems 'LAUF', 'LAEUF', and 'LIEF' are entered. The sections addressed in the reference line contain the following: 33 = the present indicative without 2nd and 3rd person, the present subjunctive, 34 = 2nd and 3rd person present indicative, 29 = imperfect indicative and subjunctive of strong inflected verbs, 31 = the strong inflected perfect participle when *sein* is used to form the perfect.

In the case of *greifen* the stems 'GREIF' and 'GRIFF' are automatically entered into the base lexicon. Section 26 contains present indicative and subjunctive with unchanging stem. Section 29 is the same as for *laufen*. Section 32 contains the strong perfect participle when *haben* is used to form the perfect.

What one must know to correctly decline a German noun is its definite article, the nominative singular, the genitive singular, the nominative plural, and the dative plural. I shall give a few examples with patterns but I shall leave out the reference line:

DER MANN	MANNES	MAENNER	MAENNERN
DER _	_ES	_(+E)ER	_(+E)ERN
DIE FRAU	FRAU	FRAUEN	FRAUEN
DIE _	_	_EN	_EN
DAS KIND	KINDES	KINDER	KINDERN
DAS _	_ES	_ER	_ERN

German adjectives differ only in their comparison forms. Here the following characteristic forms are sufficient:

LIEB	LIEBER	AM LIEBSTEN
_	_ER	AM _STEN
KURZ	KUERZER	AM KUERZESTEN
_	_(+E)ER	AM _(+E)ESTEN

A native speaker can state the characteristic forms of a verb, noun, and adjective in his language without much thought. If the option GENERATE is chosen, PLAIN also automatically generates the AL lexeme out of the basic form. By means of characteristic forms, users with no knowledge of the internal linguistic representation can quickly and effortlessly expand the vocabulary of the system. This is advantageous when PLAIN is applied by users of the second generation in order to process information of a specific subject domain. The linguist is not needed to expand the base lexicon, so that it will suit the specific application.

3.3. Valence Lexicon

Whereas the base lexicon serves to map the elementary segments of the input onto terms of the model language and, at the same time, to describe the morphology of the input language, the valence lexicon deals with the syntagmatic aspect of the lexical units. We assume that lexemes, in a more or less close connection with morphological features, have a disposition to form a syntactic construction together with other expressions which in turn are morphologically and syntactically classifiable. This disposition appears in the framework of directed trees as a potential dominance and potential dependency of the terms. Since the dominance and dependency relationships are converses of each other, it is sufficient to represent just the dominance potential.

Formally the valence lexicon is a set of trees. Valence patterns and references to valence patterns must be distinguished. Valence patterns are made up of one dominating term with a specific lexeme and a morpho-syntactic categorization and any number of subordinated terms, each containing a slot variable. There are two kinds of slots. One can be replaced in a construction with a tree, the other with a sequence of collateral trees. The user can change the symbols for the corresponding variables via the parameters SLOT and SLOTSEQUENCE. (The standard representation is '_' and '='.) In print-outs slots are accented by '<SLOT>' and '<SLOTSEQ>' respectively. Alternative valence patterns can be combined in one single list by means of the metalinguistic terms "or" (,) and "and" (&).

Valence references contain an identifying symbol in the lexeme field of the uppermost term. The standard representation is '+>'. To elucidate the function of this symbol, '<CONFER>', the Latin word for 'see', is added in the print-outs. The representation can be changed via the parameter CONFER. In general, two subtrees, whose sequence is not arbitrary, are subordinated to the dominating term. The first subtree is a description of the lists to which the reference applies. We have called it the "application part" of the reference. The second subtree contains a term which dominates a valence pattern elsewhere in the valence lexicon or which matches the application part in another reference. The term referred to by a reference was introduced above as the "referent". Several alternative or simultaneous referents can be denoted in one single reference. The system defined terms "or" (,) and "and" (&) can be used to symbolize any referent combination.

The valence lexicon is entered via the lexeme of the uppermost term of a list found in the base lexicon. Hence at first, precisely those valence patterns are looked up in which that particular lexeme is also dominating as well as those references in which the lexeme is addressed in the application part. A directory added to the valence lexicon assures that this can be done via direct access for every lexeme.

The next step is to check whether the role and the morpho-syntactic category of the dominating term in the valence pattern or in the application part of the valence reference are compatible with the respective specifications in the initial list. In the case of a reference, the expressions referred to are temporarily substituted for the list matching the application part. Valence patterns or further references are subsequently sought for this substitute. If the role or the morpho-syntactic features of a valence description are not compatible with those of a given term, then the program immediately proceeds to the next pattern or reference.

Thus lexemes are the starting points for valence determination. Restrictions arise from fixed roles or from the morphological categorization. It is noteworthy that each one of the several simultaneously possible completions of an elementary unit can have its own pattern or reference drawn up in the valence lexicon, i.e. the syntactic disposition of a certain morpho-syntactically marked lexeme can be split into several term-class relationships. All of the fitting patterns and references together yield the total pattern. Some of the possible completions might be ascribed only to one single lexeme or to a very few lexemes. This is done by providing an individual valence pattern to the lexemes in question. On the other hand, there are possibilities of completion which are shared by many lexemes or which are even regularly linked with a word class. Here, we will refer from the individual lexeme to a common pattern.

An example of individual syntactic relationships are the separable prefixes of verbs in German. For the verb *setzen* our valence lexicon of German has the following entry:

```
(a)     1  (*: setzen
        2       (, <AUT>
        3            (: simplex+)
        4            (: _ * ab <SLOT>: komp kty<5>)
        5            (: _ * auf <SLOT>: komp kty<5>)
        6            (: _ * zusammen <SLOT>: komp kty<5>)));
```

The role marker in term 1 of this valence pattern is a variable, the category is unspecified. The pattern thus applies to the lexeme 'setzen' in general, regardless of the syntactic context in which this lexeme occurs. The subordinated terms 3 - 6 are mutually exclusive; this is indicated by term 2. Thus (a) is a combination of four alternative completion patterns. In addition to the variable '_' slots 4, 5, and 6 contain selectional specifications. Accordingly, they can only be replaced by terms with the lexemes 'ab', 'auf', or 'zusammen'. Furthermore, the potential fillers must have the category 'komp kty<5>', i.e. the category of separable prefixes. Finally, the asterisk in the lexeme fields marks the filling of all slots as obligatory. (The parameter SLOTOBLIGATION can be used to select another character for representing obligatory filling.) Normally, all slots whose filling is obligatory must be occupied before the dominating term of the tree is, in turn, free to fill a slot in another tree. If no separable prefix appears with 'SETZEN' in an input that is to be analyzed, the only possibility for the further processing is with (: simplex+) as the subordinated term.

Thus pattern (a) accomplishes two things: it differentiates between the simple verb *setzen* and the compound verbs *absetzen, aufsetzen, zusammensetzen* and it creates the syntactic provisions which are needed for the dependential assignment of the prefix to the verb during the analysis.

It may seem odd that the lexical meaning of a prefix verb which is felt to be uniform should be represented in AL by two terms. However, the syntactic characteristics of German force this solution. The prefix can be located at the opposite end of the sentence with respect to the verb - a classic case of a discontinuous constituent. For the semantic processing it does not matter that certain terms of AL are unambiguous only in combination with other terms. The AL prefix (: simplex+) makes sure that, later, unambiguous rules can be formulated that are applicable to the simple *setzen* but not to the compound forms of that verb.

The lexical and dependential approach of the valence theory has never been strictly adhered to because syntactic structures exist in every language whose slots can be filled by a great variety of lexical items. Therefore, a grammar of some sort is usually considered necessary that generates the sentence structures by means of general rules. The valence descriptions of lexemes are then formulated in terms of the abstract categories of the grammar. Since a dependency grammar that generates abstract sentence structures causes formal problems, valence descriptions usually rely on a previously generated constituent structure that would somehow have a dependency structure "imposed upon" it later on.[14] In PLAIN these consequences are avoided by means of valence patterns and references.

Let us look at a few more entries in the valence lexicon of German:

---

14 See, for instance, BAUMGÄRTNER 1970, especially p. 76 and HERINGER 1970, pp. 77f., pp. 84f., pp. 237ff.

```
(b)   1  (: +> <CONFER>
      2        (*: setzen)
      3        (*: %trans));

(c)   1  (: +> <CONFER>
      2        (*: %trans: verb fin<1,4>)
      3        (*: %aktiv));

(d)   1  (: +> <CONFER>
      2        (*: %trans: verb fin<2,3>)
      3        (, <AUT>
      4             (*: %aktiv)
      5             (*: %passiv)));

(e)   1  (*: %aktiv
      2        (TRANS: _ <SLOT>: nomn cas<4> dte<2> pos<C>));

(f)   1  (*: %passiv
      2        (AGENS: _ ?praep_ag <SLOT>: prpo pos<C>));
```

Lexemes that function in references and subsequent valence patterns as substitutes for the actual lexemes are marked with a percent sign. They belong to the meta-linguistic part of the AL and are something like names of valence classes. The entry (b) states: one of the dominance potentials of 'setzen' is the same as that of '%trans'; in traditional formulation: 'setzen' is transitive. This applies without detriment to the role or the morpho-syntactic category of the term in which 'setzen' appears, since both labels are unspecified in the application part of (b). This is different in the case of (c), for here a morpho-syntactic feature is specified as a prerequisite for the reference to be applicable: 'verb fin⟨1,4⟩'. One can paraphrase (c) as follows: the valence of finite transitive verbs (= fin⟨1⟩) as well as transitive verbs in the imperative (= fin⟨4⟩) is the same as that of '%aktiv'; or in short: finite and imperative transitive verbs only occur in active constructions. In (d), features are likewise made into prerequisites. Furthermore, this reference denotes an alternative marked by term 3. Thus (d) leads to the establishment of two mutually exclusive valence descriptions, if the features in the application part apply to a given term. Freely formulated, (d) can be read: transitive verbs in the infinitive (= fin⟨2⟩) or past participle (= fin⟨3⟩) can be part of either an active or a passive construction. (e) and (f) contain the valence patterns themselves, which from 'setzen' were referred to via '%trans' and '%aktiv' or via '%trans' and '%passiv'. In the case of (e), a slot for a noun in the accusative and marked with the role symbol 'TRANS' is copied into the original list with 'setzen'. In the case of (f) 'setzen' gets a slot for a prepositional phrase in the role 'AGENS'; the preposition must belong to the selection class '?praep_ag'.

Of course, '%trans' can be referred to from any number of concrete lexemes. If one represents references as directed arcs and every entry as a node, then the structure of the valence lexicon, just like that of the base lexicon, corresponds to a complex diagram. The following illustrates this for our example:

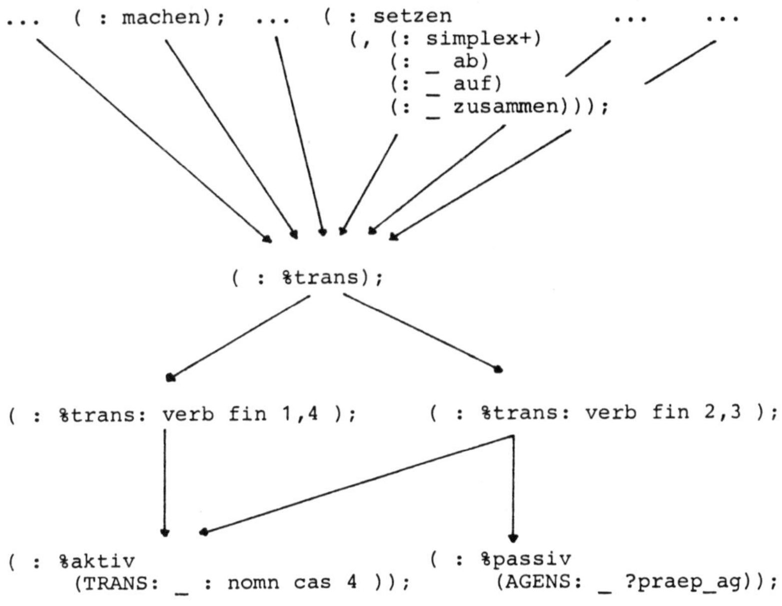
... (: machen); ... (: setzen ... ...
(, (: simplex+)
(: _ ab)
(: _ auf)
(: _ zusammen)));
(: %trans);
(: %trans: verb fin 1,4);
(: %trans: verb fin 2,3);
(: %aktiv
(TRANS: _ : nomn cas 4));
(: %passiv
(AGENS: _ ?praep_ag));

The above paraphrasing of the references and valence patterns may have seemed quite traditional. That was, in fact, intentional. For a large part, our valence lexicon is nothing but a fomalization of traditional grammatical terms such as "transitive", "active", "passive", etc. On the other hand, one can easily recognize the rewriting rules of generative grammar in the valence references. References are, so-to-speak, "tailor-made" rules.

Selectional classifications in the lexeme field of slots have proven to be useful. But in drawing up these classifications I have stuck to syntactic criteria as much as possible out of a certain scepticism towards semantic feature classification.[15] Thus '?praep_ag' is precisely the class of prepositions that can enter slots with the role AGENS, namely 'von' and 'durch'. Since often the valence categories defined by references are also suitable for selectional subclassification, PLAIN makes no formal difference between the reference to a valence pattern and the assignment of a selection class. All of the symbols that occur in references are associated with the initial term and can be used for selection. Lexemes that are referred to but for which there is no valence pattern are purely subclassifying. In order to facilitate our own understanding, we mark these expressions with '?'. Accordingly, the following selectional specifications are also part of our valence lexicon:

(g)

```
(: +> <CONFER>
     (*: von: prpo cas<3>)
     (: ?praep_ag));
```

(h)

```
(: +> <CONFER>
     (*: durch: prpo cas<4>)
     (: ?praep_ag));
```

In the course of the practical testing of PLAIN, the reference technique was further refined. The guiding principle was to achieve the greatest possible flexibility for formulating empirical findings. A few details may be mentioned. By means of references, it is possible to specify subcategories that had not yet been specified or, in extreme cases, even to completely change the category of a term. This is desirable for features that do not depend on the lexeme or on morphology but that are purely syntagmatic. Simply for reasons of clarity one would rather have these features in the valence lexicon than in the base lexicon. An example in German is the position of nominal completions, depending on whether they are to be subordinated to verbs, adjectives, or nouns. As already mentioned in 3.2. we note generally applicable position regularities in the dominating term and from there we have them copied into the corresponding slots, if necessary,

---

15 It would go too far to give my reasons for this here. See HELLWIG 1978, pp. 182ff.

by giving the slot subcategory the value 'C'. To provide the dominating term, for its part, with a positional specification, the following references, among others, exist:

```
(i)     (: +> <CONFER>
             (*: %verb: verb fin<2,3>)
             (*:: verb pos<1,2>));

(j)     (: +> <CONFER>
             (*: %verb: verb fin<4>)
             (*:: verb pos<3,4>));
```

Freely formulated, this means:

(i) Complements of verbs in the infinitive or perfect participle (= fin⟨2,3⟩) precede these verbs indirectly or directly (= pos⟨1,2⟩).

(j) Complements of verbs in the imperative (= fin⟨4⟩) follow these verbs directly or indirectly (= pos⟨3,4⟩).

This general provision frees one from considering the position regularity anew for every single slot specification.

As a matter of principle, the following stipulations apply to processing morpho-syntactic categories in valence references:

1. The main category of the application part must be identical to the main category of the initial term or it must be unspecified. If it is unspecified, the category of the initial term is used in the further process. If it is specified, the intersection of the values in the initial term and in the application part of the reference is formed for every subcategory. If the intersection is empty in any subcategory, then the reference is unusable in that particular case. Otherwise this intersection is decisive for the rest of the looking up procedure in the valence lexicon. If differing feature intersections arise from several references applied to the same initial term, the result is that one valence pattern is set up for each feature set, i.e. several alternative AL lists arise for the same NL segment.

If no category is specified for the referent of a reference, then the result of the comparison between the initial term and the application part continues to be used. If the main category is specified for the referent and is identical to the initial term, then a new intersection is formed out of the previous values and the values for the referent. This is the case in the example just discussed where 'pos⟨1,2,3,4⟩' became 'pos⟨1,2⟩' after (i) and 'pos⟨3,4⟩' after (j). Lastly, if the main category for the referent does not correspond to the original main category, then the whole category is replaced by the new category in the initial term as well. In the part of German that I have processed so far there has not yet been an occasion for such a change of categories. The relabeling would correspond to the concept of "translation" as proposed by L. TESNIERE.[16] However, the status of this concept in a theory of grammar is not quite clear.

Describing a certain completion as obligatory is done by marking the slot variable with '*' or with another symbol fixed by the user via the parameter SLOTOBLIGATION. It is practical to be able to include obligation in references, too. If necessary, one can add the obligation symbol to the application part as well as to the referring part. The symbol is treated like a normal feature in the comparison of the initial term and the application part, i.e. it must be in both or in neither. However, if one goes from a reference to the referred to pattern, then the feature is skipped in the applicability test. Instead, it is transferred to all of the slots of the pattern. Thus in many cases one can avoid setting up two patterns, one for the obligatory and one for the optional version of completion.

Sometimes not only the dominating term in the initial structure is decisive for a valence reference, but also subordinated elements, whether they be terms that stem from a lexical decomposition in the base lexicon or from previously attributed completions. One must be aware that in the course of consulting the valence lexicon first all of the direct patterns are looked up and only then are the references applied. Therefore, it is possible to incorporate previously subordinated terms in the application parts of references. For example, the valence of verbs varies depending on the separable prefix. In (a) a valence pattern with various alternative prefix slots was assigned to the lexeme 'setzen'. The following references presuppose this assignment:

---

16 Compare TESNIERE 1959, chapter 151ff.

(k)

```
(: +> <CONFER>
     (*: setzen
          (: simplex+))
     (*: %adv_dir));
```

(l)

```
(: +> <CONFER>
     (*: setzen
          (: _ zusammen <SLOT>))
     (, <AUT>
          (*: %mit)
          (*: %aus)));
```

Freely paraphrased, (k) means that *setzen* as a simplex allows a directional adverb, and (l) means that the prefix verb *zusammensetzen* allows either a prepositional phrase with *mit* or with *aus* as a completion. Compare *etwas irgendwohin setzen, etwas mit etwas zusammensetzen, etwas aus etwas zusammensetzen*. The pattern for (*: %adv_dir), (*: %mit), (*: %aus) can be found elsewhere in the valence lexicon. The general rule reads: in the application part of a reference any subordinated terms are allowed. A reference is valid for an expression if the structure of the application part is included in the structure of the expression.

Sometimes it is useful to be able to eliminate certain copies of initial lists that were set up according to a general pattern. For example, adjectival and substantival derivations from the past participle exist only for transitive and certain durative verbs, e.g. *zusammengesetztes, Zusammengesetzter*. In the base lexicon, where no distinction is made between transitive, intransitive, durative, etc., derivations from the past participle of all verbs are allowed and are labeled with the term '(FOCUS: passiv+)'. This derivation must be deleted for verbs that are specified in the valence lexicon as being intransitive. This is done by:

(m)

```
(: +> <CONFER>
     (*: %intrans
          (FOCUS: passiv+)));
```

No expression is referred to in (m). This is to be interpreted as an instruction to delete all of the initially formed lists to which the reference is applicable. Accordingly, an input such as **geschlafenes* is not accepted by the analysis program.

3.4. Analysis Algorithm

First of all, the information available in the base lexicon is obtained for every word of the input; compound words are divided into their constituents. The result is a number of initial lists whose main terms are morpho-syntactically more or less fixed. Next, syntactic information for each of the initial lists is looked up in the valence lexicon. Slots, if any, are inserted into the initial lists. When all of the building blocks have been gathered from the two lexicons, then more complex expressions are constructed step by step. In every step, a suitable list is inserted into a slot of another tree. Finally, the bracketed expressions which contain an AL representation for all segments of the input are turned out as the analysis result. One can have a listing of the steps printed that led up to the result. The result of the analysis can be stored temporarily in the data set RESLF and passed on from there to the deduction component of PLAIN. Neither the person who sets up the lexicons nor the one who makes the natural language input need actually know more than this. Nevertheless I will mention a few further details of the analysis algorithm of PLAIN below, most of which serve to optimize the process; they also to some extent have linguistic relevance.

All intermediate results of the analysis starting with the lexically assigned lists, are numbered in ascending order. They are stored in a working file (WORKF). All of the lists look for fitting slots in other lists, according to the sequence of the numbering. Constituents of compounds are combined within the word frame. Only after the word formation has been completed, i.e. after all of the segments of the compound are represented in one tree, is a further processing of the word tried. Terms that are constituents of portmanteau morphs may enter another list on their own. This list, however, can only be combined with another constituent of the same portmanteau form. Lists with unfilled but obligatory slots are likewise excluded from the search for slots. (The option FILL=OFF can be used to suspend this stipulation; this can be advantageous when examining elliptical constructions.) Marking a slot as obligatory contributes to the optimization of the analysis process, because this produces less intermediate results which have to be checked later on. However, since the necessity of filling a slot often depends on the communication situation, fairly strict limits are set for this measure. Of course, a list is also prevented from being inserted into another when both lists contain terms that have been assigned to the same segments of the input; the intersection of the segments represented by both lists must be the empty set every time.

The role in the dominating term of a tree that is to be inserted must be identical to the role in the corresponding slot term, or else one of the two role fields must contain a variable. The filling of a slot can be selectionally restricted by a lexeme. In this case a tree is inserted only when its dominating term itself contains this lexeme or when the tree has been subclassified accordingly by a reference in the valence lexicon. Selectional lexemes can also be passed on from subordinated terms to the dominating term. For this to occur the slot filled by the subordinated term must have been marked before with the value of the parameter PASSLEXEME. (The standard value of PASSLEXEME is '+'.) In this manner, any number of selectional features of a tree can be collected in the dominating term. Selectional lexemes can be negated by means of the system defined negation element (parameter NON). In this case, a tree may only fill the slot in question if the selectional lexeme has not been assigned to it. The comparison of the morpho-syntactic categories of slots and slot fillers is carried out by the special programs for subcategories, as described in 3.1.

If a tree fits into the slot of another list, then a copy of the slot list is made; the filler list is inserted into the copy; the resulting list is then added to the series of the previously produced lists. The copying of the old list guarantees that other alternatives are not blocked in the case of an incorrect assignment. As soon as a tree has been made dependent on another, all of the slots it still contains are deleted. In the receiving tree only those parts are eliminated that were identified, by means of the meta-linguistic term (,), as alternatives to the filled slot. All of the other slots of the receiving expression remain open. Hence, many different complements can be attributed to one and the same dominating term in subsequent steps. The union set of the segment positions which are represented by every newly formed structure is calculated and recorded in each step. Once the analysis program has reached the list with the highest numbering, it starts again with the first list, limiting its search range, however, to the newly added lists. This process is repeated until no more new assignments have been made while checking the whole series of lists.

The first experiences with PLAIN showed that an analysis program based exclusively on the specifications in the terms and slots produces many incorrect intermediate results. Even a large repertory of positional features does not keep lists from being assigned to other lists beyond the scope of the corresponding constituents. The range of a constituent is, at first, not at all discernible from a purely dependential point of view. See the following two expressions:

(1) der Schirm der Frau
(the woman's umbrella)

(2) der der Frau gehörende Schirm
(the umbrella owned by the woman)

With completely free slot seeking in (1) the first *der* would also be subordinated to the noun *Frau*, which is, of course, a dead end. The scope of the constituent dominated by *Frau* does not reach to the left beyond the second *der*; therefore the first *der* is not allowed to be linked with *Frau*. (2) shows that the solution does not lie in restricting the assignment of the article to the next noun in the input sequence. In (2) the range of the constituent that is dominated by the second noun, *Schirm*, includes the whole expression, so that the first word, *der*, can and actually must be subordinated to the last word in the input string. The incorrect assignments do not cause incorrect final results, but the dead ends waste computer time.

A phrase structure grammar naturally does not have such problems, since it concatenates only immediately adjacent constituents. Consequently it seemed advisable to include at least the principle of immediate constituents in the analysis algorithm though not in the description data. That was easy to accomplish; inserting a tree into the slot of another was restricted to the cases in which the corresponding segments of the input immediately follow each other. Keeping track of the represented segment positions is necessary anyway. On the other hand, discontinuous constituents must also remain analyzable. The postulated advantage of our dependential approach is that a discontinuity of the represented constituents is not excluded.

The optimized version of PLAIN adheres to the following principle: continuous analysis insofar as possible, discontinuous completion only where absolutely necessary. To realize this principle, cycles of continuous and discontinuous analysis alternate. To start with, only lists which represent adjacent constituents are combined into a new list. If a complete AL representation of the input is achieved in this way, then the program quits. If not, a cycle of discontinuous combination attempts is run through, followed by a phase in which the new constituents are again continuously linked with the others, and so on. Via the parameter DISCONTINUOUS=OFF this process can be changed in such a way that only a continuous analysis is tried, thereby considerably reducing the computer time. DISCONTINUOUS=ON has the effect that a discontinuous reading is sought even though an analysis result has already been reached.

Slots cannot be completely freely sought in a cycle of discontinuous analysis, for then we would still get the senseless intermediate results I mentioned above, whenever a continuous connection of the input is not possible. Therefore, two hypotheses about discontinuity are built into the analysis program:

(a) The segment which can not be linked continuously belongs to an adjacent constituent, but the corresponding tree is to be made dependent on one of the subordinated terms in the list and the segment correlated to the appropriate term is not located at the edge of the adjacent constituent, because otherwise it would already have been concatenated with the segment that causes the problem.

(b) Another constituent that has not yet found a slot is located between the segment and the constituent the segment belongs to.

According to hypothesis (a) lists are sought whose corresponding constituents are adjacent to the segment of the list which is currently being processed. All of the trees that were incorporated in these lists are then checked once more for slots. If a suitable slot is found, then the searching list is still inserted into the discovered tree. According to hypothesis (b) all lists whose constituents follow directly after any adjoining segment are examined for suitable slots. However, segments separated by several constituents for which no coherent analysis was yet achieved are not included in the examination. As a result of this restriction, it is rare for totally incorrect intermediate results to occur in the part of German tested so far. If one symbolizes the concatenation of segments with arches, then PLAIN can only analyze constituent relationships like (3), but not like (4).

(3)

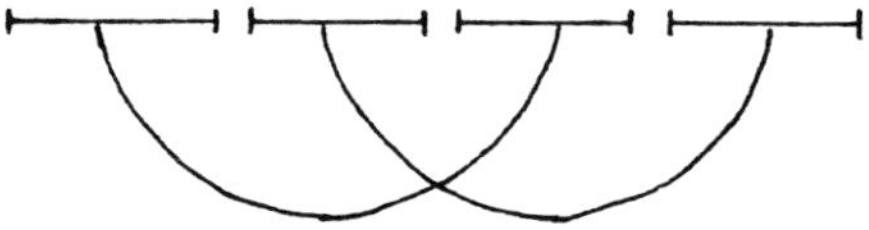

(4)

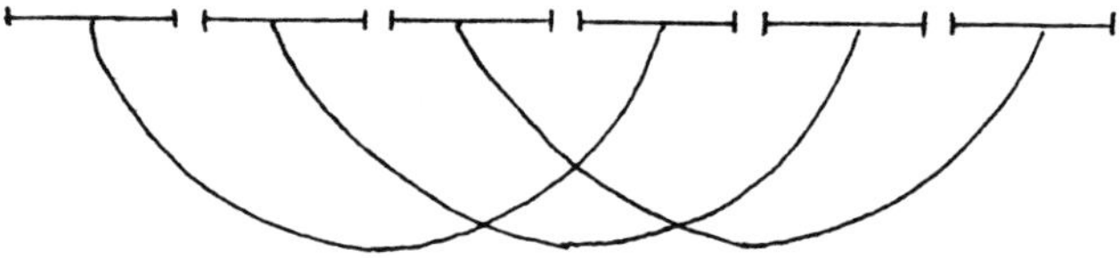

It is an unanswered empirical question whether structures occur in natural language which would require concatenations such as in (4) for their analysis.

Another problem arises from the binary nature of the analysis steps as opposed to the unrestricted branching possibilities in the dependency trees. In certain cases one and the same dependency structure can be reached via a different sequence of analysis steps, so that multiple results are erroneously arrived at. Informally illustrated, we require, for example, the following analysis result for the expression *die Anfänge der deutschen Sprache*:

(5)

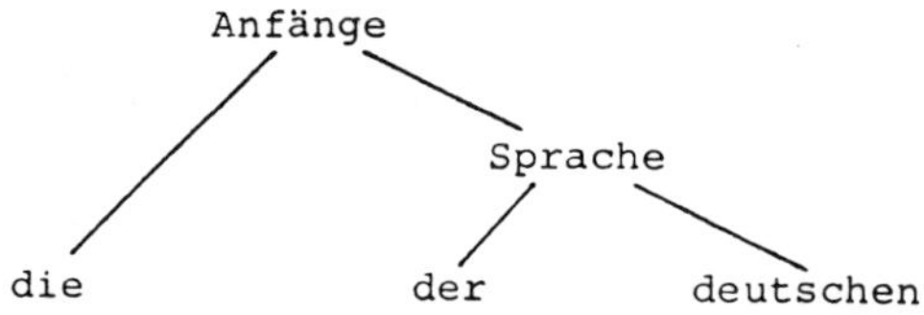

This very result can be generated in two ways (the numbers represent the numbers of the intermediately produced lists):

(6)

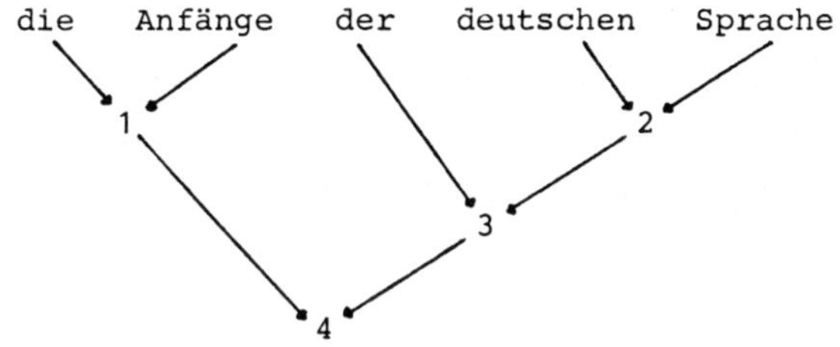

(7)

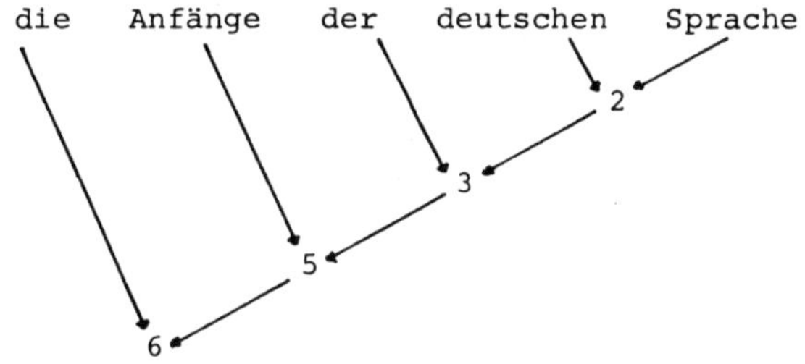

Step 5 in (7) is quite meaningful, for the expression *Anfänge der deutschen Sprache* is acceptable on its own. On the other hand, step 6 conveys nothing new as compared to 4, since *die* as well as the constituent *die deutsche Sprache* are in both cases subordinated to the word *Anfänge*. By checking the genealogy of previous results, PLAIN's analysis program recognizes this and avoids steps such as 6.

PLAIN often assigns several alternative analysis results to an NL input. That is correct if the input is indeed ambiguous. One need not depart from interpreting the translation of NL into AL as a mathematical function for this reason. The unambiguity of the mapping is maintained if one assumes that there are items in NL that are different even though they look the same. What we map from NL into AL are linguistic units as a whole, not only their outward appearance.

However, in all cases where the speakers of NL view a statement as unambiguous, multiple results of the program have to be reduced. Certain readings are unacceptable for the human hearer because the presuppositions associated with these readings cannot be made to agree with what the hearer knows about the subject area. To simulate this state of affairs with PLAIN, one would have to write rules which allow us to generate all presuppositions connected with given expressions. The presuppositions derived from each reading of an analysis would have to be checked by means of the deduction component for compatibility with the respective data base. If the negation of a presupposition linked to an input item can be logically inferred from the data base, then the corresponding reading must be eliminated from the analysis alternatives. I have not yet tried this out in practice. Theoretical considerations on the above can be found in HELLWIG 1978.

In the future the analysis procedure of PLAIN is to be further expanded. Special routines are planned to deal with complicated cases of coordination such as *er legt den Hut auf den Stuhl und die Handschuhe auf den Tisch* and to determine the anaphoric relationships of words such as *dieser, jener, ersterer, letzterer,* etc. The modular structure of the program system encourages such expansions.

3.5. An Analysis Example

The analysis component of PLAIN was tested on a corpus of 2000 technical book titles. The text type of book titles was selected because the syntactic and semantic structures that occur in them are comprehensible and because automatic title processing is one of the possible areas of application of the system. One of the input titles reads:

: WIE EIN BUCH ENTSTEHT.
(How a Book is Made)

The analysis result arrived at by PLAIN looks like this:

```
*** ANALY - RESULT OF ANALYSIS:

LIST 22:

 1  (ILLOC: titel+
 2       (THEMA: hypo+: satz typ<2> rel<5> pos<3>
 3            (PRAED: entstehen: verb per<3> num<1> fin<1>
              rel<5> pos<2> ord<3> con<1>
 4                 (TEMPS: praesens+)
 5                 (MODUS: indikativ+)
 6                 (ADVRB: wie: ptkl pty<2> rel<5> pos<1>
                   vps<1>)
 7                 (SUBJT: buch: nomn gen<3> per<3> num<1>
                   cas<1> fle<2> flk<1> dte<2> pos<2>
 8                      (NUMRS: singular+)
 9                      (REFER: ein: dete gen<3> num<1>
                        cas<1,4> fle<2> pos<2> nps<1>)))));
```

The input starts with a colon. Let us assume that, in a bibliography, this colon is the separation character between the author or editor and the title, so that the subsequent text is recognized as a title. The program system must be informed beforehand what kind of a text the input is. This is done by specifying a section of the base lexicon as the starting point for the look up routine. Each starting point section contains the words and punctuation marks which are used in a specific way in texts of the corresponding type.

The result of the analysis is a bracketed expression of an AL specially designed for German. In order to make the structure of the expression transparent, the terms are numbered and printed on separate lines. Each subordinated term is moved further to the right than the corresponding dominating term. Collateral terms are printed in the same column. If one imagines lines between each dominating term and all of its directly subordinated terms, then one can easily visualize the listing as a dependency tree that has been turned by 90 degrees as compared to the customary representation.

The fields of each term are separated from each other by a colon. Role markers are written in capitals, everything else in small letters. Lexemes that have no direct word correspondence in NL, such as 'titel+', 'hypo+', and the components of lexical decomposition 'indikativ+', 'praesens+', 'singular+' are labeled with the plus sign to keep them apart from the representations for words that exist in German, such as *Titel, Indikativ, Singular*. Aside from this the lexemes of AL in our example coincide with the primary (uninflected) form of German words.

The third field in every term contains the morpho-syntactic category. In a few terms, 1,4,5, and 8, it is empty. In such cases the second colon is also left out. In the other terms, each category is made up of a four character long symbol for a word or morpheme class and a varying number of feature specifications. (The category 'satz' that occurs in the 2nd term of the bracketed expression is also considered to be a word class. The segment that corresponds to this term in the input is the period.) Each feature specification is made up of a 3 character long designation of the feature type and of a numerical representation of the feature itself (in angular brackets).

Once one is used to the symbolism one can read the analysis result like a regular syntactic description. Element by element, the most essential statements in the bracketed expression can be paraphrased as follows:

1 This text is a speech act of the type title.

2 The title specifies the topic of the publication in the form of a hypotactic sentence with a W-pronoun.

3 The predicate of the topic outlining sentence is the lexeme 'entstehen' that appears as a finite verb in the 3rd person singular.

4 The tense of the word form of 'entstehen' is the present.

5 The mode of the word form of 'entstehen' is the indicative.

6 The lexeme 'wie' is subordinated to the predicate 'entstehen' in the role of an adverb. The word class of 'wie' is that of an adverbial particle of the W-type.

7 In the role of the subject, the lexeme 'buch' depends on 'entstehen'. The word form of this expression is that of a singular neuter noun in the nominative. The word forms of

subject and predicate are congruent in number and person.

8 The number of the noun corresponding to 'buch' is the singular. Since this is a semantically relevant syntactic feature it is, as tense and mode of the verb were, recorded in a term of its own.

9 'buch' is completed by the determiner 'ein' which indicates the extra-linguistic domain of reference of the noun. The determiner is congruent with the word form of 'buch' in gender, number, and case.

A lengthy discussion is going on as to which criteria should be used to subordinate and superordinate expressions to each other in a dependency representation.[17] I do not consider this question especially important since role markers make it possible to label any tree structure functionally in such a way that it can be semantically processed later on. In the majority of empirical cases constraints arise on their own that call for a certain dependency order. So it is unavoidable when one uses trees as a means of representation that a term which is in a direct syntagmatic relationship with two other terms must dominate at least one of those. Also, one will have to make those terms into the dominating ones whose word classes are decisive in the overall context. Sometimes such a term represents a segment that could also stand alone in the particular place - a criteria that is often suggested. However, in our example, this does not apply to any of the superordinated terms. For example, the noun *Buch* must be superordinated to the determiner *ein*, not because the distribution of *Buch* is the same as that of *ein Buch* (it is not, cf. **Wie Buch ensteht.*), but because the morpho-syntactic features that are prerequisites for nominal verb completions can easily be noted only within the category noun.

Our analysis result also contains a description of the phrase structure of the input. The hierarchy of the subtrees which make up the dependency tree can be projected onto the input string.

---

17 See HELLWIG 1978, pp. 116ff.

The result is a division into immediate constituents. The linear sequence of the constituents is indicated by the position subcategories pos, ord, vps, and nps. In addition to the information offered by a phrase structure grammar, among the immediate constituents of each projection one is always marked as being dominating. This seems to be a general desideratum.[18]

Below I shall refer to the subtrees in the analysis result by the number of the dominating term. Let us distinguish between a "segment" as a piece of the input string that correlates with one single term, and a "constituent" as the section from the input string that is assigned to a tree. Segments are to be numbered like the terms, constituents like the trees. The above bracketed expression then gives the following information about the phrase structure of the input.

1 Constituent 1 embraces the whole input. The marked immediate constituent of 1 is segment 1 (':').

2 Constituent 2 ('WIE EIN BUCH ENTSTEHT.') is an immediate constituent of 1 and directly follows (= pos⟨3⟩) the marked segment 1. The marked immediate constituent of 2 is segment 2 ('.').

3 Constituent 3 ('WIE EIN BUCH ENTSTEHT') is an immediate constituent of 2 and directly precedes (= pos⟨2⟩) the marked segment 2. The marked immediate constituent of 3 is segment 3 ('ENTSTEHT '). This is in final position with respect to the other constituents of 3 (= ord⟨3⟩).

---

18 J.J. ROBINSON 1970, pp. 259ff., describes cases where the generative transformational grammar also needs information as to which constituent is "the head of the phrase". For semantic reasons, U. WEINREICH 1966, pp. 432ff., feels a need to distinguish in his grammar between "major" and "minor" morphemes and, correspondingly, between two types of preterminal constituents. C. FILLMORE criticizes the fact that the phrase structure model does not provide the basic elements necessary to account for case relationships, already in the first pages of the article with which he introduced case grammar. See FILLMORE 1968, p. 3 and also p. 87.

4 Term 4 has no positional features and thereby shows itself to be a decomposition of the segment 'ENTSTEHT'.

5 The same applies to term 5 as to term 4.

6 Segment 6 ('WIE ') is an immediate constituent of 3. It precedes (= pos<1>) segment 3 ('ENSTEHT') and among all the other components of constituent 3, it occupies the initial position (= vps<1>).

7 Constituent 7 ('EIN BUCH ') is an immediate constituent of 3. It directly precedes (= pos<2>) segment 3. The marked immediate constituent of 7 is segment 7 ('BUCH ').

8 Term 8 arises from decomposition of segment 7.

9 Segment 9 ('EIN ') is an immediate constituent of 7 and occupies the first position (= nps<1>) among all possible IC's of constituent 7. 'EIN ' immediately precedes (= pos<2>) segment 7 ('BUCH ').

After the end of an analysis one can call up several types of documentation: a complete record of the analysis process, interesting intermediate results, etc. All of the information used during the analysis is still available in the working file (WORKF). To see how the analysis result of our example was achieved, we have a "history" of the resulting list printed. In a "history" only those steps of analysis are recorded which contributed to the construction of the list in question. The gaps in the numbering of the intermediate results show that other steps led into dead ends.

```
-----------------------------------------------------------

*** ANALY - HISTORY OF LIST  22:

LIST    1 (BUILT BY LEXICON LOOKUP) :
': '
MORPHEM(S): 1, WORD(S): 1

   1  (ILLOC: titel+
   2        (, <AUT>
   3              (TEXTC: _ * setzung+ <SLOT>: satz typ<3>
                  pos<3>)
   4              (THEMA: _ * e_frage+ <SLOT>: satz typ<1>
                  pos<3>)
   5              (THEMA: _ * w_frage+ <SLOT>: satz typ<1>
                  pos<3>)
   6              (THEMA: _ * hypo+ <SLOT>: satz typ<2> rel<5>
                  pos<3>)
   7              (THEMA: _ * setzung+ <SLOT>: satz typ<3>
                  pos<3>))
   8        (, <AUT>
   9              (TEXTC: _ setzung+ <SLOT>: satz typ<3>
                  pos<4>)
  10              (THEMA: _ setzung+ <SLOT>: satz typ<3>
                  pos<4>)));

- LOOKING FOR SLOTS WAS SKIPPED FOR THIS LIST -
-----------------------------------------------------------

LIST    2 (BUILT BY LEXICON LOOKUP) :
'WIE '
MORPHEM(S): 1, WORD(S): 01

   1  (ADVRE: wie: ptkl pty<2> rel<5> vps<1>);
-----------------------------------------------------------

LIST    6 (BUILT BY LEXICON LOOKUP) :
'EIN '
MORPHEM(S): 1, WORD(S): 001

   1  (REFER: ein: dete gen<3> num< 1> cas<1,4> fle<2>);
-----------------------------------------------------------
```

```
LIST   7 (BUILT BY LEXICON LOOKUP):
'BUCH '
MORPHEM(S): 1, WORD(S): 0001

  1  (*: buch: nomn gen<3> num<1> cas<1,3,4> flk<1> pos<3,4>
  2        (NUMRS: singular+)
  3        (REFER: _ <SLOT>: dete gen<C> num<C> cas<C>
           fle<C> dte<C> nps<1>)
  4        (OBJRL: _ <SLOT>: poss gen<C> num<C> cas<C>
           fle<C> dte<C> nps<1> ctn<1>)
  5        (OBJRL: _ %name_e <SLOT>: nomn num<1> cas<2>
           fle<3> dte<C> nps<1> ctn<1>)
  6        (OBJRL: _ <SLOT>: komp kty<2> pos<2>)
  7        (OBJRL: _ NICHT ?temploc <SLOT>: nomn per<3>
           cas<2> fle<1,2> dte<2> pos<3> erg<C>)
  8        (OBJRL: _ von_g <SLOT>: prpo pos<3> erg<C>)
  9        (SUBRL: _ ?adje_sa <SLOT>: adje gen<C> num<C>
           cas<C> fle<C> atr<1> pos<2> erg<C>)
 10        (ATTRB: = NICHT ?adje_sa <SLOTSEQ>: adje gen<C>
           num<C> cas<C> fle<C> atr<1> pos<1,2> ctn<1>
           erg<C>)
 11        (ATTRB: _ <SLOT>: komp kty<3> pos<2>)
 12        (ATTRB: _ <SLOT>: satz typ<3> pos<3>)
 13        (ATTRB: _ <SLOT>: satz typ<2> rel<3> pos<3,4>
           erg<C>)
 14        (, <AUT>
 15             (ADVRB: _ ?temploc <SLOT>: adje gen<C> num<C>
                cas<C> fle<C> pos<1,2> ctn<1> erg<C>)
 16             (ADVRB: _ ?temploc <SLOT>: nomn cas<2> dte<2>
                pos<3> erg<C>
 17                  (REFER: @_d)))
 18        (ADVRB: = ?adv_obj <SLOTSEQ>: prpo pos<C> ctn<1>
           erg<C>)
 19        (RNUMR: _ <SLOT>: numr nty<3> gen<C> num<C>
           cas<C> fle<C> pos<1,2>)
 20        (CASUS: _ ueber_akk <SLOT>: prpo pos<C>)
 21        (APPOS: _ zitat+ <SLOT>: ptkl pos<3>));

SATISFYING:

%indiv, %ueber_akk, %zit, %obj, %konkr, %attr_su, %adv_temploc,
%adv_obj, ?obj, ?edit

- NO SLOT FOUND FOR THIS LIST -
```

```
LIST   8 (BUILT BY LEXICON LOOKUP):
'ENTSTEHT '
MORPHEM(S): 1, WORD(S): 00001

   1  (*: entstehen: verb per<3> num<1> fin<1>
   2        (TEMPS: praesens+)
   3        (MODUS: indikativ+)
   4        (ATTRB: _ NICHT ?adje_sa <SLOT>: adje atr<3>
            pos<C>)
   5        (ADVRB: = ?adv_intr <SLOTSEQ>: prpo pos<C> ctn<1>
            erg<C>)
   6        (ADVRB: _ <SLOT>: ptkl pty<2> pos<C>)
   7        (, <AUT>
   8             (SUBJT: _ * <SLOT>: nomn per<C> num<C>
                 cas<1> dte<2> pos<1,2,3>)
   9             (SUBJT: _ * hypo+ <SLOT>: satz typ<2> rel<5>
                 pos<2,3>))
  10        (ADVCM: _ ?adv_kmt <SLOT>: adje atr<3> pos<C>)
  11        (CASUS: _ aus <SLOT>: prpo pos<C>));

SATISFYING:

%intrans, %aus, %verb, %attr_vb, %adv_vb, %subj, %adv_kmt

- LOOKING FOR SLOTS WAS SKIPPED FOR THIS LIST -
------------------------------------------------------------

LIST  11 (BUILT BY LEXICON LOOKUP):
'. '
MORPHEM(S): 1, WORD(S): 000001

   1  (THEMA: hypo+: satz typ<2> rel<5>
   2        (PRAED: _ * <SLOT>: verb fin<1> pos<2,3> vps<3>
            crd<3> ccn<1>));

- LOOKING FOR SLOTS WAS SKIPPED FOR THIS LIST -
                                                     --------
```

```
LIST  16 (DERIVED FROM LIST  6 AND LIST  7):
'EIN BUCH '
MORPHEM(S): 1, WORD(S): 0011

  1  (*: buch: ncmn gen<3> num<1> cas<1,4> fle<2> flk<1>
     dte<2> pos<3,4> nps<C>
  2        (NUMRS: singular+)
  3        (REFER: ein: dete gen<3> num<1> cas<1,4> fle<2>
           pos<2> nps<1>)
  4        (OBJRL: _ <SLOT>: poss gen<C> num<C> cas<C>
           fle<C> dte<C> nps<1> ctn<1>)
  5        (OBJRL: _ %name_e <SLOT>: nomn num<1> cas<2>
           fle<3> dte<C> nps<1> ctn<1>)
  6        (OBJRL: _ <SLOT>: komp kty<2> pos<2>)
  7        (OBJRL: _ NICHT ?temploc <SLOT>: nomn per<3>
           cas<2> fle<1,2> dte<2> pos<3> erg<C>)
  8        (OBJRL: _ von_g <SLOT>: prpo pos<3> erg<C>)
  9        (SUBRL: _ ?adje_sa <SLOT>: adje gen<C> num<C>
           cas<C> fle<C> atr<1> pos<2> erg<C>)
 10        (ATTRB: = NICHT ?adje_sa <SLOTSEQ>: adje gen<C>
           num<C> cas<C> fle<C> atr<1> pos<1,2> ctn<1>
           erg<C>)
 11        (ATTRB: _ <SLOT>: komp kty<3> pos<2>)
 12        (ATTRB: _ <SLOT>: satz typ<3> pos<3>)
 13        (ATTRB: _ <SLOT>: satz typ<2> rel<3> pos<3,4>
           erg<C>)
 14        (, <AUT>
 15             (ADVRB: _ ?temploc <SLOT>: adje gen<C> num<C>
                cas<C> fle<C> pos<1,2> ctn<1> erg<C>)
 16             (ADVRB: _ ?temploc <SLOT>: nomn cas<2> dte<2>
                pos<3> erg<C>
 17                  (REFER: @_d)))
 18        (ADVRB: = ?adv_obj <SLOTSEQ>: prpo pos<C> ctn<1>
           erg<C>)
 19        (RNUMR: _ <SLOT>: numr nty<3> gen<C> num<C>
           cas<C> fle<C> pos<1,2>)
 20        (CASUS: _ ueber_akk <SLOT>: prpo pos<C>)
 21        (APPOS: _ zitat+ <SLOT>: ptkl pos<3>));
```

```
LIST  17 (DERIVED FROM LIST  16 AND LIST   8):
'EIN BUCH ENTSTEHT '
MORPHEM(S): 1, WORD(S): 00111

  1  (*: entstehen: verb per<3> num<1> fin<1>
  2        (TEMPS: praesens+)
  3        (MODUS: indikativ+)
  4        (ATTRB: _ NICHT ?adje_sa <SLOT>: adje atr<3>
           pos<C>)
  5        (ADVRB: = ?adv_intr <SLOTSEQ>: prpo pos<C> ctn<1>
           erg<C>)
  6        (ADVRB: _ <SLOT>: ptkl pty<2> pos<C>)
  7        (SUBJT: buch: nomn gen<3> per<3> num<1> cas<1>
           fle<2> flk<1> dte<2> pos<2>
  8              (NUMRS: singular+)
  9              (REFER: ein: dete gen<3> num<1> cas<1,4>
                 fle<2> pos<2> nps<1>))
 10        (ADVCM: _ ?adv_kmt <SLOT>: adje atr<3> pos<C>)
 11        (CASUS: _ aus <SLOT>: prpo pos<C>));
------------------------------------------------------------

LIST  20 (DERIVED FROM LIST   2 AND LIST  17):
'WIE EIN BUCH ENTSTEHT '
MORPHEM(S): 1, WORD(S): 01111

  1  (*: entstehen: verb per<3> num<1> fin<1> rel<5> vps<1>
  2        (TEMPS: praesens+)
  3        (MODUS: indikativ+)
  4        (ATTRB: _ NICHT ?adje_sa <SLOT>: adje atr<3>
           pos<C>)
  5        (ADVRB: = ?adv_intr <SLOTSEQ>: prpo pos<C> ctn<1>
           erg<C>)
  6        (ADVRB: wie: ptkl pty<2> rel<5> pos<1> vps<1>)
  7        (SUBJT: buch: nomn gen<3> per<3> num<1> cas<1>
           fle<2> flk<1> dte<2> pos<2>
  8              (NUMRS: singular+)
  9              (REFER: ein: dete gen<3> num<1> cas<1,4>
                 fle<2> pos<2> nps<1>))
 10        (ADVCM: _ ?adv_kmt <SLOT>: adje atr<3> pos<C>)
 11        (CASUS: _ aus <SLOT>: prpo pos<C>));
--------------------------
```

```
LIST  21 (DERIVED FROM LIST  20 AND LIST  11):
'WIE EIN BUCH ENTSTEHT . '
MORPHEM(S): 1, WORD(S): 011111

  1  (THEMA: hypo+: satz typ<2> rel<5>
  2       (PRAED: entstehen: verb per<3> num<1> fin<1>
          rel<5> pos<2> ord<3> con<1>
  3            (TEMPS: praesens+)
  4            (MODUS: indikativ+)
  5            (ADVRB: wie: ptkl pty<2> rel<5> pos<1>
               vps<1>)
  6            (SUBJT: buch: nomn gen<3> per<3> num<1>
               cas<1> fle<2> flk<1> dte<2> pos<2>
  7                 (NUMRS: singular+)
  8                 (REFER: ein: dete gen<3> num<1>
                    cas<1,4> fle<2> pos<2> nps<1>)))));
-------------------------------------------------------------

LIST  22 (DERIVED FROM LIST  21 AND LIST   1):
': WIE EIN BUCH ENTSTEHT . '
MORPHEM(S): 1, WORD(S): 111111

  1  (ILLOC: titel+
  2       (THEMA: hypo+: satz typ<2> rel<5> pos<3>
  3            (PRAED: entstehen: verb per<3> num<1> fin<1>
               rel<5> pos<2> ord<3> con<1>
  4                 (TEMPS: praesens+)
  5                 (MODUS: indikativ+)
  6                 (ADVRB: wie: ptkl pty<2> rel<5> pos<1>
                    vps<1>)
  7                 (SUBJT: buch: nomn gen<3> per<3> num<1>
                    cas<1> fle<2> flk<1> dte<2> pos<2>
  8                      (NUMRS: singular+)
  9                      (REFER: ein: dete gen<3> num<1>
                         cas<1,4> fle<2> pos<2> nps<1>)))))
 10       (, <AUT>
 11            (TEXTC: _ setzung+ <SLOT>: satz typ<3>
               pos<4>)
 12            (THEMA: _ setzung+ <SLOT>: satz typ<3>
               pos<4>)));

- NO SLOT FOUND FOR THIS LIST -
  ---------------------
```

Above every intermediate result, the segment from the input is printed that corresponds to the bracketed expression below it. A sequence of '0' and '1' indicates which morpheme positions within compounds and which word positions within the total input are occupied by the analyzed expression. The sequence of '0' and '1' also shows whether the intermediate result is a continuous or discontinuous constituent.

Lists 1 through 11 contain valence descriptions of the terms that have been lexically assigned to the segments of the input. List 1 is a pattern for technical book titles. The role marker 'ILLOC' means illocution, 'TEXTC' stands for "text characterization", 'THEMA' for "topic specification". (A text characterization is a component of a title in which the type of the publication, the comprehensiveness, the purpose, etc. are described, i.e. *Einführung* (introduction), *Forschungsbericht* (project report), *kurzer Abriss für Schulen* (a primer for schools). It is important for automatic document retrieval to keep the text characterization and the topic of a document apart.) By means of term 2 in list 1 several alternative patterns are grouped together; there are 5 alternatives of main titles and 2 alternatives of optional subtitles. List 1 is thus a short form of 5 x 2 = 10 different title patterns. Slots are recognizable by the variable '_' in the lexeme field as well as by the comment '<SLOT>' that PLAIN adds in printouts. The lexical filling of all slots is precicely defined. Only trees that are dominated by a term with one of the following lexemes are eligible: 'setzung+', i.e. a phrase such as *Einführung in die Semantik* (TEXTC) or *Sprache in unserer Zeit* (THEMA), 'e_frage+', i.e. a decision question such as *Gab es eine mittelhochdeutsche Schriftsprache?*, 'w_frage+', i.e. an interrogative sentence with W-pronoun like *Was ist Syntax?*, and 'hypo+, i.e. a title like our analysis example. An asterisk in the lexeme field symbolizes that it is obligatory to fill that particular slot. As long as this has not occured, the list itself cannot enter into a slot or count as a complete analysis. The comment 'LOOKING FOR SLOT WAS SKIPPED FOR THIS LIST' draws attention to this fact.

List 2 and list 3 contain non-completable terms whose possible roles, ADVRB and REFER, are lexically fixed. This is different in the case of the term with the lexeme 'buch' described in list 7; its role in syntactic constructions can be manifold. Therefore, the first field of this term is occupied by the role variable '*', i.e. the symbol for arbitrary roles. Rather than explain the valence description of list 7 in detail, I shall just give an example with respect to evry slot. The segments that correspond to the fillers are underlined:

3 ein Buch
4 sein Buch
5 Goethes Buch
6 Uebungsbuch
7 Buch der deutschen Sprache
8 (das) Buch von der Kommunikation
9 mittelhochdeutsches (Lehr)buch
10 ausfuehrliches (Lehr)buch
11 Weißbuch
12 (ein) Buch, verfasst von ...
13 (ein) Buch, das ... enthält
15 antikes Buch
16 (das illustrierte) Buch des 19. Jahrhunderts
18 (Hand)buch für den Lehrer
19 (das) erste Buch
20 Buch über Semantik
21 (Goethes) Buch "Die Wahlverwandtschaften"

In the framework of its morpho-syntactic categorization, 'buch' shares the majority of its possible complements with other lexemes. Accordingly, list 7 was assembled via a series of references in the valence lexicon. A listing of the auxiliary symbols used in these references is to be found under the heading 'SATISFYING:'. All of these symbols remain assigned to the list. If need be, they can be used for selectional classification in the slots of other trees. By the way, no slot was found for list 7 (without determiner) in the course of the analysis. The comment added at the end of the listing draws attention to this fact.

I also illustrate the pattern of list 8 with examples of possible completions:

4 schnell entsteht (ein Buch)

5 ... entsteht unter Verwendung verschiedenen Materials
6 hier entsteht (ein Buch)
8 ein Buch entsteht
9 Was sich verkaufen läßt, entsteht
10 wahrscheinlich entsteht (ein Buch)
11 ... entsteht aus Papier und Pappe

List 11 contains the correct interpretation of the period as the closing of a special form of a topic specification that requires a constituent with a dominating verb in final position (= ord<3>).

Now a program operates on the initial lists to insert terms into slots insofar as the filler candidates meet the given requirements. In every step, precisely two trees are combined into a new list. At first the corresponding constituents have to be adjacent. During the further course of the process this requirement is relaxed in a controlled way so that discontinuous constituents can be analyzed. (In the above example discontinuous constituents do not occur.) The lists for which all word positions are marked as being filled (symbolized by '1') are considered to be a possible reading. In our case that is only list 22. Thus the input receives an unambiguous reading.

The construction of list 22 from the initial lists can be illustrated by the following diagram:

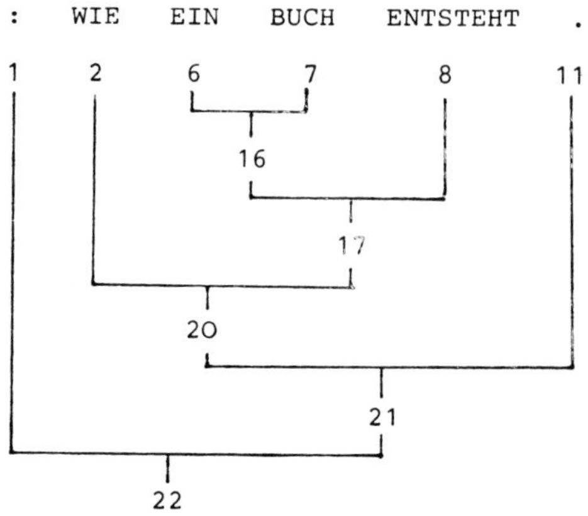

Thus outwardly the course of the analysis corresponds to a binary IC analysis. But the result is not a binary branching tree. For example, at the end the term with 'wie' and the list with 'ein' and 'buch' are both directly subordinated to the term with 'entstehen'. The analysis steps do not show up as nodes in the produced lists. Thus even with this small example, our dependential representation is already five symbols more economical than a phrase structure tree with non-terminal nodes.

4. DEDUCTION

The deduction component of PLAIN is still in the development stage. Whereas analysis with PLAIN has already been successfully tested on a considerable portion of German syntax, there are not yet systematically compiled language description data for testing the deduction component on a large scale. It is possible that a closer study of logico-semantic relationships in a particular natural language will still lead to changes in and expansions of the deduction concept of PLAIN. On the other hand, originally a few experiments in simulating inferences from German sentences led precisely to the design of an artificial language with roles and lexemes as they are assigned to the input by the analysis component. Below I shall describe how a very simple model can be constructed for at least part of natural language inferring, using the formal means of PLAIN as they exist so far.

4.1. The Deduction Principle

I use "deduction" as a collective term for all operations which, on the basis of a set of sentences (a so-called data base), result in a transition from given sentences to other sentences; the criteria for this transition is a definable meaning relationship.

Logical consequence is especially eligible as a meaning relationship. Therefore, inferences and proofs form the major part of the deductions. They are also the basis of other operations, such as question answering, paraphrasing, translation, etc. I purposely speak of sentences and not of propositions, for the deduction procedure is based on syntactic transformations of expressions and does not, as is the case with many other deduction systems, rely on a mapping of propositions into a mathematical model of possible worlds and on calculating truth values. How well my method stands up against the latter devices will have to be seen in practice.

Let us assume that D is a set of sentences that are held to be true for a certain subject domain. An exemplary linguistic deduction system is then expected to be able to carry out the following two tasks:

(i) All of the sentences k_1 to k_n that can be inferred from a new input sentence p in accordance with D are to be generated.

(ii) All of the sentences p_1 to p_m from which a new input sentence k can be inferred in accordance with D are to be generated.

The first task is that of a reproduction of possible inferences, the second task is that of assembling possible proofs.

A computer procedure that claims to be a linguistic model must not only reach the same results as human speakers who infer or prove something but it must explicitly show which rules, also language-specific ones, are behind human inferring and proving. Thus tasks (i) and (ii) must be fulfilled in such a way that the procedure provides insight into the mechanisms of natural language deduction to an extent yet to be more closely specified.[19]

---

19 A theory of argumentation has to take into account that human speakers, too, must justify their inferences or they can demand justifications from others. The discussion of the rules of argumentation can be an important component of the argumentation itself. The rules that speakers turn to in their justifications should also be the basis of the automatic deduction, in order to maintain the analogy of the model with the model object.

Techniques for finding patterns are familiar from the study of syntax. The commutation test is especially suitable for determining the syntactic constituents of sentences. One can also use this method to examine inference examples by setting up commutation classes not only with respect to the syntactic well-formedness of the sentences but also by taking care that the consequence relationship is maintained during the commutation tests in the premises and the conclusion of an inference. What we then end up with are "logical constituents".[20]

Let us take an often cited Aristotelean syllogism as an example:

(1) Alle Menschen sind sterblich.
Sokrates ist ein Mensch.
Also: Sokrates ist sterblich.

(All men are mortal.
Socrates is a man.
Thus: Socrates is mortal.)

The validity of this inference is completely independent of what the words *Mensch, sterblich, Sokrates* denote. These components of (1) can be exchanged for any others. The inference still remains valid. What cannot be changed is the sequence of the premises and the conclusion, the words *alle* and *ein*, the word *ist* in the second sentence, and the syntactic structure of the sentences insofar as the connection between the constants and the exchangeable constituents is concerned.

Thus the logical constituents of the example include the syntagmatic slots of the commutable units as well as the syntagmatic slots and lexemes of the non-replacable units. In the artificial language of PLAIN the role fields of the terms are reserved for the symbolization of logical constituency. In 2.2. I promised to provide a criteria for the assignment of roles to terms. Here it

---

20 One can find the idea of logical constituents in HINST 1974, pp. 49ff., 232ff. The method has been known since antiquity. Noteworthy, however, is the connection with the grammatical concept of constituent analysis.

is: roles are logical constituents. A role marker is the name of a logical constituent. Analogously to the syntactic constituent structure, the logical structure of immediate constituents is represented implicitly by the hierarchy of the terms and trees; the role marker of a dominating term denotes the constituent formed by the whole tree as well as the marked immediate constituent made up of just the dominating term.

If we invent symbols for the logical constituents of (1), if we replace the commutable segments with suitable variables, if we choose lexemes for the constants, and, finally, if we represent the relationship between the premises by the term (&) and the transition from the premises to the conclusion by the term (:=>), then we get the following inference pattern in AL representation:

(2)

```
(: => <REPLACE>
     (& <CON>
          (ILLOC: aussage+
               (PRAED: #2
                    (SUBJT: #1
                         (QUANT
                              (alle)))
                    (-1)))
          (ILLOC: aussage+
               (PRAED: sein
                    (SUBJT: $)
                    (PDKTV: #1
                         (REFER: ein)))))
     (ILLOC: aussage+
          (PRAED: #2
               (SUBJT: $)
               (-1))));
```

In this formula '#1' and '#2' stand for lexemes such as 'mensch' and 'sein' or 'vegetarier' and 'lieben'; '$' stands for a lexeme along with any subordinated terms such as 'Sokrates' or 'philosoph (ATTRB: beruehmt) (REFER: ∂_d)'; (-1) stands for a sequence of any subtrees such as '(PDKTV: sterblich)' or '(OBJKT: gemuese)'. Accordingly, pattern (2) also fits

(3) Alle Vegetarier lieben Gemüse.
Der berühmte Philosoph ist ein Vegetarier.
Also: Der berühmte Philosoph liebt Gemüse.

(All vegetarians love vegetables.
The famous philosopher is a vegetarian.
Thus: The famous philosopher loves vegetables.)

(2) can be interpreted as a transformation rule with two sentence descriptions, i.e. the patterns for the premises, and a construction precept, i.e. the pattern for the conclusion. The rule already suffices for simple automatic deductions. If, among the input into the system, there are two sentences which represent instances of the description part of (2), a sentence can be built according to the construction part of the rule.

In expanding the range of AL to rules, one must take care that the choice of the role markers in the valence lexicon and, as ensues from this, their occurrence in the anaysis results is compatible with the use of these symbols in the inference rules, so that no erroneous rule applications can occur. Let us assume that the following sentences are given:

(4) Alle Menschen sind gleich.
Sokrates ist ein Mensch.

(All men are equal.
Socrates is a man.)

In this case, of course, the following may not be deduced:

(5) Sokrates ist gleich.

(Socrates is equal.)

To prevent rule (2) from being applied to (4) and leading to (5), the two sentences *Alle Menschen sind sterblich* and *Alle Menschen sind gleich* must receive representations from the analysis program that are so different that it is impossible to trace them back to the same rule pattern, even though they are similar on the surface. Perhaps this can be done by introducing another subject role, in which case an appropriate formulation in the valence lexicon is to take care that the first subject type is linked with *sterblich* and the second with *gleich*. The retroaction of the deduction component onto the analysis component is clear. In comparison to traditional valence descriptions the valence lexicon receives a completely new status. It does not contain only the patterns for the syntactic construction of expressions but it is, at the same time, the place where the logical constituents, i.e. the building blocks for semantic rules, are introduced.

Examples such as (1) and (3) are so trivial from the standpoint of symbolic logic that they themselves are not yet an argument for the use of inference schemes in an automatic deduction system. Thus I would like to especially emphasize the salient point of the inference rule procedure: inference schemes on a syntactic base can be drawn up for any sentences of a particular language, regardless of the structure of the sentences and whether a translation into a familiar system of symbolic logic is easily possible or not. Whenever inferences are observable in an NL, patterns in AL can be assigned to them; the most subtle syntactic and lexical differences can be directly accounted for. This is the reason why none of the advanced devices of formal logic, such as theorem proving on the basis of the resolution principle or a model-theoretical calculus[21], were incorporated into PLAIN.

The deduction principles of universal logic systems are simple and transparent. When it is necessary to formulate general logical laws or to design and prove formal theories, the artificial languages of symbolic logic are certainly the current optimum. When such systems are applied to a natural language, the analysis component has to do the bulk of the job. It must assign expressions from the universal language of symbolic logic to the natural language input; this involves forcing every expression of the NL into an utterly foreign syntax. The direct connection between the syntax of the particular language and the possible deductions is obscured; in practice many natural language inferences are ignored simply because an adequate translation into logic calculus has not yet been successful. Just as the syntax of diverse languages has been measured by the yardstick of Latin grammar for a long time, formal logic becomes too easily a filter for the logico-semantic relationships observable in natural languages. In

21 See the survey on these devices in CHANG/LEE 1970.

syntax description it is agreed upon that every language is to be taken as a system on its own; this attitude probably also has to be taken towards logico-semantic structures.

Of course, the logical analysis of an NL must not fall behind the results arrived at in symbolic logic. What is deducible via the indirect route of a translation into a predicate calculus must also be deducible by means of the direct procedure. Especially in the development stage of an independent linguistic inference model, the agreement of the simpler cases with the law of formal logic is an indispensable touchstone. Referring to well-understood relationships in symbolic logic also facilitates the communication about the planned solution within the natural language deduction system. Therefore, I shall stick to simple examples from symbolic logic throughout the following explanation of the deduction principles of PLAIN. However, it is my hypothesis that expressions and rules of an AL that closely reflects the syntax of NL cannot only be substituted for logical formulas but that the syntactic framework within which the device works goes far beyond what can be translated into current symbolic logic.

Transformation rules such as (2) with two patterns in the description part are inconvenient in practice, because it would be awkward to single out of a large set of sentences precisely those pairs that fit such a rule. Instead, it is desirable to have transformation rules with only one pattern in the description part and, possibly, to apply several such rules successively. The organization of deductions with PLAIN adheres to this principle.

It is known that in symbolic logic every tautological expression can be transferred into a rule. If the equivalence of two expressions X and Y is a tautology, then a replacement rule of the form "X can be substituted for Y and vice versa" can be formulated. If the implication of Y by X is a tautology, then an inference rule of the form "If X can be asserted, then Y can be asserted" can be generated.[22]

Let us still remain with the syllogism as an example. If P_1, P_2 and K are patterns for any, even complex, assertions, if '&' be

22 For further details about transferring a "sentence logic" to a "rule logic", see BOCHENSKI/MENNE 1965, pp. 50ff.

the connective for logical conjunction '->' be the connective for implication, then every syllogism is based on a tautology with the following structure:

(6) $(P_1 \;\&\; P_2) \;\text{->}\; K$

According to the just formulated translation principle of tautologies into rules, the familiar inference figure arises:

(7)
$$\frac{\begin{array}{c} P_1 \\ P_2 \end{array}}{K}$$

(7) is to be read as "If a sentence of the form P_1 can be asserted and if a sentence of the form P_2 can be asserted, then a sentence of the form K can be asserted".

On the basis of familiar laws, (6) can be replaced alternatively by one of the two following formulas:

(8) $P_1 \;\text{->}\; (P_2 \;\text{->}\; K)$

(9) $P_2 \;\text{->}\; (P_1 \;\text{->}\; K)$

Always under the condition that P_1 , P_2 and K are assertions of a form such that (6), (8) and (9) are tautologies, the formulas (8) and (9) can, in turn, be transferred into rules. For example, (8) gives us:

(10)
$$\frac{P_1}{P_2 \;\text{->}\; K}$$

Now we stipulate that every declarative sentence that is stored in the data base of our system or that is newly entered is deemed to be true. To express that an assertion is false, one must form and enter the negation of the sentence. The above rule formulation "If X can be asserted, the Y can be asserted" can now be changed into "When X is given, then Y can be generated", i.e. we interpret the inference instruction as a transformation rule.

(10) is such a transformation rule. It states that when a sentence of the form P_1 is given, the implication of a sentence of the form K by a sentence of the form P_2 can be generated. Let us assume that p_1 is a sentence according to pattern P_1, p_2 a sentence according to pattern P_2, k a sentence according to pattern K. (10) can only be applied when a sentence p_1 according to pattern P_1 was actually given, i.e. whenever a sentence $p_2 \rightarrow k$ is deduced according to this rule, p_1 is true. Hence, $p_2 \rightarrow k$ is also always true within the system, insofar as this expression resulted from the previous application of (10). Therefore the deduced implication formula may likewise be reformulated as a transformation rule, namely:

(11) $$\frac{p_2}{k}$$

(10) is an analytically valid rule since it results directly from a tautology. Tautologies are true under every interpretation merely on the basis of the logical constituents they contain. Consequently, rules such as (10) belong to the language description. They can be set up independent of actual sentences which are entered into the system.

On the contrary, (11) is an empirically valid rule. It is only appropriate when p_1 was, in fact, given in the system. But whether p_1 is to be entered or not is an empirical question.

Now we have all of the prerequisites together to divide the original inference pattern (2) with two premises and one conclusion into transformation rules which are applicable one after the other. If we use '=>' as a rule symbol for rules such as (10) and '|-' as a symbol for rules such as (11), then we can formulate (2) as follows:

(12)

```
(: => <REPLACE>
     (ILLOC: aussage+
          (PRAED: #2
               (SUBJT: #1
                    (QUANT
                         (alle)))
               (-1)))
     (: |-
          (ILLOC: aussage+
               (PRAED: sein
                    (SUBJT: $)
                    (PDKTV: #1
                         (REFER: ein))))
          (ILLOC: aussage+
               (PRAED: #2
                    (SUBJT: $)
                    (-1)))));
```

(12) is an analytically valid deduction rule whose description part contains a pattern for a sentence and whose construction part contains a pattern for an empirical deduction rule. The fact that the transformation does not yield an implication in sentence form, but rather immediately generates the rule into which this special implication statement may be transferred guards against confusion with sentences that denote an implication relationship elsewhere in the system.

Let the following bracketed expression be the result of the analysis of an input into PLAIN:

(13)

```
(ILLOC: aussage+
     (PRAED: sein
          (SUBJT: mensch
               (QUANT
                    (alle)))
          (PDKTV: sterblich)));
```

According to (12) this expression receives a further representation, namely:

(14)

```
(: |-
     (ILLOC: aussage+
          (PRAED: sein
               (SUBJT: $)
               (PDKTV: mensch
                    (REFER: ein))))
     (ILLOC: aussage+
          (PRAED: sein
               (SUBJT: $)
               (PDKTV: sterblich))));
```

The transition from (13) to (14) is also justified by the fact that human language users, too, take sentences not only as situational descriptions but, at the same time, as instructions for their inferring.[23]

The input (13) could be stored in the data base of PLAIN in the form of (14). The data base then contains empirically valid deduction rules along with primitive sentences. If a sentence occurs which is an instance of the description part of (14), e.g. *Sokrates ist ein Mensch*, then this rule can be applied at will and the sentence *Sokrates ist sterblich* can be deduced.

If a sentence is to be proved in accordance with the data base, rules such as (14) can simply be reversed. The second subtree is taken as the description part, the first subtree is taken as the construction part. If *Sokrates ist sterblich* is to be verified, but if this sentence itself is not contained in the data base, then according to (14) *Sokrates ist ein Mensch* can be formed as one of the sentences from which the first sentence follows.

However, (14) is not the only instruction for inference that can be derived from (13). On the basis of the contraposition of the implication, it is also possible to infer *Sokrates ist kein Mensch* (Socrates is not a man) from *Sokrates ist nicht sterblich* (Socrates is not mortal), insofar as (13) is given in the system. Correspondingly, *Sokrates ist kein Mensch* can be proved through *Sokrates ist nicht sterblich*. In order not to have to double all analytically valid rules of the type of (12), we still go a few steps further.

In developing rules so far we had assumed a tautology with the following structure:

---

23 S.E. TOULMIN 1958, pp. 99ff., pertinently calls general and hypothetical sentences that speakers rely on in their reasoning "warrants" and "inference licenses". TOULMIN's presentation is less formal than my suggestions. There are, however, a few points in common. One can emphasize extremely the character of sentences as instructions for action by using a LISP-like notation as an artificial language. This would allow formulating and executing sentences directly as programs. A sophisticated system of this kind is C. HEWITT's PLANNER. See HEWITT 1972.

(8) P_1 -> (P_2 -> K)

On the basis of familiar laws, (8) can be replaced by

(15) P_1 -> ($\neg P_2$ v K)

'¬' is the negation sign, 'v' is the connective of the logical disjunction. Now let us stipulate that a disjunction that was deduced by means of an analytically valid rule from a sentence given in the system is represented as an empirically valid rule of a special type by replacing the connective with a rule symbol. I call the new type of an empirical deduction rule an "expansion rule", since it is used to expand the set of given sentences by other sentences that follow from the given ones or that are able to prove the given ones. The standard rule symbol for expansion rules in PLAIN is '|'.

The analytical deduction rules now have the following format:

(16) P_1 => (P_2 | K)

Assume that the sentence p_1 is given in the system and that the empirical rule generated according to (16) from p_1 is:

(17) p_2 | k

The following conventions are set up for processing empirical deduction rules like (17). Both subtrees of the rule can be taken as the description part; whichever subtree remains is the construction part. The rule is applicable for the purpose of deducing a conclusion in D when the n e g a t i o n of a given sentence matches the description part. The result is equal to the construction part. The rule is applicable for finding out sentences that can prove a given sentence in D when the given sentence matches the description part. The result is equal to the n e g a t i o n of the construction part.

Accordingly, there are four possible interpretations of (17):

from $\neg p_2$ infer k,	prove k by means of $\neg p_2$,
from $\neg$k infer p_2,	prove p_2 by means of $\neg$k.

For all four applications it is easy to look through the data base for instances.

So far we have only dealt with three-part inference schemes. But there are also inference figures with more than two premises and the individual premises themselves can be logically compounded. Traditional logic provides a solution. By means of substitution rules, which are based on tautological equivalences, every complex propositional expression can be transferred into a reduced form in which only the connectives of conjunction and disjunction appear and in which the negation sign, if it occurs, is attributed only to primitive assertions. A conjunctive normal form is the reduced form of an assertion that is made up of only conjunctions which, in turn, contain only primitive disjunctions or primitive assertions.[24] We can maintain our method of simulating inferences by means of transformations if we first put the expressions that form the basis of the empirical deduction rules into a conjunctive normal form.

Let a sentence p_1 and the following expression be given:

(18) $(a \ \& \ b) <-> c$

'a', 'b' and 'c' are assertion constants, '<->' is the connective of logical equivalence. The implication of (18) by p_1 is to be a tautology. (18) is then derivable from p_1 by means of an analytical rule. The conjunctive normal form of (18) is:[25]

(19) $(\neg a \vee \neg b \vee c) \ \& \ (\neg c \vee a) \ \& \ (\neg c \vee b)$

Internal bracketing within the conjuncts is superfluous because of the associativity of the disjunction. (In the tree representation of PLAIN there is only one term for the connective with any number of immediately subordinated subtrees for the disjuncts.) Every conjunct of (19) can now be transferred into its own expansion rule, since it is the logical law that everything that follows from any

24 Compare BOCHENSKI/MENNE 1965, pp. 53ff.

25 The formula is achieved by transformations according to the usual laws, as they are listed in BOCHENSKI/MENNE 1965, pp. 35ff.

conjunct of an assertion in conjunctive normal form follows from the assertion itself.[26]

Just like the connective of disjunction, the term with the rule symbol of an expansion rule can dominate any number of subtrees. Accordingly, an expansion rule embraces and arbitrary number of patterns. The regulation for the application of an expansion rule is refined as follows. Any subtree that is directly subordinated to the rule symbol can qualify as a description of an application instance. When checking the applicability of the rule all of the subtrees are compared with the potential instance one after the other. If an expression matches a subtree, all of the other subtrees are used for construction. If more than one tree is constructed (because the rule contained more than two patterns), then when applying the rule for the purpose of inferring, all of the newly generated trees are linked by the connective of disjunction (parameter VEL), and when applying the rule in a proof expansion, they are linked by the connective of conjunction (parameter ET).

Below there are three expansion rules that are to be drawn from (19). For each I list the possibilities of application.

(20) (| (¬a) (¬b) (c))
from a infer ¬b v c, prove ¬a by means of b & ¬c,
from b infer ¬a v c, prove ¬b by means of a & ¬c,
from c infer ¬a v ¬b, prove c by means of a & b.

(21) (| (¬c) (a))
from c infer a, prove ¬c by means of ¬a,
from ¬a infer ¬c, prove a by means of c.

(22) (| (¬c) (b))
from c infer b, prove ¬c by means of ¬b,
from ¬b infer ¬c, prove b by means of c.

Expression (18), if it is analytically derivable from a given sentence, can thus be restated in three empirically valid rules.

---

26 See BOCHENSKI/MENNE 1965, p. 56.

These rules are stored in the data base. This expands the deductive capacity of the system by 14 possible operations.

A directory associated with the data base of PLAIN makes it possible to directly reach all of the rules which contain subtrees whose uppermost term is identical to the dominating term of an expression which is to be expanded. In the case of an inference expansion, the initial expression is connected by conjunction with the constructed expressions from the rule applications. In the case of a proof expansion, the initial expression is connected by disjunction with the constructs. A repeated derivation of conjuncts or disjuncts which are already present is suppressed. When no more applicable expansion rules are found for a given expression, the program tries to expand the newly derived expressions as well, and so on. All of the rule applications are documented. In the case of the inference expansion the result is a conjunction of the initial sentence p with all sentences k_1 through k_n that follow from p in D (i.e. task i); in the case of a proof expansion the result is a disjunction of the initial term k with all sentences p_1 through p_m from which k follows in D (i.e. task ii).

The proof procedure is effective, since it proceeds from the sentence to be proved and it relies on the information on logical relationships contained in D. Therefore, the procedure only puts together sentences that, if they are given, really lead to the proof goal.[27] Within the context of question answering, the proof expansion must still be evaluated after it is compiled. On the one hand, this is done by checking the data base to see whether any sentences p_1 to p_m from which k follows are, in fact, given. On the other hand, certain analytically valid evaluation rules are applied to the expansion. In the end, all of these

27 Goal-oriented execution of proof operations is the strong point of PLANNER. See HEWITT 1972. T. WINOGRAD also uses PLANNER for deductions within his program for understanding natural language. See WINOGRAD 1971. Although there might have been short-term advantages to adapting PLAIN to a system as PLANNER, I decided to design a deduction component which reflects more closely the syntax of natural language. Otherwise an additional translation of the analyzed input into the format of PLANNER would have been necessary. However, it is not certain that such a translation is possible for all syntactic structures which occur in natural language.

rules can be traced back to the law of non-contradiction:

(23) $\neg (P \ \& \neg P)$

Evaluation rules are likewise transformation rules that, as a result, generate the system defined terms "true" or "false". Here I would like to dispense with the development of such rules from (23) as well as with a more detailed description of the evaluation of proof expansions in PLAIN. (The implementation is not yet completed.) The principle of evaluation is somewhat similar to the well-known "resolution principle" of J.A. ROBINSON.[28] The great difference from theorem proving according to ROBINSON and from similar proof procedures lies in the fact that PLAIN assembles the sentences that are candidates for a solution according to syntactic rules from the data base. In doing so, PLAIN solves the searching problem, that causes the biggest headches in theorem proving.

Just like the base lexicon and the valence lexicon, the analytically valid deduction rules must be empirically determined, formulated, and tested for every particular language. All three data sets together represent a description which earns R. CARNAP's designation "logical syntax".[29] According to an influential theory, the meaning of an expression is its use. The analytically valid deduction rules describe the meaning of a part of the AL, namely that of the logical lexemes and the syntactic structures, by showing how these language elements are to be used for inferring. Without deduction rules AL is only differentiated from NL by a more explicit syntax, whereas with deduction rules, the AL becomes a "semantic representation".

Incidently, note that we have not made provisions for identical deep structures of expressions with the same meaning. The semantic representation suggested for PLAIN is closely bound up with the surface of each NL. Meaning equivalence, like all other meaning relationships, is accounted for by deduction rules. I hope I have made it clear that G. LAKOFF's goal of showing how the grammatical

28 See ROBINSON 1965, ROBINSON 1971.

29 Compare CARNAP 1969.

and logical form of a language are related to each other can be achieved without generative semantics.[30]

But what about the interpretation of the descriptive terms, i.e. the language elements that are interchangeable in inference schemes and that show up in deduction rules only in the form of variables? For example, how is the often cited meaning relationship of *Junggeselle* (bachelor) and *verheiratet* (married) or *oculist* and *eye-doctor* to be dealt with?

R. CARNAP has pointed out that one can formulate to any desired degree of precision the relationship between descriptive terms by means of so-called meaning postulates.[31] An example given by CARNAP in predicate logic notation would read in German:

(24) Alle Junggesellen sind unverheiratet.
(All bachelors are unmarried.)

One could also translate:

(25) Wenn jemand Junggeselle ist, dann ist er unverheiratet.
(If someone is a bachelor, then he is unmarried.)

Or:

(26) Ein Junggeselle ist jemand, der nicht verheiratet ist.
(A bachelor is someone who is not married.)

The relationship of *oculist* and *eye-doctor* could be expressed in the following postulate:

(27) An oculist is either an eye-doctor or an optician.

CARNAP views his meaning postulates as analytically true statements, i.e. they are true because they express language conventions. That is precisely why he can call them postulates about meaning. But in contrast to logical particles, the decision is difficult as to which descriptive terms are analytically linked

---

30 See the first pages of LAKOFF 1970.
31 See CARNAP 1952.

together and which links only denote empirical circumstances. Does "Schwarz-Sein" (being black) belong to the language convention that is linked with *Rabe* (raven) - another meaning postulate that CARNAP sets up in the same article, or is it a circumstance that could just as easily change? Is a white raven not a raven? How can one then guarantee that fairy tales can continue to be told?

One avoids these difficulties by viewing sentences such as (24) to (27) as only empirically valid.[32] They are candidates for the data base of PLAIN, as are other sentences as well. If (24) is entered, then the result, according to all explained above, is an empirical deduction rule of the form:

(28) (| ($ ist nicht ein Junggeselle) ($ ist unverheiratet))

As far as the deductive capacity of the system is concerned, this rule achieves the same as a replacement rule on the basis of an analytically interpreted postulate. The fact that speakers do indeed utter such sentences as (26) and (27) in order to explain the meaning of *Junggeselle* or *oculist* to someone does not speak against the empirical validity of these sentences. When dealing with meaning, speakers typically talk about things and not about words. There is no reason to chose another route in PLAIN. The use of descriptive elements is given by the sentences stored in the actual data base.

Under these circumstances, the logico-semantic analysis of sentences such as (24) to (27) is most urgent. The linguist must carefully study the use of such elements as *alle, sind, wenn ... dann, ein, jemand ... der* within the context of inferences and he must write analytically valid rules by means of which, in actual cases, the empirical rules for all possible deductions are derived from sentences like those quoted above. PLAIN will already be useful in the test phase. But it is not the task of the linguist to fill the data base with information about bachelors, eye-doctors, and opticians. This can be left up to users of the second generation.

---

32 I have given a more detailed explanation for this position in HELLWIG 1978.

4.2. A Deduction Example

The following three sentences are part of the German tax laws:

(1) Wer mehr als 24000 Mark verdient, wird zur Einkommensteuer veranlagt.
(He who earns more than 24,000 Marks is assessed for income tax.)

(2) Wenn jemand Einkünfte hat und keine Lohnsteuer zahlt, dann wird er zur Einkommensteuer veranlagt.
(If a person has income and does not pay tax on wages, then he is assessed for income tax.)

(3) Unternehmer zahlen keine Lohnsteuer.
(Employers pay no tax on wages.)

The analysis program of PLAIN gives the first of these sentences approximately the following AL representation:

```
(ILLCC: aussage+
     (PRAED: werden_passiv
          (ADPRD: veranlagen
               (CASUS: zu
                    (: einkommensteuer))
               (SUBJT: hypo+
                    (PRAED: verdienen
                         (SUBJT: wer)
                         (OBJKT: mark
                              (QUANT: 24000
                                   (ADVRE: mehr
                                        (: als)))))))));
```

The analysis result is somewhat simplified here for the sake of clarity. I have left out the terms for tense, mode, and number. The morpho-syntactic categories were already deleted since they are no longer needed.

Right after the analysis, every sentence is transferred into normal form by means of replacement rules. With the option STEPS one can order a documentation of the individual rule applications. In the case of sentence (1) the listing of the replacement steps looks like this:

```
*** REPLC - REPLACEMENT OF LIST

  1   (ILLOC: aussage+
  2        (PRAED: werden_passiv
  3             (ADIFD: veranlagen
  4                  (CASUS: zu
  5                       (: einkommensteuer))
  6             (SUBJT: hypo+
  7                  (PRAED: verdienen
  8                       (SUBJT: wer)
  9                       (OBJKT: mark
 10                            (QUANT: 24000
 11                                 (ADVRB: mehr
 12                                           (: als))))))))));

*** REPLC - RULE USED FOR REPLACEMENT:

  1   (: => <REPLACE>
  2        (ILLOC: aussage+
  3             (PRAED: #1
  4                  (SUBJT: hypo+
  5                       (PRAED: #2
  6                            (SUBJT: wer)
  7                            (-2)))
  8                  (-1)))
  9        (ILLOC: aussage+
 10             (PRAED: oder_d <SYSTERM>
 11                  (CONJT: NICHT #2
 12                       (SUBJT: $)
 13                       (-2))
 14                  (CONJT: #1
 15                       (SUBJT: $)
 16                       (-1))))) ;

*** RVLST _ LIST OF VARIABLES:

      TYPE: 21  NAME: #1   REFERS TO:  2
      TYPE: 21  NAME: #2   REFERS TO:  7
      TYPE: 12  NAME: -1   REFERS TO:  3
      TYPE: 12  NAME: -2   REFERS TO:  9


*** REPLC - SUBSTITUTING LIST (  1) ACCORDING TO RULE (  9)
------------------------------------------------------------
```

```
*** REPLC - LIST AFTER REPLACEMENT:

  1  (ILLOC: aussage+
  2       (PRAED: oder_d <SYSTERM>
  3            (CONJT: NICHT verdienen
  4                 (SUBJT: $)
  5                 (OBJKT: mark
  6                      (QUANT: 24000
  7                           (ADVRB: mehr
  8                                (: als)))))))));
  9            (CONJT: werden_passiv
 10                 (SUBJT: $)
 11                 (ADPRD: veranlagen
 12                      (CASUS: zu
 13                           (: einkommensteuer))

*** REPLC - RULE USED FOR REPLACEMENT:

  1  (: => <REPLACE>
  2       (ILLOC: aussage+
  3            (PRAED: oder_d <SYSTERM>
  4                 (CONJT: -)))
  5       (: | <EXPAND>
  6            (PRAED: -)));


*** PVLST _ LIST OF VARIABLES:

      TYPE: 23  NAME: -    REFERS TO:  3
      TYPE: 23  NAME: -    REFERS TO:  9

*** REPLC - SUBSTITUTING LIST (  1) ACCORDING TO RULE (  5)
------------------------------------------------------------

*** REPLC - LIST AFTER REPLACEMENT:

  1  (: | <EXPAND>
  2       (PRAED: NICHT verdienen
  3            (SUBJT: $)
  4            (OBJKT: mark
  5                 (QUANT: 24000
  6                      (ADVRB: mehr
  7                           (: als)))))
  8       (PRAED: werden_passiv
  9            (SUBJT: $)
 10            (ADPRD: veranlagen
 11                 (CASUS: zu
 12                      (: einkommensteuer)))));

*** REPLC - REPLACEMENT TERMINATED
--------------------------------------------------------------
```

The result of the replacements is an empirically valid expansion
rule.
 The analysis of sentence (2) results in the following simplified
list:

```
 1  (ILLCC: aussage+
 2      (PRAED: wenn
 3          (ANTEC: und <SYSTERM>
 4              (CONJT: haben
 5                  (SUBJT: jemand)
 6                  (OBJKT: einkuenfte))
 7              (CCNJT: zahlen
 8                  (SUBJT: jemand)
 9                  (OBJKT: lohnsteuer
10                      (QUANT: kein))))
11          (ECSTC: dann
12              (: werden_passiv
13                  (SUBJT: er)
14                  (ADPRD: veranlagen
15                      (CASUS: zu
16                          (: einkommensteuer))))))));
```

Nine rule applications are necessary for transferring this list
into an expansion rule. It would take up too much space to print
all of the rules and the listing of the replacement steps.
Finally, the following rule is reached from sentence (2):

```
 1  (: | <EXPAND>
 2      (PRAED: NICHT haben
 3          (SUBJT: $)
 4          (OBJKT: einkuenfte))
 5      (PRAED: zahlen
 6          (SUBJT: $)
 7          (OBJKT: lohnsteuer))
 8      (PRAED: werden_passiv
 9          (SUBJT: $)
10          (ADPRD: veranlagen
11              (CASUS: zu
12                  (: einkommensteuer)))));
```

Sentence (3) is analyzed as follows:

```
 1  (ILLCC: aussage+
 2      (PRAED: zahlen
 3          (SUBJT: unternehmer
 4              (QUANT: all))
 5          (OBJKT: lohnsteuer
 6              (QUANT: kein))));
```

The result of the replacements is:

```
1   (: | <EXPAND>
2        (PRAED: NICHT sein
3             (SUBJT: $)
4             (PDKTV: unternehmer
5                  (REFER: ein)))
6        (PRAED: NICHT zahlen
7             (SUBJT: $)
8             (OBJKT: lohnsteuer)));
```

We now have three expansion rules. By entering them into the data base of PLAIN we create the provision for possible empirically valid inferences and proofs. First let us look at an example of an inference. The following sentence is newly entered and is to be considered as true:

(4) Häberle ist ein Unternehmer.
(Häberle is an employer.)

On the basis of the previously stored rules that were derived from sentences (1) through (3), the following expansion steps are made:

```
*** EXPAN - EXPANSION OF LIST (FOR INFERENCE):

  1   (ILLOC: aussage+
  2        (PRAED: sein
  3             (SUBJT: Haeberle)
  4             (PDKTV: unternehmer
  5                  (REFER: ein))));

*** EXPAN - RULE APPLIED TO SUBLIST (  2):

  1   (: | <EXPAND>
  2        (PRAED: NICHT sein
  3             (SUBJT: $)
  4             (PDKTV: unternehmer
  5                  (REFER: ein)))
  6        (PRAED: NICHT zahlen
  7             (SUBJT: $)
  8             (OBJKT: lohnsteuer)));

*** EXPAN - DERIVED LIST(S):

  1   (ILLOC: aussage+
  2        (PRAED: NICHT zahlen
  3             (SUBJT: Haeberle)
  4             (OBJKT: lohnsteuer)));
-----------------------------------------------------------
```

```
*** EXPAN - EXPANSION OF LIST:

  1  (ILLOC: aussage+
  2       (PRAED: NICHT zahlen
  3            (SUBJT: Haeberle)
  4            (OBJKT: lohnsteuer)));

*** EXPAN - RULE APPLIED TO SUBLIST (  2):

  1  (: | <EXPAND>
  2       (PRAED: NICHT haben
  3            (SUBJT: $)
  4            (OBJKT: einkuenfte))
  5       (PRAED: zahlen
  6            (SUBJT: $)
  7            (OBJKT: lohnsteuer))
  8       (PRAED: werden_passiv
  9            (SUBJT: $)
 10            (ADPRD: veranlagen
 11                 (CASUS: zu
 12                      (: einkommensteuer)))));

*** EXPAN - DERIVED LIST(S):

  1  (ILLOC: aussage+
  2       (PRAED: NICHT haben
  3            (SUBJT: Haeberle)
  4            (OBJKT: einkuenfte)));

  1  (ILLOC: aussage+
  2       (PRAED: werden_passiv
  3            (SUBJT: Haeberle)
  4            (ADPRD: veranlagen
  5                 (CASUS: zu
  6                      (: einkommensteuer)))));


*** EXPAN - EXPANSION TERMINATED
------------------------------------------------------------
```

One conclusion is deduced from a sentence in every step. The admissibility of each deduction depends on an expansion rule which, in turn, comes from one of the sentences (1) through (3). The expansion rule can be applied for the purpose of inferring, if the negation of an instance corresponds to one of the subtrees in the rule. The result of each rule application is one or more lists which were formed by the transformation of the initial list according to the pattern of the remaining subtrees in the rule. If several lists are generated by a rule application, then they are understood to be disjunctively linked together. If we mark the conclusion with 'ALSO' (THUS) and the sentence that led to the particular expansion with 'DENN' (FOR), then our deduction listing reflects the following argumentation:

1st step: Häberle ist ein Unternehmer,
ALSO zahlt Häberle nicht Lohnsteuer,
DENN Unternehmer zahlen keine Lohnsteuer.

(Häberle is an employer,
THUS Häberle does not pay tax on wages,
FOR employers pay no tax on wages.)

2nd step: Häberle zahlt nicht Lohnsteuer,
ALSO hat Häberle nicht Einkünfte
oder Häberle wird zur Einkommensteuer veranlagt,
DENN wenn jemand Einkünfte hat und keine Lohnsteuer zahlt, dann wird er zur Einkommensteuer veranlagt.

(Häberle does not pay tax on wages,
THUS Häberle does not have income
or Häberle is assed for income tax,
FOR if someone has income and pays no tax on wages, then he is assessed for income tax.)

In the case of an inference expansion, the conclusions of the individual steps are conjunctively linked, since all of the conclusions that can be drawn from a sentence are valid at the same time. Finally, PLAIN prints a survey that corresponds to a tree made up of connectives and lists. (Connectives and lists are numbered through. The subordination relationship is indicated by 'SUB' and the number of the superordinated connective. In the listing, the connective of conjunction is represented by 'und', the connective of the disjunction is represented by 'oder_d'.)

```
*** RESEX - RESULTS OF INFERENCE:

CONNECTIVE   1: und <SYSTERM>

LIST   2 (SUB   1):

  1  (ILLCC: aussage+
  2       (PRAED: sein
  3            (SUBJT: Haeberle)
  4            (PDKTV: unternehmer
  5                 (REFER: ein))));

LIST   3 (SUB   1):

  1  (ILLCC: aussage+
  2       (PRAED: NICHT zahlen
  3            (SUBJT: Haeberle)
  4            (OBJKT: lohnsteuer)));

CONNECTIVE   4 (SUB   1): oder_d <SYSTERM>

LIST   5 (SUB   4):
  1  (ILLCC: aussage+
  2       (PRAED: NICHT haben
  3            (SUBJT: Haeberle)
  4            (OBJKT: einkuenfte)));

LIST   6 (SUB   4):

  1  (ILLCC: aussage+
  2       (PRAED: werden_passiv
  3            (SUBJT: Haeberle)
  4            (ADPRD: veranlagen
  5                 (CASUS: zu
  6                      (: einkommensteuer)))));
```

To illustrate a proof expansion we ask the system the following question:

(5) Wird Häberle zur Einkommensteuer veranlagt?
(Will Häberle be assessed for income tax?)

Before PLAIN attempts to answer a question, the deduction program generates the corresponding declarative sentence. Which terms of a question correspond to which terms of a declarative sentence is specified by the linguist, as the first user of PLAIN. (This is done via the parameter EQUATION.) The declarative sentence is then expanded as follows:

given sentence with 'FALLS' (IF), then the listing of the expansion reflects the following problem explication:

1st step: Häberle wird zur Einkommensteuer veranlagt,
FALLS Häberle mehr als 24000 Mark verdient,
DENN wer mehr als 24000 Mark verdient, wird zur Einkommensteuer veranlagt.

(Häberle is assessed for income tax,
IF Häberle earns more than 24,000 Marks,
FOR he who earns more than 24,000 Marks is assessed for income tax.)

2nd step: Häberle wird zur Einkommensteuer veranlagt,
FALLS Häberle Einkünfte hat
und Häberle nicht Lohnsteuer zahlt,
DENN wenn jemand Einkünfte hat und keine Lohnsteuer zahlt, dann wird er zur Einkommensteuer veranlagt.

(Häberle is assessed for income tax,
IF Häberle has income
and if Häberle does not pay tax on wages,
FOR when someone has income and pays no tax on wages, then he is assessed for income tax.)

3rd step: Häberle zahlt nicht Lohnsteuer,
FALLS Häberle ein Unternehmer ist,
DENN Unternehmer zahlen keine Lohnsteuer.

(Häberle does not pay tax on wages,
IF Häberle is an employer,
FOR employers pay no tax on wages.)

The sentences derived in the individual steps are linked disjunctively with the original sentence. The outprint of the expansion result contains a precise survey of the logical connections between the original and the generated lists:

```
*** RESEX - RESULTS OF EXPANSION FOR PROOF:

CONNECTIVE   1: oder_d <SYSTERM>

LIST   2 (SUB   1):

  1  (ILLCC: aussage+
  2       (PRAED: werden_passiv
  3            (SUBJT: Haeberle)
  4            (ADPRD: veranlagen
  5                 (CASUS: zu
  6                      (: einkommensteuer)))));

LIST   3 (SUB   1):

  1  (ILLCC: aussage+
  2       (PRAED: verdienen
  3            (SUBJT: Haeberle)
  4            (OBJKT: mark
  5                 (QUANT: 24000
  6                      (ADVRB: mehr
  7                           (: als))))));

CONNECTIVE   4 (SUB  1): und <SYSTERM>

LIST   5 (SUB   2):

  1  (ILLCC: aussage+
  2       (PRAED: haben
  3            (SUBJT: Haeberle)
  4            (OBJKT: einkuenfte)));

CONNECTIVE   6 (SUB   4): oder_d <SYSTERM>

LIST   7 (SUB   6):

  1  (ILLCC: aussage+
  5       (PRAED: NICHT zahlen
  6            (SUBJT: Haeberle)
  7            (OBJKT: lohnsteuer)));

LIST   8 (SUB   6):

  1  (ILLCC: aussage+
  2       (PRAED: sein
  3            (SUBJT: Haeberle)
  4            (PDKTV: unternehmer
  5                 (REFER: ein))));
```

The result is in its entirity a tree made of connectives and lists. The structure of this tree is elucidated by the following diagram:

(6)

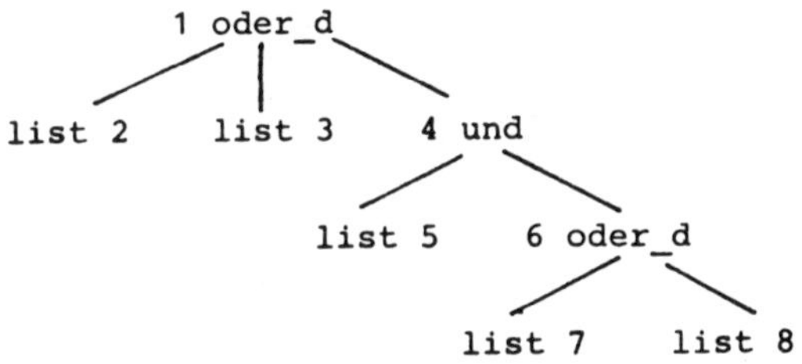

In order to answer question (5), the above expansion is evaluated. If list 2 or list 3 is given in the data base, or if list 5 and either list 7 or list 8 are given, then the question can be answered affirmatively, since if one of the disjuncts of a proof expansion is true, then the disjunction that was generated as the result of the expansion is true, too.

In contrast to other deduction procedures that produce only a truth value or quit without a result, the syntactic expansion method has an important advantage. Even if none of the disjuncts are given in the data base, the expansion does show at least under which conditions the question could be answered affirmatively. The system can formulate counter-questions from the sentences that were generated in the expansion. Assume that sentence (4) (Häberle is an employer) has been stored in the data base. This sentence verifies list 8 of the proof expansion. After diagram (6) only a verification of list 5 is then still necessary in order to be able to answer question (5) affirmatively. Just like a human question-answerer, e.g. a tax consultant, who is missing certain information, PLAIN also asks back by formulating list 5 in question form:

(7) Hat Häberle Einkünfte?
(Does Häberle have income?)

Perhaps the user who asked question (5) knows the answer to (7) himself. In this case he can be served even though the data base does not contain enough information to answer the question directly. Finally, the listings of expansions that correspond to non-answerable questions are a valuable guideline for the administrators of an information system as to which information still has to be obtained and entered into the data bank in order to satisfy the customers.

5. IMPLEMENTATION

The author developed PLAIN on an IBM 370/168 at the University of Heidelberg. At present, the program system is made up of 6 main procedures and some 50 subroutines. The programs are written in PL/1. PLAIN is mainly conceived for interactive use. Of course, the programs can also be submitted to batch operation in order to process large amounts of data. Approximately 90 commands are available for carrying out a dialogue with PLAIN. The execution of the commands can be varied with almost 100 options and parameters.

Essentially, the main programs achieve the following:

DFN ("define")
definition of morpho-syntactic categories;
definition of rules insofar as they have not been supplied standardly;
permanent change of the representation of system defined terms;
changing and printing roles, lexemes, and categories.

LEX ("lexicon")
setting up, changing, and printing the base lexicon and the valence lexicon.

UBS ("update base")
setting up and changing the data base (or the valence lexicon;

address oriented or pattern oriented looking for entries in the data base (or the valence lexicon).

PBS ("print base")
printing the contents of the data base (or the valence lexicon);
setting up a sorting file for specific elements from the base (or the valence lexicon);
printing the contents of a data set according to the sorting file.

ANA ("analyze")
analyzing the input text and, if desired, storing it in a file of results.

DED ("deduce")
reading artificial language expressions from the file of results of ANA, from the data base, or from direct input;
various operations of pattern matching;
applying replacement rules;
carrying out inference and proof expansions;
evaluating proof expansions, answering questions.

Another main procedure is planned for the near future:

LMA ("lemma")
automatic compilation of the lexeme occurrences in texts by consulting just the base lexicon or on the basis of full analysis;
KWIC printing of text according to the compiled lexemes.

PLAIN will shortly be taken up into the program library of the Institute for Communication Research and Phonetics at the University of Bonn. The use of this library is open to interested scientists. Linguists who would like to use PLAIN for research purposes can contact Dr. P. Hellwig, Germanistisches Seminar der Universität Heidelberg, Postfach 105 760, D-69 Heidelberg, Germany.

REFERENCES

ABRAMOW, B. 1971: "Zur Paradigmatik und Syntagmatik der syntaktischen Potenzen". In HELBIG 1971, pp. 51 - 66.

ADMONI, W.G. 1966: *Der deutsche Sprachbau*. 2nd edition, Moscow, Leningrad.

BANERJEE, N. 1977: "CONDOR - Communication in Natural Language with Dialogue Oriented Retrieval Systems". In W. SCHNEIDER/ H. SAGVALL (Ed.): *Computational Linguistics in Medicine*. Amsterdam, New York, Oxford.

BAUMGÄRTNER, K. 1970: "Konstituenz und Dependenz. Zur Integration der beiden grammatischen Prinzipien". In H. STEGER (Ed.): *Vorschläge für eine strukturale Grammatik des Deutschen*. Darmstadt.

BERRY-ROGGHE, G.L./H. WULZ 1978: "An overview of PLIDIS. A problem solving information system with German as query language". In L. BOLC (Ed.): *Natural Language Communication with Computers*. Berlin, Heidelberg, New York, pp. 87 - 132.

BOCHENSKI, I.M./A. MENNE 1965: *Grundriß der Logistik*. 3rd edition, Paderborn.

BROCKHAUS, K. 1971: *Automatische Sprachübersetzung. Untersuchungen am Beispiel der Sprachen Englisch und Deutsch*. Braunschweig.

CARNAP, R. 1952: "Meaning Postulates". *Philosophical Studies 3*, pp. 65 - 73.

CARNAP, R. 1969: "The Logical Syntax of Language". In T.M. OLSHEWSKY (Ed.): *Problems in the Philosophy of Language*. New York.

CHANG, C.L./R. LEE 1970: *Symbolic Logic and Mechanical Theorem Proving*. New York.

ENGEL, U./H. SCHUMACHER 1976: *Kleines Valenzlexikon deutscher Verben*. Tübingen.

FILLMORE, C.J. 1968: "The Case for Case". In E. BACH/R.T. HARMS (Ed.): *Universals in Linguistic Theory*. New York, pp. 1 - 88.

GAIFMAN, H. 1965: "Dependency Systems and Phrase-Structure Systems". *Information and Control 8*, pp. 304 - 337.

HAYS, D.G. 1964: "Dependency Theory. A Formalism and Some Observations". *Language 40*, pp. 511 - 525.

HABEL, Ch./A. SCHMIDT/H. SCHWEPPE 1977: *On Automatic Paraphrasing of Natural Language Expressions*. Semantic Network Project. Report No. 3/77. Institut für Angewandte Informatik. Technische Universität Berlin.

HELBIG, G. 1971 (Ed.): *Beiträge zur Valenztheorie*. The Hague.

HELBIG, G./W. SCHENKEL 1973: *Wörterbuch zur Valenz und Distribution deutscher Verben*. 2nd edition, Leipzig.

HELLWIG, P. 1977: "Dependenzanalyse und Bedeutungspostulate - eine Alternative zur generativen Transformationsgrammatik". *Linguistische Berichte 52*, pp. 32 - 51.

HELLWIG, P. 1978: *Formal-desambiguierte Repräsentation. Vorüberlegungen zur maschinellen Bedeutungsanalyse auf der Grundlage der Valenzidee*. Stuttgart.

HELLWIG, P.: "PLAIN - Ein Programmsystem zur Sprachbeschreibung und maschinellen Sprachbearbeitung". *Sprache und Datenverarbeitung*. To appear.

HERINGER, H.-J. 1970: *Theorie der deutschen Syntax*. Munich.

HEWITT, C. 1972: *Description and Theoretical Analysis (Using Schemata) of PLANNER: A Language for Providing Theorems and Manipulating Models in a Robot*. M.I.T. Artificial Intelligence Laboratory. AD - 744 620.

HINST, P. 1974: *Logische Propädeutik. Eine Einführung in die deduktive Methode und logische Sprachanalyse*. Munich.

ISACENKO, a.V./H.-J. SCHÄDLICH 1966: "Untersuchungen über die deutsche Satzintonation". *Studia Grammatica VII*. Berlin.

KRALLMANN, D. 1978 (Ed.): *Kolloquium zur Lage der linguistischen Datenverarbeitung*. LDV-Fittings e.V., Universität Essen, Postfach 6843, D-43 Essen.

KRATZER, A./E. PAUSE/A.v. STECHOW 1974: *Einführung in Theorie und Anwendung der generativen Syntax*. Zweiter Halbband: Anwendung. Frankfurt/M.

LAKOFF, G. 1970: "Linguistics and Natural Logic". *Synthese 22*, pp. 151 - 271.

ROBINSON, J.A. 1965: "A machine-oriented logic based on the resolution principle". *Journal of the A.C.M. 12*, pp 23 - 41.

ROBINSON, J.A. 1971: "Building Deduction Machines". In N.V. FINDLER/B. MELTZER (Ed.): *Artificial Intelligence and Heurictic Programming*. Edinburg, pp. 3 - 13.

ROBINSON, J.J. 1970: "Dependency Structures and Transformational Rules". *Language 46*, pp. 259 - 285.

SFB 99 FORSCHUNGSBERICHT 1976: *Kontextfreie Syntaxen für Fragmente der Sprachen Deutsch, Englisch, Französisch, Russisch*. Sonderforschungsbereich 99 Linguistik, Teilprojekt A2 Automatische Übersetzung, Forschungsbericht 1.11.1973 - 31.3.1976. Teil II. Universität Konstanz, Postfach 7733, D-775 Konstanz.

SOMMERFELDT, K.E./H. SCHREIBER 1974: *Wörterbuch zur Valenz und Distribution deutscher Adjektive*. Leipzig.

SOMMERFELDT, K.E./H. SCHREIBER 1977: *Wörterbuch zur Valenz und Distribution der Substantive*. Leipzig.

TESNIÈRE, L. 1959: *Eléments de syntaxe structurale*. Paris.

TOULMIN, S.E. 1958: *The Uses of Argument*. Cambridge.

WEINREICH, U. 1966: "Explorations in Semantic Theory". In T.A. SEBEOK (Ed.): *Current Trends in Linguistics*. Vol. III, The Hague, pp. 395 - 477.

WINOGRAD, T. 1971: *Procedures as a Representation for Data in a Computer Program for Understanding Natural Language*. M.I.T. Artificial Intelligence Laboratory, AI TR-17, Cambridge Mass.